EU Committees:
Social Regulation,
Law and Politics

EU Committees:
Social Regulation,
Law and Politics

Edited by
CHRISTIAN JOERGES
and
ELLEN VOS

HART PUBLISHING
OXFORD – PORTLAND
1999

Hart Publishing
Oxford and Portland, Oregon

Published in North America (US and Canada) by
Hart Publishing
c/o International Specialized Book Services
5804 NE Hassalo Street
Portland, Oregon
97213-3644
USA

Distributed in Netherlands, Belgium and Luxembourg by
Intersentia, Churchillaan 108
B2900 Schoten
Antwerpen
Belgium

Distributed in Australia and New Zealand by
Federation Press
John St
Leichhardt
NSW 2000

Hart Publishing is a specialist legal publisher based in Oxford, England. To order
further copies of this book or to request a list of other publications please write to:

Hart Publishing, 19 Whitehouse Road, Oxford, OX1 4PA
Telephone: +44 (0)1865 434459 Fax: +44 (0) 1865 794882
email: hartpub@janep.demon.co.uk

British Library Cataloguing in Publication Data
Data Available

ISBN 1-901362-68-X (cloth)

Typeset in Sabon
by John Saunders Design & Production, Reading
Printed in Great Britain on acid-free paper
by Biddles Ltd, Guildford and Kings Lynn.

Foreword and Acknowledgements

This book stems from two research initiatives. One originated in Florence, Italy, the other in Bremen, Germany. The core event of the activities undertaken at the European University Institute was a conference on "Social Regulation Through European Committees: Empirical Research, Institutional Politics, Theoretical Concepts and Legal Developments" supported by the Institute's Research Council and the Robert Schuman Centre. Drafts of most of the contributions to this volume were presented at that occasion. But this event needs to be seen in a broader context. Both editors have been dealing with substantive and institutional aspects of European regulatory policies for many years; their work was embedded in research networks at the EUI comprising professors and research students both from the Law and the Political Science Departments. The interdisciplinary approach of this book, the analytical bases and normative orientations of many contributions (at any rate those of the editors) owe much to this intellectual background.

The second *locus studiae* was the Centre of European Law and Politics (ZERP) in Bremen where the *Volkswagen-Stiftung* supported, through a generous grant, a long-term research project on "The Assessment of the Safety of Technical Consumer Goods and of Risks to Health of Foodstuffs in the Praxis of European Committees ('Comitology')" directed by Christian Joerges. Although research in Bremen had a strong empirical component, it was by no means restricted to this aspect. If this book manages to improve our awareness and understanding of the activities of European committees in general and comitology in particular, the credits should go to both institutions. They should also go to many individuals who have already helped, by means of their advice, with the intellectual design of this project; to the participants of the conference in Florence who have reacted constructively to our suggestions regarding their contributions and who supported a lengthy editing process. Particular thanks go to Josef Falke, Marlies Becker, Chris Engert, Monika Hobbie, Mel Kenny and Stephen Vousden for all their help in the editing of this book. Many thanks go to our publisher Richard Hart for his truly professional patience and understanding.

Bremen/Florence/Maastricht, February 1999.

Christian Joerges and Ellen Vos

Contents

Section 2 *Institutional Controversies*

Section 4 *Comitology in the Perception of Political Science*

Section 5 *Comitology in the European Polity*

Abbreviations

AG	Advocate General
BSE	Bovine Spongiform Encephalopathy
Bull. EC	*Bulletin of the EC*
BverfG	Bundesverfassungsgericht
BverfGE	Entscheidungen des BverfG
CAP	Common Agricultural Policy
CEN	Comité Européen de Normalisation
CENELEC	Comité Européen de Normalisation Electrotechnique
CFSP	Common Foreign and Security Policy
CML Rev	*Common Market Law Review*
COREPER	Committee of Permanent Representatives
DG	Directorate General
DIN-Mitt.	DIN Mitteilungen
EC	European Community
ECJ	European Court of Justice
ECR	*European Court Reports*
ECSC	European Coal and Steel Community
EEA	European Environment Agency
EEC	European Economic Community
ELJ	*European Law Journal*
ELR	*European Law Review*
EMEA	European Agency for the Evaluation of Medicinal Products
EU	European Union
EuR	*Europarecht*
Euratom	European Atomic Energy Community
EuZW	*Europäische Zeitschrift für Wirtschaftsrecht*
EWG	Europäische Wirtschaftsgemeinschaft
ff.	and following pages
FIUs	Financial Information Units
GATT	General Agreement on Tariffs and Trade
GMOs	Genetically Modified Organisms
GMMOs	Genetically Modified Micro-organisms
IGC	Intergovernmental Conference

JCMS	*Journal of Common Market Studies*
JEPP	*Journal of European Public Policy*
MEP	Member of the European Parliament
MLR	*The Modern Law Review*
NvCJD	New variant form of Creuzfeldt-Jacob Disease
OJ	Official Journal of the European Communities
OVPIC	Office of Veterinary and Phytosanitary Inspection and Control
PVS	Politische Vierteljahresschrift
QMR	Qualified Majority Rule
QMV	Qualified Majority Voting
RabelsZ	*Rabels Zeitschrift für ausländisches und internationales Privatrecht*
RMC	*Revue du Marché Commun*
RTD Eur	*Revue Trimestrielle de Droit Européen*
SCF	Scientific Committee on Food
SEA	Single European Act
StCF	Standing Committee on Foodstuffs
StVC	Standing Veterinary Committee
SVC	Scientific Veterinary Committee
UCLAF	Anti-Fraud Co-ordination Unit
WTO	World Trade Organisation
ZaöRV	*Zeitschrift für ausländisches öffentliches Recht und Völkerrecht*
ZLR	*Zeitschrift für das gesamte Lebensmittelrecht*

Tables

Numbering of the Treaty on European Union and the EC Treaty
before and after entry into Force of the Amsterdam Treaty

A. Treaty on European Union

Before	After	Before	After
TITLE I	TITLE I	Article J.15	Article 25
		Article J.16	Article 26
Article A	Article 1	Article J.17	Article 27
Article B	Article 2	Article J.18	Article 28
Article C	Article 3		
Article D	Article 4	TITLE VI (***)	TITLE VI*
Article E	Article 5		
Article F	Article 6	Article K.1	Article 29
Articlc F.1 (*)	Article 7	Article K.2	Article 30
		Article K.3	Article 31
TITLE II	TITLE II	Article K.4	Article 32
		Article K.5	Article 33
Article G	Article 8	Article K.6	Article 34
		Article K.7	Article 35
TITLE III	TITLE III	Article K.8	Article 36
		Article K.9	Article 37
Article H	Article 9	Article K.10	Article 38
		Article K.11	Article 39
TITLE IV	TITLE IV	Article K.12	Article 40
		Article K.13	Article 41
Article I	Article 10	Article K.14	Article 42
TITLE V (***)	TITLE V	TITLE VIa (**)	TITLE VII
Article J.1	Article 11	Article K.15(*)	Article 43
Article J.2	Article 12	Article K.16(*)	Article 44
Article J.3	Article 13	Article K.17(*)	Article 45
Article J.4	Article 14		
Article J.5	Article 15	TITLE VII	TITLE VIII
Article J.6	Article 16		
Article J.7	Article 17	Article L	Article 46
Article J.8	Article 18	Article M	Article 47
Article J.9	Article 19	Article N	Article 48
Article J.10	Article 20	Article O	Article 49
Article J.11	Article 21	Article P	Article 50
Article J.12	Article 22	Article Q	Article 51
Article J.13	Article 23	Article R	Article 52
Article J.14	Article 24	Article S	Article 53

B. Treaty establishing the European Community

Before	After	Before	After
Before	*After*	*Before*	*After*
PART ONE	PART ONE	Article 17 (repealed)	—
Article 1	Article 1	Section 2 (deleted)	—
Article 2	Article 2	Article 18 (repealed)	—
Article 3	Article 3	Article 19 (repealed)	—
Article 3a	Article 4	Article 20 (repealed)	—
Article 3b	Article 5	Article 21 (repealed)	—
Article 3c (*)	Article 6	Article 22 (repealed)	—
Article 4	Article 7	Article 23 (repealed)	—
Article 4a	Article 8	Article 24 (repealed)	—
Article 4b	Article 9	Article 25 (repealed)	—
Article 5	Article 10	Article 26 (repealed)	—
Article 5a (*)	Article 11	Article 27 (repealed)	—
Article 6	Article 12	Article 28	Article 26
Article 6a	Article 13	Article 29	Article 27
Article 7 (repealed)	—		
Article 7a	Article 14	CHAPTER 2	CHAPTER 2
Article 7b (repealed)	—	Article 30	Article 28
Article 7c	Article 15	Article 31 (repealed)	—
Article 7d (*)	Article 16	Article 32 (repealed)	—
		Article 33 (repealed)	—
PART TWO	PART TWO	Article 34	Article 29
Article 8	Article 17	Article 35 (repealed)	—
Article 8a	Article 18	Article 36	Article 30
Article 8b	Article 19	Article 37	Article 31
Article 8c	Article 20		
Article 8d	Article 21	TITLE II	TITLE II
Article 8e	Article 22	Article 38	Article 32
		Article 39	Article 33
PART THREE	PART THREE	Article 40	Article 34
TITLE I	TITLE I	Article 41	Article 35
		Article 42	Article 36
Article 9	Article 23	Article 43	Article 37
Article 10	Article 24	Article 44 (repealed)	—
Article 11 (repealed)	—	Article 45 (repealed)	—
CHAPTER 1	CHAPTER 1	Article 46	Article 38
Section 1 (deleted)	—	Article 47 (repealed)	—
Article 12	Article 25		
		TITLE III	TITLE III
Article 13 (repealed)	—	CHAPTER 1	CHAPTER 1
Article 14 (repealed)	—		
Article 15 (repealed)	—	Article 48	Article 39
Article 16 (repealed)	—		

Before	After	Before	After
Article 49	Article 40	Article 73k (*)	Article 63
Article 50	Article 41	Article 73l (*)	Article 64
Article 51	Article 42	Article 73m (*)	Article 65
		Article 73n (*)	Article 66
CHAPTER 2	CHAPTER 2	Article 73o (*)	Article 67
		Article 73p (*)	Article 68
Article 52	Article 43	Article 73q (*)	Article 69
Article 53 (repealed)	—		
Article 54	Article 44	TITLE IV (**)	TITLE V
Article 55	Article 45		
Article 56	Article 46	Article 74	Article 70
Article 57	Article 47	Article 75	Article 71
Article 58	Article 48	Article 76	Article 72
		Article 77	Article 73
CHAPTER 3	CHAPTER 3	Article 78	Article 74
		Article 79	Article 75
Article 59	Article 49	Article 80	Article 76
Article 60	Article 50	Article 81	Article 77
Article 61	Article 51	Article 82	Article 78
Article 60	Article 50	Article 83	Article 79
Article 62 (repealed)	—	Article 84	Article 80
Article 63	Article 52		
Article 64	Article 53	TITLE V	TITLE VI
Article 65	Article 54		
Article 66	Article 55	CHAPTER 1	CHAPTER 1
		SECTION 1	SECTION 1
CHAPTER 4	CHAPTER 4		
		Article 85	Article 81
Article 67 (repealed)	—	Article 86	Article 82
Article 68 (repealed)	—	Article 87	Article 83
Article 69 (repealed)	—	Article 88	Article 84
Article 70 (repealed)	—	Article 89	Article 85
Article 71 (repealed)	—	Article 90	Article 86
Article 72 (repealed)	—		
Article 73 (repealed)	—	Section 2 (deleted)	—
Article 73a (repealed)	—	Article 91 (repealed)	—
Article 73b	Article 56	SECTION 3	SECTION 2
Article 73c	Article 57		
Article 73d	Article 58	Article 92	Article 87
Article 73e (repealed)	—	Article 93	Article 88
Article 73f	Article 59	Article 94	Article 89
Article 73g	Article 60		
Article 73h (repealed)	—	CHAPTER 2	CHAPTER 2
		Article 95	Article 90
TITLE IIIa (**)	TITLE IV	Article 96	Article 91
		Article 97 (repealed)	—
Article 73i (*)	Article 61	Article 98	Article 92
Article 73j (*)	Article 62		

Before	After	Before	After
Article 99	Article 93	Article 109k	Article 122
		Article 109l	Article 123
CHAPTER 3	CHAPTER 3	Article 109m	Article 124
Article 100	Article 94	TITLE VIa (**)	TITLE VIII
Article 100a	Article 95	Article 109n (*)	Article 125
Article 100b (repealed)	—	Article 109o (*)	Article 126
Article 100c (repealed)	—	Article 109p (*)	Article 127
Article 100d (repealed)	—	Article 109q (*)	Article 128
Article 101	Article 96	Article 109r (*)	Article 129
Article 102	Article 97	Article 109s (*)	Article 130
TITLE VI	TITLE VII	TITLE VII	TITLE IX
CHAPTER 1	CHAPTER 1	Article 110	Article 131
Article 102a	Article 98	Article 111 (repealed)	—
Article 103	Article 99	Article 112	Article 132
Article 103a	Article 100	Article 113	Article 133
Article 104	Article 101	Article 114 (repealed)	—
Article 104a	Article 102	Article 115	Article 134
Article 104b	Article 103		
Article 104c	Article 104	TITLE VIIa	TITLE X
CHAPTER 2	CHAPTER 2	Article 116 (*)	Article 135
Article 105	Article 105	TITLE VIII	TITLE XI
Article 105a	Article 106		
Article 106	Article 107	CHAPTER 1 (***)	CHAPTER 1
Article 107	Article 108	Article 117	Article 136
Article 108	Article 109	Article 118	Article 137
Article 108a	Article 110	Article 118a	Article 138
Article 109	Article 111	Article 118b	Article 139
		Article 118c	Article 140
CHAPTER 3	CHAPTER 3	Article 119	Article 141
Article 109a	Article 112	Article 119a	Article 142
Article 109b	Article 113	Article 120	Article 143
Article 109c	Article 114	Article 121	Article 144
Article 109d	Article 115	Article 122	Article 145
CHAPTER 4	CHAPTER 4	CHAPTER 2	CHAPTER 2
Article 109e	Article 116	Article 123	Article 146
Article 109f	Article 117	Article 124	Article 147
Article 109g	Article 118	Article 125	Article 148
Article 109h	Article 119		
Article 109i	Article 120	CHAPTER 3	CHAPTER 3
Article 109j	Article 121	Article 126	Article 149

Before	After	Before	After
Article 127	Article 150	Article 130s	Article 175
		Article 130t	Article 176
TITLE IX	TITLE XII		
Article 128	Article 151	TITLE XVII	TITLE XX
		Article 130u	Article 177
TITLE X	TITLE XIII	Article 130v	Article 178
Article 129	Article 152	Article 130w	Article 179
		Article 130x	Article 180
TITLE XI	TITLE XIV	Article 130y	Article 181
Article 129a	Article 153		
		PART FOUR	PART FOUR
TITLE XII	TITLE XV	Article 131	Article 182
Article 129b	Article 154	Article 132	Article 183
Article 129c	Article 155	Article 133	Article 184
Article 129d	Article 156	Article 134	Article 185
		Article 135	Article 186
TITLE XIII	TITLE XVI	Article 136	Article 187
Article 130	Article 157	Article 136a	Article 188
TITLE XIV	TITLE XVII	PART FIVE	PART FIVE
Article 130a	Article 158	TITLE I	TITLE I
Article 130b	Article 159	CHAPTER 1	CHAPTER 1
Article 130c	Article 160	SECTION 1	SECTION 1
Article 130d	Article 161	Article 137	Article 189
Article 130e	Article 162	Article 138	Article 190
		Article 138a	Article 191
TITLE XV	TITLE XVIII	Article 138b	Article 192
Article 130f	Article 163	Article 138c	Article 193
Article 130g	Article 164	Article 138d	Article 194
Article 130h	Article 165	Article 138e	Article 195
Article 130i	Article 166	Article 139	Article 196
Article 130j	Article 167	Article 140	Article 197
Article 130k	Article 168	Article 141	Article 198
Article 130l	Article 169	Article 142	Article 199
Article 130m	Article 170	Article 143	Article 200
Article 130n	Article 171	Article 144	Article 201
Article 130o	Article 172		
Article 130p	Article 173	SECTION 2	SECTION 2
Article 130q (repealed)	—	Article 145	Article 202
		Article 146	Article 203
TITLE XVI	TITLE XIX	Article 147	Article 204
Article 130r	Article 174	Article 148	Article 205
		Article 149 (repealed)	—

Before	After	Before	After
Article 150	Article 206	SECTION 5	SECTION 5
Article 151	Article 207		
Article 152	Article 208	Article 188a	Article 246
Article 153	Article 209	Article 188b	Article 247
Article 154	Article 210	Article 188c	Article 248
SECTION 3	SECTION 3	CHAPTER 2	CHAPTER 2
Article 155	Article 211	Article 189	Article 249
Article 156	Article 212	Article 189a	Article 250
Article 157	Article 213	Article 189b	Article 251
Article 158	Article 214	Article 189c	Article 252
Article 159	Article 215	Article 190	Article 253
Article 160	Article 216	Article 191	Article 254
Article 161	Article 217	Article 191a (*)	Article 255
Article 162	Article 218	Article 192	Article 256
Article 163	Article 219		
		CHAPTER 3	CHAPTER 3
SECTION 4	SECTION 4	Article 193	Article 257
		Article 194	Article 258
Article 164	Article 220	Article 195	Article 259
Article 165	Article 221	Article 196	Article 260
Article 166	Article 222	Article 197	Article 261
Article 167	Article 223	Article 198	Article 262
Article 168	Article 224		
Article 168a	Article 225	CHAPTER 4	CHAPTER 4
Article 169	Article 226		
Article 170	Article 227	Article 198a	Article 263
Article 171	Article 228	Article 198b	Article 264
Article 172	Article 229	Article 198c	Article 265
Article 173	Article 230		
Article 174	Article 231	CHAPTER 5	CHAPTER 5
Article 175	Article 232		
Article 176	Article 233	Article 198d	Article 266
Article 177	Article 234	Article 198e	Article 267
Article 178	Article 235		
Article 179	Article 236	TITLE II	TITLE II
Article 180	Article 237	Article 199	Article 268
Article 181	Article 238	Article 200 (repealed)	—
Article 182	Article 239	Article 201	Article 269
Article 183	Article 240	Article 201a	Article 270
Article 184	Article 241	Article 202	Article 271
Article 185	Article 242	Article 203	Article 272
Article 186	Article 243	Article 204	Article 273
Article 187	Article 244	Article 205	Article 274
Article 188	Article 245	Article 205a	Article 275
		Article 206	Article 276

Before	After	Before	After
Article 206a (repealed)	—	Article 227	Article 299
Article 207	Article 277	Article 228	Article 300
Article 208	Article 278	Article 228a	Article 301
Article 209	Article 279	Article 229	Article 302
Article 209a	Article 280	Article 230	Article 303
		Article 231	Article 304
PART SIX	PART SIX	Article 232	Article 305
		Article 233	Article 306
Article 210	Article 281	Article 234	Article 307
Article 211	Article 282	Article 235	Article 308
Article 212 (*)	Article 283	Article 236 (*)	Article 309
Article 213	Article 284	Article 237 (repealed)	—
Article 213a (*)	Article 285	Article 238	Article 310
Article 213b (*)	Article 286	Article 239	Article 311
Article 214	Article 287	Article 240	Article 312
Article 215	Article 288	Article 241 (repealed)	—
Article 216	Article 289	Article 242 (repealed)	—
Article 217	Article 290	Article 243 (repealed)	—
Article 218 (*)	Article 291	Article 244 (repealed)	—
Article 219	Article 292	Article 245 (repealed)	—
Article 220	Article 293	Article 246 (repealed)	—
Article 221	Article 294		
Article 222	Article 295	FINAL	FINAL
Article 223	Article 296	PROVISIONS	PROVISIONS
Article 224	Article 297		
Article 225	Article 298	Article 247	Article 313
Article 226 (repealed)	—	Article 248	Article 314

(*)   New Article introduced by the Treaty of Amsterdam.
(**)   New Title introduced by the Treaty of Amsterdam.
(***) Chapter 1 restructured by the Treaty of Amsterdam.

Table of Cases

Table of Treaties

Table of EC Secondary Legislation

Table of National Legislation

SECTION 1

Introduction

1

Bureaucratic Nightmare, Technocratic Regime and the Dream of Good Transnational Governance

*Christian Joerges**

1. Contextualising the Comitology Complex

Comitology[1] marks the transformation of the "old" European Economic Communities into a European polity. Committees are an institutional means of creating policy for the European internal market that involves not only a plethora of policy objectives, regulatory techniques and specific structures of governance, but also a perceptible legitimacy problem. Consequently, comitology challenges the very foundations on which traditional legal and political analyses of the EC rest. The purpose of this book, therefore, is to form a bridge across the chasm dividing politics and the law so as to understand the comitology complex more comprehensively.

2. Social Regulation and Internal Market Policy: Re-regulation and Re-politicisation

The intensification of European internal market policy during the 1980s has often been characterised as an exercise in "negative" integration. Since Tinbergen invented the concept of negative integration,[2] it has been used to serve several goals of political discourse. Indeed, at first blush, the

* Professor of Law, European University Institute, Florence. I would like to thank Stephen Vousden for his intensive editorial work on my English
[1] This term is widely used for the whole spectrum of committees although the Council Decision 87/373/EEC concerns only the procedures for the exercise of implementing powers conferred on the Commission, (1987) OJ L 197/33; the Commission's draft proposal of 16 July 1998, (1998) OJ C 279/5, sticks to that terminology.
[2] See Tinbergen (1965).

eloquent rhetoric that is intended to distinguish between integration oriented "merely" to removing non-tariff barriers to trade and "positive" integration designed to develop European policies, seems perfectly reasonable and analytically even convincing.[3]

However, on closer inspection, the use of the positive/negative dichotomy is beguiling not least because it leads to two kinds of misconceptions. First, negative integration suggests a rather myopic vision of establishing uniform market conditions as in some way paying tribute to pre-legal "freedoms". But this has the deleterious effect that the politically creative elements involved in removing barriers to trade disappear from public view. Secondly, and this is just as damaging to understanding the famous dichotomy, even when analytically carefully defined, the dichotomy will be difficult to apply to the real world of European intervention in the regulation of the internal market; how is one to distinguish a "negative" policy, aimed at removing legal differences, from a "positive" policy, aimed at determining what laws are to be replaced or removed. Again, viewing the phenomenon of harmonisation through the bi-focal lens of positive and negative integration merely constructs an understanding of EC intervention that conceals an awareness to the regulatory interests held by the Member States when they produce policy decisions claiming to implement the economic freedoms contained in the Treaties.[4]

The dichotomy has become part of the ideological rhetoric of market integration and has thus exercised a profound effect on the understanding of the emerging European polity. The now legendary internal market initiatives of the 1980s were, at the time, viewed by sceptical and partisan commentators alike, as a two-pronged strategy combining an implementation of the freedoms guaranteed in the EC Treaty and the European principle of "mutual recognition"[5] to overcome the national regulatory discretion that littered the path towards integration. However, this two-pronged legal strategy of deregulation failed to clear through the pile of regulatory provisions that acted as non-tariff barriers to trade, and instead, and indeed rather perversely, the strategy only assisted in the construction of new "European" arrangements that "re-regulated"[6] the path trodden by the Member States as they trudged their way off to the European market.

Two observations can be made at this point on the context of surrounding the regulatory route chosen by the Member States. The first concerns the "level" or "stringency" of regulatory policy. The Treaty stipulated that the harmonisation measures needed to "complete the internal market" should aim at "a high level of protection" as a *legal* requirement

---

[3] In this sense, for example, Scharpt (1997a: chapter 2).

[4] See Joerges *et al* (1988: 178 ff.) with references.

[5] See the notorious (over-)interpretation of the legendary 1979 *Cassis de Dijon* judgment by the Commission, (1980) OJ C 256/2.

[6] See the debate commented in Majone (1990).

pursuant to Article 100a (3) EC. Most observers underline that this requirement has in fact been achieved.[7] Of course, identifying a particular level of protection, and making a distinction between stricter and more lax rules, is an enterprise riddled with so many problems that it seems more appropriate to view the whole "high" level objective debate as a "modernisation" strategy. This strategy happened to fit rather well with the conditions for EC institutional action: Article 100a (3) EC only required the Commission to present regulatory proposals that could secure a qualified majority. However, as soon as the Commission began to pursue "positive" integrative strategies, they encountered resistance from the different national regulatory traditions and interest groupings that were included in the European structure. This resistance meant that the Commission could not adopt any obviously national model when launching a proposed piece of regulatory legislation because this would not have been conducive to generating sufficient consensus within the Council. Thus, the Commission had to propose legislation as some "objective" and "neutral" mediation between the goal of market integration and that of guaranteeing protective interests like health and safety, the environment, and consumer protection.

If such objective neutrality becomes a commonly shared objective, how can its implementation be furthered? One conceptual response to this question has been proffered by Giandomenico Majone. The central thesis of Majone is that the EC should, and indeed must, confine itself to essentially technical corrections to market failure. The corrections must be oriented to efficiency criteria, in the broadest sense of the meaning, and they must also refrain from all distributive activities.[8] Majone does not deny that policy options to a particular regulatory standard will have disparate impact on some regions, or indeed on Member States, nor does he ignore the fact that in the event of a dispute, the actors concerned will assert their interests through their governments or other national agents. Consequently, Majone is concerned primarily with the conditions for ensuring the success of Community policies even if this is at the expense of deliberately neglecting policy areas which are fraught with diplomatic tension such as those with potentially distributive objectives. Against this theoretical backdrop, it comes as no surprise to read that Majone adopts a particularly narrow view of what constitutes "social regulation".[9]

---

[7] For product safety law see in detail Joerges *et al* (1988) and Joerges (1990); on safety at work see Eichener (1993) and Bücker (1997); on foodstuffs law see, for example, Hufen (1993) and now in more detail Schlacke (1998). For a markedly sceptical view of environment policy on the example of the UVP directive see now Albert (1998), who admittedly neglects the – now outdated – institutional context.

[8] The term "social regulation" denotes not the whole of social policy, but "merely" so-called "quality-of-life issues such as risk, consumer safety, the environment or the protection of diffuse interests and non-commodity values"; so runs Majone's (1996a) definition; see earlier Majone (1993a).

[9] Majone (1993b); see Majone (1996a: 285 ff.).

Readers of this book will realise to what degree Majone's work has influenced academic perceptions of European market building strategies. They will also encounter two objections to his theses. The severity of the criticisms are closely related to the object of this book's concerns with the "constitutional" dimensions and the problem-solving capacity of the EC comitology system. First, it is important to note that no national constitutional state has ever given *carte blanche* to expert committees. Indeed, even at Community level, the normative, ethical, cultural and political dimensions of risk assessment have all combined to militate against a delegation of risk management to purely "technocratic" expert bodies and have almost certainly precluded the option of establishing one single institution that would be able to come up with uniform decisions which are socially acceptable within the entire internal market. This situation is loaded with far-reaching implications for the design of the EC institutional structure as it is precisely because risk assessments also include politico-normative considerations that the committee system must mediate between "universal" European-wide criteria and national concerns. Recognising this need within the regulatory risk assessment system clearly prevents the EC from ever developing a central authority that would be politically unaccountable.[10]

The second criticism of Majone's work concerns his treatment of distributive considerations. In Majone's view, it is the insulation of social regulation from distributive objectives which constitutes its non-political nature. This dichotomy between a-political social regulation and political distributive politics seems highly artificial and misleading. It simply cannot be denied that regulatory standards do have important economic implications which rank high on the agenda of political actors. An insulation of internal market policies from distributive concerns needs therefore to be grounded on normative reasons and compensated by broader strategies.[11] Even where the insulation of social regulation from distributive concerns can be justified, social regulation retains a "political" dimension. The reality of the development of the EC regulatory system is at any rate such that it would seem rather naive to believe that regulatory bodies will themselves be "apolitical". On the contrary, the issues committees are to deal with tend to become more and more political – numerous examples of this development are to be found in the regulation of genetic engineering, foodstuffs and nutritional policy and even in health and safety at work.

When the two queries are coupled together and seen in the light of the ethical and normative dimensions to risk assessments which are being taken in complex social regulation, then the explosive growth of the comitology system cannot be understood as the growth of technocratic governance, and it is equally deceptive to justify the delegation of this task

---

[10] Joerges/Neyer (1997a: 278).

[11] See Joerges/Neyer (1997a: 295-298).

to some European agency in the manner of Majone's. The scale of the "repoliticisation" phenomenon is such that it presents an enormous problem of whether the current institutional framework is appropriately equipped to cope with the technically complex, economically important and politically sensitive dimensions of Europe's internal market.

3. Legal and Institutional Options

From the historical description of the Commission's role in the comitology system and the nexus to the institutional developments of the Treaty revisions, it is clear that the continual deepening of market integration has always been associated with an expansion of the institutional frameworks designed to achieve regulatory ends. Furthermore, given the disparate configurations of interests within the EC framework, it is not surprising that the design of the committees varies considerably. However, there are three patterns for European social regulation, limited but not determined by the institutional peculiarities of the Community, that deserve particular attention. The three forms clearly demonstrate the interdependencies between the institutional alternatives, the definitions of regulatory problems, and also the indispensability of practical, normative arguments.

3.1 Mutual Recognition Regulatory Competition

One institutional alternative is to abandon "positive" EC policy in favour of the "mutual recognition" of national provisions. This policy is founded on information policy measures and consistent product liability law.[12] However, even though the role of mutual recognition attracted a great deal of theoretical attention, it has failed in practice to govern the field of social regulation. The failure does not come as any great surprise given that there is no legal system which could function with regulatory policies that are immune from the concerns about risks to health and the environment. Notwithstanding the deregulatory rhetoric involved in the construction of the single market, it has never been conceivable that the market could be "completed" merely by deregulating risk controls – and if any further proof of this assertion were needed, then the regulatory catastrophe surrounding the BSE "mad cow" disease serves as a case in point of how tearing down the boundaries between markets not only yields economic advantage but also raises intensely complicated social problems.

---

[12] As in fact was said at the time by the Wissenschaftlicher Beirat beim Bundesministerium für Wirtschaft (Scientific Advisory Council at the Federal Ministry of Economics) (1986); on the later debate, see Gerken (1995).

3.2 Agencies

Another institutional option is to establish agencies. Independent regulatory agencies, already an option firmly established in the USA, have been
advocated by Majone as being an institutional priority for the EC.[13]
Majone claims, in theoretical and normative-constitutional terms,[14] that
the delegation of regulatory powers to non-majoritarian institutions
"internally" stabilises commitments from political short-termism, and
"externally" acts to enhance the credibility of programmatic commitments.[15]

The institutional option would amount to a "renunciation of power" by
politically accountable actors and could only be acceptable if a type of
technocratic self-restraint could be imposed on the agencies. Furthermore,
the agency option would require the tasks of the agencies to be clearly
defined by legislative requirements and the practice of regulatory activity
would have to satisfy procedural standards that could be substantiated,
monitored and subject to review by courts.[16]

The reality of the European agencies which have been established so far
cannot meet these concerns. The London Pharmaceuticals Agency, which
was created in 1993,[17] remains essentially tied to the committee structure
that it was designed to replace.[18] Indeed, this inability to gain the genuine
legal regulatory competence that has been granted to their American
cousins, forms a criticism that can be levelled at all the new European
agencies for they are all auxiliary institutions satiating the Commission's
appetite for prepared information. Notwithstanding the success of the
Commission's efforts to curtail and limit the autonomy of European
agencies, the Commission may enjoy a false sense of security because it has
created a regulatory scenario resembling that of Goethe's "Sorcerer's
Apprentice".

3.3 Committees

The final institutional option is committees. The apparently irresistible rise
of the committee system as a forum for, and form of, regulatory policy for
the internal market appears at first sight to be an obvious precept for
functionalist reason. It was not a coincidence that the committee system
was first developed under the auspices of the most intensively regulated

---

[13] See references in notes 8 and 9, above.

[14] See the analysis by Everson (1995a).

[15] Most recently, see again Majone (1998).

[16] See Majone (1993b) and the analysis by Everson (1995a) and (1998).

[17] The "European Agency for the Evaluation of Medicinal Products" (EMEA), set up by
Council Regulation (EEC) 2309/93, (1993) OJ L 214/1. Details in Gardener (1996); Vos
(1999: 203 ff).

[18] See, for example, Dehousse (1997: 254 ff.) and earlier Joerges (1991a).

sector of the European economy: agriculture.[19] A pattern of regulatory behaviour emerged as the EC realised that regulating policy sectors required constant "accompaniment" to guarantee the necessary consent being generated among the Member States to implement the programmes without establishing genuine European powers of administration. However, although this regulatory path cannot be explained completely by these general considerations, it does seem safe to mention three observations at this point for they are reflected throughout the contributions to this book.

The committee system can be characterised as a form of action through which the Community executes long-term policy goals. Even though the form of "comitology" bears the imprints of recent internal market policy, it must be analysed in the context of the creation and "management" of the market; that is to say, that comitology must be connected with the specific rationality patterns and content of regulating the market.

The committee system must be considered as an institutionalisation of the European internal market which is specific to the Community. It is clear that the practical shape of the committee depends on the tasks associated with market integration and of course, these can change over time. As a result, the committee structure itself must remain supple and have a flexible internal structure that can meet the ever changing demands of performance capacity which the institutions of the EC place upon it.

Finally, the committee system is, without doubt, a specific form of Community governance, or of market management, which carries enormous "constitutional" significance.

4. A Contest or a Concert of Disciplines? From Cacophony to Polyphony

Comitology forms a battle ground for the EC institutions but because the scale of the conflict is now so large, it is dangerous to leave the analysis to one solitary author or indeed to one academic discipline. This assertion does not suggest in the least that mono-disciplinary analysis has no contribution to make to understanding the comitology phenomenon, because that would ignore the reality that each of the social sciences has elucidated specific and salient aspects of the comitology problem; but it does acknowledge that each discipline has its idiosyncratic research obsessions. For lawyers, comitology represents a strengthening of the administrative branch of government which seems to escape parliamentary control and even appears to elude the scope of judicial review to which national regula-

---

[19] See Bertram (1967); Falke (1996: 138 ff.).

tion is subject within the legal systems of the Member States. For political scientists, the problem seems completely different: comitology confronts their discipline with the simultaneous presence of intergovernmentalist bargaining and the construction of supranational institutions. As such, comitology stubbornly refuses to be pigeonholed into the classical paradigms of integration theories. Institutional economic analysis must either criticise the establishment of this comitology complex or simply remain dumbfounded by its continued success.[20]

Acknowledging the weaknesses of the individual social sciences permits the deployment of a multidisciplinary research agenda that pays attention to the ingenuity of practice and seems better equipped to meet the many challenges posed by comitology. To acknowledge this potential is not to equate the factual with the normative but to ensure that the academic analyses and suggestions relate to the reality of social regulation in Europe's internal market. The inclusion of the regulatory actors themselves thus serves a threefold purpose. First, it exposes their activities to academic criticism. Secondly, the accounts of the actors serve to show that understanding comitology from a legal formalist perspective would simply be inadequate. And thirdly, it should persuade political scientists to take Law and its factual power more seriously. Thus, increasing awareness to the problems of traditional paradigms ought to bridge the gaping chasm between analytical and normative approaches to integration studies and, in turn, this should sustain the search for a "constitutional" perspective on European governance advocated by the editors along with many other contributors to this book.

5. Institutional Conflicts and the Europeanisation of Administrative Practices

The legal analysis of the committee system has traditionally focused on the repeated and continuous conflict between the EC institutions.[21] The escalation of the dispute resulted in: attention from the Court in the context of the *Meroni* (or anti-delegation) doctrine; a legally-binding institutional balance of powers;[22] a debate on the new version of Article 145 of the Single European Act[23] and relatively successful attempts of the European

---

[20] See Steunenberg *et al* (1997).

[21] For details on this, see Bradley, in this volume; Vos, in this volume.

[22] Case 25/70, *Einfuhr- und Vorratsstelle für Getreide und Futtermittel* v. *Köster, Berodt & Co.* [1970] ECR 1161; Case 23/75, *Rey Soda* v. *Cassa Conguagli Zucchero* [1970] ECR 1279; Case 5/77, *Tedeschi* v. *Denkavit* [1977] ECR 1555.

[23] The complaint brought by the European Parliament against the Council's Comitology resolution was rejected by the ECJ as inadmissible, without going into the legal questions of Comitology (Case 302/87, *Parliament* v. *Council (Comitology)* [1988] ECR 5615; Case C-70/88, *Parliament* v. *Council* [1990] ECR I-2041.

Parliament towards enhancing its own legal position within the comitology procedures.[24]

There has been another series of decisions which even though less spectacular than the legal fireworks of the institutional conflict they are no less important because they go to the heart of what may be described as the "procedural modalities" of the committee system.[25] The number of decisions[26] that deal directly with the committee procedure is surprisingly small but there are passages in the judgments which are of fundamental importance to European "social regulation" because they contain the procedural requirements for arriving at, and justifying, decisions. The passages in these judgments may contain the potential to develop requirements so as to increase the transparency of the system and also approach some recognition of participation rights.

The contributions which open this book capture both of these developments. *Ellen Vos* sets in this introductory section the general frame of the comitology debate in terms of the institutional balance of powers and the doctrine of subsidiarity when she examines the legal technicalities and peculiarities associated with the comitology system. The book then focuses in part 2 on the positions of the individual institutions. The cautious and thoughtful restatements of the positions of the European Commission, in the piece by *Giuseppe Ciavarini Azzi*, and the Council, in the contribution by *Jean-Paul Jacqué*, can in part be explained by the fact that these contributions were written during the height of the Intergovernmental Conference which subsequently failed to come to grips with the comitology problem.[27]

The book then shifts its attention to the potential of the institutions to meet the challenge. In the analysis of *Kieran St C Bradley*, who several years ago delivered probably the most detailed legal basis for the position of the European Parliament on the subject of comitology,[28] there is a sceptical and colourful account of the arguments that were proposed by the institutional actors, especially the Parliament. Indeed, he suggests that even though the Parliament has always claimed a greater role, the validity of this claim can be doubted for the Parliament may not be interested in good governance but rather only interested in its own institutional survival. Furthermore, Bradley extends his scepticism to deny generous readings of the ECJ judgments which could be interpreted as demonstrating a willing-

---

[24] See, in particular, the *modus vivendi* agreed between EP, Council and Commission on 20 December 1994, (1996) OJ C 102/1.

[25] On this see already Joerges (1997); Joerges/Neyer (1997a: 284 ff.).

[26] See, in particular, Case C-269/90, *Hauptzollamt München-Mitte* v. *Technische Universität München* [1991] ECR I-5469, at I-5499, and Case C 212/91, *Angelopharm* v. *Freie und Hansestadt Hamburg* [1994] ECR I-171.

[27] See the Commission's recent Proposal for a Council Decision laying down the procedures for the exercise of implementing powers conferred on the Commission, above, note 1.

[28] Bradley (1989); (1992) and (1997).

ness to discipline the institutions. Somewhat surprisingly but, I would like to add, rightly, he also underlines the "constitutional" dimensions of comitology and advocates that the institutional actors ought to be allowed to "write their own script". Interestingly his proposition results in a high level of responsibility being placed on the judiciary assuming that judges will realise "constitutional moments" and act accordingly.

The book then covers the contribution of *Graham R Chambers* who looks at how the European Parliament met the considerable challenges that resulted from the BSE "mad-cow" crisis. The BSE crisis, although not a crisis of comitology as a whole, did bring to the fore some very serious failures in the risk management regime governing the agricultural sector. The failures of risk management can be traced not only to defects in one Member State but also those that exist at European level. The response of the European Parliament to the crisis certainly established its credibility to act as a guardian of the concerns of European citizens by using and at the same time transforming its right to investigation into a means of initiating a European-wide critical debate through which at the end of the day both European and national officials were held politically accountable.

The book then turns its attention to the second, and seemingly more mundane, set of legal issues: the "administrative" or "technocratic" dimension to comitology. The comitology procedures normally produce implementing decisions concerning directives or regulations and as such, comitology may be seen as handing down "rules". Sometimes characterised by lawyers as "executive law making",[29] these rules may even affect individual actors quite directly – notwithstanding their often uncontroversial subject-matter. The technocratic dimension to comitology seems to lend itself to belonging to the traditional domain of administrative law and of all the contributions to this book, *John A E Vervaele's* contribution comes closest to this strategy. He captures a species of governance which involves the intergovernmental elements and he picks up on this theme but then also emphasises essential differences between fully-fledged federations and the EU. On this basis, he advocates that the EU should concentrate on building non-hierarchical co-operative networks.

The two other contributions to Part 4 go much further still towards reforming the technical dimension to comitology – indeed, these contributions question the utility of established models of administrative law. *Renaud Dehousse* adopts a functional approach and includes quite pragmatic deliberations in order to express his reservations about any European counterpart to the American Administrative Procedures Act and the strengthening of Parliamentary oversight. Indeed, his functional approach goes so far as to reflect seriously held concerns about the specific nature of the European polity and suggests a furthering of transparency, a greater openness of the

[29] Falke/Winter (1996).

comitology procedures and the development of additional procedural rules regulating the interface between comitology, committees and civil society at large. Essentially, Dehousse is striving towards the establishment of genuinely transnational structures of governance.

The piece by *Karl-Heinz Ladeur* is radical in a different respect: it leaves behind traditional models of administrative law in two fundamental ways. First, Ladeur conceptualises even "national" administrations as operating in "heterarchically" linked networks rather than as some hierarchically structured body which would be entrusted with the task of implementing given public interests. Consequently, and this itself forms the second departure from traditional thinking, he argues that the "Europeanisation" of administrative functions is but one further step in an ongoing progression which may even improve the problem-solving capacities of the EC merely because it will build up a greater potential for the gathering and improvement of knowledge under conditions of uncertainty.

6. Comitology as Perceived by Political Science

A standard question in political science is "into which paradigm of integration research does comitology fall?" Does the European Council's defence of the comitology system and the transposition of the 1987 Comitology Decision[30] amount to a complete confirmation of the practical relevance of intergovernmentalism?[31] Or is comitology more accurately described as fitting a neo-functionalist paradigm of an intensified co-operation between national administrations and the Commission? Or should comitology be viewed as a phenomenon which expresses Majone's assertion that the EC develops non-majoritarian institutions?[32] Each of the contributions to this book transcends the traditional dichotomies associated with integration research. The contributions are very sensitive to the importance of the institutions, the role of ideas and the normative components of social and political processes. As a lawyer, one may ask: how do their perceptions of institutions relate to the world of law; and do their conceptualisations of the normative dimensions of social action adequately capture activities within the legal system? Even though the individual contributors would propose slightly different answers to these questions, they all remain political scientists in that their responses aim at *explanations* of comitology and its decision-making practices.

This section of the book opens with two case studies on comitology by *Christine Landfried* and Thomas Gehring. Landfried examines the area of bio-technology which, by its very nature, contradicts the assumption that

---

[30] See note 1, above.
[31] As most recently in Pollack's principal/agent model (1997).
[32] See Majone (1996a: 285 ff.); see also Bach (1992) and (1993).

the European Union could function as a purely "technocratic" regime. Whereas this dimension of her argument appears rather obvious, the message in her analysis is far more challenging. The analysis reveals that politically thorny issues are often presented as purely technical questions. Thus, the way in which Europe responds to ethically and normatively controversial issues results in specific and sometimes opaque models of committees. On the basis of this knowledge, Landfried does not condemn this state of the Union but rather advocates far greater transparency and democratic decision-making that is founded on the polycratic nature of the European polity.

Thomas Gehring's analysis concerns the specific features of committee governance. There are two premises underpinning his research. First, committees only matter if the behaviour of actors inside the committee room is different to that which they display outside. Secondly, Gehring's analysis assumes that it is possible to identify and understand distinct patterns of interaction among these actors. From these premises, his analysis proceeds to deploy the conceptual distinction between "arguing" and "bargaining" to two types of committees: one committee with weak decision-making powers, the other with strong decision-making powers. His findings appear at first sight paradoxical: "arguing" prevails only in weak committees but the peculiar thing is that the value of arguing ensures that these weak committees assume a specific authority which secures their continued influence. In comitology procedures, where the mandate of the committee has been specified with some precision, any delegation of decision-making functions shifts the discourse into arguing. His analysis confirms the idea that the weak "advisory" committee was asked originally for *expert* opinions on technically complex matters – opinions which are largely insulated from either controversy concerning distribution or from large-scale political fights. In this way, the committee system could deliver common positions which were stable and which the political process found difficult to reject in the broader political process of bargaining. Indeed, Gehring's analysis lends some empirical credence to calls by Majone and others for the establishment of "strong" regulatory "non-majoritarian" institutions. However, on the basis of Gehring's analysis, it seems unlikely that bargaining could be substituted for by arguing because of the distributive implications of process regulation (rather than product regulation) even where implementing tasks would be delegated to "strong" committees.

Jürgen Neyer advocates a different case.[33] Neyer takes issue with the intergovernmentalist heritage which belies so many integration studies – including that of Gehring. Furthermore, Neyer also distances himself from the functionalist heritage, that inspires the protagonists concerned with viewing the EC as a collection of supranational and apolitical administra-

---

[33] See only Joerges/Neyer (1997a) and (1997b).

tive bodies. It is precisely because Neyer views comitology analytically as an integral part of genuinely transnational structures of governance that he can address a fresh cluster of institutional and normative issues. Neyer presents a cautious identification of "deliberative" processes within comitology. Neyer's concept of deliberation resembles Gehring's concept of arguing in that Neyer's concept means entrusting regulatory decision-making powers to independent experts who are insulated from distributional concerns. However, because Neyer acknowledges the non-technocratic nature of the comitology complex, his institutional and normative proposals differ markedly from any non-majoritarian thought.

Two further contributions look at comitology from abroad and from above. *Michelle Egan* and *Dieter Wolf* take the regulatory functions of the committee system seriously and literally. They interpret comitology in the light of the rich American arsenal of theories conceptualising the relationship between politics and administration based on experience with regulatory policy. Even those readers who believe in the distinctness of the European experience will find their comparative effort illuminating. *Wolfgang Wessels* pioneered research on European committees many years ago[34] and has reflected upon them ever since.[35] I refrain from commenting upon his remarks about his disciplinary colleagues or his scepticism towards black letter lawyers. Suffice it to underline that his "fusion thesis" is intended to cover much broader fields than the mere Europeanisation of social regulation and that his approach coincides with the analytical tools and normative perspectives of many contributions to this book which seek to conceptualise the functioning and the legitimacy of "administrative" activities outside or beyond the state.

7. Constitutionalising Committee Governance

If this book promises interdisciplinary research, then why are the contributions partitioned according to the accounts of the institutional actors, legal scholars and political scientists? The answer to this question is brief but it involves thorny issues[36] concerning the century-old schism between the normative and doctrinal approach to legal problems that contrasts so sharply with the external observations and explanations of legal events propounded by political scientists. Nevertheless, the collection of legal contributions confirmed the degree to which legal conceptions must refer to normative legal premises and the collection of contributions by political scientists document an involvement in normative discourse. Consequently even though the texts were compartmentalised, intellectual counterparts

---

[34] See Institut für Europäische Politik (1989).
[35] Wessels (1996) and (1998).
[36] See for a more comprehenive discussion Joerges (1996a).

can be identified and parallels between the often conflicting paradigms can be detected both in orientation and in their interpretation of minor problems.

The contributions gathered in Part 5 advocate a further "meta-disciplinary" step. They argue that Law matters to the integration process both as a fact (the normative deploying factual power)[37] and as a norm (the social impact of law depending on the "quality" of its contents). They search for a constitutional perspective that legitimises European governance and which is simultaneously capable of disciplining the real world of political conflict. Even though there is thus a perceptible theoretical and methodological convergence between us, this did not guarantee a unanimous judgment on the comitology complex. My own contribution seeks to elaborate a vision of "deliberative supranationalism" with a twofold basis in (national) constitutional states and emerging "deliberative" transnational patterns of interaction.[38] The Law matters in this vision because its task is not to establish some transnational "administration" but rather it is to ensure "good governance" of the common market which is responsive to the normative concerns and economic interests that are represented within European societies. As such the law's task is to mitigate between the basis of shared substantive principles and procedures controlling parochial interest representation and a furthering of the deliberative decision-making processes. *Michelle Everson*'s search for a constitutionalised administrative law dismisses the national state (including its *Volkswirtschaft*) a touch more radically; in her readiness to accept the emergence of a non-comprehensive non-statal transnational polity, Everson remains indebted to Majone's understanding of the European Community as a "fourth branch of government";[39] in her insistence on the social embeddedness of this "market polity", she strives for the resurrection or defence of democratic rather than technocratic legitimacy. Do such suggestions overinterpret the importance of the comitology complex, as Jachtenfuchs argues?[40] There are many good reasons to remain sceptical as to any generalising conclusions based upon rather thin evidence. The existence of "infranational" patterns nurturing the emergence of governance structures outside the constitutional state and beyond the traditional notions of European supranationalism seem undisputable – and hence the imagining in theory, and establishment in practice, of the constitutionalising of such orders is an irrefutable challenge.

With *Joseph H H Weiler*'s "Epilogue" the whole endeavour undertaken in this book gets a final tilt. On the one hand, Weiler confirms without any

[37] *"Die faktische Kraft des Normativen"* – to turn Georg Jellinek's famous and dubious theorem upside down.

[38] See Joerges/Neyer (1997a); Joerges (1997).

[39] Majone (1994a).

[40] Jachtenfuchs (1998).

reservation the factual importance ascribed to the comitology phenomenon in this project, and his depiction of its analytical and normative challenges is nothing less than dramatic. His reservations, however, relate to normative values of comitology as acknowledged in conceptualisations like that of this author. The belief in the factual impact of legally protected standards of reasoning ("*die faktische Kraft des Normativen*"), Weiler argues, is misguided; "deliberative supranationalism" either asks for the recognition of the normative power of the factual ("*die normative Kraft des Faktischen*") or, what is just as bad, promotes regulatory ideas which are conceptually empty and hence tend to camouflage real-world processes.

To place *Adrienne Héritier* in the final section outside her disciplinary *Heimat* is not to claim that her approach must be complementary to the lawyers' concerns with the social functions and normative properties of their beloved object of study. What seems nevertheless striking are parallels in Heritier's characterisation of the European polity and the motivation underlying the assignment of constitutionalising functions to law-making processes. A "polity in flux", continuously requiring institutional innovations and inevitably combining problem-solving endeavours with the search for legitimate governance structures cannot get away with subterfuge and camouflage techniques; it will have to design frameworks structuring the legitimacy of its permanent transformation. An, at best, utopian suggestion and/or near-to-impossible task? If this book makes readers aware of such dimensions within its, at first sight, rather mundane and technocratic subject, it has fulfilled its tasks.

2

EU Committees: the Evolution of Unforeseen Institutional Actors in European Product Regulation

Ellen Vos[*]

1. Introduction

Committees have operated within the Community's institutional structure since the Community's inception. As the 1972 Vedel Report stated,

> "[o]nce the Community institutions began to function, practice quite naturally gave birth to bodies for which no provision was made initially".[1]

Committees are an *ad hoc* institutional evolution meeting the, at times unexpected, functional demands of an ever-expanding European Community for technical information and expertise. The "birth" of committees generally responds to the triplicate need to achieve effective and efficient Community decision-making, to ensure the continuing presence of the Member States within the Community decision-making process and to include the views of socio-economic parties. In Brussels jargon, this plethora of committees is often referred to as "comitology". This term is also used in a stricter sense, encompassing only those committees composed of national representatives who assist the Commission in the exercise of its implementing powers. At present approximately 477 committees are listed on the Community budget.[2] Today, committees play an ever greater role within the Community decision-making process. The

---

[*] Lecturer in European Law, University of Maastricht.
[1] Report of the Working Party on the Enlargement of the Powers of the European Parliament, set up by the Commission in 1972 quoted by Lauwaars (1979: 365).
[2] It is noteworthy that the Community budget gives an overview of committees which are expected to meet and therefore does not include "dormant" committees. See SEC(89) 1728 final, 5. See also Falke (1996). Other authors, however, make different estimates, each based on different calculations. For example, Buitendijk and van Schendelen calculate approximately 1,000 committees. Buitendijk/van Schendelen (1995: 40).

increasing need of the Community to implement its own legislation and to manage the internal market leads to more committee-based decision-making.[3] The substantive increase in the importance of committees is revealed within the EU budget which discloses that in the years 1980 to 1989 annual Community expenditure on committees increased from approximately 3,8 million to 8 million ECU, whilst for 1998, this expenditure amounted to 19,5 million ECU.

This essay examines committees as an institutional model of Community regulatory policies, and analyses the main legal problems to which committees have given rise. In particular, the dispute surrounding the legality of committees composed of national representatives which must be consulted by the Commission in the exercise of its implementing powers is addressed. Delegation of implementing powers to the Commission, which is subject to review and oversight by these committees, it has been argued, upset the institutional balance of powers, interfering particularly with the Commission's right of decision and the Parliament's power of control. Subsequent to the Maastricht Treaty, such committees have once again become the focus of debate since the Parliament repeated its desire to be involved in the implementation of Community decision-making, this time strengthened by its co-legislative powers. Importantly, the call for a new Comitology Decision by the Intergovernmental Conference following the Treaty of Amsterdam keeps the institutional debate on comitology going, and this is intensified by the recent proposal of the Commission. In this context, this analysis aims to establish both a framework for the other contributions in this book and to underline the question of committees' legitimacy in this debate. Examination will focus on one specific field of regulatory politics: social or risk regulation, which is the main field of interest throughout this book. This field is mainly concerned with regulatory protection against risks to human health and safety and the environment.[4] In this field, the specific nature of risk regulation, requiring individual and flexible decision-making, has forced the Commission to become increasingly active. As a result, committee-based decision-making is gaining in importance. In conclusion, some suggestions for improvement will be advanced.

2. The Birth of Committees

The resort to committees by the Community institutions dates back to the 1960s, when the Council, urgently needing to reduce its workload in implementing the Community's agricultural policy, decided to delegate certain

[3] See Figures 2 and 3 of the contribution by Dehousse, in this volume.
[4] This terminology originates, in particular, from the USA. See, for example, Sunstein (1990) and Reagan (1987).

discretionary powers to the Commission.[5] Faced, however, with strong national resistance to an unconditional delegation of powers to the Commission, the Council obliged the Commission to consult a committee made up of national representatives prior to adopting any decision. Where this committee (by qualified majority voting) agreed upon the Commission measure or failed to reach a decision, the Commission was free to adopt the measure. However, when this committee rejected the draft decision, the Commission had to refer the matter back to the Council. Hence, under this so-called "management committee procedure" the Council retained its oversight powers, being able to take a different decision on the basis of a qualified majority. Another committee procedure (the "regulatory committee procedure") was introduced in 1968 and placed more onerous constraints on the Commission's exercise of implementing powers. In the years which followed, more of these committees, together with less powerful "advisory committees", were created by the Council in a variety of areas. Encouraged by the Paris Summit of 1972, which called for the increased participation of economic and social interests in the Community policy-making process,[6] the Commission created committees composed of interested representatives in specific fields. Furthermore, committees were also resorted to by the Commission in an attempt to satisfy its anxious demand for technical and scientific information. The expansion of Community activities has meant that an ever greater number of committees is involved in the preparation and implementation of Community policies.

3. Classification of Committees

From a legal policy perspective committees may be classified according to three criteria: a) binding nature of the consultation, b) the legal basis of committees and c) committee functions.

3.1 *Binding Nature of the Consultation*

According to the first criterion, committees can be divided into committees whose consultation is compulsory in the procedure for drafting Community legislation, and committees whose consultation is not compulsory.[7] Depending on the weight of their opinion, the first category of committees can be further subdivided into *advisory*, *management* and *regulatory* committees. This twofold distinction, however, is not rigid: committees may be transferred to the first category should either the

---

[5] See Bertram (1966-67); Schindler (1971) and Schmitt von Sydow (1973).
[6] Sixth General Report of the EC of 1972, 11.
[7] Such a division is adhered to in the Community budget.

Community legislature or the Court decide that their consultation needs to be made obligatory.[8]

3.2 *Legal Basis*

Under the second classification, committees may be divided into committees set up by a Council act, and committees set up by a Commission act. The first are established by a separate act of the Council, or are included in a Council (and Parliament) act regulating a specific subject-matter. The latter are, in general, created by a specific Commission act. In general, committees set up by Council act, in order to assist the Commission in implementation, need to be consulted in the decision-making procedure, whilst other committees, commonly set up by the Commission, do not require compulsory consultation.

3.3 *Functions*

In functional terms, three types of committees can be distinguished: scientific committees, interest committees and policy-making/implementation committees, each of which correspond with the different aspects of regulatory decision-making. The composition of the committees varies in accordance with their function. Scientific committees are composed of independent scientific experts. Interest committees consist of the representatives of the various interest groups, whilst policy-making/implementation committees are composed of the representatives of the Member States. Committees composed of scientific experts have been created by the Commission in response to the need for expertise and their recommendations form the basis of any decision. These committees thus operate both in the preparatory and in the implementing phase. Committees composed of representatives of socio-economic interests groups have been set up where the Commission wanted to hear a wider body of opinion. Committees composed of national representatives operate mainly in the implementing phase of the decision-making process, where the Council has delegated powers to the Commission. Obligatory consultation of such committees by the Commission follows a specific procedure.[9]

---

[8] See Case C-212/91, *Angelopharm* v. *Freie und Hansestadt Hamburg* [1994] ECR I-171. For example, the Scientific Committee on Food was considered so important as to make consultation obligatory, see, for instance, Article 6 of Council Directive 89/107/EEC on food additives authorised for use in foodstuffs intended for human consumption, (1989) OJ L 40/27.

[9] See section 4.1.

4. Institutional Challenges

Not surprisingly, the insertion within the Community's institutional structure of bodies not foreseen by the Treaties gave rise to various legal and institutional challenges. Given the general Community rule that, should the Council retain implementing powers at the Community level,[10] such powers should be delegated to the Commission, it has often been argued that the oversight of Commission activities by management and regulatory committees distorts the institutional balance of powers within the Community. In contrast to the opinions given by advisory committees, the opinions of the management and regulatory committees may not simply be ignored. For example, should the Commission wish to diverge from an opinion of a regulatory committee, it must refer its own draft measures back to the Council. This requirement, it has been argued, detracts from the Commission's independent right of decision and thus from the Parliament's right of control. These problems surfaced when the Community sought to streamline the presence of committees within the Community's institutional structure in order to achieve the goals of the internal market more efficiently.

4.1 Article 145 Third Indent and the 1987 Comitology Decision

The cumbersome and time-consuming nature of the "traditional" approach to market harmonisation which became apparent during the 1980s led the Community to seek a new strategy to achieve its precious aim of an integrated internal market. Inspired by the *Cassis de Dijon* ruling of 1979,[11] the Commission launched a new strategy in its White Paper on the completion on the internal market in 1985.[12] In this document the Commission introduced an integration strategy along the lines set out in the "New Approach to Technical Harmonisation and Standards", in which it would only harmonise trade barriers, justified under Article 36 EC, limiting itself to drafting legislative essential safety requirements and referring to technical standards, to be produced by the European standardisation bodies.[13] In tandem with its institutional corollary, the SEA's Article 100a which introduced qualified majority voting, this New Approach was designed to accelerate the decision-making procedure and make it at the same time more efficient.[14] Fast and efficient decision-making was also to be accomplished through a more rational and disciplined process of

---

[10] Rather than leave the matter of implementation to the Member States.

[11] Case 120/78, *Rewe-Zentrale AG* v. *Bundesmonopolverwaltung für Branntwein* [1979] ECR 649.

[12] COM(85) 310 final.

[13] Council Resolution on a New Approach to Technical Harmonisation and Standards, (1985) OJ C 136/1.

[14] See in more detail, Joerges *et al* (1988); Lauwaars (1988) and Vos (1997a).

delegating implementing powers to the Commission. To this end, a third indent was inserted into Article 145 EC, which obliged the Council to delegate implementing powers to the Commission, and at the same time demanded that it introduce formal and streamlined committee procedures.

Following heated conflicts which subsequently arose on the committee procedures to be introduced among the Community institutions, the Council finally adopted Decision 87/373/EEC, commonly termed the Comitology Decision.[15] This Decision consolidated the three classical procedures which had grown out of established Community practice, supervising the implementing powers delegated by the Council to the Commission by advisory, management and regulatory committees, with the management and regulatory committee procedures being further subdivided into an (a) and (b) variant. In addition, the Comitology Decision provided for a safeguard committee procedure. The complexity of the procedures requires a brief description.

4.1.1 Procedure I: the Advisory Committee Procedure

The advisory committee procedure requires the Commission to consult a committee for an opinion. This committee consists of representatives of the Member States and is chaired by a Commission representative. The latter submits the draft measures to the committee which delivers its opinion within a time limit laid down by the chair according to the urgency of the matter. If necessary, the committee adopts its opinion through a vote. The opinion is recorded in the minutes of the committee and each Member State may have its position registered in these minutes. When adopting its final decision, the Commission must take the "utmost" account of the committee's opinion and further inform the committee of the manner in which its opinion has been taken into account.

4.1.2 Procedure II: the Management Committee Procedure

The management committee procedure largely reproduces the traditional formula established in the agricultural area. Under this procedure, the Commission is required to consult a committee composed of representatives of the Member States and chaired by a representative of the Commission. The Commission representative submits a draft of the measures proposed for adoption to the committee which, in turn, delivers its opinion within a time limit laid down by the chair according to the urgency of the matter. The opinion of the committee is adopted by a qualified majority in accordance with Article 148 (2) EC, in the context of which the chair does not have a vote. Subsequently, the Commission adopts the measures, which have immediate effect. However, if these measures are not in accordance with the opinion of the committee, the Commission is

---

[15] (1987) OJ L 197/33.

obliged to communicate them to the Council forthwith. In such cases, there are two possible procedures. Under variant (a), the Commission may defer the application of the measures which it has decided upon, for a period not longer than one month from the date of communication to the Council. Within this period, the Council may take a different decision by qualified majority. Under variant (b), the Commission is obliged to defer application of the measures for a period to be laid down in each Council act of up to a maximum of three months from the date of communication to the Council. Within this period the Council may adopt a different decision by qualified majority.

4.1.3 Procedure III: the Regulatory Committee Procedure

The regulatory committee procedure varies from the management committee procedure in that, if the Commission wishes to adopt measures which are not in accordance with the committee's opinion, or in the absence of an opinion, it must without delay submit to the Council a proposal of the measures to be adopted. The Council then acts by qualified majority. In this case too, two variants exist. Variant (a) (*filet*) requires that if, on the expiry of the time limit laid down in each Council act (a maximum of three months from the date of referral to the Council), the Council has not acted the Commission then adopts the proposed measures. Variant (b) (*contre-filet*) stipulates that if, on the expiry of the time limit laid down in each Council act (up to a period of three months from the date of referral to the Council), the Council has not acted the proposed measures are adopted by the Commission, save where the Council has decided against the said measures by simple majority.

4.1.4 Safeguard Procedure

The safeguard procedure may be applied where the Council confers on the Commission the power to decide on safeguard measures. In accordance with the procedure, the Commission notifies the Council and the Member States of any decision regarding safeguard measures. In its enabling act, the Council may stipulate that, before adopting this decision, the Commission must consult the Member States in accordance with procedures to be determined in each case. Any Member State may refer the Commission's decision to the Council within a certain time limit to be determined in the act in question. This procedure, too, has two variants. In accordance with variant (a) the Council may take a different decision if it acts by qualified majority within a certain time limit determined in the main act. Under variant (b) the Council may, by qualified majority, confirm, amend or revoke the decision of the Commission within a certain time limit. If, within this period, the Council has not acted, the Commission decision is deemed to be revoked.

4.2 The Modus Vivendi

The Comitology Decision, however, failed to resolve the brewing controversy between the Community institutions. In particular the Commission
and the Parliament were upset to see the regulatory committee procedure
(especially in its *contre-filet* variant) included in the Decision notwithstanding their vehement protests. Subsequent to its unsuccessful attempt to
attack the validity of the Comitology Decision before the European Court
of Justice (ECJ),[16] the Parliament formally requested the Commission to be
informed of all Commission proposals submitted to advisory, management
or regulatory committees, which resulted in the adoption of the "Plumb-
Delors" agreement.[17] By virtue of this agreement, the Commission was
from now on obliged to forward to the Parliament all draft measures
referred to committees, with the exception of routine management
documents of a limited period of validity or of minor importance, and
proposals whose adoption is complicated by considerations of secrecy or
urgency. In practice, however, this strategy, too, was rather unsuccessful
since the Commission forwarded very few documents,[18] often leaving the
Parliament very little time to react, whilst the Parliament itself failed to
properly enforce this agreement.

However, although its initial judicial and political campaign against the
regulatory committee procedure had failed, the Parliament was soon
supplied with an opportunity to oppose the use of regulatory committee
procedures. After finally having been given co-legislative powers under a
co-decision procedure (obligatory for *inter alia* Community acts under
Article 100a EC) by the Treaty of Maastricht,[19] the Parliament argued that
Article 145 third indent EC did not apply to measures adopted jointly by
the Parliament and the Council, but only to acts derived solely from the
Council.[20] Accordingly, it consistently rejected any Commission proposals
for joint Parliament and Council Directives under Article 100a EC.[21] To
overcome this decisional deadlock, the Council was finally forced to
negotiate with the Commission and Parliament, which resulted in the

---

[16] Case 302/87, *Parliament v. Council (Comitology)* [1988] ECR 5615.

[17] Jacobs/Corbett/Shackleton (1994: 234).

[18] This may partly be due to the fact that not every Commission official knew that this
procedure existed. This was admitted in several interviews which I conducted with
Commission officials.

[19] See Bradley (1992: 696) and Bradley/Feeney (1993: 405).

[20] Resolution of the Parliament, (1994) OJ C 20/176. See also the 1993 De Giovanni
Report of the Committee on Institutional Affairs on questions of Comitology relating to the
entry into force of the Maastricht Treaty, Doc. A3-417/93, PE 206.619/fin.

[21] See in particular the bargaining on mechanical coupling devices, recreational craft and
the open network provision (ONP) of voice telephony discussed by Earnshaw/Judge (1995:
634-636). See, also Falke/Winter (1996).

conclusion of a *modus vivendi* in December 1994.[22] Under this *modus vivendi*, the Commission is obliged to forward copies of draft measures sent to committees to the appropriate parliamentary committee. Largely mirroring and reinforcing the Plumbs-Delors agreement, the *modus vivendi* contains one important additional element: the Council is obliged to consult the Parliament should a committee have failed to reach agreement, and the Commission be forced to refer a proposal to the Council. Although the very general formulation of this agreement gives room for various interpretations, in practice, the *modus vivendi* has achieved its aim of unblocking the decision-making procedure and developing (apparent) agreement amongst the institutions on comitology. Although the 1996/97 IGC failed to consider comitology as a topic in need of Treaty amendment, it did call upon the Commission to submit a proposal to amend the Comitology Decision to the Council by the end of 1998[23] (see below).

5. The ECJ's Attitude towards Committee Procedures

5.1 *Approval of the Committee Procedures*

As a response to the functional demands of the European Community for rapid and expert-led decision-making in the process of market integration, committees have been given legal approval by the ECJ. The legality of the use of the management committee procedure was contested immediately following its introduction. In *Köster*, this procedure was argued to be contrary to the EC Treaty, since it not only interfered with the Commission's independent right of decision, but also because the use of a body not foreseen by the EC Treaty would distort the established institutional relationship between the Commission and the Council.[24] The ECJ, however, failed to find any legal objection to the oversight of Commission implementing powers by committees. It emphasised that a delegation of powers to the Commission under Article 155 EEC was entirely optional, and that consequently Article 155 EEC did not preclude the Council from subjecting delegated powers to detailed rules for their exercise. Following this logic, the ECJ concluded that the management committee procedure played an important role, ensuring permanent consultation between Council and Commission, and allowed the Council greater room to both delegate powers and to retain control over such powers, possibly even substituting its action for that of the Commission.

---

[22] *Modus vivendi* between the European Parliament, the Council and the Commission concerning the implementing measures for acts adopted in accordance with the procedure laid down in Article 189b of the EC Treaty, (1996) OJ C 102/1.

[23] Declaration no. 31 to the Treaty of Amsterdam.

[24] Case 25/70, *Einfuhr- und Vorratstelle für Getreide und Futtermittel* v. *Köster, Berodt & Co.*, [1970] ECR 1161.

Since ultimate decision-making power did not rest with the relevant committee, but remained either with the Council or the Commission, the ECJ held that the resort to management committees was not contrary to the Community's institutional balance under Article 4 EC.[25] The legality of this procedure was further confirmed by the Court in *Rey Soda*.[26]

In its subsequent case-law, the Court tackled various other objections raised against comitology, concluding in each case that they were unfounded. For example, in *Tedeschi*, the Court rejected fears that comitology might, rather than accelerate, paralyse the Community decision-making process; concluding that the *contre-filet* variant of the regulatory committee procedure would not necessarily lead to decisional impasse, since the Commission was always free to submit a new proposal.[27] Similarly, comitology was held not to interfere with the Commission's independent activities under Article 205 EC. In *Fisheries*,[28] the ECJ confirmed a broad interpretation of the concept of "implementation" within Article 145 third indent EC, and approved the Council's use of a management committee procedure within the Commission's budgetary powers under Articles 203 EC and 205 EC. In *Parliament* v. *Council*, the ECJ investigated the question of whether the Council might alter a Commission proposal for a management committee into a regulatory committee procedure (*filet* variant) without re-consulting Parliament.[29] Although it did recognise that the choice between the various types of committees could have a substantive effect upon the decision-making process, it nevertheless held that *in casu* this choice had not decisively affected the overall balance of powers.[30]

5.2 Committee Activities Reviewed

Recently, both private parties and Member States have become increasingly aware of the possibility of using the committee procedures as a means of attacking the validity of committee-based Commission decisions. Consequently, despite its initial general and superficial attitude towards committees, the ECJ has been forced to take a closer look at the functioning of committees and in particular their internal rules of procedure.[31] Recent

[25] Ibid., at 1171. See also Case 30/70, *Scheer* v. *Einfuhr- und Vorratstelle für Getreide und Futtermittel* [1970] ECR 1197, at 1208-1209.

[26] Case 23/75, *Rey Soda* v. *Cassa Conguaglio Zucchero* [1975] ECR 1279, at 1301. See also joined Cases 279, 280, 285 and 286/84, *Rau and others* v. *Commission (Christmas butter)* [1987] ECR 1069.

[27] Case 5/77, *Tedeschi* v. *Denkavit Commerciale Srl.* [1977] ECR 1555, at 1580.

[28] Case 16/88, *Commission* v. *Council (Fisheries)* [1989] ECR 3457.

[29] Case C-417/93, *Parliament* v. *Council (TACIS)* [1995] ECR I-1185. See also Case C-156/93, *Parliament* v. *Commission (organic production)* [1995] ECR I-2019.

[30] Case C-417/93, above, note 29, paras 25 and 26.

[31] See also Bradley, in this volume.

judgments point out that although committee opinions cannot be formally reviewed by the ECJ, in practice, committee activities seem no longer to escape judicial review. Although in *Accrington Beef* the ECJ was still unwilling to go into procedural details,[32] more recently, the ECJ was prepared to take a closer look at committee rules, examining in detail various drafts of the regulation and the minutes of the relevant management committee although it concluded that the committee procedure had been observed.[33] In the *Construction Products* case the ECJ went even further.[34] In this case, Germany clearly indicated its desire to be taken seriously in the participation of the Commission's decision-making through the Standing Committee on Construction Products by attacking a Commission Decision[35] which implemented the Construction Products Directive.[36] It accused the Commission of not having sent the German version of the draft Commission Decision within the prescribed time-limit of 20 days. In addition, Germany argued that the Commission had completely disregarded its express request to postpone voting at the meeting of the Standing Committee; a possibility allowed for in the rules of procedure in case of delay. The Commission, however, replied that the German delegation had received an English version of the draft decision and that it was unreasonable to request postponement one day before the meeting. Faced with this clear disregard of procedural rules, the ECJ decided this time to teach the Commission a lesson. It first confirmed that the sending of an English version of the document in question was contrary to Article 3 of Council Regulation no. 1 on the languages to be used by the Community[37] according to which documents which are sent by a Community institution to a Member State need to be drafted in the language of that State.[38] The ECJ continued by examining the requirements stipulated in the Rules of Procedure of the Standing Committee, in particular, the requirement to send the document to the offices of the Permanent Representatives of the Member States and to their representatives on the Committee, together with the requirement that there was no possibility of shortening the period of notice of 20 days. It held that these requirements were designed to ensure that Member States had enough time to study the documents, which could be particularly complex and require time for discussion between the different administrative authorities or consultation of external experts.[39] Hence, from these requirements

---

[32] Case C-241/95, *The Queen* v. *Intervention Board for Agricultural Produce, ex parte: Accrington Beef Co. Ltd and Other* [1996] ECR I-6699, para 43.

[33] Case C-244/95, *Moskof AE* v. *Ethinikos Organismos Kapnou* [1997] ECR I-6441, para 46. See also Case T-218/95, *Azienda Agricola "Le Canne" Srl* v. *Commission* [1997] ECR II-2055, para 56.

[34] Case C-263/95, *Germany* v. *Commission (Construction Products)* [1998] ECR I-441.

[35] (1989) OJ L 40/12.   [36] (1995) OJ L 129/23.

[37] Special Edition (1952-1958) OJ 59.   [38] Case C-263/95, above, note 34, para. 27.

[39] Ibid. para. 31.

together with the fact that the vote had not been postponed despite
Germany's explicit request, the ECJ concluded an infringement of essential
procedural requirements and annulled the Commission's Decision.

6. Risk Regulation through Committees

On the basis of the ECJ's case law, committees are formally-speaking legal
bodies which do not interfere with the Community's institutional structure. Such a conclusion, however, does not explain why such bodies might
be considered an appropriate method by which to satisfy the Community's
regulatory needs. Importantly, it does not tackle the concerns of legitimacy
raised in relation to committees. These issues will therefore be addressed in
this section.

6.1 The Community as Risk Regulator

Although the founders of the Community primarily focused their attention
on the creation of an "Economic" Community,[40] the Community has
gradually become a "true" regulator of intricate health and safety aspects
of consumer products. The Community's involvement in these issues has a
dual basis: on the one hand, it stems from the Community's continuous
effort to achieve the internal market, and on the other hand, it has evolved
as an independent Community goal. Consequently, the Community needs
to deal with risk assessment of specific products or substances (measuring
the risk associated with specific products/substances) and risk management
(deciding what to do about the risks which the assessment reveals). Hence,
risk regulation sees "objective" scientific values intertwined with more
normative considerations.[41] The acceptability of risks must therefore be
weighed against normative values which are often strongly rooted in
national traditions and cultures. This explains *inter alia* the difficulties the
Community faces in regulating risk. Committee structures of risk regulation must therefore address the tensions arising from the opening up of
markets on the one hand and the need to respond to "legitimate" regulatory concerns on the other.[42]

The increasing importance of the Community as a risk regulator and,
thus, the role of committees in this field is most clearly demonstrated by
the BSE crisis,[43] which propelled the Community and its committee-based
decision-making into severe crisis and led to the explicit insertion by the

[40] Although it is true that Article 2 EEC already mentioned as one of the objectives of the
Community an accelerated raising of the standard of living.

[41] See, in more detail, Vos (1999).

[42] Joerges (1997: 322).

[43] See on the BSE crisis, Chambers, in this volume.

Amsterdam Treaty of the obligation on the Commission to base its internal market proposals on new scientific evidence into paragraph 3 of Article 100a EC.

6.2 *Legitimacy of Community Risk Regulation*

Traditionally the democratic nature of the Community has been measured against the degree to which the Parliament was able to participate in the legislative process. More "recent" legitimacy concerns have arisen with the delegation of ever-more discretionary powers to the Commission. This tendency is closely connected with the general crisis of the representative parliamentary democracy model which may be observed at national level. This situation can be explained as follows. In most national concepts of the Rule of Law, citizens can only be bound by laws. These laws derive their legitimacy from the representative character of a legislature, which is directly elected. Rules issued by government or administration obtain indirect legitimacy as the latter are deemed to act solely on the basis of laws adopted by the legislature. Yet, the requirements of the modern welfare state have led to a general withdrawal of the legislature in favour of the administration and non-governmental actors. The wide degree of discretion delegated to the administration may accordingly be argued to have weakened the administration's claim to be acting solely on the basis of the legislature's duly enacted laws and, thus, to have undermined administrative legitimacy. This explains the search for additional means by which to enhance administrative legitimacy.[44] Here administrative law is increasingly concerned with the provision of a surrogate political process to ensure the fair representation of a wide range of affected interests in the process of administrative decision-making.[45] Such additional measures include greater democratic and judicial control, increased transparency, greater expertise and stronger participation of citizens in the decision-making process, by means of representative interest groups, open hearings and public debate.

Not a state, but a system of multi-level governance, the Community is beset by additional difficulties inherent in the need to respect the regulatory concerns of the Member States and the differing linguistic and cultural systems and the "representativity" of socio-economic interests. Importantly, risk regulation should be recognised as a process permeated by policy considerations[46] and thus also leave room for the participation of political actors together with socio-economic interests, originating from the entire Community. Therefore, contrary to the non-majoritarian approach to market integration which holds that the integrated market can

---

[44] See, in this context, Everson (1998).
[45] Stewart (1975: 1670). See also Everson (1998).
[46] See, for example, also Shrader-Frechette (1991: 190 and 218).

be managed in isolation from political concerns by non-majoritarian technical experts, in particular independent agencies,[47] in my opinion, for risk regulation to be legitimate, it cannot be left to technocrats/experts alone but needs to be decided by political (national representatives) and socio-economic actors. Although this contribution does not go so far to attempt to resolve the "pressing problem" of what weight to attach to the various interests (national, Community, public and private interests),[48] it does aim to emphasise the need for the participation of and deliberation with such interests. It is against these co-ordinates that the operation and/or desirability of committees must be viewed.

6.3 The Participation of Member States in Risk Regulation through Committees

6.3.1 Policy-making/implementation Committees

Increasing implementation of risk regulation at Community level raises the question of what role is left for the Member States. The search for legitimate risk regulation by the Community/Commission is based on the main premise that the Member States are an essential basis of the Community and that consequently their participation in balancing political interests at the Community level is desired. The Member States' concern to be involved in Community risk regulation is not to be seen as just a matter of promoting national protectionist interests, but is much more the inevitable result of the fact that risk assessment and management are so complex, uncertain and controversial that they cannot be conducted without reference to normative social values. Policy-making/implementation committees may on the one hand augment the legitimacy of Community decision-making by guaranteeing on-going national influence and form an appropriate way of including the interests of the Member States in risk management and of addressing subsidiarity concerns. Such committees may now be argued to form a bridge

---

[47] See, in particular, Majone (1996a). Agencies can be distinguished from committees in that they possess legal personality and, supported by their own administrative structures, have a degree of administrative independence. The agency model, foremost advocated by G Majone, is based upon non-majoritarian thinking, preferring administrative market integration to be carried out by fully independent agencies, and bringing together technical and economic expertise. However, the agencies currently operating within the Community structure are not (yet) independent regulatory agencies in the American sense. The agency model adopted in the Community does, by no means, exclude resorting to committees. On the contrary, most agencies are actually based on committees or require resort to committees. Just as scientific committees, they produce information, which potentially leads to more informed decision-making, although they are more visible than committees, which possibly facilitates the political oversight and transparency of their activities. In general, decision-making is (formally) left to the Commission together with policy-making/implementation committees.

[48] See Everson, in this volume.

between the horizontal and vertical distribution of powers between Community and national levels, thus developing multi-level policy-making.[49]

In this context, comitology-based decision-making in the food sector has been argued to enhance legitimacy and constitute "deliberative supranationalism". This view, advocated most notably by Christian Joerges, is based upon the idea that market integration and risk regulation cannot be left to scientific and market actors alone but require political guidance.[50] It does not consider the supranational law of the EU as a set of rules which has precedence over and pre-empts national systems, but it emphasises the manner in which the actual law is produced. Law, in this view, derives its validity and legitimacy from the deliberative quality of its production.[51] Although this view largely neglects the importance of deliberation with civil society and citizens in general in risk regulation, I do agree with the idea that the building of a European polity cannot take place without the participation of and deliberation with Member States. Logically, participation and deliberation with Member States should apply to the implementation of Community risk regulation and can be appropriately achieved through committees. This plea for the participation of and deliberation with Member States can be founded on several normative and pragmatic arguments, which I briefly present below.

a) The Institutional Balance of Powers

First, the involvement of the Member States in the implementing phase of Community legislation may be explained by a "Member State-oriented" understanding of the principle of the institutional balance. Such an interpretation of the institutional balance of powers mainly holds that for a comprehension of the full complexity of the Community's institutional structure, the principle of the institutional balance of powers must also include the balance between the Community and the Member States.[52] The principle of the institutional balance of powers, as developed by the ECJ,[53] means that each Community institution must exercise its powers with due regard for the powers of the other institutions.[54] The strict division of powers between the institutions, however, may be argued to be a reflection of the Member States' concern that the integrity of their own powers be maintained; and thus acts as a shield against too great an institutional

---

[49] See Sauter/Vos (1998) and, in general, Scharpf (1994).

[50] See Joerges, in this volume.

[51] Joerges/Neyer (1997a).

[52] See Vos (1999: 83ff.). See also Everson (1995: 196-198).

[53] See, Case 9/56, *Meroni & Co., Industrie Metallurgiche, S.p.A. v. High Authority of the ECSC* [1957-58] ECR 133 and Case 10/56, *Meroni & Co., Industrie Metallurgiche, S.p.A. v. High Authority of the ECSC* [1957-58] ECR 157.

[54] See, for instance, Case C-70/88, *Parliament v. Council (Chernobyl)* [1990] ECR I-2041, at I-2072.

concentration of powers, particularly within the hands of the Commission. A broad, "Member State-oriented", understanding of this principle, there-fore, explains why it is necessary not only to give the Member States and their national institutions a voice in the legislative process, but also to allow them a degree of influence over the process of the implementation and application of Community law. Where powers are exercised by an intergovernmental institution such as the Council (in co-decision with the Parliament) this control is ensured. Yet, where—retaining implementing powers at Community level—the Council and the Parliament delegate such powers to the Commission, national influence is no longer guaranteed. From this perspective, the altering of the balance of powers in favour of the Community and, ultimately, of the Commission may explain the Member States' insistence on an ongoing role in such "Community" activity. It is especially in this latter situation, in which powers are increasingly exercised by the Commission, that Member States want to restore their influence.[55] Seen in this light, the principle of the institutional balance of powers may explain the irresistible rise of committees composed of national representatives within the Community setting.

In this way, the principle of the institutional balance accommodates the recognition of transnational governance structures between the Community and the Member States, which are based on a spirit of co-operation and deliberation. This Member State-oriented interpretation of the institutional balance of powers is therefore by no means "a dangerous concept since it provides a justificatory framework of the bewildering quantity of committees".[56] It does not necessarily lead to a "bewildering quantity" of committees, but possibly leads to an increased and reinforced role of committees. In the area of foodstuffs, for example, increased reliance on committees in risk regulation does not lead to more committees but to a greater role for the Standing Committee on Foodstuffs. This is not to say that the current situation as regards committees is perfect: a more disciplined use of committees through procedural rules is necessary.[57]

Interestingly, the ECJ seems recently to have taken a step in the direction of such a "Member-State oriented" interpretation of the institutional balance of powers. In *Regione Toscana* v. *Commission*,[58] the ECJ reiter-ated its earlier decision in *Région Wallonne* v. *Commission*[59] that it did not have jurisdiction to take account of actions brought by persons other than

---

[55] *Contra*: Prechal (1998: 284). She argues that "instead of helping to avoid the concentra-tion of powers, the introduction of the interests and concerns of the Member States into the notion of institutional balance is producing the opposite effect, in particular strengthening the position of the Council, with as a possible result the further intergovernmentalisation of the Community".

[56] Prechal (1998: 284).

[57] See section 8.

[58] Case C-180/97, [1997] ECR I-5247.

[59] Case C-95/97, [1997] ECR I-1789.

a Member State or a Community institution and referred the case to the Court of First Instance. It concluded from the general scheme of the Treaties that the term "Member State" for the purpose of the institutional provisions (particularly, those relating to proceedings before the courts) refers only to government authorities of the Member States and does not include the governments of the regions or autonomous communities. It then underlined, and this is the most interesting part, that if the contrary were true,

> "(...) it would undermine the institutional balance provided for by the Treaties, which determine the conditions under which the Member States, that is to say the States party to the Treaties establishing the Communities and the Accession Treaties, participate in the functioning of the Communities".[60]

b) *The Sui Generis Character of the Community*

Furthermore, the need for participation of the Member States stems from the specific character of the Community. The Community is not a state.[61] Instead, it can be identified as a system of multi-level or transnational governance. Governance in such a system, with a non-hierarchical structure, can only be accomplished through co-operation among power holders, which are both the Member States and the Community institutions.[62] The multi-level approach perceives decision-making by different levels of government and shifting fields of competence[63] and appears to be compatible with the conservation of national administrative powers and the assumption of national powers by the Community.

c) *National Constitutions*

In addition, the continuing interest of the Member States in risk regulation is understandable in view of the fact that many countries are required by their national constitutions to provide for the health and safety of their citizens.[64] The view that the nation-state is obliged to protect the health and safety of its citizens has been developed, in particular, in the German literature. The German Basic Law, for example, can be interpreted as laying down an obligation on the German State to protect human health and safety.[65]

---

[60] Case C-180/97, above, note 58, para 6.
[61] See, on the desirability of European statehood, the recent discussion by Mancini (1998) and the reply by Weiler (1998).
[62] See, for example, Joerges/Neyer (1997a).
[63] Marks/Hooghe/Blank (1996); Curtin (1999).
[64] See Micklitz (1991) and Micklitz/Roethe/Weatherill (1994).
[65] Article 1 I, in combination with Articles 2 II and 14 of the Basic Law. See Micklitz (1991). Importantly, in several acts the recognition of the precautionary principle as a legal principle also points in this direction.

d) Article 36 EC and Secondary Community Law

It must be emphasised that both primary and secondary Community law recognise the responsibility of Member States for human health and safety. Foremost, Article 36 EC explicitly stipulates that Member States may adopt measures constituting trade barriers provided that they are justified for reasons of *inter alia* the protection of health and life of humans. This responsibility is further laid down in many Community acts on health and safety issues.

e) The Specific Nature of Risk Regulation

The normative, ethical, cultural and political dimensions of risk regulation make themselves strongly felt at Community level: not only do they speak against the delegation of risk assessments entirely and exclusively to expert bodies but they also render it highly unlikely that one single body (the Commission) will be able to come up with uniform decisions which are in any way socially acceptable throughout the whole internal market.[66] Member States may accordingly be argued to have a very strong interest in health and safety matters. Seen in this light, it would thus seem expedient to ensure that the increased transfer of implementing powers to the Community level, be accompanied by the evolution of mechanisms (committees and agencies) which allow the Member States to retain a degree of influence over the exercise of such powers.

f) Procedural Subsidiarity

The need to include the Member States in Community risk regulation may also be viewed as a means of engaging subsidiarity. In view of the political character of subsidiarity it may be argued that the decision on the level at which specific tasks can best be achieved should be left to the political process.[67] This does not, however, mean that the subsidiarity principle is completely irrelevant. It clearly announces the message that Member States should not be excluded from the process of creating a European Union based upon the rule of law, democratic principles and solidarity. Therefore other means of implementing the philosophy of subsidiarity have been pointed out, underlining its procedural dimension which not only takes into consideration the level at which decisions are taken, but also how and in what way decisions are drafted.[68] Mechanisms which provide for co-operation between all the levels concerned might address Member States' concerns for unnecessary Community activities. The committee procedures might now be argued to perform precisely this function: they enable Member States to exercise on-going control over the

[66] See Joerges/Neyer (1997a).
[67] See, also, Dehousse (1994a: 119).
[68] See Dehousse (1994a: 124-125) and Bankowski (1997).

decision-making process whilst, at the same time, secure constant co-operation between all the authorities concerned. Likewise, agencies could also serve this purpose.

g) Compliance

Non-compliance is amongst the factors which push the Community in its third phase of integration towards ever-increasing activity in the field of risk regulation.[69] Importantly, it is no longer a phenomenon restricted to the confines of recalcitrant states.[70] Therefore, from a more pragmatic viewpoint too, Member States' participation in Community risk regulation would be necessary, since the production of regulatory provisions is of little use where these rules are not complied with by Member States. The need for co-operation and deliberation with the Member States is accentuated by the large extent of mutual distrust between national administrations. These problems may be overcome by also allowing Member States to participate in the implementing phase (by means of committees or agencies).

6.3.2 Secrecy of Committee Activities

Hence, policy-making/implementation committees may be an appropriate means to include Member States in Community risk regulation. However, although such committees are flexible, fit easily within Commission decision-making and offer a platform for problem-resolution and discourse, they may themselves create certain problems. From the perspective of transparency, these committees leave much to be desired. For example, their flexibility creates uncertainty about their precise activities and membership. Only through empirical research may some of this notorious obscurity be unveiled.[71] Hence, the obscure operation and the uncontrolled proliferation of committees within the Community institutional structure must be criticised as greatly detracting from the clarity of European decision-making. Here there is a clear need for more transparency and access to committee documents. Furthermore, the manner in which committees are composed and/or operate, often depends solely on the "goodwill" of the Community institutions, and in particular upon that of the Commission which possesses the administrative leeway to disrupt committee activities.[72]

6.4 Science-based Decision-making through Committees

6.4.1 Compulsory Consultation of Scientific Committees?

Until the outbreak of the BSE crisis, scientific committees received little

---

[69] See Joerges/Vos (1999).
[70] Mendrinou (1996: 4).
[71] See Joerges (ed.) (1998). Also, Vos (1999).
[72] See, in more detail, Vos (1999: 131–184).

attention from both the Community institutions and academics.[73] However, in the aftermath of the BSE scandal, the importance of scientific committees has become readily apparent. This episode has contributed to the overall awareness that where the Community has been forced to deepen its activities in the field of risk regulation, it has also been faced with a concurrent need for increased scientific expertise. This has in turn led to an increasing reliance upon the *ad hoc* scientific committees set up by the Commission for the very purpose of providing it with technical informa-tion and expertise. In some fields, such as foodstuffs, the Community legis-lature has itself made the consultation of scientific committees compulsory. The ECJ's jurisprudence indicates support for this development. In *Angelopharm*, which tackled the Cosmetics Directive,[74] the Court ruled that as the purpose of the scientific committee set up in this case was to provide the Commission with the assistance and information necessary to examine complex scientific and technical problems, the consultation of this committee should be mandatory in all cases, even if the text of the relevant directive was ambiguous on this point.[75] From this ruling it might be deduced that where the Commission has set up a scientific committee to ensure that its measures have a scientific basis, to take account of the most recent scientific and technical research, and to ensure that only measures are adopted which are necessary to protect human health, the Commission is obliged to consult this committee.[76]

Is this conclusion still valid in the BSE aftermath? Here, particular notice must be taken of Commission Decision 97/579/EC on scientific committees.[77] This Decision was part of the set of measures rapidly taken by the Commission in response to the accusations levelled by the Parliament of a lack of transparency and of manipulation.[78] It explicitly stipulates that the scientific committees must be consulted in the cases laid down by Community legislation. From this, it could be concluded that in other cases consultation would not be obligatory. However, even where Community legislation is silent on this point, consultation of scientific committees on issues which affect consumer health and safety should be preferred. First, it would ensure that the scientific advice resorted to is based on the principles of excellence, independence and transparency which are explicitly adhered

---

[73] See, however, Joerges/Ladeur/Vos (eds.) (1997).

[74] Case C-212/91, above, note 8.

[75] It was uncertain whether the consultation of the Scientific Committee for Cosmetics was necessary in every case or only at the request of either the Commission or a Member State.

[76] See, also Joerges, in this volume. More doubtful: Bradley, in this volume.

[77] Article 2 (1) of Commission Decision 97/579/EC setting up Scientific Committees in the field of consumer health and safety, (1997) OJ L 237/18.

[78] Parliament Resolution on the results of the Temporary Committee of Inquiry into BSE, (1997) OJ C 85/61.

to by Decision 97/579/EC, and is not dependent on an *ad hoc* approach of the Commission. Second, this would enable the Commission to fulfil its obligation under the new text of Article 100a (3) inserted by the Amsterdam Treaty to take account of "any new development based on scientific facts".

6.4.2 Excellence, Independence and Transparency of Scientific Expertise

Subsequent to the BSE crisis the Commission has developed a more coherent approach to the operation of scientific committees. The functioning of these committees is based on the *excellence* of their members (risk evaluation is undertaken by eminent scientists), their *independence* (to ensure that the scientists are free from conflicting interests) and the *transparency* of their activities (ease of access to information on the activities of the committees and their advice).

In accordance with the principle of excellence, the Commission has itself set selection criteria for the appointment of the committee members. Consequently, a selection jury composed of members of the Scientific Steering Committee (which co-ordinates the scientific committees)[79] will give "preference" to candidates who possess:[80] professional experience in the field of consumer health and more specifically in the areas covered by the field of competence of the committee concerned; experience in risk assessment; experience in delivering scientific opinion at national or international level; professional experience in a multidisciplinary and international environment; attested scientific excellence; experience in scientific management.

As regards the principle of independence, Commission Decision 97/579/EC determines that the members of the scientific committees act "independently of all external influence".[81] To this end, committee members must annually inform the Commission of any interests which might be considered prejudicial to their independence, and they (as well as external experts) have to declare at each meeting any specific interest potentially conflicting with their independence. Of further importance for the independence of committees is that their agenda is drawn up by the Committee itself and not by the Commission. Although provisions on this point are lacking, this has already occurred in practice. More transparency on the activities of the scientific committees is ensured through publication of their membership, agendas, minutes and opinions (including minority opinions) whilst respecting the need for commercial confidentiality.[82] In

---

[79] Commission Decision 97/404/EC setting up a Scientific Steering Committee, (1997) OJ L 169/85.

[80] These criteria are laid down by the Commission in the Call for expressions of interests for the post of member of one of the Scientific Committees, as published on the Internet: http://europa.eu.int/comm/dg24/health/sc/call_en.html.

[81] Article 6 (1) of Commission Decision 97/579/EC, above, note 77.

[82] Article 10 of Commission Decision 97/579/EC, above, note 77.

this connection, particular use is made of the Internet.[83] For an effective use of the principle of transparency in this field, however, it does not suffice just to have a homepage on committees on the Internet; for example, the Commission should also be committed to update regularly the information provided and put new information on it, which seems, at present, not always to occur.

Although these criteria are certainly acceptable, the question nonetheless arises (precisely in view of the BSE disaster) whether the Commission should be allowed to draw up its own rules—some of which are not even set forth in a decision but are instead placed in a Commission publication looking for candidates for committees. Here, general principles which stipulate under which conditions and which principles the Commission should carry out its (implementing) tasks should be laid down by the Community legislature.

6.5 The Participation of Civil Society in Risk Regulation through Committees

To a certain extent, the "deliberation" which takes place through the committees resembles the regulatory practices of both the American Food and Drug Agency and the Environmental Protection Agency which support a negotiation model of hazard assessment and management, as advocated by some social studies of science.[84] This model, however, is specific in so far as it refers to the need for negotiation with citizens. In the search for a more democratic and procedural account of rationality so as to reflect the human dimensions of risk assessment and management, the model recognises that the process of risk assessment is highly value laden and needs the explicit consent of those who are most vulnerable to risks, i.e. the users of products. In this context, negotiation, rather than mere expert decision-making, is argued to be of vital importance for ensuring free, informed consent in situations of controversial risks.[85] However, in the Community context, "deliberation" through committees in, for example, the food sector at present includes solely the negotiation process between scientists, national representatives and the Commission.[86]

The question arises whether Community risk regulation should, aside from to Parliament and governmental representatives of Member States, also include negotiation and deliberation with "civil society" (that is, non-governmental) actors,[87] and therefore with the citizens of the

[83] See http://europa.eu.int/comm/dg24/health/sc/index_en.html (homepage for the scientific committees).

[84] See Jasanoff (1990: 234 ff.) and Shrader-Frechette (1991: 206 ff).

[85] Shrader-Frechette, in the context of environmental protection (1991: 169-218).

[86] Joerges/Neyer (1997a).

[87] Curtin (1999).

Community.[88] This question must be affirmatively answered for several reasons. First of all, as decision-making increasingly takes place at the Community level and since risk regulation is recognised as being a matter which requires flexible and speedy decision-making and because this is seen as a task properly assigned to the Commission, the direct roles of the Parliament representing the European citizens and possibly of the Economic and Social Committee (ESC) in the decision-making process is diminishing.[89] This trend underlines the crisis of the model of representative parliamentary democracy in favour of a participatory democracy model. At the same time, interest participation at the Community level enables the various interested citizens to free themselves from imposed national traditions and values. In addition, the normative character of risk regulation together with the potential of technocratisation of Community risk regulation makes the participation of other "non-scientific" interested parties in risk regulation increasingly important. Here, the limits of science together with the normative character of risk assessment require foodstuffs not to be regulated solely by scientific experts and/or national and European bureaucrats in a closed and often secretive, albeit deliberative, circle. By means of participation the widening gap between the Community institutions and citizens[90] may be countered.

In practice, the Commission has not only attempted to increase efficiency, flexibility and rationality through the inclusion of scientific expertise by means of committees in the decision-making process, but has also sought acceptance for its decisions through the inclusion of interest committees in decision-making. These committees are composed of the various relevant protagonists of civil society and resemble "little ESCs". Analysis of the manner in which such interest committees currently participate in Community risk regulation has revealed its shortcomings.[91] In the food sector, for example, the Commission created the Advisory Committee on Foodstuffs in 1975.[92] At present, however, this Committee is not active, since the Commission currently does not convene this Committee. The non-consultation of this Committee by the Commission is confirmed by recent empirical research and may be explained by the fact that the Commission is no longer in need of information about the different viewpoints through this Committee, as it is now approached directly by the interested parties concerned.[93] Clearly, those who will lose most from this

[88] See on this topic, Everson, 1999, in this volume.

[89] See, in this context, also the Herzog report of the Parliamentary Committee on Institutional Affairs on participation of citizens and social players in the Union's institutional system, 29 October 1996, A4-0338/96.

[90] See on this issue, Dehousse, in this volume.

[91] See Vos (1999: 173–177).

[92] Commission Decision 75/420/EEC, setting up an Advisory Committee on Foodstuffs, (1975) OJ L 182/35, amended by Commission Decision 78/758/EEC, (1978) OJ L 251/18.

[93] See Joerges/Neyer (1997a: 279).

development are the consumers, who, in comparison with industry, are already greatly under-represented. The question must be asked whether it is feasible and worthwhile intensifying the consultation of this Committee, for example, by giving the Committee the right to request the Commission to be consulted[94] and/or make its consultation obligatory.[95] This will largely depend on whether and what kind of choice on citizen participation in Community health and safety regulation is selected. In any event, it is clear that this Committee could not be the sole form of interest participation, since it poses by its very definition the general problem of "representativity"; the Committee does, for example, not include representatives of environmental organisations and gives the Commission the exclusive powers to select the interests represented. Consultation of such a committee as the sole representative body of civil society would thus inevitably risk excluding other interested parties.[96] These difficulties underline the need for further means of enabling a wider consultation of all parties concerned. Examples of such mechanisms might be a more systematic use of green papers[97] and the institution of a type of public notice and comment procedure, such as the one set forth under the US Administrative Procedures Act[98] publishing decisional intentions in the Official Journal and inviting all interested parties to make their observations or comments known. The role of the Internet in this as a means of facilitating the participation of citizens in Community decision-making should not be underestimated.[99]

7. Comitology Revisited

7.1 The Commission's Proposal of 16 July 1998

Summoned by the IGC in a declaration to the Amsterdam Treaty, the Commission has recently presented its proposal for a revision of the committee procedures.[100] Cautiously, it advocates simplification of the

---

[94] This has been granted to the advisory committee in the agricultural sector by Article 1 (3) of Commission Decision 98/235/EC on the advisory committees dealing with matters covered by the common agricultural policy, (1998) L 88/59.

[95] See the ESC Opinion on the Commission's Green Paper on Food and its New Approach to Food Safety, (1998) OJ C 19/61.

[96] Therefore I speak of *participation* and not of *representation* of interested parties.

[97] See already Communication from the Commission to the Council and the European Parliament on the operation of the Community's internal market after 1992. Follow-up to the Sutherland report, SEC(92) 2277 final, 5-6. See also Communication from the European Commission to the Council on the Priorities for Consumer Policy, 1996-1998, COM(95) 519 fin.

[98] 5 USC Sec. 553(c). See Breyer/Stewart (1992) and Baldwin (1995: 75 ff.).

[99] See Weiler's proponency of Lex Calibur, Weiler (1997).

[100] (1998) OJ C 279/5.

committee procedures. The proposal eliminates the various variants, but retains the safeguard procedure. The most important changes to the procedures as proposed by the Commission are as follows:

a) Advisory Procedure

The advisory committee procedure remains the same except for the elimination of the requirement that the opinion is recorded in the minutes and that each Member State can ask that its position is recorded in the minutes. This omission can be understood in the light of Article 7 of the proposal which stipulates that each committee shall adopt its own rules of procedure.

b) Management Procedure

The two variants of the current procedure have merged into one single management committee procedure. It stipulates that the Commission may (instead of must) adopt measures which immediately apply. If these measures are not in accordance with the opinion of the committee, they must be communicated by the Commission to the Council. In that case, the Commission may defer the application of the measures for a maximum of three months. Within this period, the Council may take a different decision by qualified majority.

c) Regulatory Procedure

The changes to the regulatory committee procedure are the most drastic. If the measures proposed by the Commission are not in accordance with the committee opinion or if the committee failed to deliver an opinion, the Commission does not adopt the measures. In this case, the Commission may present a proposal in accordance with the normal Treaty decision-making procedures.

d) Safeguard Procedure

The two variants of the safeguard procedure, too, have fused into one procedure. The text now stipulates that any Member State may refer the Commission's decision on safeguard measures (before adopting this decision the Commission may still be required to follow specific procedures) to the Council within a specific time limit. The Council may take a different decision within the time limit specified in the main act by qualified majority.

Importantly, the Commission's proposal indicates some kind of hierarchy rules as to when the specific procedures need to be prescribed. According to the Commission, the management committee procedure must be used for implementation or management measures, and in particular those relating to common policies such as the common agricultural policy, to the implementation of programmes with significant budgetary implications, or to the grant of substantial financial support. The regulatory committee procedure, on the contrary, should be used for measures of general scope designed to apply, update or adapt essential provisions of basic instruments, whilst the advisory committee procedure must be used where the management or regulatory committee procedures are not or are no longer considered appropriate. The safeguard procedure may be applied where decision-making power is delegated to the Commission.[101] The proposal furthermore addresses the inter-institutional debate. It stipulates that the European Parliament shall be informed of committee procedures on a regular basis: it receives agendas of committee meetings, draft measures submitted to the committees for the implementation of the measures adopted under co-decision. In addition, it must be informed whenever the Commission transmits any measure or any proposal for a measure to the Council.[102]

7.2 Suggestions for Improvement

In view of the institutional sensitivity of the whole issue, it is not surprising that the Commission has remained quite cautious in its proposal. The proposal is to be welcomed for retaining the three committee procedures[103] and abandoning the *contre-filet* procedure. In addition, committees are now obliged to draw up rules of procedure which would, for example, also include rules on the language in which the Commission needs to send its draft decisions. Furthermore, the proposal meets the criticism expressed in relation to the current Comitology Decision for leaving unaffected the existing procedures,[104] in that it requires that all existing committee procedures be brought in line with the new committee procedures.[105]

The proposal is, however, disappointing in several other aspects. First, it fails to lay down provisions on the openness of committee activities. Although the "success" of deliberation admittedly depends on a certain degree of confidentiality of the environment in which deliberation takes place,[106] this should not prevent committee activities from being brought

---

[101] Article 2 of the Commission's proposal, above, note 100.

[102] Article 7 of the Commission's proposal, above, note 100.

[103] Having one single committee procedure, as the Parliament proposed in its preparatory documents on the IGC, would probably have meant that the advisory committee procedure would have been abandoned, a procedure which in some fields is both well established and widely accepted. See European Parliament Committee of Institutional Affairs, Report on the European Parliament's opinion for the IGC (Article N of the TEU) and assessment of the work of the Reflection Group (rapporteurs Dury and Maij-Weggen), 5 March 1996, A4-0068/96/Part B, 48.

[104] See the Parliament's critique in its Institutional Affairs Committee Report on the executive powers of the Commission (Comitology) and the role of the Commission in the Community's external relations (Rapporteur: Roumeliotis), 19 November 1990, Doc. A 3-0310/90, PE 141.457/fin, 11.

[105] Article 8 of the Commission's proposal, above, note 100.

[106] Joerges/Neyer (1997a).

out into daylight (such as the American "sunshine committees").[107] Greater transparency could be ensured by the publication of the dates of the meetings and agenda, as well as the committee members, whilst open ("enlarged") meetings could be organised with interested parties. In addition, it is clear that although the Commission intends to clarify and structure the use of the procedures, the wording of the text is not without ambiguity and provides food for multiple interpretation. For example, it will not always be possible to draw a clear line between implementation and management measures and measures of general scope designed to apply, update or adapt essential provisions of basic instruments.

Furthermore, the role of the Parliament remains limited to one of control by means of information. As in the Plumb-Delors agreement, no reference is made to the position of the Parliament when it has severe objections to the committee opinions or the draft Commission proposal. In this regard, it should be conferred a right of "revocation".[108] Such a right could enable Parliament to require the Commission to interrupt its decision-making procedure and to refer the matter back to the Community legislature under a simplified co-decision procedure. Where the Commission fails to agree with the management or regulatory committee, the overall logic behind committee procedures would seem to indicate that the matter must again be referred to the Community legislature; i.e. in cases of measures adopted under co-decision (Article 100a EC) to both the Council and the Parliament.[109] For the management procedure, the proposal however confirms the existing text which only mentions reference to the Council. For the regulatory committee procedure, it indeed accepts this logic although it refers to the normal legislative procedures (in case of internal market measures this would mean the normal co-decision procedure under Article 189b EC). Yet, for efficiency reasons together with the fact that these measures are implementing measures of general rules, of which the "fundamental elements"[110] are already considered by the Community legislature, a strongly simplified form of co-decision within strict time-limits should here be adopted. Moreover, in view of the fact that the safeguard procedure in practice is hardly used and in matters touching upon health and safety issues resort is habitually had to regulatory committees, it would be important in cases of disagreement with the committee or the lack of a committee opinion, that the Commission be able to adopt temporary measures in relation to emergency situations endangering human health and safety.

---

[107] See Federal Advisory Committee Act, section 10, 5 USCS Appx (1994).

[108] See also Neyer, in this volume.

[109] See, also, Falke/Winter (1996: 578-580). See, in this context, the practice in some Member States of the parliament retaining some form of involvement in the executive rule-making; Jacobs/Corbett/Shackleton (1994: 235) and Ladeur (1996a: 257).

[110] See *Köster*, above, note 24.

8. Concluding Remarks: Towards a European Administrative Procedures Act?

In the area of risk regulation, committees arguably re-establish the Community balance of powers by compensating for the increasing transfer of formal implementing powers to the Commission and pragmatically by securing subsidiarity, herewith creating a framework for co-operative and deliberative multi-level policy-making. Yet, it is true that committees have several deficiencies. For example, where policy-making/implementation committees are often very secretive and neither their activities nor their members are made public, the need for greater transparency and for more information as to committee membership and activities becomes particularly clear. Until the outbreak of the BSE crisis, the improvised origins of committees determined that committees' procedural rules were either *ad hoc* or developed through the Court's jurisprudence. However, the BSE crisis has clearly demonstrated that where important political interests are at stake, the *ad hoc* approach followed by the Commission to (scientific) committees is not sufficient to guarantee decision-making free from manipulation and capture. This is underlined by the fact that in such situations even the scientists are likely to be subject to powerful political pressure, as was openly admitted by scientists working on the BSE case within various scientific committees. This makes the need for enhanced legitimacy and greater transparency of committee activities even more imperative. It further highlights the need for the development of a rationality based on "objective" and refined scientific expertise.

In response to the BSE crisis, the Commission has, in fact, presented a more coherent approach to food safety based on true "principles", namely, the excellence, independence and transparency of scientific advice delivered by the scientific committees. Although these criteria are certainly to be welcomed, doubts arise (precisely in view of the BSE disaster) whether the Commission is the appropriate institution to draw up its own rules. Here, general principles which stipulate under which conditions and to which criteria the Commission should refer in carrying out its (implementing) tasks should be laid down by the Community legislature. In addition, the Commission's new approach only addresses scientific advice given by the scientific committees and does not extend these principles to the rest of the process of risk regulation. It thus fails to take account of the role of Member State representatives within the relevant policy-making/implementation committees or of interest group representatives within the relevant interest committees.

Consequently, the incoherence which has resulted from the essentially pragmatic approach of the Community institutions to comitology now needs to be compensated for through the setting up of a more general mechanism to ensure more openness and legitimacy in regulatory decision-making as well as greater consistency and generality of application. The Commission's proposals for a revision of the Comitology Decision only address these issues to a certain extent. The drafting of these and other principles on scientific expertise may lead to the establishment of a kind of European administrative procedures act. Such an act could include, for example, the composition of committees, the appointment of the members, public meetings and access (such as the American "sunshine" committees), publications, quality of expertise and hearing rights. Importantly, the drafting of such an act would need to address the question of how interested citizens may participate in Community risk regulation to ensure its legitimacy. Here, the limits of science together with the normative character of risk assessment require foodstuffs not to be regulated solely by committees composed of scientific experts and/or national and European bureaucrats in a closed and often secretive, albeit deliberative, circle. To this end, one may consider institutionalised interest participation through committees combined with the establishment of a public notice and comment procedure. This may contribute to the opening up of a truly Community-wide public debate on the risks inherent to consumer products; a debate noticeable at present only for its absence. Disciplined through such rules, committees may constitute an appropriate medium for regulating risks.

SECTION 2

Institutional Controversies

3

Comitology and the European Commission[*]

Giuseppe Ciavarini Azzi[**]

1. Introduction

The Committee system has grown to the point of attracting the sustained attention of the academic world. In the discussion surrounding the committees which fall under the auspices of the Commission, there are generally two different phenomena which are in the mind of commentators. On the one hand, there exist committees set up by the Commission to organise the consultations it holds in connection with exercising its power of initiative. Clearly, these committees have a purely consultative role. On the other hand, there is a sizeable number of committees created by the Council and made up of Member State representatives. Most of these committees assist the Commission in exercising the implementing powers conferred on it, and operate according to detailed provisions laid down by Community legislation (comitology). In these cases, consultation is a mandatory obligation placed upon the Commission. The entire panoply of these committees constitutes the main vehicle for institutionalised dialogue among the Commission, national administrations and the socio-economic environment in Member States. In my contribution, I shall consider both types of committees, on the understanding that the second type will take up more of our attention as it is an element of the debate on the reform of the institutions.

2. The Consultative Committees set up by the Commission

These committees have the task of organising and systematising the consultative activities performed by the Commission in order to develop its initiatives. Of course, this does not prevent much of this activity being entrusted to non-institutionalised bodies such as private or governmental groups of

[*] Translation by Iain L. Fraser, Florence.
[**] Director, Secretariat-General, European Commission. The opinions expressed are the author's own and do not commit the institution to which he belongs.

experts but, in principle, these committees meet at the Commission's request and their opinions are not binding on the Commission. The Commission's wish to be firmly rooted in the reality of social and business life explains the wide diversity of types and membership of committees. They may be *ad hoc* or standing committees, their members may be independent experts or national civil servants (attending in a personal capacity), and the social partners may be involved (on an equal-representation basis). The only general rule is that there is no general rule.

In 1995, for example, there were 57 consultative committees which met on subjects as diverse as the agricultural sector, the common organisation of the market, and the social and employment policy area, to discuss measures which resulted in the Employment Confidence Pact being presented to the European Council held in Florence in June 1996. All of the consultations which the Commission conducts with these committees increase the legitimacy of the Commission's proposals but it should not be forgotten that the Commission alone adopts this position within the framework of its exclusive political responsibility.

3. Comitology

The Council has established committees from the very early days of the Community. The participants in the committees are the representatives from the Member States who assist the Commission in its implementing tasks. There is a mandatory obligation to consult these committees. The "Comitology Decision" of 13 July 1987[1] regulates the majority of these committees, it accomplished the goal of a simplification in the committee system by reducing to seven the number of procedures (advisory (I), management (II), regulatory (III) and safeguard, the later three with one variant each). However, in the Commission's view, two problems remained: firstly, it regards inclusion of variant (b) of the regulatory procedure – the famous "*contre-filet*" (double safety net) – as "illogical since it can lead to a situation in which no decision is taken", as the Commission repeated in its report to the Reflection Group on the 1996–1997 IGC.[2] For this reason, it has always refused to bring it into its proposal. Secondly, the Commission has deplored the absence of explicit reference in the text of the Comitology Decision to the preponderant emphasis placed on the advisory committee procedure in the area of the internal market.

In 1995, the number of committees established by the Council and with which the Commission had to consult, totalled 224. The Comitology Decision governed 141 of these committees. I feel that it is important to

[1] Council Decision 87/373/EEC, (1987) OJ L 197/33.
[2] Commission Report of 10 May 1995.

stress three aspects of the current state of development: first, the choice of comitology procedure; secondly, the daily operation of the committees; and finally, the problems raised by the European Parliament.

The choice of comitology procedure led to the Commission stressing, in its report to the Reflection Group of the IGC, that "the multiplicity of types of procedure available too often generates long discussion, sometimes of principle, on which one to adopt in each case, slowing down the legislative process".[3] In fact, at COREPER or in the conciliation committees of the co-decision procedure disputes are frequent over what procedure to adopt, where the real issue is sometimes not relevant to the substance of the text. Apart from the accumulated delays, this practice also leads to perverse effects: given the difficulties of coming to agreement on a formula for a committee, the Council sometimes ends up reserving implementing powers to itself instead of delegating these powers to the Commission as provided for in the Treaty. This temptation is present for the European Parliament, too, given that acts are taken by co-decision. Finally, the Commission also sees itself sometimes compelled to split its proposal in order to allow a majority decision to be reached on the substance of the act, while maintaining its opposition to regulatory Procedure III-b (*"contre-filet"*). The risk of polluting the area of qualified majority decision by unanimity voting where the issue is purely procedural is thus a real one. There is, therefore, an obvious need emerging to simplify procedures, if possible in the context of a better articulation for Community acts.

The daily functioning of the committees also deserves attention. In practice, the Commission feels that the comitology procedure has, in technical terms, enabled and facilitated a fruitful collaboration between its services and those Member State administrations which are most often faced with having to apply, on the ground, the implementing measures adopted at Community level. Thousands of administrative acts have thus been adopted following opinions by these committees.

The figures shown in Table 1 confirm this assessment. For instance, in 1995 there were only seven cases of referral to the Council (five under Procedure III-a and two under Variant III-b) all because of absence of opinions from the committees consulted. Only one case led, as the Commission feared, to absence of decision (additives in animal feed: authorisation for avoparcine). This figure is all the more modest if it is borne in mind that the 141 committees forming part of the comitology that met in 1995 gave 2951 opinions, none of which was unfavourable to the Commission proposal. In 332 cases, the committee gave no opinion (324 of them in the management committee procedure and eight in the regulatory committee procedure). Let us note, however, that the large number of favourable opinions and the small number of referrals to

---

[3] Ibid.

Council even in the context of the "regulatory" procedures does not necessarily mean that the latter procedures are, in all cases, best suited to
ensuring the adoption of committee decisions.

4. The European Parliament and Comitology

The European Parliament has raised two main points in its criticism of the
functioning of the comitology procedures: on the one hand, it complained
of lack of information and transparency surrounding the work of these
committees, and on the other, it asked to have a power of legislative control
over implementing measures based on an act taken by co-decision equal to
that of the Council.

The Commission has displayed sensitivity to the problem of transparency
in the work of the committees. To offer a remedy, Parliament and
Commission arrived in 1988 at what is known as the "Plumb-Delors" agreement,[4] containing provisions ensuring the forwarding to Parliament of draft
implementing acts of the Commission with general scope. This agreement
followed by the "Klepsch-Millan" agreement, has been applied.

In recent years, especially 1995 and 1996, the European Parliament has
used its prerogatives in the budgetary area to put pressure on the
Commission and the Council so as to secure further, regular information
on the work of the committees. Concerned both to advance along the road
of transparency and to appease an inter-institutional conflict that risked
endangering the good operation of the committees, and after having
contacted the Council on the aspects coming within its province, the
Commission took initiatives which move in the direction of Parliament's
demands. For instance, it drew up in June 1995 a report for the European
Parliament on the committees' activities,[5] and it forwards to Parliament
since December 1996 the agendas and the results of votes for the management and regulatory committees.[6]

It is clear that all these initiatives presuppose greater centralisation
within the Commission of information relating to the committees. The
Commission has taken measures in this direction while safeguarding
decentralised administration of the committees. These do not, after all,
constitute a block, but have to meet specific needs of their own in each of
the Community policies.

Once co-decision became a reality, the European Parliament asked to be
able to exercise political control over the activity of implementing acts
taken by co-decision. We are all familiar with the inter-institutional debate

---

[4] See Jacobs/Corbett/Shackleton (1994: 234).
[5] "Fonctionnement des comités en 1995 – Note de synthèse", 28th June (SEC (96) 1998).
[6] Samland-Williamson "agreement".

that resulted from this demand. To find a solution, the Commission, in May 1994, presented a proposal for an inter-institutional agreement, taking over much of Parliament's demands. The tough negotiations that ensued finally led in December that year to the signing of a *modus vivendi*,[7] pending the 1996–97 IGC. This consists essentially of rules for informing and consulting the European Parliament in connection with all draft implementing acts of general scope related to the co-decision procedure.

The *modus vivendi* which came into formal operation only after ratification by all the three relevant institutions in April 1996, has without doubt enabled Parliament to enjoy greater access to information on the subject.

5. A New Comitology Decision

Despite initiatives on the part of the Commission,[8] the 1996–1997 IGCs decided not to deal with the comitology issue by changing the Treaty itself. Instead, a declaration attached to the Final Act in Amsterdam asked the Commission to submit a proposal amending the 1987 "Comitology Decision". In response, the Commission transmitted to the Council its proposal for a new comitology decision in July 1998.[9]

This was no easy task though. As the Treaties were not amended in this respect, the room for manoeuvre in a legal sense was very limited: Article 202 of the EC Treaty (formerly Article 145) being unchanged, and in the absence of any hierarchy of norms, the Commission nevertheless had to propose a text bringing the Community implementation system more closely into line with the new institutional balance.

The European Parliament, although having no formal involvement other than to be consulted, played a key role in the negotiations: by blocking half of the appropriations available for committees in the 1999 budget and delaying its opinion until the last legislative session, in May 1999, it applied pressure by all available means in order to make its position clear to the Member States.

After a year of negotiations, the Council finally adopted unanimously, in June 1999, the new "Comitology Decision",[10] thereby revamping considerably the 1987 system.

First and foremost, the European Parliament was given a right of scrutiny over the executive institutions (the Commission and, in certain

[7] (1996) OJ C 1⌐

[8] Commission Opinion for the Intergovernmental Conference 1996, "Reinforcing Political Union and Preparing for Enlargement" of February 1996, COM(96)90, I, 3, 22. Commission "non paper" submitted to the IGC in April 1997.

[9] (1998) OJ C 279/5.

[10] See Annex 3. Council Decision 1999/468/EC, (1999) OJL 184/23

situations, the Council). This right of scrutiny will enable the Parliament, under the co-decision procedure, to alert the executive body if it considers that an implementing measure encroaches on the legislative sphere. The Commission was ready to establish such a right by unilateral commitment; the Council finally accepted that such a mechanism should be made official in the form of a new textual provision.

Alongside this right of scrutiny, the Commission also made provision, in the new decision, for Parliament to be kept informed, thus indicating a willingness to "tidy up" agreements reached in the past (Plumb-Delors, Klepsch-Millan, *Modus vivendi*, Samland-Williamson). Certain aspects of the decision go even further than the Commission's proposal. In a broader sense, the decision responds to criticism likening committee procedures to a closed, even secret system: documents discussed in committees will henceforth be accessible to the general public, with a register being provided to that end; the Commission will also draw up an annual report on committees activities.

A degree of simplification of the system has been achieved by doing away with the 1987 decision's "variants". The range of possible formulas is thus reduced to three main procedures – advisory, management and regulatory, plus one safeguard procedure – in place of the seven variants under the current system.

In a declaration, the Council and the Commission have also proposed that a thorough cleanup be swiftly undertaken by aligning all existing procedures with the new-type formulas. This vital legislative task will require co-operation with Parliament so that debates on matters of substance are not reopened and the reform can proceed speedily.

It is only regrettable that the Commission's original proposal, aimed at radically simplifying the regulatory procedure by removing the "*filet*" (safety net) and "*contre-filet*" (double safety net) was not adopted. The final outcome reflects a difficult balance between the three institutions;[11] the Commission's proposal would, though, have constituted a step towards better separation of powers at Community level.

Finally, criteria are also introduced to guide the legislator choice of procedure. As regards co-decision in particular, this measure should facilitate the adoption of basic instruments by removing the purely institutional matters that complicate debates on the substance of legislation.

The success of the new system can only be properly judged in the medium term. Let the system be set up, so that we can appreciate its advantages.

---

[11] See in this connection the relevant declarations published in the C series of the Official Journal. (1999) OJC 203/1.

Table 1 *Functioning of Comitology in 1995*

Examination of the functioning of the committees in 1995 shows that:

– for all the committees forming part of the comitology that met in 1995 (141), 3283 mandatory consultations were held. 2951 opinions were given:

- 158 under the consultative procedure;
- 1678 under the management procedure, variant (a);
- 553 under the management procedure, variant (b);
- 364 under the regulatory procedure, variant (a);
- 196 under the regulatory procedure, variant (b);
- 2 under the safeguard procedure;

– in the consultations there was no clause of an unfavourable opinion. On the other hand, there were 332 cases of absence of opinion (for lack of an adequate majority, or because the deadline set had been exceeded). These break down as follows:

- 296 under the management procedure, variant (a);
- 28 under the management procedure, variant (b);
- 5 under the regulatory procedure, variant (a);
- 3 under the regulatory procedure, variant (b).

Following these consultations, the Council was involved in 1995 in 7 cases:

– 5 under Procedure IIIa;
– 2 under Procedure IIIb.

It will be noted that the number of cases where the Commission had to make a referral to the Council is limited. Moreover, of the 7 cases referred to the Council, it should be noted that:

– in one case* (IIIa), the Council amended the Commission proposal by unanimity; in one case** (IIIb), the Council decided by simple majority against the Commission proposal, so that there was an absence of decision;

– in the five other cases (four IIIa*** and one IIIb****), the Council was unable to decide and it was the Commission that took the final decision.

---

* Labelling of certain foodstuffs with mandatory indications.
** Additives to animal feed (authorisation for avoparcine).
*** Introduction of a monitoring system in relation to the United Arab Emirates. Three cases of recognition of standards establishing the management specification for environmental systems.
**** Setting of ceilings on residues of veterinary medicaments in foodstuffs of animal origin (ban on dimetridazole).

4

Implementing Powers and Comitology*

*Jean-Paul Jacqué***

1. Introduction

The question of powers to implement Community norms is at the core of the Community institutional debate.[1] The material implementation of Community norms is normally a matter for Member States, on the classic principle of indirect administration. Article 5 EC, moreover, binds Member States to take all proper measures for ensuring the implementation of obligations resulting from the acts of Community institutions. It normally happens, and it is frequently the case, that normative implementation when applying to the Community norm implies the adoption of an implementing act. This act is adopted by the Member States, who are best placed to assess the ways the Community norm should be applied in the context of their national legal systems. The Commission sees this, moreover, as an application of the principle of subsidiarity, and it is this view that underpinned its proposals on the hierarchy of norms in connection with the intergovernmental conference that led to the Treaty on European Union. It, in fact, proposed that measures implementing Community laws be taken either by Member States or by the Commission. As Jacques Delors stated:

"(. . .) the law would be implemented:
- either directly by national authorities – most of them by the parliaments; here the point would be to adopt the essential function of the directive, to give it its original meaning, leaving the choice of ways to attain the objective open; in this case, national parliaments are necessarily involved in the Community process, instead of being, as all too often at present, mere recording chambers;
- or the law is implemented by a Commission regulation, but only for those aspects calling for the involvement of uniform rules; again, this implementation by the Commission is subordinate to a possibility of reservation by the

* Translation by Iain L. Fraser, Florence.
** Professor, Director in the Legal Service of the Council of the European Union. The opinions expressed are the author's own and do not commit the institution he belongs to.
[1] On comitology, see C Reich (1990); Meng (1998); Ehlermann (1988); Blumann (1988).

Community legislator with the effect of converting the disputed regulation into a Commission proposal subject to the legislative procedure".[2]

2. Implementation of Community Legislation

The Commission proposals were not followed at the intergovernmental conference, but the principle that the implementing of Community legislation is a matter for Member States has never been challenged. Moreover, the rule of proportionality contained in the last sub-paragraph implies that Community intervention should not exceed what is necessary to attain Treaty objectives, and the exercise by the Community of its implementing powers is subject to this rule. The adoption of implementing measures ought, therefore, to be left to the Member States wherever Community intervention is unnecessary within the meaning of Article 3b EC.

It is not a matter of indifference to establish that in principle the adoption of implementing measures is a matter for the Member States, since the consequence is that where these measures are adopted at Community level it is entirely legitimate for Member States to wish to retain a special right of oversight in respect of a process that naturally concerns them and in this case tends to escape them.

2.1 The Initial Position in the Treaty of Rome

Originally, the issue was governed by Article 155, paragaph 4, EEC, according to which, the Commission shall "exercise the powers conferred on it by the Council for the implementation of the rules laid down by the latter". The implementing power thus belongs to the Council unless it decides to delegate all or part of it to the Commission. On the basis of this provision, a very important practice emerged. Its essential feature was, prior to taking a measure for delegation, to be accompanied by the obligation to consult committees made up of Member State representatives, with, in some cases, a right of reservation for the Council in the event of disagreement between the committee and the Commission.

This practice, known by the name of comitology, had given rise to vigorous criticism for amounting, in certain cases, to dispossessing the Commission of the powers that had been delegated to it. The Court of Justice, however, recognised the validity of comitology procedures in the case of the so-called "management" committees in *Köster*:

> "Article 155 provides that the Commission shall exercise the powers conferred on it by the Council for the implementation of the rules laid down by the latter.

---

[2] Contribution to the debate on the Principle of Subsidiarity, held at EIPA, Maastricht, on 21 March 1991.

This provision, the use of which is optional, enables the Council to determine any detailed rules to which the Commission is subject in exercising the power conferred on it. The so-called management committee procedure forms part of the detailed rules to which the Council may legitimately subject a delegation of power to the Commission. (…) The function of the management committee is to ensure permanent consultation in order to guide the Commission in the exercise of the powers conferred on it by the Council and to enable the latter to substitute its own action for that of the Commission. The management committee does not, therefore, have the power to take a decision in place of the Commission or the Council. Consequently, without distorting the Community structure and the institutional balance, the management committee machinery enables the Council to delegate to the Commission an implementing power of appreciable scope, subject to its power to take the decision itself if necessary."[3]

However, as Community legislation developed, the need to expand delegation to the Commission made itself felt, in order for Council to concentrate its effort on the legislative function and to save the time it was devoting to considering measures concerned with implementing powers. The need to accomplish the ambitious programme to complete the internal market by 1 January, 1993 helped to stress the importance of refocusing the Council's legislative activity. Moreover, it appeared desirable to bring some order into the various procedures framing the implementing powers, the diversity of which had grown over time. The Single European Act was to bring about this restoration of order.

2.2 Implementing Powers After the Single European Act

The third indent of Article 145 was introduced by the Single European Act, whereas Article 155 remained unchanged. Article 145, paragraph 3, brought two essential changes.

2.2.1 Assignment of Implementing Powers and their Extent

First, Article 145, paragraph 3, establishes the principle of assigning implementing powers for Community acts to the Commission. It uses the word "shall", stating that the Council shall "confer on the Commission, in the acts which the Council adopts, powers for the implementation of the rules which the Council lays down". The normal state of affairs is, therefore, the delegation of powers to the Commission. This interpretation is confirmed *a contrario* by the third sentence of the paragraph, which provides that the Council may, in specific cases, reserve the right to exercise implementing powers to itself. The implication is that in all other cases power to take implementing measures is conferred on the Commission. This is indeed the view that the Court has of Article 145, paragraph 3, EC, as expressed in

---

[3] Case 25/70, *Einfuhr- und Vorratsstelle für Getreide und Futtermittel* v. *Köster, Berodt & Co.* [1970] ECR 1161.

Case 16/88,[4] where it stressed that these specific cases must be covered by a detailed statement of reasons. One cannot, however, draw the conclusion, as some authors do, that one might establish a typology of cases where the Council can reserve implementing powers. To be sure, the Court called for detailed grounds, but it is doubtful that it would interfere on a question of appropriateness, such as whether the Council ought to reserve its implementing powers or not.[5] This is an assessment that is up to the legislature, with the Court confining itself to verifying the existence of the stated reasons and their appropriateness to the provision disputed. Thus, classically, the Council reserves implementing powers for certain rules in the agricultural area,[6] conferring the power to implement the other rules on the Commission.

2.2.2 General Scope

Second, the scope of the rule set by Article 145 EC is general. However, the Commission, pursuant to Article 205 EC, holds the power to implement the budget. Hence, the question was raised as to whether the Council had the power to frame the Commission's financial implementing power by committee procedures. The Court gave the notion of implementation a broad interpretation as applying to the adoption both of general measures and of individual decisions. It felt that the provisions of Article 145 EC, given their importance and their place in the Treaty, ought also to apply in the area of financial implementation,[7] despite the provisions of Article 205 EC, which are to be interpreted in accordance with the general nature of Article 145 EC.

[4] Case 16/88, *Commission* v. *Council* [1989] ECR 3457.

[5] See, for example, Blumann (1994: 122 ff.), who feels that the Council cannot reserve implementing powers except on grounds of the high politicisation of a matter, risks of resistance by certain states or the fully integrated nature of the matter to be implemented. It is hard to see how the Court's control could manage to be exercised in such cases. Nor is it very likely that they would appear in that form in the stated reasons in the document.

[6] The basic regulation generally provides that in this case the Council shall adopt implementing rules by the majority provided for in Article 43, but without consulting Parliament. This procedure has, on several occasions, been accepted by the Court. See, in particular, Joined Cases C-63/90 and C-67/90, *Portugal and Spain* v. *Council* [1992] ECR I-5073, and Case C-417/93, *Parliament* v. *Council*, [1995] ECR I-1185, in which the Court stressed that: "[t]he procedure by which the Council adopts regulations relating to a Community policy, on a proposal from the Commission and after consulting the Parliament, applies solely to the basic regulations containing the essential elements of the matter to be dealt with and the provisions implementing those regulations may be adopted by the Council according to a different procedure".

[7] Hence, the Court ruled in Case 16/88 that: "[i]t must be stressed in that regard that the Commission's power to implement the budget is not such as to modify the division of powers resulting from the various provisions of the Treaty which authorise the Council and the Commission to adopt generally applicable or individual measures within specific areas, such as Article 43, which is in issue in the present case, and from the institutional provisions of the third indent of Article 145 and Article 155". Case 16/88, above, note 4, at 3486.

The implementing power cannot relate to all the elements of a Community regulation. In every case, only the Council can lay down the essential elements of the matter. As the Court stressed in the *Köster* case:

"[i]t cannot, therefore, be a requirement that all the details of the regulations concerning the Common Agricultural Policy be drawn up by the Council according to the procedure in Article 43. It is sufficient for the purposes of that provision that the basic elements of the matter to be dealt with have been adopted in accordance with the procedure laid down by that provision".[8]

This requirement is intended to preserve the institutional balance. It is not for the Council to abandon power to legislate in an area, by conferring it on the Commission. Moreover, by so acting in an area in which Parliament has the power to take part in legislative procedure, it would deprive Parliament of the possibility of exercising its prerogatives were the essential elements of a policy not to be contained in the act itself.

However, the Court's case law has interpreted the notion of essential elements in a manner favourable to the Commission. Thus, in Case C-240/90, the Court felt that the essential rules were those intended to translate the fundamental guidelines of a Community policy,[9] leaving very broad room to the implementing power. Similarly, the Comitology Decision specified in Article 1 that where it conferred implementing powers on the Commission, the Council should specify the essential elements of these powers.[10] The Court found that such precision was not necessary, and that an empowerment worded in general terms was sufficient. It deduced that the Commission could, within the framework of its implementing powers, lay down penalties for Member States to apply to operators committing irregularities even though the basic regulation did not so empower it.[11]

3. The Comitology Procedures

Article 145 EC introduces the comitology procedures into the Treaty, reflecting the will to bring order into these by averting the creation of new procedures whenever the Council in a specific act confers implementing powers on the Commission.

[8] Case 25/70, above, note 3.

[9] Case C-240/90, *Germany* v. *Commission* [1992] ECR I-5383.

[10] Council Decision 87/373/EEC, (1987) OJ L 197/33.

[11] Hence, "[s]ince the Council has laid down in its basic regulation the essential rules governing the matter in question, it may delegate to the Commission general implementing power without having to specify the essential components of the delegated power; for that purpose, a provision drafted in general terms provides a sufficient basis for the authority to act. That principle is not affected by the aforementioned decision. As a measure of secondary law it cannot add to the rules of the Treaty, which do not require the Council to specify the essential components of the implementing powers delegated to the Commission". Above, note 9, at I-5435.

It provides that the Council may impose certain requirements on the exercise of implementing powers. It specifies that these procedures must be consistent with principles and rules to be laid down in advance by the Council, acting unanimously on a proposal from the Commission and after obtaining the opinion of the European Parliament. The Decision reflected in Article 145 EC was adopted by the Council on 13 July 1987.[12]

It follows from the Treaty that the Comitology Decision is exhaustive and that one cannot use the absence of parallelism of forms in Community law as a basis for delegating from it by creating a new procedure when adopting a regulation or directive. This interpretation follows from the use of the terms "laid down in advance" in Article 145 EC. The wording of Article 145 EC thus implies that any comitology procedure inserted into an act must have been laid down in advance of the adoption of the act. Should it appear necessary to have recourse to a new procedure, the Comitology Decision ought first to be amended. The procedures introduced by this Decision are exhaustive.

The choice of implementing procedure follows the procedure laid down for adopting the basic act that it is inserted in. It is, thus, for the Commission to include in its proposal a provision enabling empowerment, accompanied where necessary by one of the comitology procedures provided for by the Comitology Decision. If the Council wishes to have recourse to a different procedure, it should amend the Commission proposal unanimously, pursuant to Article 189a (1) EC, unless the Commission itself agrees to amend its proposal. Even if the Council amends the Commission proposal in relation to comitology, it is possible that it may be obliged to consult Parliament again, since the Court, in some cases, considers that an amendment to comitology may be regarded as affecting a substantial feature of the act. For the Court, reconsultation is appropriate where the amendment adopted in relation to the type of committee decisively affects the overall balance of powers between the Commission and the Council as it emerges from the proposal. The Court does not go any further in its analysis, but in this specific case the amendment was not found to have to give rise to reconsultation, although the Council had adopted a regulatory committee, variant (a), whereas the proposal was for a management committee, variant (a).[13] Moreover, in the cases where the Article 189b (co-decision) procedure applies, Parliament plays an important part in choosing

[12] Above, note 10.

[13] Case C-417/93, above, note 6. In his Opinion to this Case, Advocate General Léger gave a more precise idea of what, in his view, cases of reconsultation should be: "[t]here is, in my view, a substantial difference between the committee of an advisory nature in Procedure I and the committees provided for by Procedures II and III, since the first excludes any decision-making power of the Council. There is also a substantial difference between committees of type II(a), II(b) and III(a) on the one hand, and type III(b) on the other. The latter procedure alone can lead to a deadlock, since the Council can block any decision by simple majority". (paras 90 and 91).

the implementing procedure. It is, moreover, because of the implementing procedure adopted in the Council's Common Position that the proposal for a directive relating to voice telephony was rejected.[14]

The Comitology Decision limits the types of committee to three, the latter two having variants. Type I procedure is the advisory committee. The Commission has to bring before the committee, made up of Member State representatives and chaired by the Commission, the draft implementing measures to be adopted. The committee gives an opinion. The Commission takes the greatest account of this opinion and informs the committee of the way it has taken account of this opinion. In this framework, the Commission retains the fullest freedom. It is, therefore, not surprising that this is the formula it favours. In a joint declaration on the final act of the Single European Act, the Intergovernmental Conference invited,

> ". . . the Council to give the Advisory Committee procedure in particular a predominant place in the interest of speed and efficiency in the decision-making process, for the exercise of the powers of implementation conferred on the Commission within the field of Article 100 a of the EEC Treaty".

Despite this declaration, Commission proposals favouring an advisory committee have often not been followed by the Council. Procedure II, called the "management committee", gives the Council a power of reservation. The committee gives its opinion by qualified majority (Article 148 (2) EC). Member States representatives' votes are accordingly weighted pursuant to that Article. After the committee's opinion, the Commission adopts immediately applicable measures. However, in the case of an unfavourable opinion from the committee, the Commission may postpone, for a maximum of one month, the application of the measures, and the Council, deciding by qualified majority, may, within this month, take a different decision (variant a). In variant (b), the Commission must postpone application of the measures for a time set in the act, which may not exceed three months, during which time the Council may, by qualified majority, take different measures. This procedure, which has been accepted by the Court,[15] ensures that in every case the implementing measures will enter into force within a set time. One may also note that absence of the committee's opinion is tantamount to a positive opinion.

Procedure III, called the "regulatory committee", was the one most criticised by the Commission and Parliament when it was adopted. The latter even introduced an appeal for annulment of the Decision because of this procedure. The appeal was pronounced inadmissible by the Court, on the ground that Article 173 EC did not give Parliament active legitimation.[16]

---

[14] See, in particular, Earnshaw/Judge (1995).

[15] Case 25/70, *Köster*, above, note 3.

[16] Case 302/87, *Parliament* v. *Council* [1988] ECR 5615. This was before the development in the Court's case law in relation to Parliament's active legitimation. It is, in any case, uncertain whether the case would have been declared admissible after the development in the case

In this procedure, in the case of absence of opinion or negative opinion by the committee, the Commission cannot decide the measures to adopt but must make a proposal to the Council. If the Council does not adopt this proposal by qualified majority within a time set in each act, which does not exceed three months, the Commission adopts the proposed measure. This is variant (a), called the "*filet*", since there is a safety net (*filet de sécurité*) that ensures that eventually the implementing measures will be taken. In variant (b), called the "*contre-filet*", the Council has the possibility, within a time limit laid down in the act that cannot exceed three months, of opposing, by simple majority, the measures adopted by the Commission. The drawback with this variant is the possibility of ending in a situation of blockage, preventing the adoption of implementing measures. Thus, the Commission has never proposed this variant.

It should be noted that the Council's right of reservation in Procedure III is not afforded only by a negative opinion from the committee, but also by an absence of opinion. However, whereas in Procedure II the Council may depart from measures adopted by the Commission by qualified majority, it may do so in Procedure III only unanimously, since it has before it a Commission proposal; the real difference in terms of Council powers between Procedure IIb and Procedure IIIa is, therefore, not very important.

Additionally, Parliament has maintained that Procedure III contravenes the Treaty, since it deprives the Commission, particularly in variant (b), of the power of adopting the implementing measures that had been conferred on it by the basic act. This criticism can hardly stand up to the text of Article 145 EC or the Court's ruling in the *Köster* case.[17]

In practice, as the Commission notes in a support on the functioning of the Treaty on European Union, the procedures work well. Out of 200 committees able to block a decision, and out of several thousand opinions, there have only been six cases of referral back to the Council, and none led to blockage of the decision.[18]

To be sure, it has been asserted that the absence of blockage has to do with the fact that the Commission produces implementing measures with a content unlikely to be opposed on the committee, so as to avert any decision by the Council. The cost of comitology would, then, be a certain self-censorship by the Commission. But in this area, it is up to the Commission to exercise its responsibility fully. Since the Member States are responsible for the material implementation of the measures, it is legitimate for their concern to be taken into account in developing these measures. What use would there be in adopting measures that would subsequently prove impossible to implement? Moreover, in more political

law, since it would have been necessary for Parliament to show how the 1987 Comitology Decision affected the prerogatives granted it by the Treaty.

[17] Above, note 3.

[18] SEC(95) 731 final, para 52.

terms, as we have seen earlier, the implementing powers normally belong to Member States. It is, therefore, legitimate where these measures are adopted at Community level to allow Member State representatives, who make up the committees, the right to be consulted on these measures.

4. Comitology Following the Treaty of Maastricht

4.1 Article 145 Third Indent EC

The Treaty of Maastricht did not amend Article 145 EC. The Intergovernmental Conference, which had proposals in this direction before it from both Parliament[19] and the Commission[20] in the context of the debate on the hierarchy of acts, refused to do so. However, Parliament drew on the creation of a new legislative procedure, the Article 189 b procedure, to relaunch the debate on comitology.

In fact, for the European Parliament, Article 145, third indent EC is not applicable to measures implementing acts based on Article 189 EC. These acts are adopted by Parliament and Council. But Article 145 EC only covered acts adopted by the Council alone, as shown by the use of the wording "in the acts which the Council adopts". The Commission, for its part, felt that there was a *lacuna* in the Treaty in terms of implementing measures for acts adopted according to the Article 189b procedure. For the Council, these arguments are unfounded. The Intergovernmental Conference had before it proposals to amend Article 145 EC, and did not follow them up. It is clear that the authors of the Treaty wished to preserve the existing position. Moreover, in formal terms, acts adopted according to the Article 189b procedure are indeed acts adopted by the Council, as shown by the wording used in all the legal bases that refer to the Article 189b procedure: "the Council, deciding in accordance with the Article 189b procedure". There is, therefore, no question of a Treaty *lacuna*, and Article 145 EC does apply to all Council acts, including those adopted in accordance with the Article 189b procedure. In Case C-259/95, the Court agreed with the Council's interpretation of Articles 145 and 189b EC, and rejected the more literal interpretation given by the Parliament.[21]

In any case, Parliament's prerogatives in relation to comitology were not negligible. The choice of detailed rules for implementing the act is made in accordance with the co-decision procedure. The Commission proposals before the committee may be challenged by Parliament in the context of

---

[19] See paras 24-27 of Parliament's Resolution of 11 July 1990, (1990) OJ C 231/97.

[20] See the Commission's contributions to the Intergovernmental Conference, EC Bull suppl. 1/91, 115-121. The Commission proposed deleting Article 145, third indent, conferring implementing powers on the Commission and providing for a right of reservation by Council and Parliament.

[21] Case C-259/95, *European Parliament* v. *Council* [1997] ECR I-5303.

the political control it exercises over the Commission's management. Finally, should it feel that the implementing act exceeds the powers laid down in the basic act, it has, by Article 173 EC, the power to invoke the Court of Justice.[22]

4.2 Institutional Dispute

The dispute between the Council and Parliament threatened to compromise the functioning of the co-decision procedure, since Parliament threatened to reject any act subject to co-decision that called on a type III procedure for its implementation. To avoid such an outcome, the Commission proposed an inter-institutional agreement providing, in cases of co-decision, for the adoption of an act involving measures of a normative nature for the conferment on the Commission of the power to adopt the implementing measures subject to the European Parliament being offered an opportunity by the majority of its members, and the Council by qualified majority, to reject the act, in which case the Commission could either adopt a new act or submit a proposal for an act to Parliament and Council, which would decide in accordance with the Article 189b procedure.[23] However, this proposal was not acceptable to the Council since it assumed the existence of a *lacuna* in the Treaty and the possibility of filling that *lacuna* by an interinstitutional agreement. The Council felt that there was no *lacuna* and that an inter-institutional agreement in this area would have constituted a formal breach of the Treaty. Moreover, it was very hard to reject an implementing measure adopted by the Commission, since it required agreement from Parliament and Council, something likely to happen very rarely, thus leaving great freedom to the Commission. In fact, under cover of contributing to resolving a dispute, the Commission was first and foremost seeking to free itself of the constraints of the 1987 Comitology Decision and secure largely uncontrolled implementing powers to itself.

4.3 The Modus Vivendi

Finally, the dispute was to be resolved by the three institutions negotiating among themselves a *modus vivendi* which left intact the provisions of the Comitology Decision and specified that nothing in it prejudiced the legal positions of the three institutions, since in its own terms it merely constituted guidelines.[24] This *modus vivendi* essentially provides for broad infor-

---

[22] Case C-303/94, *Parliament* v. *Council* [1996] ECR I-2943.

[23] See draft interinstitutional agreement between the European Parliament, the Council and the Commission on the implementing powers for acts adopted jointly by the European Parliament and the Council in accordance with the procedure provided for in Article 189b of the Treaty setting up the European Community, SEC(94) 645 final.

[24] (1996) OJ C 102/1.

mation to Parliament by the Commission on its draft-implementing measures. For the Council, it will not, in the event of reservation, proceed with adopting an act of general scope except after informing Parliament, setting a reasonable time for it to give an opinion, and, should Parliament's opinion be negative, subsequently taking note of Parliament's viewpoint so as to seek a solution in an appropriate framework. This involvement of Parliament would have to be speedy, since it is specified that in any case the measure is to be adopted within the time limits laid down in the basic act. It is, therefore clear that disagreement by Parliament does not prevent the Council from deciding the way it wants. Moreover, it is stated that the problem will be given consideration at the next intergovernmental conference, at the request of the Commission, Parliament or several Member States. The consequence of this *modus vivendi* is to organise a permanent procedure enabling Parliament's viewpoint to be secured, and a solution to be sought with it in the event of disagreement where the Council is inclined to intervene in the context of Procedures II and III, and only where adoption of an act of general scope is involved. Given the small number of cases in which this situation arises, the *modus vivendi* is likely to be applied only rarely.

5. Comitology Post-Amsterdam

The 1996/97 IGC abandoned the Comitology issue since the Member States once again concluded that it would not to be desirable to amend Article 145 EC, but possible to revise the Comitology Decision. Consequently, a Declaration which was integrated into the Final Act of Amsterdam invited the Commission to submit a pertinent proposal. The Commission complied with this request in July 1998.[25] The Commission proposal seeks to simplify the procedures and tries to rationalise the use of the different types of committees. With regard to the first point, the initiative is successful; as to its second objective, however, the contents of the proposal raise more problems than they seem to resolve; what will attract even more attention, is the possibility of substituting in certain cases the regulatory procedure by a recourse to the legislative procedure. This possibility profoundly modifies the institutional balance; this will certainly provoke interesting debates both within the Council and between Council and Parliament.

We refrain from commenting upon the Commission's proposal, but simply indicate that it may seem difficult to accept that the executive power attributed to the Council by Article 145 EC could be exercised by the legislature. On the other hand, if and because an executive procedure

[25] (1998) OJ C 279/5. For a detailed analysis, see Kortenberg (1998).

which is to modify or adapt a text has to be adopted by the legislature, the principle of institutional balance does not militate against such association and its procedural implications.

5

Institutional Aspects of Comitology: Scenes from the Cutting Room Floor

Kieran St Clair Bradley[*]

According to Hollywood lore, sequences shot for a film, in some cases vital (or at least useful) to a proper understanding of a character or the plot may be left out of the version edited for general release.[1] To the eternal chagrin of the actors and script-writers concerned, the extirpation of such sequences need not be related to their artistic merit, but may reflect other concerns, particularly of those pulling the purse-strings, such as the length of the movie or the likely box-office returns. So it is with the former cult feature, "The Return of the Comitology Debate", now showing to packed audiences at an epistemic theatre near you, from which a number of potentially relevant, if perhaps rather recondite, institutional and legal aspects appear to be missing or incompletely covered. The present essay does not therefore aim to provide any comprehensive overview of the place of committees in general, or of Comitology in particular, in the institutional scheme of the European Community/Union, but seeks rather to restore to their rightful place some of these scenes from the cutting room floor.

1. The Modus Vivendi: a Mess of Pottage?

While Community law sets its face against attaching too much importance to the denomination of an instrument as distinct from its contents, it can hardly be an accident that the text concerning Comitology in co-decision to which the representatives of the European Parliament, the Council and the Commission appended their signatures on 20 December 1994 was not even

---

[*] *Referendaire* at the European Court of Justice, Luxembourg. The views expressed are personal.
[1] One, perhaps rather inappropriate, example was reported in *The Observer* on 1 March 1998, concerning the showing on British television of 10 minutes of footage omitted from *The Exorcist* when it was released in 1973.

graced with the title of "interinstitutional agreement" or "declaration" as is usual in such cases.[2] The choice of *"modus vivendi"* might be taken as implying something well short of an "agreement", which betokens a meeting of minds, or even of an agreement to disagree, such as the 1966 Luxembourg Compromise. In the circumstances, it could be read as indicating a failure to agree on the parameters of the dispute, with an acceptance of the fact that political life and legislative activity must nonetheless go on. Hence the guidelines the *modus* establishes are expressly "intended to overcome the difficulties which have arisen" in the adoption of acts under co-decision, but "in no way prejudice the position of principle expressed by the three institutions". The *modus vivendi* sought to bring interinstitutional peace; it might fairly be asked at what price and at whose expense.

The background is fairly simple; the co-decision procedure introduced by the Maastricht Treaty allows Parliament a veto over the content of legislation adopted under this procedure, a facility which it exercised systematically as regard Comitology provisions during the first year of operation of the new procedure.[3] Parliament's legal justification was that the third indent of Article 202 (ex-Article 145) EC, which had not been amended, only applied to "acts which the Council adopts", while acts under co-decision are adopted by Parliament and the Council jointly (see, for example, the first paragraph of Article 230 (ex-Article 173) EC). The soundness of this view has been thrown into question somewhat by an *obiter dictum* of the Court in a judgment of 2 October 1997.[4] In rejecting a challenge by Parliament, on the grounds of a faulty legal basis, to a Council Decision on an information system regarding home and leisure accidents, the Court held that the expression

> "[acts] of the Council, without further qualification, are those adopted by that institution, either alone or together with the Parliament under the co-decision procedure (...) acts adopted jointly by the Council and the Parliament are regarded as acts of the Council".

Be that as it may, Parliament's use of the co-decision procedure to block Comitology provisions was less the reflection of its adherence to a particular interpretation of the Treaty than of its willingness to use legal means to achieve political ends.

The *modus vivendi* poses two dangers for Parliament's margin for manoeuvre in the co-decision procedure; the first is that it is not worth the paper on which it is written, the second is that it is. The *modus* provides a mechanism by which Parliament is informed of draft implementing legislation by the Commission, and is consulted by the Council whenever a "draft

---

[2] The latest publication of the *modus vivendi* in the Official Journal is accompanied by one of each, (1996) OJ C 102/1, 2 and 4, respectively.

[3] Bradley (1997: 238–240).

[4] Case C-259/95 *European Parliament* v. *Council (Home Accidents)* [1997] ECR I-5303.

[5] Ibid., at para 26.

general implementing act" is referred to it as a result of a negative, or no, committee opinion. Apart from this consultative mechanism, the Commission is required to "take account as far as possible of any comments by the European Parliament and [to] keep it informed at every stage of the procedure (...) so as to enable the Parliament to assume its own responsibilities in full knowledge of the facts". It neither guarantees that Parliament's views will be taken into account, nor ensures Parliament any real influence over the content of the implementing legislation; the wording of the obligation on the Commission to take account of Parliament's views is reminiscent of the so-called "aerosol formula" included in the advisory committee procedure, so rarely favoured by the Council, while the assumption by Parliament of its own responsibilities can only refer ultimately to the right to adopt a motion of censure against the Commission or to start legal proceedings to protect its position, which Parliament did not need the *modus* to bestow upon it. The limitation to "general implementing acts", apart from introducing ambiguity where there was none before, ignores the fact that other implementing acts can prove equally or more controversial.[6] Perhaps most important of all, the *modus* provides no means by which Parliament can verify that the other institutions respect their obligations, and leaves its application, in effect, to the good will of the Council and the Commission.[7]

The other matter which arises in connection with the *modus* is its legal value, and in particular whether Parliament could rely upon it as a ground for the annulment of an implementing act which has been adopted in breach of the consultation procedure it establishes. An alternative, and rather more problematic, scenario would arise where Parliament sought to challenge basic legislation containing Comitology provisions adopted by the Council after having applied the *modus vivendi* to the letter.

To date, the Court of Justice has been somewhat reluctant to recognise consultation obligations other than those expressly provided for in the Treaty or enabling legislation. In the *Isoglucose* cases, the Court was careful to specify that "[due] consultation of the Parliament *in the cases provided for by the Treaty*" was an essential procedural formality.[8] Contrariwise, in the *Migrant Policy* cases, the Court refused to read into Article 118 EEC a requirement that the Commission consult the Economic and Social Committee on a proposed decision organising co-operation between the Member States on certain social policy matters, despite an eloquent plea in favour of this view from Advocate General Mancini.[9]

[6] See the very specific authorisation of transgenic maize, discussed at section 2, below.

[7] On the application in practice of this and other interinstitutional agreements on Comitology, see Bradley (1997: 235–238). For a concrete example of a parliamentary consultation under the *modus*, see (1998) OJ C 167/187.

[8] Case 138/79, *Roquette Frères* v. *Council* [1980] ECR 3333, at 3360 (emphasis added).

[9] Joined Cases 218, 283 to 285 and 287/85, *Germany and others* v. *Commission* [1987] ECR 3203, at 3256 and 3243-3244, respectively.

If the *modus* were to be considered for the purposes of argument an interinstitutional agreement, it would, in accordance with the *FAO Voting Rights* case, have to satisfy two criteria to be deemed to have legal effects: the text would have to represent the fulfilment of a duty of co-operation, and demonstrate an intention on the part of the institutions concerned "to enter into a binding commitment towards each other".[10] There can be little real doubt that the operation of the co-decision procedure is subject to a duty on the institutions to co-operate with each other, both as a matter of practice and as a matter of law. The practical necessity to co-operate was recognised, and to some extent regulated, by the two interinstitutional agreements concluded on 25 October 1993 on tripartite talks before the adoption of the Council's common position and on the operation of conciliation committees in co-decision.[11] The Court would almost certainly apply its case-law on the consultation and budget procedures in this regard, to the effect that

> "inter-institutional dialogue (...) is subject to the same mutual duties of sincere co-operation as those which govern relations between Member States and the Community institutions".[12]

The question of the extent to which the *modus* can be said to fulfil such a duty is somewhat less evident; it expressly imposes duties on the Commission and the Council, but none on Parliament. The wording of the text could reasonably be interpreted as manifesting an intention on the part of those concerned to conclude a legally binding agreement. Therefore, at least in so far as it fulfils a duty to co-operate, the *modus* is well capable of having binding legal effects.

Where Parliament considers that either the Commission or the Council has adopted implementing legislation without respecting the *modus*, it would have a possible cause of action under Article 230 (ex-Article 173) EC. It is significant in this regard that neither this provision nor the Court's case-law restricts Parliament's prerogatives to those which it derives directly under the Treaty, and, indeed, Parliament enjoys a number of important, largely supervisory, prerogatives under secondary law, such as the decision on the parliamentary right of inquiry.[13] Given the rather formal character of the obligations imposed by the *modus* on the Council and the Commission,

---

[10] Case C-25/94, *Commission v. Council (FAO Voting Rights)* [1996] ECR I-1469, at I-1510 (para 49).

[11] (1993) OJ C 329/141.

[12] Case C-65/93, *Parliament v. Council (GSP)* [1995] ECR I-643, at I-668 (para 23); notwithstanding a Council request for urgent consideration of a proposal for an annual regulation on tariff preferences, Parliament had postponed the delivery of its opinion at the December part-session for reasons which the Court felt qualified to describe as "wholly unconnected with the contested regulation" (para 26).

[13] Decision 95/167/EC, Euratom, ECSC, (1995) OJ L 113/2.

it is on the other hand difficult to see why these institutions would not comply with such obligations scrupulously, particularly in a case where the content of the implementing measure is likely to be controversial.

What, however, of the case where Parliament and the Council are *ad idem* on the content of primary legislation, and the Council, pleading, for example, urgency, adopts the measure where Parliament's approval on a joint text has been withheld because this contains a Comitology provision?[14] In accordance with the third indent of Article 202 (ex-Article 145) EC, the Council is obliged to confer implementing powers on the Commission, except where it reserves these to itself; in accordance with the *Home Accidents* case, this obligation applies to acts adopted under co-decision; in accordance with the reasoning of the *FAO Voting Rights* case, the *modus vivendi* is capable of having legal effects. It is true that the *modus* imposes no express obligations on Parliament, but can it realistically be interpreted, in the light of the "*mutual* duties of sincere co-operation", as a series of unilateral obligations by the Council and the Commission, with no parliamentary *quid pro quo*?

It is also true that the right of Parliament to block Comitology provisions under co-decision is bestowed directly by the Treaty, under Article 251 (ex-Article 189b) EC; this may not, however, be sufficient to guarantee the success of any annulment proceedings it might initiate against a Council act adopted in such circumstances. After all, the fact that Parliament's right to consultation derives directly from the Treaty did not prevent the Court rejecting its challenge to a Council regulation adopted without its opinion, where the Court considered Parliament had "failed to discharge its obligation to co-operate sincerely with the Council".[15] In the light of these provisions and this case-law, it is not entirely implausible that the Court would conclude that the *modus vivendi* constitutes the fulfilment of an interinstitutional duty of co-operation, and that in signing up Parliament agreed not to block the inclusion of normal Comitology provisions in acts adopted under co-decision; "[in] these circumstances, the Parliament [would] not [be] entitled to complain of the Council's failure" to respect the terms of Article 251 (ex-Article 189b) EC.[16] While such a case could have been made out even in the absence of the *modus*, the Council's position would appear

---

[14] This is merely a concocted scenario for the purposes of illustrating the possible ramifications of the *modus vivendi*; it is not suggested that the Council would adopt such a course of conduct.

[15] *GSP* Case, above, note 12, at I-669 (para 27).

[16] *GSP* Case, above, note 12, at I-669 (para 28); the Court might be all the more tempted to so conclude if the dispute, as is often the case, were between committee procedures II(b) and III(a) (see section 2, below), though the point is equally valid where Parliament seeks simply to delete any such procedure. Obviously any defence by Parliament of committee procedure II would be inconsistent with its interpretation of the third indent of Article 145 EC.

to be much stronger with Parliament's signature on the dotted line; has Parliament sold its birthright for a mess of pottage?

2. The Difference between Comitology Procedures: II(b) or not II(b)?

One of the problems with Comitology which the 1986 SEA set out to tackle was that of deciding which particular procedure should apply for each type of implementing decision. Thus the third indent of Article 202 (ex-Article 145) EC provides that the supervisory procedures which the Council can impose on the Commission "must be consonant with principles and rules to be laid down in advance by the Council". It is notorious that the 1987 Comitology decision omits to provide any such principles governing the selection of committee procedure.[17] In its report on the application of the Treaty on European Union, the Commission recommended that

> "the 1996 Conference would be well advised to do away with Comitology in its present form. The reason is not that Comitology, as it stands, has not functioned or is functioning inadequately (...) [but that] too much time and energy is being lost in individual cases by interinstitutional quarrels as to which variant to choose out of the broad Comitology range".[18]

The Westendorp Report failed to reach a consensus on the reform of the Comitology system, though noting a large majority in favour of the simplification of "the present committee procedure," (*sic*) "which is already complicated and confused and will not survive beyond the next enlargement".[19] It also adverted to the "need to improve the quality of the rules adopted under these procedures". Perhaps wisely in the circumstances, the IGC restricted itself to inviting the Commission to submit to the Council by the end of 1998 a proposal to amend the Comitology decision.

While the broad outlines of the Comitology system are well known, its operation in practice has given rise to perplexity even in the most elevated circles; Weiler's description of Comitology as "a phenomenon which requires its very own science which no single person has mastered"[20] time and again proves apt. Descriptions of Comitology do not always distinguish clearly between the legal impact of opinions delivered by management and regulatory committees, particularly as regards the difference between a draft measure and a Commission proposal. One otherwise very reliable study states that where a particular regulatory committee does not

---

[17] Council Decision 87/373/EEC, (1987) OJ L 197/33; Bradley (1997: 252).

[18] Timmermans (1996: 140).

[19] Report of the Reflection Group for the IGC chaired by Westendorp, Brussels, 5 December 1995, reprinted in Winter (1996: 509-510) (paras 127 and 128).

[20] Weiler (1995b: 6).

approve the Commission's proposal,

> "the issue is transferred to the Council which ... may adopt a different measure with qualified majority".[21]

This description is somewhat misleading, as the Council may only amend the Commission proposal by unanimity.[22] For its part, the Court of Justice has held that there is no substantial difference between a management committee type II(b), and a regulatory committee type III(a), though acknowledging in the same judgment that

> "the choice of one type of committee or another, in so far as it involves different decision-making procedures and a different division of powers between the Commission and the Council, may have a decisive influence on the operation of the arrangements in question".[23]

It is possible to construct an argument[24] to show that there is no difference, as the Court has held, between committee types II(b) and III(a), at least as long as there are fewer than 61 votes against the Commission's proposal. The argument, which is premised on the assumption that the Council will vote the same way as the supervisory committee, runs as follows:

– where there are not more than 25 votes against the Commission's proposal, the Commission can go ahead under either procedure, as there are not enough votes against to refer the matter to the Council;
– where there are more than 25 votes but fewer than 62 votes against: under II(b), the Commission can adopt its measures; under III(a), the Commission must submit a proposal to the Council, but as the Council is not unanimous, it will neither adopt the proposal nor be able to amend it, and hence the Commission will be able to adopt its original proposal on the rebound, as it were.

Apart from the fact that it does not apply where there are more than 62 votes against in committee, this reasoning is flawed in at least four respects. In the first place, the assumption that the Council will always vote in the same way as the supervisory committee is problematic. If this were so in practice, then the Council would in effect have delegated decision-making powers to the committee, in contravention of the principle of institutional balance, as interpreted by the Court in *Meroni*.[25] In any case, in the absence of any legal requirement or similar arrangement, such as an interinstitutional agreement to this effect or specifying that the committee's decisions

---

[21] Ballmann (1996: 14).

[22] Article 250 (Article 189a(1)) EC.

[23] Case C-417/93, *European Parliament* v. *Council (TACIS)* [1995] ECR I-1185, at I-1218.

[24] I am indebted to Piet Van Nuffel of the Institute for European Law at the Katholieke Universiteit Leuven for his insightful suggestions in this regard.

[25] Case 9/56 *Meroni SpA.* v. *High Authority* [1957-58] ECR 133, at 152; see also Bradley (1992: 698-699).

are to be treated as if they emanated from the Council,[26] the difference between decisions of the two bodies remains legally significant. Secondly, under procedure III(a), abstentions count against the Commission, which therefore requires at least 62 positive votes, rather than merely less than 25 negative votes as in II (b). Thirdly, the fact that it may be difficult for the Council to overturn the Commission's position under a particular procedure does not mean that there is no difference between this and a procedure where the Commission acts alone; the Council might, for example, prefer to adopt a compromise measure (unanimously) rather than that proposed by the Commission. Finally the significant difference in this analysis ignores the "dissuasive effect" of each procedure; it is clearly much easier for the Commission to avoid a reference to the Council under II(b) than under III (a), and it is difficult to believe that this factor has no impact on the content of its draft measures/proposals.

The minutiae of the operation of committee procedures are not just lawyers' quiddits and quillets. As long as the Comitology system remains in place, these apparently slight differences can have a fundamental effect on the outcome of the legislative procedure; indeed, they seem to come into play particularly where the substantive outcome is controversial. The implications of each procedural nuance will need to be carefully evaluated in any reform of the Comitology decision. Moreover, as regards the relative strength of the position of each of the institutions concerned under these procedures, things are not always what they seem.

This last point can be illustrated by the procedure leading to the adoption of Commission Decision 97/98/EC[27] requiring France to consent to the marketing of genetically modified ("transgenic") maize notified by Ciba-Geigy (now Novartis). Council Directive 90/220/EEC on the release into the environment of genetically modified organisms ("GMOs")[28] allows the competent authority of a Member State to authorise the marketing of transgenic products, unless the competent authority of another Member State raises objections; in this case the power of decision falls to the Commission under a regulatory committee procedure, type III(a), the "GMO committee". Following objections by a number of Member States, France referred the request for a marketing authorisation for transgenic maize to the Commission with a positive assessment. In the Committee, six Member States voted for authorisation (34 votes), four voted against (21 votes), with four abstaining (27 votes) and one submitting an invalid vote (5 votes). In the absence of a positive opinion, the matter was referred to the Council. There the opposition to the Commission's proposal was much firmer, with 13 Member States expressing disapproval, one abstaining and, surprise

---

[26] The scenario is not quite so fanciful as it might appear; see the facts of the *FAO Voting Rights* case, above, note 10.
[27] (1997) OJ L 31/69.   [28] (1990) OJ L 117/15.

surprise, France in favour. Failing unanimity, the matter reverted to the Commission which, unshackled of the bonds of the GMO Committee, granted the authorisation requested in January 1997, notwithstanding widespread public and political disapproval.[29]

That the supervision of the GMO Committee and the Council's power of veto were unable to prevent the Commission proceeding with the authorisation is not so extraordinary as it might at first appear. After all, an authorisation request only reaches the Commission and the GMO Committee if at least one Member State is in favour (the referring Member State) and one or several Member States are against (the objecting state(s). Where the committee fails to agree with the Commission's proposal, this will then come before the Council, where unanimity is inherently improbable, given the existence of two opposing, and by now probably entrenched, views. The net result is that, except where the Member State which has originally proposed or opposed the authorisation request changes its position in order to permit unanimity in Council, the Commission cannot in practice fail, whatever it proposes.

For decisions of this kind, which are essentially limited to the approval or rejection of a request for authorisation on which the Member States disagree, the regulatory committee procedure renders the Council veto useless in practice. The Council's position would, in all probability, have been stronger under the management committee procedure.[30] Given the clear sensitivity of the matter under consideration, at least some of the Member States which voted in favour of the authorisation in committee might have been prevailed upon to vote against, if only to let the Council have its say; as it was, nine delegations in the committee commanding 53 votes between them did not approve of the authorisation. The Council was clearly willing, and under a management committee procedure would have been able, to overturn the Commission's determined position in favour of authorisation.

3. *Angelopharm*: an End to Bald Assertions?

Though a favourite technique of lawyers everywhere engaged in litigation, a legal argument or hypothesis based on a citation from a court judgment detached from its context should in principle be treated with a degree of reserve, if not downright scepticism. This is particularly so of judgments of

---

[29] See also Bradley (1998: 211–215), and Case C-6/99 *Association Greenpeace France*, pending [(1999) OJ C 71/17].

[30] Type II(b), as type II(a) only allows the Council an *ex post facto* review; there would be little point, from the point of view of environmental protection, in refusing a market authorisation after the event. In its proposal to amend Directive 90/220, the Commission opted for committee procedure type III (b) [(1998) OJ C 139/9].

the European Court of Justice, which are drafted in a style which goes from economical through terse to laconic. Not all of its pronouncements constitute great statements of principle, and it is usually possible to distinguish the kernel of the Court's reasoning from the supporting explanations and observations to sift the prescriptive from the merely descriptive. Difficult cases may, however, arise, where an appreciation of the exact scope of a Court dictum requires account to be taken of the entirety of the context, including submissions made orally, and where more may be read into the wording of the judgment than is justified in the circumstances.

One such case is what has been described as the "meta-positive principle" apparently laid down by the Court in *Angelopharm*.[31] There the Court held, in paragraph 31 of its judgment, that

> "the drafting and adaptation of Community rules governing cosmetic products are founded on scientific and technical assessments which must themselves be based on the result of the latest international research".

Having noted that, by its own admission, the Commission was unable to carry out such assessments, the Court went on to hold that the sonorously-titled Committee on the Adaptation to Technical Progress of the Directives on the Removal of Technical Barriers to Trade in the Cosmetic Products Sector (hereinafter, for convenience, the "Cosmetics Adaptation Committee") was "similarly not in a position to make such an assessment". In reaching this conclusion, the Court noted that the Cosmetics Adaptation Committee

> "must, in the nature of things and apart from any provision laid down to that effect, be assisted by experts on scientific and technical issues delegated by the Member States".

The statement that committees such as the Cosmetics Adaptation Committee must "in the nature of things" have access to such expert assistance has been hailed, in a captivating analysis by Joerges, as a new dawn in the integration of scientific expertise in social regulation "designed to promote the adequacy of regulatory policies by ensuring that they take 'the latest international research' into account".[32] While Joerges might be considered the leader of the pack in this regard, his view has been followed or adopted independently by a considerable number of other commentators in this area, including Neyer,[33] Vos,[34] Falke,[35] Ballmann,[36] Docksey and Williams,[37] though not, apparently, the Commission's Legal Service.[38]

---

[31] Case C-212/91 *Angelopharm* v. *Hamburg* [1994] ECR I-171.

[32] Joerges (1997: 314).   [33] Joerges/Neyer (1997a).   [34] Vos (1997b: 212).

[35] Falke (1996: 150-151).   [36] Ballmann (1996: 26).

[37] "The judgment (...) has revolutionised the status of such groups in the decision-making process": Docksey/Williams (1997: 142-143).

[38] Joerges/Neyer (1997a: 281).

In a more recent gloss on the judgment, Joerges and Neyer are careful to disclaim any

> "suggest[ion] that the authority of the ECJ is backing our vision of a law of transnational governance, which would avoid both the pitfalls of intergovernmentalism and the building up of a centralised technocratic governance structure".[39]

The *Angelopharm* horse has, however, well and truly bolted and it is therefore necessary to evaluate its chances of reaching the finishing line.

The 1976 Cosmetics Directive set up the Cosmetics Adaptation Committee to supervise the adoption by the Commission of certain implementing measures under a regulatory committee procedure.[40] Article 8 (2) as subsequently amended specified that the implementing measures were to be adopted "after consultation of the Scientific Committee for Cosmetology at the initiative of the Commission or of a Member State". The twelfth adaptation Directive, adopted in 1990 without any consultation of the Scientific Committee,[41] prohibited the use in cosmetics of 11 alpha OHP, the main ingredient in Setaderm, marketed by Angelopharm as a product to combat hair loss.[42] Angelopharm challenged the German provisions implementing the twelfth adaptation Directive before the competent administrative court, which referred a number of questions concerning the validity and interpretation of that directive to the Court of Justice.

The principal question considered by the Court was whether the consultation of the Scientific Committee was obligatory, and hence whether the 1990 Directive was invalid. The Commission and the intervening governments argued that the committee need only be consulted in accordance with Article 8 (2) if a Member State or the Commission so requests, and no such request had been made. The Court however noted that

> "the article can also be interpreted as meaning that it is for the Commission or the Member States to take the initiative to convene the Scientific Committee, which must be consulted in all cases" (paragraph 26).

Unable to come to any viable conclusion on the basis of a comprehensive examination of the text alone, including the different language versions of the relevant provision and a comparison with other provisions on the consultation of the Scientific Committee, the Court turned its attention to the role of the Committee in the amendment of the Annexes to the Directive.

It was in this context that the Court observed that the scientific and technical assessments on which the Community rules are founded "must be based on the results of the latest international research". However, the

---

[39] Ibid., 287.   [40] (1976) OJ L 262/169.

[41] Commission Directive 90/121/EEC, (1990) OJ L 71/40.

[42] According to expert evidence submitted to the national court, Setaderm "did not constitute a danger to human health but did not have any demonstrable effect on hair growth" (*Angelopharm* Case, above, note 31, para 8).

Court did not reach such a conclusion *proprio motu*, but was merely paraphrasing the eighth and ninth recitals in the preamble to the Cosmetics Directive, and the fifth recital in the preamble to the twelfth adaptation directive. The former note that adaptations may have to be made to "the determination of methods of analysis (...) on the basis of the results of scientific and technical research" and that "technical progress necessitates rapid adaptation of the technical provisions defined in this Directive", while the latter refers to "the latest scientific and technical research" as justifying authorisation to use certain products in cosmetics, subject to specified limitations and requirements. This is clear from paragraph 31 of the judgment, which is often cited without its key opening phrase, "[as] is emphasised in particular in the preambles to Directives 76/768, 82/368 and 90/121". If Community rules, at least in the cosmetics sector, must be founded on scientific research, it is because the Council has so determined, rather than because such a requirement is imposed by some revolutionary new principle of Community law against which the validity of such rules could be judged.

Equally unrevolutionary in this regard is the Court's finding that the adoption of implementing measures required the prior consultation of the Scientific Committee. Joerges has suggested that the wording of the relevant provision was not so ambiguous.[43] The question of whether a particular provision is ambiguous or not is, of course, a matter of appreciation. On the other hand, the Court's finding in regard to the ambiguity of Article 8 (2) of the Cosmetics Directive could hardly be said to be wholly implausible, and even if it were, this would not affect the Court's separate finding on the role of the Scientific Committee in the adoption of implementing measures on cosmetic products. Once again, the Court sought merely to draw certain conclusions from the text of the Directive, particularly regarding the interpretation of the procedural provisions which were designed to guarantee that Community cosmetics rules are based on scientific and technical assessments. The United Kingdom had apparently argued at the oral hearing that the Cosmetics Adaptation Committee would be assisted by the appropriate experts, and hence that the consultation of the Scientific Committee would not be necessary in order to ensure an adequate scientific basis for implementing legislation. Advocate General Jacobs agreed with this conclusion. He also considered that the interventions of the Cosmetics Adaptation Committee and the Scientific Committee in the adoption procedure served different purposes, that the former was part of the mechanism of Member State control of the Commission while the latter was an optional supplement, and concluded that it was "clear that an actual consultation of the Scientific Committee is not a necessary part of such control".[44]

---

[43] Joerges (1997: 314).
[44] *Angelopharm* case, above, note 31, at I-187 (para 38).

The Court, however, turned the United Kingdom argument on its head; *notwithstanding* the fact that the Cosmetics Adaptation Committee had access to scientific expertise "in the nature of things and apart from any provision laid down to that effect", the Court implicitly did not accept that this was sufficient to ensure compliance with the scientific requirements of the Directive. The Court held as follows:

- the task of the Scientific Committee was to enable the Community institutions "to determine, from a fully informed position, which adaptation measures were necessary" (judgment, paragraph 34);
- this Committee had been created "in order to provide the Commission with the assistance necessary to examine the complex scientific and technical problems entailed by the drafting and adaptation of Community rules on cosmetics" (paragraph 35);
- in fact, the Committee "made it possible to ensure that the measures had a scientific basis, that they took account of the most recent scientific and technical research and that only prohibitions necessary on grounds of public health were imposed" (paragraph 36).

As the purpose of consulting the Scientific Committee matched "the objective, pursued by the Cosmetics Directive, of protecting human health", the Court concluded that "consultation of the Committee must be mandatory in all cases", and annulled the Directive accordingly.

It is highly significant that, in ruling on the consultation requirement, the Court paid careful attention to the composition and role of each committee. That the Cosmetics Adaptation Committee was assisted by experts (possibly even the same experts, wearing a different hat, who sat on the Scientific Committee) did not provide a legal guarantee that the level of scientific reliability required by the Directive identified in paragraph 36 of the judgment could be achieved. The Cosmetics Adaptation Committee was in effect recognised as a political body, whose members act under instruction ultimately from their national governments; nothing in its composition or functioning ensured that members would listen to, or would be able to comply with, scientific advice. The soundness of the Court's analysis in this regard has subsequently been confirmed, albeit in a rather different context.[45]

In the present case, "the nature of things" was less a "meta-positive principle" than an *obiter dictum*, proffered with a view to refuting an argument against the mandatory character of the consultation of the Scientific Committee on Cosmetology. It seems likely that the Court was aware of the necessity to "promote the adequacy of regulatory policies", as Joerges has suggested;[46] it is, however, open to doubt that it thereby created either a new standard of legality against which delegated legisla-

---

[45] See section 4, below.   [46] Joerges (1997: 314).

tion could be judged, or a general duty for the Commission to consult scientific committees irrespective of the terms of the powers, granted by the Treaty or basic legislation, under which the Commission acts, as some of the comments on this judgment might lead one to believe. The Court was concerned in this case primarily with the existence and respect of procedural requirements imposed by the Cosmetics Directive; had Article 8 (2) omitted any reference to consultation of the Scientific Committee, it is difficult to see by virtue of what legal principle the Court might have questioned the validity of the adaptation directive.

The alternative interpretation of *Angelopharm* suggested above does not, of course, undermine the general thrust of Joerges' analysis or the utility of his insights; it seeks instead to bring the general level of expectation regarding the case-law of the Court down to a more realistic level. The search for a "meta-positive principle" is surely a useful exercise; it may be that the new Article 6, which the Treaty of Amsterdam introduces into the EC Treaty, would provide one suitable candidate. This provision would require that environmental protection requirements be integrated into virtually all areas and stages of the activities of the Community institutions; the definition of the Community's environmental policy already requires, by virtue of Article 174(3) (ex-Article 130r(3)) EC that the Community "take account of (...) available scientific and technical data". In its amended version, Article 95(3) (ex-Article 100a(3)) also requires the institutions to take account of "any new development based on scientific facts". The *Walloon waste* case[47] could also be seen as already providing some favourable indications in this regard. The general application of such a principle is clearly not far away.

4. British Beef Certificates – "Best in the World!": the Role of Scientific Committees

In his empirical assessment of Comitology and other committees, Falke notes that

> "[a] limited number of scientific committees assists the Commission in dealing with difficult questions concerning the production, composition and use of certain substances".[48]

Nine are listed, including the Scientific Committee for Cosmetology already mentioned above: of these, the Scientific Committee for Food ("SCF") may be considered the paradigm, in terms of its composition, role and operation, as well as the most successful, in terms of the acceptance of its authority by the other institutions.[49] Events which have come to light in

---

[47] Case C-2/90, *Commission* v. *Belgium* [1992] ECR I-4431; see also Joerges (1997: 313).
[48] Falke (1996: 143).   [49] See Gray (1998).

the last few years have, however, given rise to serious doubts about the reliability of the scientific advice coming from one such committee, and, by extension, of the scientific committee system as it now stands.

The SCF was first established by Commission Decision 74/234/EEC, and re-established by Decision 95/273.[50] Its members, who may number up to 20, are nominated by the Commission "from highly qualified scientific persons having competence" in the food safety field; the three-year mandate is renewable. Article 2 provides that the Commission shall consult the committee whenever a legal act so requires, and may consult it on "any other problem relating to the protection of the health and safety of persons arising or likely to arise from the consumption of food, in particular on nutritional, hygienic and toxicological issues". While the committee is empowered to draw the Commission's attention to any such problem, this falls short of a full right of initiative, as under Article 9 (1) its deliberations "shall relate to the requests for opinion put by the representative of the Commission". Meetings of the committee and its working groups are convened by the Commission, representatives of which attend the meetings, provide the secretariat, and fix a deadline (if any) for the adoption of an opinion; the Commission may also invite outside experts to participate in the examination of subjects within their field of special competence. Committee opinions are as a general rule adopted by consensus, in the absence of which the Commission representative draws up a report setting out the diverging positions; in each case, they are published. A new provision in the 1995 Decision seeks to reinforce the independence of the committee by obliging members to notify the Commission of possible conflicts of interest both on an annual basis and as they arise in the context of particular discussions. This supplements a practice adopted by the SCF since the mid-1980s whereby members were expected to declare any interest they may have had in a particular topic under discussion; a member in this position would not chair the relevant working party, though could participate in the discussion at the discretion of the chairman.[51] A recital in the preamble to the 1995 Decision declares that "scientific advice on matters relating to food safety must, in the interests of consumers and industry, be independent and transparent".

The Court has in the past been sensitive to the utility of such committees. In the area of food safety, for example, the Court has acknowledged that, in the absence of harmonised Community provisions, the Member States are entitled to decide on the level of protection they wish to ensure, subject to the Treaty requirements on the free movement of goods. In *Motte*, the Court noted that "for those purposes, Member States must take into account the results of international scientific research and, in particular, the work of the Community's (*sic*) 'Scientific Committee for Food'",

[50] (1974) OJ L 136/1 and (1995) OJ L 167/22.
[51] Gray (1998: 76).

though taking pains to emphasise that "the opinions of that Committee do not have binding force" and "cannot therefore abrogate the responsibility of national authorities for the protection of health in the absence of binding rules and effective supervisory measures at the Community level".[52] Quoting from a 1980 SCF report, the Court concluded that Member States could impose an authorisation procedure which sought to establish whether the use of a particular food additive corresponded to an identifiable need. Similarly, in the "German beer" case, the Court ruled that in order to determine whether a particular additive presented a risk to public health and met such a need, the Member States were obliged to take account of "the findings of international scientific research and in particular the work of the Community's Scientific Committee for Food".[53]

The Court has subsequently clarified that this requirement does not imply a duty on the Member States to consult specialist Community committees. In *Delattre*, a national court was faced with a difference in the classification of certain products, which were considered foodstuffs or cosmetics in Belgium but medicinal products in France.[54] The Court held that

"[in] applying the definition of medicinal product given in Article 2 (1) of Directive 65/65, the Member States must take account, as is the general rule in such matters, of the results of international scientific research and, in particular, the work of specialised Community committees (...) However, no legislation requires them to consult such committees before taking a decision concerning a particular product".[55]

For his part, Advocate General Tesauro had opined that consultation of the special committees was not an appropriate way of avoiding differing classifications of the same product, and noted that the committees' opinions would not in any case be binding on the Member States.[56]

The political institutions have also accepted in effect the authority of the SCF for matters within its remit. Council Directive 89/107/EEC on food additives in foodstuffs intended for human consumption,[57] for example, provides for the adoption of a variety of implementing provisions, either by a legislative procedure under Article 95 (ex-Article 100a) EC, or by a regulatory committee procedure, under the aegis of the Standing Committee on Foodstuffs. Article 6 of the Directive provides rather sweepingly that "[provisions] that may have an effect on public health shall be adopted after consultation with the Scientific Committee for Food", presumably before these are proposed to the Standing Committee or the

[52] Case 247/84, [1985] ECR 3887, at 3904 (para 20).
[53] Case 178/84, *Commission* v. *Germany* [1987] ECR 1227, at 1274 (para 44); see also 1276 (para 52).
[54] The committees cited in the question were in fact Comitology, rather than scientific, committees, but the principle at issue here was the same.
[55] Case C-369/88 [1991] ECR I-1487.   [56] Ibid., para 11, I-1517.
[57] (1989) OJ L 40/27.

European Parliament and the Council, as the case may be.

This cosy picture of the scientific respectability of the Community's legislative processes has been shattered by revelations made to the European Parliament's inquiry committee on BSE.[58] The Scientific Veterinary Committee (SVC) was set up by Commission Decision 81/651/EEC,[59] its members are nominated by the Commission "from highly qualified scientific persons having competence in the fields" of animal health, veterinary public health and animal welfare. According to the findings of the inquiry committee:

— the BSE sub-group of the Animal Health section of the SVC was at all material times chaired by a United Kingdom member, and its meetings were numerically dominated by United Kingdom nationals; in 1994 the Chairman had acted as rapporteur for the sub-group to the SVC; the inquiry committee took the view that "[the] preponderance of UK scientists and officials, therefore, meant that the SVC tended to reflect current thinking at the British Ministry of Agriculture, Fisheries and Food";[60]

— the Commission was in effect obliged to base its proposals for implementing legislation on the conclusions of the SVC, in order to obtain the requisite level of support in the Standing Veterinary Committee (StVC);[61] notwithstanding this practice, the StVC was not always properly informed by the Commission of the work of SVC;

— the Commission did not publish the opinions of members or experts who dissented from the conclusions of the majority of the SVC; moreover, on one occasion the Director-General of DG VI (Agriculture) of the Commission rebuked the German Health Minister in stern terms because German officials had refused to toe the Community line on BSE at a meeting of the Office International des Epizooties;

— at no time during the four-year period from mid-1990, did the Council examine the question of BSE; this the inquiry committee found to constitute a reprehensible delegation of the Council's responsibilities to the StVC; furthermore, the StVC did not keep minutes of its meetings, only brief summaries which it refused to transmit to the inquiry committee.

So scandalised was Parliament at the operation of the committee system that it even merited a mention in its resolution of 19 February 1997 on the

---

[58] EP Doc A4-0020/97/A.   [59] (1981) OJ L 233/32.

[60] See above, note 58, at 10 (para 5); see also ibid., 16 (para 2).

[61] This was the first regulatory committee to operate with a so-called *contre-filet* (equivalent to the type III(b) procedure). This expression is generally translated as being a "safety net", though in fact it is more in the nature of a ripped net through which Commission initiatives can fall to perdition.

BSE crisis, along with swingeing condemnations of the United Kingdom government, the Council and the Commission; Parliament took the view that "lack of transparency and manipulation of the committees dealing with veterinary and health issues were a major contributory factor to the crisis".[62]

Parliament's damning conclusions on the operation of the BSE sub-group should be put in perspective. Given the incidence of BSE in the United Kingdom compared to the other Member States, it is unsurprising both that the United Kingdom members of the BSE sub-group should count amongst the most assiduous attenders of its meetings,[63] and that one of their number should take the chair. On the other hand, veterinary science is far from being so certain or so safe as the general public would wish to believe,[64] while risk regulation frequently involves calculations of a kind which politicians feel they are better able to make than scientists, however expert. The history of the Community ban on the use of growth hormones in beef production[65] and the handling of the BSE affair illustrate that, while "there is no such thing as German physics or European mathematics,"[66] national governments can come to diametrically opposite conclusions to those of other governments on the basis of the same scientific evidence. The evaluation of a new set of facts and the definition of the proper course of conduct to adopt necessarily involve a certain degree of judgement; the procedures by which such decisions are taken should at least guarantee that the views of no one scientific grouping, particularly those who are most intimately involved, be allowed structural predominance. Regardless of the scientific validity or otherwise of the positions taken by the BSE sub-group, suspicion concerning its lack of independence could be said to have infected the entire decision-making process, much as the disease may have infected the food chain.

5. Judicial Review of the Comitology System: Integrating Legal Experience into Scientific Decision-making

It is, in principle, not possible to challenge directly in legal proceedings any decision of a committee, whether this is scientific, advisory or Comitology in character.[67] Legislation under a Comitology procedure, which is perforce adopted by either the Commission or the Council, is nonetheless

---

[62] (1997) OJ C 85/61.

[63] There was a suggestion that committee members from some other Member States were impeded from attending by the Commission's arrangements for reimbursing expenses: See above, note 58, at 26 (para 6).

[64] Gray (1998: 73–75).   [65] Case 68/86, *United Kingdom* v. *Council* [1988] ECR 855.

[66] Joerges (1997: 297).

[67] See, for example, the order of the Court of First Instance of 12 March 1997 in Case T-149/96 *Coldiretti*, dismissing as manifestly inadmissible an annulment action in so far as it was directed against the StVC (unpublished).

subject to judicial review at Community level on the grounds set out in Article 230 (ex-Article 173) EC, in line with the Court's much-quoted, if rather optimistic, assertion that "the Treaty established a complete system of legal remedies and procedures designed to permit the Court of Justice to review the legality of measures adopted by the institutions".[68] Thus the Court has frequently had occasion in the past to review delegated legislation for its compatibility with the Treaty and/or enabling legislation.[69]

While the Court has long sought to ensure respect for procedural requirements set out in enabling legislation,[70] it was not clear until recently whether its review extended to respect for the internal rules of procedure of Comitology committees, particularly in the light of *Accrington Beef*.[71] There the applicants had argued that the Commission had failed properly to consult the beef management committee, by submitting its proposal at the last minute in the absence of any real urgency, thereby depriving the members of the opportunity of considering its opinion or consulting the meat trade. In its observations, the Commission argued, somewhat complacently, that

"the Management Committee was consulted in this case and gave a favourable opinion (...) the circumstances in which a favourable opinion is given are a matter for the Committee".[72]

The Court found it "sufficient to note" that the committee had given a favourable opinion, adding that the relevant provisions did "not restrict the time permitted to elapse between the referral to the management committee and the issue of its opinion".

Whatever the possible merits of this plea,[73] the Court's reasoning is somewhat thin. The fact that the committee had given a favourable opinion was not contested and is of dubious relevance; nor was the Commission regulation challenged because the opinion was late. The Commission's view that the length of time allowed the committee for consideration was not subject to judicial review is doubtful as a matter of general law; in the *UK Fisheries* case, for example, the Court rejected as unsatisfactory consultation by the defendant Member States which did "not allow the Commission to weigh up all the implications of the provisions proposed and to exercise properly the duty of supervision devolving

[68] Case 294/83, *Les Verts* v. *Parliament* [1986] ECR 1339, at 1365 (para 23).

[69] See Bradley (1992: 700-702).

[70] See, for example, Case 55/87, *Moksel* v. *BALM* [1988] ECR 3845, at 3873-3874 (paras 25 to 30).

[71] Case C-241/95, *Regina* v. *Intervention Board for Agricultural Produce, ex parte Accrington Beef and others* [1996] ECR I-6699.

[72] Report for the hearing, at I-12.

[73] The applicants had adduced no evidence to demonstrate that the committee had in fact not been properly consulted in the light of market conditions then prevailing and the procedural possibilities under the committee's rules.

upon it".[74] In *Accrington*, the Court did not address the issue of whether the Commission had, in adopting the contested regulation, complied with Article 3 of the internal rules of the beef committee, which provides a minimum period of time for committee consideration except in the case of urgent measures.

A number of perspectives have been opened up by the *Moskof* and *Construction Products* cases. In the former,[75] the Court dealt in detail with a complaint that the Commission had adopted a measure after having withdrawn the proposal, and hence that the management committee had not been properly consulted. To this end, the Court examined various drafts of the contested regulation, as well as the committee's minutes, before concluding that the Commission's course of action had not affected "the proper functioning of the Management Committee procedures".[76]

The facts of the *Construction Products* case are somewhat more complex.[77] The 1989 Construction Products Directive set up a standing committee on construction for the adoption of certain implementing provisions under a regulatory committee procedure.[78] For such measures, the rules of procedure of the committee provided that the draft provisions be sent to the committee members and to the permanent representations of the Member States 20 days before the meeting at which their adoption was scheduled. Where the time-limit was not respected, the Member State could request the postponement of consideration of the item to a later meeting. On 30 November 1994 the Commission adopted Decision 95/204/EC, despite the fact that the German-language version of the draft provisions had not been sent to the German permanent representation, and had only been sent to the German members of the standing committee 19 days before the meeting. Germany requested postponement of the item before the meeting, and, when the Commission went ahead with the vote, initiated annulment proceedings.

The Court held that the requirement that the draft provisions be sent to both the committee members and the permanent representations, and the absence of any possibility for the Commission to shorten the period of notice,

> "is a sufficient indication of the intention to ensure that Member States should have the time necessary to study these documents, which may be particularly complex and may require considerable contact and discussion between different administrative authorities, or consultation of experts in various fields or of professional organisations".[79]

---

[74] Case 804/79, *Commission* v. *United Kingdom* [1981] ECR 1045, at 1077 (para 35).

[75] Case C-244/95, *Moskof* v. *Ethnikos Organismos Kapnou* [1997] ECR I-6441.

[76] Ibid., para 40.

[77] Case C-263/95, *Germany* v. *Commission* [1998] ECR I-441.

[78] Council Directive 89/106/EEC, (1989) OJ L 40/12.

[79] *Construction Products* case, above, note 77, para 31.

Without addressing itself expressly to the question of the legal value of the rules of procedure of the construction committee, the Court annulled the decision for infringement of an essential procedural requirement, in that the Commission had not respected the period of notice and had ignored Germany's minuted request that the item be postponed.

Taken together, these cases demonstrate the degree to which the activities of Comitology committees are subject to (indirect) judicial review, to complement, or perhaps compensate for, the limited degree of political supervision currently provided for. While not necessarily in a position to ensure respect for scientific criteria *per se*, in strictly enforcing the procedural rules governing the functioning of committees, the Court is seeking to ensure that the interests such criteria seek to protect are, or may be, taken into account, in the same way as it seeks to ensure that the interests represented by the political institutions and bodies are not ignored in the legislative process.

6. The Final Take

In many of the areas of regulation in which Comitology and scientific committees play a major role, the Community institutions have in effect abdicated their substantive decisional powers in favour of the committees, while retaining legal and political responsibility. In the exercise of the latter, the Community legislature relies on procedural conditions to ensure compliance with the scientific criteria in which it places so much faith;[80] according to the view espoused above, this is also the general thrust of *Angelopharm* and the *construction products* case. The question arises as to whether these procedural conditions, and particularly the internal rules of the committees concerned, and the record of the activities of such committees, are sufficiently accessible to permit judicial review at the suit of those whose interests are directly affected by decisions based on the conclusions of such committees.[81] Without prejudice to the much larger question of the codification of the Community's administrative law,[82] the political institutions could pay considerably more attention to such matters in adopting basic legislation either delegating legislation under Comitology procedures or regulating the activities of scientific committees in general.[83]

[80] Directive 90/220/EEC on the deliberate release of GMOs into the environment, on which the transgenic maize authorisation was based, is a prime example of an almost exclusively procedural measure.

[81] On access to committee documents, see Case T-188/97, *Rothmans v. Commission*, pending [(1997) OJ C 252/38].

[82] See the special issue of the *ELJ* on this topic, 1997, 3:3.

[83] On the latter point, Article 6 of Commission Decision 97/404/EC setting up a scientific steering committee ("SSC") to co-ordinate the work of the six committees providing advice

Judicial review is, of course, no substitute for political accountability, and the BSE and transgenic maize controversies could be seen as demonstrating that both the scientific and Comitology committee systems are reaching the limit of their public acceptability. The process of Treaty reform over the last decade or so has made some progress towards improving the Community's rather patchy record in the area of ensuring some degree of democratic legitimacy for the adoption of primary legislation.[84] It would ill serve the Community now to ignore the same democratic imperatives in the increasingly important area of secondary legislation and administration.

It has already been observed that the Comitology phenomenon was an organic development of the Community's institutional structures not foreseen by the authors of the Treaty.[85] The SEA sought to prune a system whose growth had become unruly and inconvenient. In adopting a decision in 1987 which provided a series of complex procedures without indicating when each was to apply, the Council managed to get the worst of both worlds, ossifying in a quasi-constitutional norm the disadvantages of the previous situation, while preventing further organic development. The invitation of the IGC to the Commission to prepare a reform of the Comitology decision, while, strictly speaking, unnecessary,[86] is nonetheless a valuable opportunity for the political institutions to regulate, rationalise and de-mystify this area of institutional activity, rather than leaving it to the vagaries of interinstitutional agreements and practice, and/or litigation at the Court of Justice.

Two matters in particular bear consideration in this regard.[87] In the first place, with the benefit of half a lifetime's experience of Comitology and, perhaps more importantly, more than ten years' experience of the application of the Comitology Decision, the Commission must, surely, be in a position to identify different categories of delegated decision on the basis of objective factors such as their urgency, their normative or executive character, or their political sensitivity, in order to propose principles for the choice of committee procedure.[88] It is on this basis that the Commission

on consumer health matters stipulates that the SSC's rules of procedure shall be publicly available, and that its work satisfy *inter alia* the principle of transparency [(1997) OJ L 169/85].

[84] The preamble to the Treaty on European Union declares the Member States' desire to "enhance further" (*sic*) "the democratic and efficient functioning of the institutions".

[85] Bradley (1992: 719). Joerges/Neyer (1997a) has been summarised as "arguing that Comitology is a metaphor for the whole of EU governance and constitutional development" (Everson, 1998).

[86] Rather than complaining about Comitology as it has done regularly since about 1990, the Commission could have presented such a proposal for reform at any time.

[87] See also the guidelines for institutional responses proposed by Joerges (1997: 322).

[88] Since this chapter was drafted, the Commission has indeed proposed criteria, albeit of a most generic character ((1998) OJ C 279/5); see House of Lords (1999) and Hoffmann and Töller (1998), and cf. 'Helmut Kortenberg' (1998).

will be able to propose, and the Council decide, whether, or in what circumstances, the specific features of the existing committee procedures should be maintained: the requirement to defer the application of implementing measures, the necessity for a qualified majority in favour before the Commission can act, the notorious *contre-filet* and, most significantly from the Commission's point of view, the unanimity requirement in Council on referral. Secondly, and in line with the declared attachment of the European Union to the principle of democracy, it is high time the Commission and the Council allowed the European Parliament, as well as the Member State administrations, some form of supervisory role in the area of delegated legislation, rather than merely reacting to various forms of parliamentary pressure.[89] It is significant that the third indent of Article 202 (ex-Article 145) EC as it stands would not preclude such a role for Parliament, without any Treaty amendment being required. In this regard, the institutional actors are, exceptionally, allowed to write their own script.

[89] On parliamentary pressure, see Bradley (1997: 238-239 and 241-243).

6

The BSE Crisis and the European Parliament

Graham R Chambers[*]

1. Introduction

"The tumult and the shouting dies, the Captains and the Kings depart".[1]

The European Parliament's Special Inquiry Committee into BSE[2] and the follow-up Committee to monitor the implementation of its recommendations[3] have flung their last accusations, interrogated their last witnesses and produced their reports from the tons of evidence accumulated. As the dust settles it is perhaps worthwhile to cast an eye over the new landscape being revealed. It has been a fascinating experience and a very important one in the development of democratic accountability in the European Union.

The Inter-institutional Agreement which accompanied the Maastricht Treaty widened the scope of operation of European Parliament Inquiry Committees – increasing their powers and resulting influence.[4] The summoning of former Commissioners and current national ministers and officials to give evidence before the Committee itself broke new ground.

Since the European Parliament was created it has proved itself adept at exploring and exploiting creative new ways of using existing Treaty and ancillary provisions to extend its power and influence into new areas. Like water seeping into the cracks of a granite monolith, then freezing and expanding, the result, over time, is a shattering of solid rock. The conse-

---

[*] Principal Research Administrator in the Directorate-General for Research of the European Parliament covering health and consumer issues and member of the Secretariat of the Special Inquiry Committee into BSE. Any opinions expressed are those of the author and do not necessarily reflect the views of the European Parliament, its Committees or its individual Members.

[1] From Rudyard Kipling's poem *Recessional*.

[2] (1996) OJ C 261/132.

[3] COM(97) 509 final.

[4] See, *inter alia*, Decision 95/167/EC, Euratom, ECSC of the European Parliament, the Council and the Commission on the detailed provisions governing the exercise of the European Parliament's right of inquiry, (1995) OJ L 113/2.

quences of the work of the Special Inquiry Committee[5] and the follow-up
Committee which followed it are no less ground-breaking. This is
especially the case in the area of agriculture, where the legislative influence
of Parliament is still very limited. The "conditional" motion of censure on
the Commission, though constitutionally a nonsense,[6] follows in this
European Parliament tradition of exploiting new methods to gain influence.

2. The Spread of BSE

The appearance of Bovine Spongiform Encephalopathy in the UK and its
inexorable spread through the 1980s and 1990s into a major epidemic has
had far reaching effects. It has, for the time being, destroyed the image of
"the roast beef of Old England" throughout the world. It has shaken and
possibly cracked the pillars of the Common Agricultural Policy (CAP) and
damaged the Commission, which escaped the European Parliament
Motion of Censure in February 1997[7] only by submitting to a close
European Parliament scrutiny of its services and promising extensive
reform. In addition, the crisis not only epitomised, but added to the factors
of turbulence and complexity which have long characterised the UK's
relationship with the European Union.

More profoundly, the development of the crisis was in great part determined by these very same factors. Certainly the BSE crisis will be cited for
a long time to come as a seminal event in the history of the European
Union, comparable perhaps with the French "empty chair" policy of the
late 1960s. For academics, the crisis provides a text-book example of the
capacity of multi-level governance to respond to a crisis situation.

The statement in the UK House of Commons in March 1996 about a
possible link between BSE and the "new variant" form of Creuzfeldt-Jacob
Disease (nvCJD) turned a veterinary problem into a public health problem.
Young people seem to be falling victim to a disease which has historically
only affected people five decades older. At the moment it is impossible to
predict what the extent of nvCJD might be in the human population, but
the worst-case predictions are frightening.[8]

Public health and food safety, which were gradually creeping up the political agenda of both the European Union and its Member States, have been

[5] Report on the alleged contraventions or maladministration in the implementation of
Community law, in relation to BSE, without prejudice to the jurisdiction of the Community
and the national courts, of 7 February 1997, AU-0020/97A, PE 220.544/fin/A.

[6] Westlake (1997).

[7] Parliament Resolution on the results of the Temporary Committee of Inquiry into BSE,
(1997) OJ C 85/61.

[8] At the end of March 1999, the total number of definite and probable cases of nvCJD in
the UK stood at 40.

thrust into the foreground as a result of this crisis. The previously cosy relationship between agriculture and food has been altered fundamentally.

The BSE crisis has thrown a powerful spotlight onto intensive agricultural practices and the mechanisms of the Common Agricultural policy which encourage them to produce cheap food for mass markets. For many consumers, the revelation which turned them away from beef (or meat in general) was not necessarily the calculation that they stood a significant chance of developing nvCJD, but the realisation that agro-industry was producing beef by feeding ground-up dead cattle to live ones (turning herbivores into carnivores and carnivores into cannibals, as some observers put it). The rendering industry which, viewed in one way, is a valuable tool for recycling protein and dealing in Europe with 12 million tonnes a year of animal waste which otherwise has to be disposed of, is an industry which operates in the shadows of public knowledge. Very few people want to know what happens there. The link between the bright red, clean meat which appears on white plastic trays wrapped in cling film on supermarket shelves and the animals – stunned, killed, bled, eviscerated and sawn up on production lines in the slaughterhouse – has not been obvious to the public now for many years. BSE let some light into this corner and the public, for the most part, did not like what was revealed.

Perhaps the strangest thing about BSE is why it happened in an EU Member State that had always been known for the efficiency of its agriculture and the high quality of its veterinary services. It is a new and very strange disease. The pathogen is not yet definitively identified, the pathology is unclear, the source uncertain and so far the link with nvCJD circumstantial rather than causal.

The question of food hygiene all along the line from "stable to table" has been brought to the attention of the public and the legislator very forcefully in recent years by a succession of scares and tragedies. Salmonella in eggs and poultry, listeria in cheese, e-coli bacterial infection in meat and meat products and BSE have all highlighted the question of hygiene in slaughterhouses and in factories and butcher's shops. On the one hand, the increased scale of production and distribution enables the building and fitting out of larger, more modern and, in principle, more hygienic premises, on the other hand increased scale and centralisation of production brings with it related problems of hygiene control and wide geographical distribution of any pathogen which does slip through the net.

3. The Impact of the BSE Crisis on the EU

Quite apart from the more general questions raised by the whole issue of BSE, its effect on the European Union, the CAP and the Commission has been considerable. One observation which has been made is that there was a disaster waiting to happen in the field of food hygiene and had it not been BSE, it might well have been something else.

The mobilisation of all available Commission resources for the rapid completion of the internal market during the latter part of the 1980s, impelled as it was by political and economic imperatives, left little possibility for the necessary control mechanisms for policing the internal market to evolve, especially in the area of food safety. The quest for subsidiarity fuelled largely by a public perception (especially in the UK) that the Commission in particular was too big and too powerful, made any attempt to obtain additional resources and staff difficult. The scandals which led in April 1999 to the resignation of the Commission were, in large part, the result of over-reliance on outside contractors and sub-contractors – itself the result of a freeze on recruitment of permanent staff. The single market – with its abolition of internal frontiers and checks was introduced largely without the accompanying changes needed to police it properly.

Responsibility for health protection was divided amongst many DGs of the Commission, in none of which it was a true priority. The responsibility for veterinary questions lay exclusively with the Directorate-General for Agriculture, even in the case of a potential zoönosis.

One of the most telling pieces of evidence given to the Inquiry Committee was that provided by Guy Legras, the Director-General for Agriculture who began his statement by declaring that his first priority in his job was the protection of public health.[9] Quite obviously this was a nonsense. The first priority of the Director-General for Agriculture must, by definition, be the protection of farmers. What his statement illustrated very well was the inherent conflict of interest where food and health matters and the protection of food markets are the responsibility of the same person.

Agriculture is by far the biggest and most powerful Directorate-General of the Commission employing nearly 1,000 administrative grades and deploying 40 billion ECU per year. Agriculture also occupies a special place in the Treaties whereby the involvement of the European Parliament is still limited to simple consultation (no power to alter legislation) and the budget, classified as "compulsory expenditure" is largely ring-fenced from Parliamentary scrutiny. The largest European Community policy of all is arguably the least *communautaire*. The principal reason for this is that the Commission, whose historic role is that of "honest broker", has simply not been able to prevail over the very powerful agricultural lobbies of the Member States. It remains something of a mystery as to why an industry, which in most Member States now employs a very small percentage of the working population, retains so much lobbying power in national government cabinets. The result is that the CAP, more than any other policy, is a creature of the Council (either the agriculture Council, or for serious

[9] Report of the Inquiry Committee, above, note 5, Part B.

matters, the European Council itself). It is still largely a system of multilateral trade-offs between states, where national interest rules above all.

With regard to inspection, there was an attitude on the part of the UK veterinary authorities of ill-concealed hostility to EU veterinary inspectors looking at BSE issues on the ground and an alleged statement to the effect that BSE was "a political issue". This meant that there were no inspections by the Commission between 1990 and 1994 – crucial years in the development of the UK epidemic. Such inspections might have discovered that the UK cattle identification scheme worked better in theory than in practice, that the meat and bone meal causing the problem was still being produced (theoretically for non-ruminants), and that it was cross-contaminating ruminant feed in the UK and still being exported to the rest of Europe inadequately labelled and traced to end-use.

Other Member-States seemed happy, for the most part, to keep the problem entirely a British one, to keep the spotlight away from any BSE cases in their own backyard, for economic reasons. Measures proposed by the Commission on the basis of the precautionary principle (banning all bovine and ovine offals, banning the use of meat and bone meal for all animals eaten by man, etc.) were initially rejected by various Member States for the same economic reasons. All in all, it seems that in this time of crisis, "Europe" came apart.

4. BSE and Comitology

The BSE saga has revealed the fact (little known to the public) that the Commission, in its decision making, operates through the curious (and curiously named) system of "comitology". Comitology is "Eurospeak" for the variety of committees and procedures used in the implementation of EU legislative acts. Comitology has also been irreverently described as the arcane science of understanding the way in which the whole system works!

The comitology process was devised when the Council began delegating executive powers to the Commission. It was first introduced in 1962 to implement a series of Council regulations organising the market in agricultural products. The Single European Act added a third indent to Article 145 EEC, which reads:

"the Council shall (...) confer on the Commission, in the acts which the Council adopts, powers for the implementation of the rules which the Council lays down. The Council may impose certain requirements in respect of the exercise of these powers. The Council may also reserve the right, in specific cases, to exercise directly implementing powers itself".

On 13 July 1987 the Council used this text as the basis for adopting what is known as the Comitology Decision, laying down the procedures for the exercise of the implementing powers conferred on the Commission.[10]

Essentially "comitology" was invented because the Council was simply not able to take decisions on a day-to-day basis on a plethora of technical matters. Devolving such decisions entirely to the Commission would have given the Commission far too much untrammelled power in the eyes of the Member States. The way around this was to construct a system of committees of experts and national representatives structured so as to give the Council the possibility of controlling the procedure at arm's length and, in certain cases, of taking the issue back to the Council itself. Comitology is thus, in a constitutional sense, "the Council in the Commission". Council and Member State sources might describe it (in private) as part of the constitutional fudge which glues the Union together by filling the fundamental gulf between federalism and intergovernmental co-operation. Like fudge, it doesn't make a very stable glue when the temperature rises!

The Commission is far from being the all-powerful and almighty institution sometimes portrayed in the press. In any case, it has neither the in-house staff nor expertise necessary to take decisions in all of the highly technical areas of the internal market and so has to rely on committees of experts.

In the case of BSE the Committees concerned were the Standing Veterinary Committee[11] and the Scientific Veterinary Committee.[12] Both of these Committees are made up principally of veterinarians and came under the aegis of the DG for Agriculture.

These experts who make up the committees are appointed by the Member States. In the Standing Committees they are usually senior scientists in late-career administrative roles. This is also true to some extent of the Scientific Committees which advise the Standing Committees. The scientists involved are, almost by definition, part of the scientific establishment. It is rare for scientific iconoclasts or "boat-rockers" to achieve senior positions of this kind. Votes are taken in the Management (Standing) Committees and the votes are weighted in the same way as in the Council. The Standing Committees have been suspected for quite some time of being little more than a mini Council of Ministers, where national policy and national attitudes reign and where the members are effectively given their instructions by their respective agriculture ministries. The Standing Committee procedures have been the object of criticism by the European Parliament for decades.[13] Parliament is particu-

---

[10]   Council Decision 87/373/EEC, (1987) OJ L 197/33. See, in detail, Vos, in this volume.

[11]   Council Decision 68/361/EEC setting up a Standing Veterinary Committee, (1969) OJ L 255/23, amended by Council Decision 81/477/EEC, (1981) OJ L 186/22.

[12]   Commission Decision 81/651/EEC establishing a Scientific Veterinary Committee, (1981) OJ L 233/32.

[13]   See, *inter alia*, Bradley, in this volume.

larly unhappy about the lack of transparency and the secretiveness of the committee meetings and the lack of representation by consumer and other interested parties.

The evidence given to the Inquiry Committee on BSE revealed that relations with the Member States' veterinary inspectorates became difficult once the BSE problem had become "political".[14] Revelations about the workings of "comitology" showed the powerlessness of the Commission vis-à-vis the Member States and the markets in the one area where the Commission is generally assumed to be all-powerful, namely agriculture. The fact that the Standing Veterinary Committee divided more or less on national lines was not surprising, but that this tendency had infiltrated the Scientific Veterinary Committee was somewhat shocking.

No votes are taken in the Scientific Committees, discussion merely continues until a compromise is reached. Although it is possible for a minority opinion to be registered, this rarely happens. In the case of the Scientific Veterinary Committee, a minority view was registered by a German government toxicologist with observer status in that Committee. The discussion concerned the parts of BSE-infected cattle which could be infective to humans and the treatment of carcasses to remove such parts. The toxicologist did not agree with the compromise reached by the Committee and insisted that his view be recorded as a minority opinion. When he expressed his views in other scientific forums, the Director-General for Agriculture wrote a letter to the German Health Minister asking him to ensure that the toxicologist concerned "shut up" – since his view did not coincide with the compromise reached in the Scientific Veterinary Committee. The legal and moral implications of this are, to say the least, disturbing.

"The European Union (. . .) is an Unidentified Political Object"

Jacques Delors

It is instructive at this point to illustrate the complications introduced by a system of multi-level governance. The scope and reach of collective institutions is determined by the extent of shared governance agreed by Member States, which varies according to policy areas, country and time (...) the agricultural policy area can be viewed as a "governance regime" or sub-system governance. Its institutional set-up in terms of decision-making bodies and multi-level administrative organisation conforms to the model of overlapping circles of governance.[15]

The peculiar features of the UK political system, including as it does the sovereignty of Parliament at the centre of an (unwritten) constitution, collective Cabinet responsibility and (increasingly theoretically) ministerial responsibility for the actions of departments lead to a situation where

---

[14] Above, note 5.
[15] H Wallace (1996c: 39).

ministers of agriculture and health cannot openly disagree.[16] Such is not
the case in Germany, for example, where a federal system and coalition
government are the norm.

There will always be a conflict between precautionary measures to
protect the health of the public and commercial market considerations.
Such a conflict is quite legitimate. What is abnormal is when the conflict is
resolved within, rather than between, centres of power. In the Commission,
as in the UK, the balance between these considerations was struck within
the Directorate-General (or Ministry) for Agriculture and more particularly within the BSE sub-committee of the Scientific Veterinary Committee
by middle-level civil servants, rather than between Directors-General or
between the respective Commissioners at the top table.

Indeed, one of the problems highlighted by the BSE investigation is the
over-specialisation of the scientific committees and the risk of allowing a
problem such as BSE to be dealt with by a sub-committee composed
entirely of veterinarians and preponderantly of one nationality – in this
case British.

The result was that the BSE sub-committee tended to reflect the mind-set
and attitude of the UK Ministry of Agriculture, which in turn was heavily
influenced by political considerations concerning Europe resulting from
the deep and fundamental split within the governing Conservative party
and indeed the Cabinet, which made its attitude regarding Europe and BSE
sometimes bizarre to the point of paranoia.

Scientifically, there seems to have been a lack of a sufficiently broad
approach to a very difficult problem. Of course everyone has a PhD in
hindsight, but dealing with BSE via a preponderantly British sub-
committee of veterinarians was unnecessarily limiting. A general problem
with modern science is the increasing degree of specialisation and lack of
cross-fertilisation. Veterinarians tended to think of BSE entirely as an
animal disease and also tended to think of it as "scrapie in cattle". This
approach, combined with a degree of wishful thinking in the UK and other
Member State ministries of agriculture and a deep "Euro-paranoia" at the
highest levels of the former UK Government, combined to create a "fog"
through which it was difficult to penetrate.

In marked contrast to the Directorate-General for Agriculture, the
Directorate-General for Consumer Protection had about forty administrative grades and a budget of roughly one two-thousandth that of agriculture, and this was a considerable improvement from what existed only a
few years previously. Public Health is still a Directorate within the
Directorate-General for Social Affairs and Employment (itself not one of
the most influential within the Commission). It developed out of Health
and Safety at Work provisions in the early EEC Treaties and its influence,

---

[16] Thise (1996-97).

vis-à-vis the Directorates-General for Agriculture and Industry, was revealed during the BSE hearings as predictably insignificant, indeed a suitable comparison might be with Sherlock Holmes's "dog which did not bark during the night". In fact the dog did bark, but it was a lapdog rather than a hound and nobody took any notice.

The Office of Veterinary and Phytosanitary Inspection and Control (OVPIC) was created in 1991 within the Directorate-General for Agriculture (DG VI) by combining an existing inspectorate with the secondary legislation unit. The logic behind this decision was that the secondary legislation unit could adapt legislation in the light of what the inspectors discover. What the inspectors look for would in turn be determined by the secondary legislation. The question of conflict of interest given so close a relationship did not at the time, with the imminent approach of the single market, appear so important.

At the Brussels Summit of 29 October 1993 the European Council decided to move OVPIC to Ireland, seemingly as part of an overall political deal in which, among other share-outs, the Plant Variety Rights Office[17] went to Angers (the home constituency of the French foreign minister). The decision appears to have had little to do with criteria of efficiency or good budgetary management, since the operational capability of the Inspectorate would patently be damaged. There is precedent for the "pork-barrel" share-out of *agencies* between Member States, but there is none for an integral part of the Commission. With what legal precedent or justification the European Council could relocate an integral part of the Commission's services to Ireland is unexplained, but the decision appears to have been made with the connivance (active or passive) of the then Irish Commissioner for Agriculture, Ray McSharry. This may explain why the Commission is unwilling to question it, despite its obvious illogicality.

Three years elapsed before the Commission finally produced its Proposal[18] to implement the decision of the European Council to move OVPIC. During that time, the Commission had started to move the veterinary inspectorate to Dublin, as a temporary measure while awaiting availability of the final site chosen by the Irish Government at Grange, in County Meath. The Commission Proposal was to create a Veterinary and Phytosanitary Inspection Agency, something which was neither proposed, nor accepted by the European Council.

The Commission claimed in its proposal that its motives for proposing an Agency included greater transparency and accountability. The arguments however were weak and there is little evidence to suggest that the creation of an Agency would, in itself, produce these effects. Apparently, the reason behind the proposal for an Agency was that the

---

[17] See Council Regulation (EC) 2100/94, (1994) OJ L 227/1.
[18] COM(96) 223 final.

European Council decision to transfer OVPIC in its entirety to Ireland posed considerable problems for the Commission. The inspectors themselves spend up to 200 days a year on mission world-wide (the total number of countries they now need to visit is 146). The air connections from Dublin complicate matters to some extent, but the chief complaint voiced by the inspectors is that, for practical reasons of organisation of the inspections, they need close contact with the Missions to the EU of the countries they visit – and these are all in Brussels.

In the meantime, the Commission proposed to split the inspection and legislative functions of OVPIC. The inspectorate has now been transferred to DG XXIV, whereas the legislation unit remains in DG VI in Brussels, thus ensuring a separation of powers.

The Commission proposal for an Agency was made with Article 43 EC as a legal base, giving Parliament the right of consultation only. However, Parliament had another weapon at hand in the Budget and Budgetary Control Committees, neither of which liked the proposal for an Agency and which were willing to withhold budgetary credits as a means of expressing their disapproval. As a result of this the proposal was withdrawn.

The Temporary Inquiry Committee into BSE uncovered the parlous state of OVPIC (the EP had already drawn attention to this in Resolutions following the Pimenta report on hormones in 1987[19] and the Garcia-Vasco report on BSE in 1990[20]). Attention was drawn to the staffing problems, inability to obtain budgetary resources to adequately carry out its tasks and the consequent poor morale of the staff. M Legras, Director-General of DG VI, estimated that 100 inspectors were necessary to carry out the tasks assigned to OVPIC; OVPIC had between 10 and 15 in the period 1990-1994.

One problem highlighted by the BSE Inquiry Committee was the difficulty of obtaining sufficient funding and staff for OVPIC as part of DG VI. Not only were the other DGs of the Commission reluctant to grant additional funds to DG VI – already the biggest and richest Directorate-General, but there was an apparent lack of enthusiasm at the highest political level to increase the effectiveness of the veterinary inspectorate. Whether the budgetary problems experienced by OVPIC as part of DG VI will disappear now that OVPIC moves to DG XXIV remains to be seen.

5. Reform of the Commission

Both Consumer Protection and Public Health at Commission level have suffered from "Cinderella syndrome" for years, being relegated to "bolt-on" and "soft" policy status – observatories, public perception campaigns,

---

[19] (1992) OJ C 13/480.   [20] (1993) OJ C 42/273.

information packs and suchlike "conscience candy". However, even before the BSE crisis, things had begun to change. Consumer protection had graduated from a service within the DG for Environment to an independent "horizontal" consumer policy service headed ultimately by a Director-General. Since this tended to be ignored equally by all concerned, it was transformed into a Directorate-General (number XXIV) in 1995.

If the work of the BSE Inquiry and "follow-up" Committee can be likened to the Labours of Hercules, then we could say that it has had the effect of diverting a river through the Augean Stables of the Commission's veterinary services and the "Stygian morass" of comitology.

As a result of the BSE crisis and more particularly the European Parliament's Inquiry Committee, DG XXIV has now been considerably reinforced and renamed "Consumer and Health Protection". All seven scientific committees concerned with consumer safety have been moved from the DGs for agriculture and internal market to DG XXIV. In addition, the scientific committees have been completely renewed through an EU-wide call for highly qualified candidates. Their composition is publicly known and their deliberations will be made public.[21] A co-ordinating "Scientific Steering Committee" will now ensure that excessive specialisation does not result in a narrowing of viewpoint.[22]

The Commission has even suggested moving towards the creation of a European homologue of the United States' Food and Drug Administration (proposed by the EP Environment Committee years ago) and even reform of the CAP and the extension of co-decision with the EP to the CAP. This is highly unlikely in the short or medium term, given the powerful national interests involved, but a continuing problem with BSE and the beef market, particularly if more cases start to be discovered elsewhere within the European Union together with future enlargement of the EU to the east, will probably make serious reform unavoidable in the long term.

Although the scientific committees now come under DG XXIV, the relevant standing committees still come under DG VI. At least we have greater transparency as far as the scientific committees are concerned and where there is conflict between the two, the public will be aware of it. In other words, should the standing committee go against the advice of the scientific committee it will have to explain why and the issue will ultimately have to be resolved between the Commissioners, or the Councils responsible for Agriculture and Public Health. This is altogether a healthier situation than that which previously existed.

The questioning of witnesses by the Inquiry Committee into BSE was particularly intense and it was perhaps natural that the focus of its most

[21] Commission Decision 97/579/EC setting up Scientific Committees in the field of consumer health and safety, (1997) OJ L 237/18.

[22] Commission Decision 97/404/EC setting up a Scientific Steering Committee, (1997) OJ L 169/85.

severe interrogation should be the Commission (the easiest target). The Committee demanded (and was shown, in camera) the Commission's own highly critical report on its veterinary services carried out by the Inspectorate-General of Services. Analysis and criticism of individual actions and lack of action was undertaken. More importantly as a *quid pro quo* for withholding the Motion of Censure on the Commission, Parliament's Committee obtained a degree of micro-management of the Commission's actions in this area never before seen. The Inquiry Committee and its successor, the BSE follow-up Committee, effectively had a considerable say in the detail management decisions taken by the Commission in reforming its services, even to the extent of commenting upon disciplinary measures taken by the Commission against individuals.

It remains to be seen whether such hands-on control by Parliament will compromise the delicate institutional relationship which is at the heart of parliamentary control over the executive and whether the ability of Parliament to "turn the screws" on the Commission, yet not on the Council or the Member States, could distort the delicate, though fluid, balance of the institutional triangle. This question is all the more pertinent following the resignation of the Commission in March 1999 as a direct result of pressure from the European Parliament.

SECTION 3

Comitology as an Administrative Task

7

Towards a Regulation of Transitional Governance? Citizen's Rights and the Reform of Comitology Procedures

*Renaud Dehousse**

1. Introduction

The discussion on comitology's legal status is by no means a new feature of the European institutional debate. A shift of emphasis, however, has occurred in recent years. For about three decades, the discourse had focused on a demarcation of the competences of the Council and Commission in the implementation of "primary" Community legislation and on comitology's role in the basic institutional balance established by the EC Treaty.[1] In this earlier period, efficiency concerns were regularly voiced. Inter-institutional quarrels as to which procedure was to be chosen were thought to be the source of considerable delay in the legislative phase, leading the Commission to make comitology one of its main war-horses in the years of the internal market programme.[2] More recently, the legitimacy of comitology has come to the fore as a major issue. Even since the European Parliament gained greater legislative power under the Treaty on European Union, it has challenged comitology as incompatible with its new institutional role stressing, *inter alia*, the undemocratic character of a system in which obscure committees, primarily composed of national bureaucrats, play a central role in the rule-making process.[3] Moreover, the

* Professor of Law, Director of the European Centre, Institut d'Études Politiques, Paris. I am grateful to Daniel Bodansky, Christian Joerges and Ellen Vos for comments on an earlier draft, and to Francesca Bignami and Cosimo Monda for their assistance in revising it. I also have a huge debt towards Carol Harlow and Martin Shapiro, whose manifold objections were of great help.

[1] Case 25/70, *Einfuhr- und Vorratsstelle für Getreide und Futtermittel* v. *Köster, Berodt & Co.* [1970] ECR 1161. See Blumann (1988).

[2] Ehlermann (1987).

[3] Bradley (1997); Blumann (1996).

BSE crisis revealed the risk of committee "capture" by specific interests.

The purpose of this contribution is not to explore in detail the various legal problems surrounding comitology. Rather, adopting a broader perspective, it will try to identify the structural causes that explain the shift from efficiency to legitimacy concerns in discussions on comitology and to consider various ways of enhancing comitology's legitimacy. While my comments will be confined to comitology proper (the web of committees that assist the Commission in the implementation of Community legislation), some of the ideas could probably be of use for other types of committees that operate at European level.

2. Regulation by Committees: Institutional Discourse and Political Reality

Comitology, like any form of governance, must be analysed in light of the functional reasons that have underpinned its development. Like much modern legislation, Community legislative rules are often incomplete and the reasons for this are manifold. The complexity of the Community legislative process makes it unwise to try to decide on everything at the legislative stage – even assuming that this would be possible, which is not always the case. It may also be more expedient politically to defer contentious items to a subsequent stage of the policy process. Last but not least, the technical character of the issues addressed may require a further input from scientific experts. A similar need may also arise when basic rules must be adapted to changing conditions, a common situation in an era of rapid technological change. Community legislation must therefore often be supplemented or updated by secondary rules. In addition, in some areas, the actual application of Community rules may require centralised decisions: this is notably the case when Community funds are distributed (for example in the framework of research and development programmes) and when producers seek a European authorisation for their products, as is now possible in relation to certain kinds of pharmaceuticals.[4]

Although Article 155 EC provided from the outset that the Commission could be entrusted with implementation powers, it was soon perceived that committees, mostly composed of national experts, were necessary to assist the Commission in this task. This innovation was dictated not only by national governments' wish to keep an eye on the Commission, but also by the technical character of many decisions. The Commission can only count on a small staff – roughly equivalent in numbers to that of a middle-sized

---

[4] Council Regulation (EEC) 2309/93, laying down Community procedures for the authorisation and supervision of medicinal products for human and veterinary use and establishing a European Agency for the Evaluation of Medicinal Products, (1993) OJ L 214/1.

European city – and therefore does not always have the expertise needed to dispose of the thousands of issues delegated to it.

All these elements are reviewed here simply to stress that comitology, which has at times been depicted as a kind of institutional hydra, is to a large extent a natural development. Any system of two-tiered government, particularly when it opts for decentralised implementation of rules adopted at central level, as has been the case in the EC, will be inclined to develop structures of this kind, as can be seen in the emergence of "executive federalism" in Canada[5] or of *"Politikverflechtung"* in Germany.[6]

This notwithstanding, the institutional discourse on comitology has been rather conflictual, particularly after the Single European Act. The Commission has made no secret of the fact that it regards the most restrictive forms of committee control – in particular the *contre-filet* variant of the regulatory committee procedure laid down in the 1987 Comitology Decision[7] – as an excessive intrusion into its powers, which could hamper the adoption of implementing measures or even affect the legislative process. The Single European Act's failure to simplify comitology procedures was one of the main reasons for the Commission's initial reservations concerning that Treaty.[8] Up to the Treaty of Maastricht, the Commission had kept insisting on the necessity of a significant overhaul of Community procedures.

However, the Commission's choice of comitology procedure in its legislative proposals is often in contrast with its public rhetoric. While it has repeatedly blamed the Council for ignoring the Single European Act's preference for the advisory committee procedure in the internal market sector,[9] the Commission appears to bear part of the responsibility, as it has proposed other procedures in over 25% of the relevant cases.[10] Likewise, despite its declared aversion to regulatory committees, the Commission itself proposed almost 40% of the regulatory committee procedures enacted by the Council in the period between July 1987 and July 1995.[11] Apparently, institutional concerns play less of a role than official statements would suggest. The Commission is frequently prepared to compromise on comitology procedures, if this will result in the Council's agreement on delegation of implementation powers being obtained.

This pragmatism may be explained by the consensual nature of the committees' work. The available data suggest a rather smooth exercise, where acute conflicts are a rare event. Indeed, out of the thousands of decisions taken by the Commission in co-operation with committees in the years 1993 to 1995, in only six cases did the Council intervene because of disagreement between the Commission and the relevant committees.[12]

[5] Smiley (1980).   [6] Scharpf/Reissert/Schnabel (1976).
[7] Council Decision 87/373/EEC, (1987) OJ L 197/33.
[8] Ehlerman (1987).   [9] See SEC(90) 2589 final, 7.   [10] Dogan (1997).   [11] Ibid.
[12] *Reinforcing Political Union and Preparing for Enlargement*, Commission Opinion for the Intergovernmental Conference 1996 (1995).

Moreover, the accounts of committee members suggest that votes tend to be a rare event, and that the Commission, which chairs these meetings, exerts considerable influence over the committees' work. Undoubtedly, the smooth functioning of comitology proceedings is positive for decision-making efficiency. However, it does not follow that this will necessarily strengthen the overall legitimacy of the system, as shall now be seen.

3. The Legitimacy of Comitology Procedures

Comitology's legitimacy is not merely a normative issue: it is likely to become a political problem. The Maastricht ratification debates have made it plain that large segments of the European populace do not recognise the legitimacy of European policy-making processes. So far, discussion on how to improve the legitimacy of European institutions has essentially focused on the powers of the European Parliament. Legislative procedures, however, are but one (admittedly important) part of the decision-making process. Now that the legislative framework for the internal market is nearly complete, there seems to be a deceleration in the Community's legislative activities. Figure 1 shows that the number of primary legislative proposals has declined in recent years.

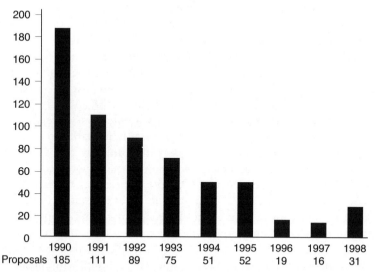

	1990	1991	1992	1993	1994	1995	1996	1997	1998
Proposals	185	111	89	75	51	52	19	16	31

Figure 1 *Proposals of primary legislation introduced by the European Commission*

Sources: Reinforcing Political Union and Preparing for Enlargement Commission Opinion for the Intergovernmental Conference 1996, 1995, p. 87, for years 1990-1995; COM (95) 512 final for year 1996; SEC(96) 1819 final for year 1997; http://europa.eu.int/comm/off/work /1998/index_fr.htm. for year 1998.

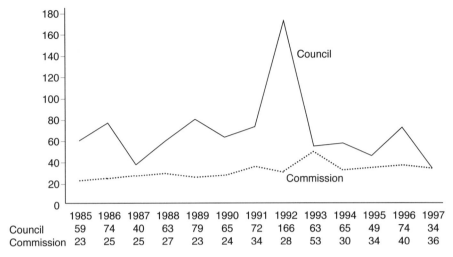

	1985	1986	1987	1988	1989	1990	1991	1992	1993	1994	1995	1996	1997
Council	59	74	40	63	79	65	72	166	63	65	49	74	34
Commission	23	25	25	27	23	24	34	28	53	30	34	40	36

Figure 2 *Number of Directives adopted by the European Institutions*

Source: General report of Activities of the EC. Data retrieved from CELEX, the interinstitutional computerised system on community law, excluding instruments not published in the OJ and instruments listed in light type (routine management instruments valid for a limited period). For years 1993 to 1997, directives adopted by the European Parliament and Council in accordance with the co-decision procedure are included in the category "Council".

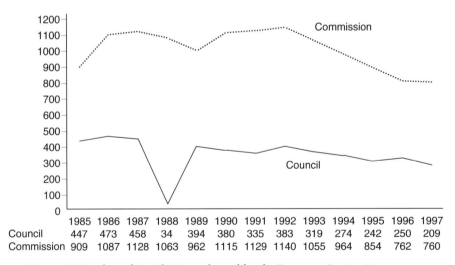

	1985	1986	1987	1988	1989	1990	1991	1992	1993	1994	1995	1996	1997
Council	447	473	458	34	394	380	335	383	319	274	242	250	209
Commission	909	1087	1128	1063	962	1115	1129	1140	1055	964	854	762	760

Figure 3 *Number of Regulations adopted by the European Institutions*

Source: General report of Activities of the EC. Data retrieved from CELEX, the interinstitutional computerised system on community law, excluding instruments not published in the OJ and instruments listed in light type (routine management instruments valid for a limited period). For years 1993 to 1997, regulations adopted by the European Parliament and Council in accordance with the co-decision procedure are included in the category "Council".

It would be wrong to conclude from this that the overall volume of Community regulatory activity is declining. Indeed, the overall volume of Commission rule-making, most of which takes place in the comitology framework, seems to be increasing, as shown in Figures 2 and 3.

The Commission has long been – and by far – the main producer of Community regulations. Moreover, in 1997, the number of directives adopted by the Commission exceeded for the first time that of directives adopted by the Council.

The combination of these two trends – the decline of purely legislative activity, and the growth of secondary rule-making – suggest that a growing number of salient political issues are likely to arise in the post-legislative phase, be it in rule-making or the concrete application of Community rules. Should a given product be authorised? What kind of precautionary measures are needed to protect human health where scientific doubts are raised concerning our dietary habits? The management phase may gain even more importance in the future, as the Treaty of Amsterdam has enhanced the powers of the Community to deal with what is known as "risk regulation" in areas such as human health, consumer policy and environmental protection.[13] As risk regulation decisions are often made on the basis of complex scientific evidence, they cannot always be made *in abstracto*, once and for all, in legislation, but rather require individual, *ad hoc* decisions to be taken by administrative bodies.

If this analysis is correct, committees are likely to be the forum for a growing number of important decisions at European level in the years to come. However, the way they operate may be a source of a host of legitimacy problems. First, the system is striking in its opacity. Who does what and how is nearly impossible to tell for a lay audience. This lack of transparency may undermine the authority of Community decisions: citizens may find it difficult to accept decisions based on recommendations from obscure bodies, the composition and functioning of which remain a mystery. Secondly, it is not clear that the social prestige of committee members will be sufficient to command obedience. While scientific experts may derive some authority from their technical knowledge, bureaucrats are the focus of widespread mistrust in European countries. Thirdly, the little we know of the way comitology works may also become a source of concern. The convergence of concerns, interests and language among experts which is said to be the hallmark of comitology seems to enable the system to operate fairly smoothly.[14] However, while positive from the standpoint of efficiency, this consensus may undermine the legitimacy of the system, as it can easily be depicted as one more instance of power in the hands of a closed circle of élites. The risk of collusion is quite real: can experts be regarded as neutral in areas where research is largely financed by

---

[13] Dehousse (1998b); Ludlow (1997).
[14] Joerges/Neyer (1997a).

industry? Can we really assume that they will not be influenced by their national origins? The BSE crisis has shown that issues of this kind are far from academic and they must be addressed if comitology is to be based on firmer ground for the purpose of increasing its legitimacy.

How may this objective be achieved? Generally speaking, five different types of arguments are traditionally used to legitimise bureaucratic processes.[15] Given the specificity of the Community regulatory process, it would be wrong to assume that they can be mechanically transposed to the European level. However, they furnish good yardsticks for assessing the legitimacy of bureaucratic decisions taken at that level.

- The "legislative mandate" approach is the most traditional. Parliament is seen as the main repository of legitimacy and the administration must strive to achieve the objectives that are set out in governing legislation.
- In the "accountability or control" model, legitimacy is grounded in the fact that the administration is somehow under control: that it is held accountable for its decisions by a representative body (generally the legislature) or by courts.
- The "expertise" claim stresses that as a result of their technical character, many decisions cannot be taken by the legislature: expert judgment is needed to assess the respective merits of competing options, and experts must be granted sufficient discretion.
- The "procedural" approach emphasises the fairness of decision-making processes. It demands that consideration be given to the interests of persons affected by administrative decisions. Procedures designed to associate such persons to the decision-making process are therefore viewed as essential. The procedures tend to vary according to the kind of decisions that are taken. Under "due process" requirements, administrative bodies must consider the interests affected by individual decisions. As regards rule-making, the same concern for fairness may lead to the adoption of rules guaranteeing transparency and participation or consultation rights.
- *Efficiency* is also often claimed as a grounds for legitimacy, particularly in recent times, as the ability of government structures to deliver results is becoming increasingly important. While there are many ways of defining efficiency, two meanings are particularly relevant for our purposes: decision-making efficiency (the ability to take decisions when needed) and substantive efficiency, i.e. the ability to take the "right" decisions.

---

[15] I am using here in a slightly adapted fashion a terminology borrowed from Baldwin (1995: 41-45).

Obviously, these approaches are not necessarily mutually exclusive. Accountability and control can be used to monitor the effective implementation of legislative mandates or the compliance with the procedural requirements of the "due process" model. Likewise, the resort to experts is often advocated on efficiency grounds, and can be balanced through various accountability techniques. Nevertheless, there are clear differences among various claims. The degree of discretion required in the "expertise" model is at odds with the idea of exhaustive legislative mandates. Similarly, the vision of the public interest inherent in the "legislative mandate" approach often assumes the existence of a collective body – the people – whose interests are represented by Parliament, while the "procedural" model is informed by a more polycentric vision of the polity, in which the coexistence of a wide variety of interests, which must all be given due consideration, is acknowledged.

At this stage, my concern is not to endorse any one of these models, but rather to discover how suitable they may be, given the specific character of Community decision-making. I will take as a starting point the limits of an approach that would rest exclusively on the "expertise" model. Involving experts at various levels of the decision-making process is undoubtedly necessary, particularly when the decisions to be taken have a sizeable technical content, as is often the case at the European level. Providing much-needed expertise is clearly an important achievement of the European committee system. It can even be argued that the quality of deliberations among experts will not only contribute to the quality of the regulatory process, but also to its legitimacy, as was suggested by Joerges and Neyer.[16] Yet, granting experts *carte blanche* is likely to be unpopular in a period of widespread mistrust of technocrats of all kinds. Right or wrong, lay people may also have views on the decisions to be taken, and insist that they too should be considered.

Our reflections should therefore focus on the remaining approaches. Various versions of the "legislative mandate" and the "accountability" models have been invoked by those who argue that the European Parliament, now that it has acquired the status of a co-legislator in many areas, should have more power over delegated legislation. Both types of arguments are part of the same, *supranational* avenue: the European Parliament, it is said, being the institution most representative of the European people at large, should play a greater role in overseeing comitology. In contrast, as was just indicated, the *procedural* model rests on a radically different vision of legitimacy, one which would require the opening of comitology to representatives of all interests affected by its decisions. Each of these two options will now be reviewed in turn.

---

[16] Joerges/Neyer (1997a).

4. The Supranational Avenue: Legislative Mandates and Parliamentary Control

Since the introduction of co-decision in 1993, the European Parliament has insisted on being treated as a Council co-equal in supervising Commission implementing decisions. It has strongly opposed management and regulatory committees, which it regards as a way of circumventing its newly acquired legislative powers: in the four years since co-decision was introduced, comitology was an issue in about two-thirds of the dossiers that were subjected to the conciliation procedure. Disagreement over the proper implementing procedure was also at the root of Parliament's rejection of the Directive on voice telephony – the first time that Parliament used its co-decision prerogatives to reject a Council common position.

There are several ways in which the European Parliament could become more closely involved with the decisions currently being taken within the comitology framework. The first, "legislative mandate", approach would suggest that the current balance between legislation and administrative decisions be altered in order to ensure that the most salient policy decisions are taken as legislative measures. A return to legislative policy-making is a technique widely advocated in order to combat the growing influence of bureaucracies.[17] Surely, it would be historically incorrect to describe comitology as having robbed the European Parliament of its legislative prerogatives, as comitology predates Parliament's rise to the status of a full-fledged legislature. However, MEPs have consistently called for a clearer delineation between decisions that can be taken through comitology and those that require a proper legislative procedure,[18] a position that underlies Parliament's support for a clear hierarchy of Community acts. The European Court of Justice (ECJ) itself has suggested that "the *basic elements* of the matter to be dealt with" must be adopted in accordance with the legislative procedure laid down by the Treaty, while "the provisions implementing the basic regulations" may be adopted according to a different (i.e. comitology) procedure.[19]

However, there seem to be clear functional limits to what can be achieved along these lines. As indicated above, it is not always possible for legislation to anticipate all the problems that may arise in the implementation phase. Parliaments may lack the time or the necessary expertise to solve all problems in advance, and they may find it expedient to delegate part of the problem-solving task to implementing agencies. Moreover, the borderline between policy choices and implementation "details", between legislation and administration, is often blurred when scientific or technical choices

[17] Lowi (1979).
[18] Bradley (1997: 234).
[19] Case 25/70, above, note 1 (emphasis added).

must be made. Prior to the BSE crisis, who would have thought that animal feed was an issue that would gain considerable public attention?

Parliamentary control over the executive seems equally difficult to adapt to the specific features of Community governance. While at national level, parliamentary control over the administration is a by-product of its authority over the cabinet via the institution of ministerial responsibility, no such thing exists at European level. Although Parliament has gained considerable power over the Commission in the post-Maastricht years, formally comitology committees are not under the Commission's authority. The vertical chain of command thought to exist at national level (parliament-executive-bureaucracy) is broken at European level, where delegated legislation is, at least partly, in the hands of networks of national experts. The European Parliament's role must be adapted to this network-based reality if it is to be of more than symbolic relevance.

Parliament's response to this structural difficulty has been to put pressure on the Commission, as the latter plays a leading role in implementation procedures, and appears to be extremely influential in comitology committees. The Plumb-Delors agreement of 1987 stipulated that the Parliament would be notified by the Commission of most draft implementing measures. These were then to be forwarded to the responsible parliamentary committee so that it could voice its concerns whenever necessary. Clearly, the effectiveness of such an agreement depends primarily on the Commission's willingness to keep the Parliament informed and to take its views into account. In both respects, the first years of the agreement have been rather disappointing: many drafts have not been sent to the Parliament and, in all but a handful of cases, parliamentary committees have failed to react.[20] The strengthening of Parliament's grip over the Commission in the post-Maastricht years leaves room for hope that its access to comitology materials will improve. Even if this were to occur, however, a question would still remain: how should Parliament process this information, and react if need be? Here, two problems must be addressed: lack of time and expertise. Can Parliament effectively scrutinise the hundreds of decisions adopted each year by committees, given its heavy agenda and complex organisation? Will MEPs have the relevant expertise?

Entrusting supervision to Parliamentary committees, decided in the wake of the Plumb-Delors agreement, is a sound division of labour. Members of committees are likely to be better equipped than many of their colleagues to make sense of the technical issues addressed in draft implementing measures; further, decentralisation is needed to deal with the masses of documents involved. But what kind of relationship should be established between Parliamentary committees and their counterpart(s) in the web of comitology committees?

---

[20] Bradley (1997: 237); Jacobs/Corbett/Shackleton (1995: 254-55).

Interestingly, Parliament's ambitions seem to have increased in parallel with the emergence of its legislative profile. Parliament has at times expressed an interest in being more closely involved with the work of committees, for example, by including its own observers in the committees.[21] This proposal raises a delicate but fundamental issue: in a system where influence appears to be directly related to the degree of expertise enjoyed by the various participants in the debate,[22] what can be the impact of elected representatives, namely politicians? True, the European Parliament could set up its own expert networks to control the work of committees. But in terms of legitimacy, the "value-added" of another layer of experts would be rather thin. Rather than have politicians clothe themselves as technical experts, as they at times seem tempted to do,[23] would it not be preferable to limit their role to a number of basic policy choices and to grant them the right to intervene when issues they deem fundamental arise in the implementation phase? Indeed, Parliament's most recent thinking seems to favour an improvement of the *modus vivendi* signed in 1994 with the Council.[24] Rather than systematically participating in the adoption of implementing legislation, it would be given the right (on a par with the Council, one can assume) to step in whenever it feels a political input is needed.[25]

Admittedly, such a division of labour would better correspond to the respective functions of legislature and executive in modern societies. Of particular importance, given the technical character of many issues tackled within European committees, is the Parliament's power to hold hearings. This technique could be used more systematically, as a means of obtaining independent expertise and facilitating a dialogue with interested parties. It would also enable the Parliament to exert greater control over the Commission, as the latter would be called upon to react to the views expressed by witnesses. Furthermore, hearings would very likely attract media attention to particular issues, thereby contributing to improved public awareness of the decisions taken at the European level. Such an approach, which emphasises accountability and the European Parliament's function as a forum where the important political issues of the day can be debated, would be better suited both to the structure of comitology as a system of regulatory networks, and to the technical character of the issues tackled through comitology, than parliamentary involvement in the day-to-day work of committees.

But would enhanced monitoring by a supranational legislature suffice as a grounds for legitimacy? There are reasons to be sceptical. Representative democracy has become the focus of widespread criticism in Western Europe, where it is often perceived as a system that enables a cartel of elites

---

[21] Bradley (1997: 234).   [22] See the analysis of Eichener (1992).
[23] Landfried (1997).   [24] (1996) OJ C 102/1.   [25] Bradley (1997: 253).

to exert tight control over the policy agenda.[26] Arguably, the gap between the rulers and the ruled may be even wider at the Community level. To many European citizens, the Parliament still appears a remote assembly, whose work remains largely unknown and whose members do not always represent the mood of the populace. More importantly, in a system where primary allegiances remain firmly rooted at the national level, national ties may prove to be more important than the supranational logic of parliamentary democracy. To put the matter bluntly, German or Danish consumers might feel more effectively represented by, say, a delegate from a national consumer organisation involved in committee proceedings, than by a similar association of Greek or Portuguese MEPs.

Reflections on the legitimacy of the European policy process must also come to terms with the polycentric character of the European populace. Not only is there no European *demos*,[27] but "we the people" cannot simply be read in the plural as a reflection of the coexistence of different states within the European Union. The truth is that the *peoples* of the Member States, too, are a kaleidoscope of regions, cultures and interests not always identified with the state apparatus, and can all legitimately claim to voice their views and be heard at the European level. After all, even at national level, the reductive nature of representative democracy, distorted even further by the structure of many electoral systems, makes it impossible for parliaments to mirror perfectly the broad range of interests and feelings that coexist within a single polity. Hence the attractiveness of alternative forms of legitimation, which provide for some form of direct participation of affected parties in the decision-making process.

5. The Transnational Avenue: Transparency, Openness and Proceduralisation

I have argued that several of the approaches traditionally used in order to legitimate delegated legislation are ill-adapted to the specific needs of comitology. Reliance on the expertise model is no longer sufficient in a world where technocracy has become the focus of much criticism. Legislative mandates cannot always be sufficiently clear, as it is impossible to consistently set down precise standards and objectives. Although more promising, the accountability claim remains elusive, as Parliamentary control over comitology decisions is still far from effective. Additional techniques ought therefore to be considered if the legitimacy of comitology is to be put on firmer ground.

Given the growing gap between citizens and government in Europe, one such technique might be to empower all the parties affected by comitology

26 Mény (1998).   27 Weiler (1995a).

decisions to express their concerns before the relevant committees. The main advantages of such an approach would be twofold. An extensive dialogue with the various segments of civil society would obviate some of the shortcomings of representative democracy at the European level.[28] It might also improve public awareness of the issues discussed at the European level, thereby contributing to the emergence of a truly pan-European public sphere.

From the standpoint of openness to the populace at large, the present situation is defective in several respects. First, information on the actual operation of committees is difficult to find. The total number of committees remains a mystery.[29] In 1994, Parliament had to freeze a share of the appropriations for committees in order to obtain more information from the Commission on the number of meetings and their work output.[30] Committees' rules of procedure are difficult to get hold of. When formal rules do exist, they appear to focus on the internal operation of committees: the main target is regulating the deliberation among experts, i.e. relationships between the Commission and national representatives.[31] In contrast, little or no attention is paid to the relationship between the comitology web and the outside world. Provisions on the consultation of affected parties are striking in their absence. True, in some areas, committees have been created specifically for the purpose of allowing organised interests to give their input. In the food sector, for example, an *ad hoc* committee has been set up to represent the views of various socio-economic interests. Yet the Advisory Committee on Foodstuffs offers a good illustration of the limits of what have been achieved so far.[32] As its members are appointed by the Commission, the latter may privilege certain interests; it is striking that representatives of environmental interests have been excluded. Moreover, the committee can only act at the Commission's request, which explains why it has remained inactive for long periods.

Rather than *ad hoc* representative fora, greater openness in the work of *all* committees is needed. This could be achieved with a standard set of procedural rules regulating the interface between comitology committees and civil society at large.[33] What kind of principles should these rules

---

[28] See Curtin (1999).

[29] See, for example, Vos (1997b: 213); Falke (1996: 136-137).

[30] Bradley (1997: 242).

[31] See the Rules of Procedure of the Standing Committee on Foodstuffs, a consolidated version of which has been prepared by the Commission (III/3939/93; SJ/260/90-EN of 11 May 1993).

[32] Commission Decision 75/420/EEC, (1975) OJ L 182/35; amended by Commission Decision 78/758/EEC, (1978) OJ L 251/18. See the analysis of Vos (1999: 175-177).

[33] This would not prevent the Community legislator from foreseeing exceptions for some kinds of decisions: standard rules would apply only in the absence of specific procedural provisions in Community primary legislation.

contain? Without entering into a detailed examination of the question, it may be useful to point out some basic elements. Thus, for instance, the agenda of committee meetings, the draft proposals to be discussed, and the minutes should all be made public.[34] Interested persons should be given the opportunity to express their views on any item on the agenda; public hearings could even be envisaged for matters of particular importance. Committees should also be required to explain the considerations that underlie their eventual choices.

A procedural approach of this nature, with its participatory ethos, would bolster the legitimacy of comitology. It should not however be seen as an alternative to parliamentary control. On the contrary, proceduralisation, because it would foster public debate, might significantly reinforce the accountability of committees vis-à-vis the European Parliament, provided the latter is granted the power to review comitology decisions. One can imagine, for instance, that if a committee were to overlook the concerns of, say, consumer groups, Parliament might be interested in knowing why. In this case, procedural and accountability concerns, far from being at odds with one another, would actually be mutually reinforcing.

How could such a proceduralisation be brought about? A number of commentators have warned against the danger of "ossification" of administrative procedures through codification in a legislative act.[35] It is fair to say that both the ECJ and the Court of First Instance have displayed a growing awareness of the necessity to protect "process" rights such as the right to be heard and the duty to state reasons, when individual rights are directly affected by Community decisions.[36] However, the approach contemplated here is less defensive. It is not motivated as much by a concern for individual rights as by a desire to ensure greater openness and more public participation in committee decision-making. Court decisions are necessarily *ad hoc*, rendered in concrete cases; they are therefore not the best avenue for injecting new principles into decision-making processes. Moreover, the overall object of the exercise should not be forgotten. What matters for legitimacy purposes is not only that justice be done, but also that it be *seen* to be done. Put together, these considerations point in the same direction: the best way to introduce the principles discussed here would be through a framework act that would be adopted in the most solemn (visible) of manners and that would apply to all committee proceedings.

[34] This could be achieved by exploiting the potential of the Internet. See in this respect the proposals put forward by Joseph Weiler (1997: 150, 153).

[35] Schwarze (1992); Harlow (1996).

[36] See, for example, Case C-269/90, *Hauptzollamt München Mitte* v. *Technische Universität München* [1991] ECR I-5469; Case T-364/94, *France Aviation* v. *Commission* [1995] ECR II-2845 and the comments by Nehl (1997).

6. The Need for a "Soft" Proceduralisation

It should be kept in mind that procedural requirements traditionally carry a twofold risk: that of imposing undue expense on rule-makers by encouraging legalism, and that of opening up the door to forms of aggressive judicial review, which may ultimately lead to judicial discretion replacing that of the administration. The American experience is quite telling in this respect. The US Administrative Procedures Act provisions on rule-making are quite general. Agencies are obliged to give notice that they are contemplating new rules, provide an opportunity for the public to comment on draft rules, and furnish a statement of purpose with the final rule. These minimal requirements were not adopted with a view to curtailing agencies' discretion; courts were merely allowed to strike down rules that were "arbitrary and capricious". Yet, on the basis of these few provisions, some courts of appeal have radically transformed the rule-making process.[37] Agencies have been ordered to engage in a structured dialogue with interested parties, a dialogue which must be documented in rule-making records. Statements of basis and purpose have been used by courts to control both the quality of the dialogue and the reasons given by agencies, so that

> "[f]ar from having to demonstrate only that it has not been arbitrary and capricious, the agency must persuade the court that it has made the best rule that it possibly could".[38]

This evolution illustrates the fact that the borderline between procedure and substance is a thin one. Hence the question: by regulating the interface between comitology and interested parties, are we not opening the door to the legalisation of comitology proceedings, leading to the development of adversarial proceedings within committees and judicial interference with committee choices? Will the development of legal disputes, some of which might simply serve the dilatory aims of adverse parties, not hamper decision-making?

Clearly, this prospect is alarming for the Union. Because of its nature as a consensus-based system, comitology would be likely to suffer even more than American regulatory agencies from excessive legalisation since consensus-building among the experts would become more difficult. The increase in transaction costs might ultimately threaten the overall efficiency of the system. Thus, in the name of legitimacy, one would compromise the system's ability to deliver good rules within reasonable time spans. That would be paradoxical, as the legitimacy of modern governance is as much a matter of *outputs* as of *inputs*.[39] However, how real is the risk?

---

[37] See in general Stewart (1975); Shapiro (1988).
[38] Shapiro (1996a: 39).   [39] See Scharpf (1996a).

First, procedural rules of the kind contemplated above, rules that would require greater openness and transparency in committee proceedings, essentially provide for a wider variety of inputs before decisions are made. Decisions, however, would still be taken by committee members and therefore the quality of discussion among experts, which is said to be one of comitology's positive achievements, should not change dramatically. Secondly, the emphasis should be strictly on procedures, and judicial review of the merits of comitology decisions should be excluded. Clauses that might be perceived by courts as an invitation to engage in substantive scrutiny – such as the clause on "arbitrary and capricious" rules in the US Administrative Procedures Act – should therefore be avoided.[40]

True, the American example has shown that the legalisation of rule-making is more a product of judicial behaviour than of formal requirements. Courts may, if they so wish, exploit even the most lenient requirements to justify more aggressive scrutiny. At the European level, therefore, the real question is whether the ECJ and the Court of First Instance are likely to follow the path of their US counterparts and use procedural requirements to monitor more closely the substance of comitology decisions. Although it is impossible to give a clear-cut reply, some points are worth mentioning. First, would committees be exposed to judicial censure if they failed to comply with procedural requirements? The difficulty here stems from the fact that comitology committees do not formally decide but merely adopt an opinion which conditions the Commission's margin of manoeuvre. Currently, the only act against which an appeal could be lodged would be the Commission's ultimate decision. However, recent developments in Community case law suggest that Community courts may be willing to accept that procedural flaws at earlier stages of an administrative proceeding, be it at national[41] or at Community level,[42] can lead to the annulment of the Commission's final decision. In *Technische Universität München*, the University of Munich, which had applied for an exemption from customs duties on the import of an electron microscope, had not been given the opportunity to submit observations to the group of experts advising the Commission on the existence of an equivalent apparatus within the Community. Although the technical debate occurred, by the Commission's own admission, exclusively within the expert group[43] the ECJ considered that procedural flaws at earlier stages of the procedure could somehow be imputed to the

---

[40] Interestingly, even in the United States, some scholars have advocated a retreat from "arbitrary and capricious" review and greater deference to agency decisions. See Pierce (1996: 200) and the comments by Francesca Bignami (1999).

[41] Case T-364/94, above, note 36.

[42] Case C-269/90, above, note 36.

[43] The Commission had indeed admitted that it always followed the opinions of the group of experts. See para 21.

Commission.[44] The Court held that, although the applicable regulation did not provide for such a hearing:

> "the person concerned should be able, *during the actual procedure before the Commission*, to put his own case and properly make his views known on the relevant circumstances and, where necessary, on the documents taken into account by the Community institution (...) (emphasis added)".[45]

Thus, if comitology procedures were to be codified, a similar reasoning might lead the Court to annul Commission decisions on the basis of procedural irregularities in committee deliberations.

Does it automatically follow that one would run the risk of unwanted judicial interference? This seems rather doubtful in the present circumstances. The ECJ has become a rather heterogeneous body. Not only are all nationalities of the Union represented under its auspices, but judges are characterised by a wide array of professional backgrounds and (one might assume, given the way they are appointed) political preferences. This, combined with the consensual character of decision-making, renders judicial activism less probable than with smaller, more homogeneous courts, where judges' preferences can more easily find their way into decisions. Secondly, the ECJ has displayed a clear reluctance to censure the policy choices made by the political institutions, particularly in areas where they enjoy discretionary powers.[46] This is not to say that the Court will never annul decisions of the Council or the Commission, but rather that as a rule, when it does so, its rulings appear more inspired by procedural considerations than by substantive concerns. This long-standing tendency has become, if anything, even more accentuated in recent years,[47] leading occasionally to criticism of the Court for its unwillingness to question choices made by Community institutions.[48] The Court's case law on subsidiarity[49] and that of the Court of First Instance on access to documents held by Community institutions[50] evidence a reluctance to

---

[44] Nehl (1997: 108).

[45] Case C-269/90, above, note 36, at para 25.

[46] This tendency has been quite strong in the Court's case-law on proportionality. In a case which concerned *inter alia* a decision of a management committee, the ECJ stressed that: "as the evaluation of a complex economic situation is involved, the Commission and the Management Committee enjoy, in this respect, a wide measure of discretion. In reviewing the legality of the exercise of such discretion, the Court must confine itself to examining whether it contains a manifest error or constitutes a misuse of power or whether the authority did not clearly exceed the bounds of its discretion". (Case 29/77, *Roquette v. France* [1977] ECR 2545, para 43).

[47] See Dehousse (1998a).

[48] See, for instance, the *Banana* case, Case C-280/93, *Germany v. Council* [1994] ECR I-4973 and the discussion in Everling (1997).

[49] See, for example, Case C-233/94, *Germany v. Parliament and Council* [1997] ECR I-2405. For a more general discussion, see de Búrca (1998).

[50] Case T-194/94, *John Carvel and Guardian v. Council* [1995] ECR II-2765 and Case T-105/95, *WWF v. Commission* [1997] ECR II-313.

transform procedural requirements into an instrument of substantive review. Given this background, it would be somewhat surprising to see the Court engage in detailed scrutiny of committees decisions or even to impose an exacting dialogue with private interests.

Admittedly, proceduralisation puts a premium on organisational and legal resources, which are unevenly distributed.[51] This, however, should not be viewed as a decisive argument against more openness. Under the present system, characterised as we saw by the opacity and lack of accountability of comitology proceedings, "strong" interests already have access to information and are able to influence decision-makers, be they members of parliaments or bureaucrats, at national or European level.[52] It is unlikely that the adoption of procedural rules would exclusively or indeed mainly favour such interests. At the same time, however, positive measures aimed at improving representation of diffuse interests, are needed to prevent proceduralisation from being mere *"trompe l'oeil"* (eye-wash) and to ensure that it actually benefits European citizens at large.

7. Conclusion: Comitology Paradoxes

Comitology is a world of paradoxes. While it appears to be growing both quantitatively and qualitatively, comitology often is ignored in discussions on the legitimacy of European policy-making, which is still heavily focused on legislative procedures. The debate among the Council, Commission and Parliament on the proper role of committees is often conflictual; yet the day-to-day work of committees seems rather consensual. Notwithstanding a widespread disenchantment with the way the European policy process operates, each institution continues to seek to maximise its own influence. All appear relatively unconcerned with creating channels through which European citizens may voice more directly their views.

This contribution has advocated a radically different approach to comitology reform, in which interested citizens would be given a say in committee deliberations. Yet, the procedural avenue outlined here, with its emphasis on transparency and openness, should not be seen as an alternative to the political control exercised by the Council and the European Parliament. On the contrary, the emergence of a public debate on committee decisions might reinforce political control, thereby contributing to the emergence of a transnational public sphere.

Can enhanced legitimacy be obtained without simultaneously threatening the efficiency of the present system? To be sure, this is a formidable problem because the proceduralisation of committee work carries a twofold risk of excessive legalisation and judicial interference. I have tried to show that given the great heterogeneity of the Community, the risk of

---

[51] Stewart (1990: 346).   [52] Mazey/Richardson (1993).

judicial activism is less acute than in other systems. This is not to say that the problem should be overlooked. On the contrary, a systematic survey of means of avoiding these two evils should be undertaken. The purpose of legal procedures should be to ensure the fairness of the decision-making process, not paralyse it, nor serve as a Trojan horse for judicial policy-making. At the same time, in view of the widening gap between citizens and representative institutions, it is counterproductive to use dangers of that kind as a scarecrow in support of maintaining the status quo.

8

Shared Governance and Enforcement of European Law: From Comitology to a Multi-level Agency Structure?

John A E Vervaele*

1. Sovereignty and Enforcement

Until quite recently enforcement in the Community was not an issue in the legal debate. The Community was engaged in system building, formulating policies for negative and positive integration in order to build an internal market predicated upon the free movement of goods, persons, services and capital, and working out the necessary regulatory programmes for achieving these objectives. In the last decade, however, implementation and enforcement of Community law has become one of the Community's priorities. In this sense, the Community may be likened to the building of a house, which, once completed, requires the observance of rules, maintenance and competent management (compliance). This metaphor at once indicates that the inhabitants of this European house, the Community institutions and the Member States, face a task and that this task also relates to the constitutional structure and legitimacy of the Community legal order.

The EC Treaty paid little regard to the particularities of enforcement of Community law (with the exception of direct enforcement of competition and merger law under Articles 85-87 EC). At the outset, Community law simply assumed that the Member States were the appropriate institutions to implement and enforce Community law and could be relied upon to do so. Direct enforcement by the Community institutions was and remains an exception to this general assumption. The execution of this enforcement authority by the Member States,[1] subsequently reshaped by the European Court of Justice (ECJ) into an enforcement duty[2] pursuant to Article 5 EC,

---

* Professor of Law, University of Utrecht and College of Europe, Bruges.
[1] Case 50/76, *Amsterdam Bulb BV* v. *Produktschap voor Siergewassen* [1977] ECR 137.
[2] Case 14/83, *Von Colson and Kamann* [1984] ECR 1891 and Case 68/88, *Commission* v. *Greece* [1989] ECR 2965.

bore the stamp of discretionary authority under which the Member States decided which enforcement tools they wanted to apply: whether they wanted to enforce Community law by means of preventive or repressive means; through a compliance of command and control approach, or by means of private law, administrative law, criminal law, or rather by means of a combination of these possibilities. In short, the Member States had institutional autonomy as regards enforcement of Community law. There was no shared enforcement governance or shared enforcement practice between the Community and the Member States.

However, during the past 10 to 15 years, some important developments have taken place in this field.[3] The Community had to confront the discrepancy in enforcement practice between the Community level and national level; the implementation and enforcement chain, from instituting rules to sanctioning breaches, having been fractured by hierarchical, institutional divisions and by divided competences. There was a clear need to intensify relationships and interventions and to streamline the regulation and implementation process. Enforcement became a real policy problem. Therefore, despite the fact that the Treaty remained unrevised as regards enforcement competences, case law and subordinated legislative activity have resulted in Community powers increasingly penetrating one of the bastions of national sovereignty, the coercive and sanctioning powers of the Member States. From that perspective enforcement became a part of policy implementation: charged with enforcing substantive norms. That means that the classic functions of the policy chain (policy development, policy decisions, policy implementation, policy evaluation) became increasingly penetrated by "European" influence and that the notions of shared and multi-level governance were introduced in order to develop an integrated norm-setting, implementation and enforcement policy.

This contribution therefore aims to examine in what way enforcement authorities[4] are involved in shared and multi-level governance in the context of the European Union. The courts, although potentially actors in the enforcement process, fall outside the scope of this contribution although the ECJ's role in establishing shared governance[5] and co-operation is discussed. Furthermore this examination is limited to the enforcement of obligations

---

[3] J.A.E. Vervaele (ed.), Compliance and Enforcement of European Community Law, Kluwer European Monographs, 20 (The Hague, London, Boston, Kluwer Law International, 1999) 426pp.

[4] In the broad interpretation of the concept of enforcement, from the legislative to the operational level.

[5] Shared governance is not a legal term. In Community legislation only the concepts of "co-operation" and partnership are used. However, co-operation is not limited to mere collaboration between states, but includes a shared responsibility for implementation and enforcement in the whole Community area. See, for example, the ruling of the ECJ in Case C-9/89, *Spain* v. *Council* [1990] ECR I-1383.

upon citizens and the corporations and not the Member States themselves.[6]
It is against these co-ordinates that enforcement is evaluated, a context in
which committees can play an important role when interpreted broadly,
ergo as forms of shared governance and co-operation, in which the national
administrations and European institutions share competence and responsibility for policy development, policy decision and/or policy implementation.[7] In this sense committees form one of the important aspects of the
emerging federal construction of the European Community; fulfilling a
wide variety of policy functions as well as being crucial for the representation of interests, information gathering and effecting transnational interaction in networks. Moreover, they play a substantive role in institutional
checks and balances between the Commission and the Council and between
the Community and the Member States.

2. The Concept of Enforcement

All theoretical conceptions of (indirect) administration of Community law[8]
include both implementation and enforcement aspects. Enforcement of
Community law deals with the enforcement of regulatory programmes,
which is part of the implementation of EC policy. Enforcement is always
linked to the substantive rules to be enforced (the policy-area) and is highly
dependent on the implementation of rules. In that sense there is a strong
link between norm-setting, implementation and enforcement. Hence, law
enforcement comprises preventive and repressive monitoring, investigating
and sanctioning substantive norms. Such activities require their own
enforcement rules concerning the competences of enforcement agencies,
the sanctions against and duties of the economic actors, etc. Imposing
these enforcement rules, the so-called "regulatory enforcement framework", is a duty for the legislature and consists of defining the normative
framework. The second step involves practical application of the enforcement rules, which is done by administrative inspectorates, judicial investigative bodies and the police. This is the first stage of the operational level.
The second stage at the operational level consists of the work of the
judiciary, in imposing or reviewing sanctions and measures.

---

[6] Herewith excluding, for example, the clearance of accounts and division of financial
responsibilities in the framework of own resources, agriculture subsidies (EAGGF) or structural funds subsidies.

[7] For the purpose of this contribution, the distinction between advisory, management and
regulatory committees, as laid down in Council Decision 87/373/EEC on comitology (1987)
OJ L 197/33, is too limited. Rather, committees are viewed to include all types of working
parties/expert groups and special committees both at Commission level and at that of the
Council (or even the European Parliament).

[8] See Daintith (1995).

3. Division of Legal Powers and Shared Governance

Implications or effects of institutional provisions are often difficult to foresee. But they can be observed *ex post*. The gradual development towards shared governance has occurred through both case law concerning Article 5 EC and secondary legislation.

3.1. *Case Law on Article 5 EC*

The ECJ has, pursuant to the principle of Community loyalty in Article 5 EC, developed the enforcement duty of both Member States and the Community. In principle Member States remain primarily responsible for enforcing Community law and are free to choose the means of enforcement. However, the ECJ restricts this choice by means of several requirements. It subjects the execution of institutional autonomy to qualitative criteria which are based on Community law principles. First, the choice of the enforcement means must guarantee the *effet utile* of Community law by aiming at effectiveness and dissuasion while at the same time observing the principle of proportionality. In addition, the enforcement action must be non-discriminatory and allow for assimilation. This means, according to the Court, that:

"(...) Article 5 of the Treaty requires the Member States to take all measures necessary to guarantee the application and effectiveness of Community law. For that purpose, whilst the choice of penalties remains within their discretion, they must ensure in particular that infringements of Community law are penalised under conditions, both procedural and substantive, which are analogous to those applicable to infringements of national law of a similar nature and importance and which, in any event, make the penalty effective, proportionate and dissuasive."[9]

These requirements constitute a further development of the *Rewe* principles.[10] It is obvious that these ECJ criteria turn the Member States' freedom of choice into a freedom determined by objectives linked to Community law principles. Furthermore, the observance of these requirements leads, to an extent, to the harmonisation of the enforcement regimes and enforcement efforts of the Member States; the first step towards a more integrated approach to the legal enforcement of Community law.[11] The ECJ not only sets rules as regards effectiveness and harmonisation but also as regards co-operation. The same Community loyalty provision of Article 5 EC is used as a statutory basis to oblige Member States to co-operate in enforcement actions, even those encompassing judicial or criminal law co-operation

[9] Case 68/88, above, note 2.   [10] Case 33/76, *Rewe* [1976] ECR 1989.
[11] Gröblinghoff (1996).

within the scope of the Member States' freedom of choice regarding enforcement instruments.[12] The ECJ also pointed out that the duty to co-operate is mutual: and lies not only as between the Member States (horizontally) and between the Member States and the European institutions (vertically), but also between the European institutions themselves.[13]

3.2. Secondary Legislation

In addition, the Council and Commission also have prescribed enforcement obligations towards the Member States and economic operators. Such obligations illustrate that even if enforcement of Community law is and remains the competence of the Member States, this does not mean that the Community has no responsibility whatsoever for ensuring compliance with Community law. On the contrary, we can observe a Community regulatory competence to impose enforcement duties on the Member States. For nearly a decade, far-reaching supervision and sanction duties have been included in sectoral regulations. Such rules may be laid down in directives used as enforcement instruments (for example, obligatory licences that can be suspended or withdrawn). For example, rules lay down detailed requirements as to who is competent to carry out inspections, the form and frequency of inspection, who is competent to impose sanctions and the severity of the sanctions. Numerous examples hereof may be found in agricultural policy,[14] own resources[15] and structural funds.[16] Hence, instead of freedom of choice as regards enforcement, such detailed requirements constitute conditional enforcement with only limited discretionary power for the Member States.

Moreover, the Commission monitors the compliance of Member States with Community law on the basis of its supervisory powers under Articles 145 and 155 EC. This is a form of direct enforcement, which is to some extent comparable with the competences of the Commission in the area of competition law, although limited to the monitoring/inspection side of enforcement (excluding sanctions). These powers are developed in

[12] Case C-9/89, above, note 4.

[13] Case C-2/88, *Zwartveld* [1990] ECR I-3365.

[14] Council Regulation (EEC) 595/91 concerning irregularities and the recovery of sums wrongly paid in connection with the financing of the common agricultural policy and the organisation of an information system in this field and repealing Regulation (EEC) 283/72, (1991) OJ L 67/11 and Council Regulation (EC, Euratom) 2988/95 on the protection of the European Communities financial interests, (1995) OJ L 312/1.

[15] Council Regulation (EEC, Euratom) 1552/89 implementing Decision 88/376/EEC, Euratom on the system of the Communities' own resources, (1989) OJ L 155/1 and Council Regulation (EEC, Euratom) 1553/89 on the definitive uniform arrangements for the collection of own resources accruing from value added tax, (1989) OJ L 155/9.

[16] Commission Regulation (EC) 1681/94 concerning irregularities and the recovery of sums wrongly paid in connection with the financing of the structural policies and the organisation of an information system in this field, (1994) OJ L 178/43.

secondary legislation relating to the general sector in question (own resources, agricultural expenditure (EOGF), structural funds) and are therefore quite diverse. For some market regulations, such as olive oil, wine and tobacco, these powers are specifically determined.[17] In contrast, for inspections in relation to fraud the 1996 framework Regulation concerning on-the-spot checks and inspections by the Commission is limited to the protection of the Community's financial interests.[18]

3.3. Levels of Enforcement

With regard to the above-mentioned case law and legislation, I distinguish three levels which are not necessarily chronological and may overlap.

3.3.1 Elaboration of Common Regulatory Rules and Standards for Enforcement

A first level which can be distinguished is that of the common regulatory rules and standards for enforcement developed through harmonisation. This harmonisation process, limited to the standardisation part of enforcement, was shaped during the 1980s and 1990s partially on the basis of ECJ criteria but primarily based on secondary legislative stipulations as regards steering instruments that can also function as enforcement instruments (suspension and withdrawal of licences; reclaiming subsidies) and as regards administrative supervision and sanctioning tools in the fields of agriculture and fisheries and of structural funds.[19] It is remarkable that own resources, customs policy, the internal market and adjacent policy areas (especially the environment) lag behind in this respect.[20] Such pro-active Community harmonisation based on "positive integration" has relied exclusively on non-criminal law enforcement tools. As regards the criminal law field, the necessary political will has been virtually non-existent so that no Commission proposal has survived negotiations within

---

[17] Council Regulation (EEC) 2262/84 laying down special measures in respect of olive oil, (1984) OJ L 208/11, Council Regulation (EEC) 2048/89 laying down general rules on controls in the wine sector, (1989) OJ L 202/32 and Commission Regulation (EEC) 85/93 concerning control agencies in the tobacco sector, (1993) OJ L 12/9.

[18] Council Regulation (Euratom, EC) 2185/96 concerning on-the-spot checks and inspections carried out by the Commission in order to protect the European Communities' financial interests against fraud and other irregularities, (1996) OJ L 292/2. See J A E Vervaele (1998). See, in more detail, section 5.2.

[19] Case C-240/90, *Germany* v. *Commission* [1992] ECR I-5383 and Council Regulation (EC, Euratom) 2988/95, above, note 13.

[20] In the framework of the Customs 2000 programme, a joint position in the third pillar (Co-operation in the field of Justice and Home Affairs), Article 12 provides for the introduction of administrative customs sanctions. The European Parliament Committee of Inquiry into the Community Transit System, 1997, PE 220.895/FIN in its recommendations even requires the establishment of a European Customs Office with far-reaching operational enforcement competences.

the Council.[21] The development of a common regulatory framework for enforcement should be the basis for mutual trust and must avoid fostering negative or positive enforcement competition between regulatory approaches.

3.3.2 Mutual Recognition of Enforcement Systems

A second level is the mutual recognition of national enforcement systems and actions and therefore not only seeks standardisation of enforcement but also the pragmatic application of enforcement. Examples hereof are the withdrawal of customs' licences of import/export companies by a Member State which is recognised by all Member States,[22] or the execution by the Member State under whose flag a fishing vessel sails of an administrative fine for breach of Community fishing regulations imposed by another Member State.[23]

3.3.3 Enforcement Co-operation

The third level concerns certain forms of operational co-operation between enforcement authorities: enforcement co-operation. This presumes the development of a common regulatory framework for enforcement co-operation. Within the first EC pillar, for example, this has occurred within the framework of specific regulations for agriculture and customs[24] and for tax matters.[25] In other areas such co-operative frameworks have been established on the basis of memoranda of understanding or third pillar or international conventions. Such frameworks define the tools of co-operation: mutual assistance, joint investigations, common enforcement policy (task forces, etc.). Based on this regulatory framework, enforcement authorities co-operate and in a number of cases develop into networks. Some of these networks subsequently turn into independent agency-like structures or true agencies.

---

[21] Vervaele (1992) and (1994a).

[22] See Council Regulation (EEC) 2913/92 establishing the Community Customs Code, (1992) OJ L 302/1 and Commission Regulation (EEC) 2454/93 laying down provisions for the implementation of Council Regulation (EEC) 2913/92 establishing the Community Customs Code, (1993) OJ L 253/1.

[23] Council Regulation (EEC) 2847/93 establishing a control system applicable to the common fisheries policy, (1993) OJ L 261/1.

[24] Council Regulation (EC) 515/97 on mutual assistance between the administrative authorities of the Member States and co-operation between the latter and the Commission to ensure the correct application of the law on customs and agricultural matters, (1997) OJ L 82/1.

[25] See, for example, Commission Regulation (EEC) 218/91 establishing unit values for the determination of the customs value of certain perishable goods, (1991) OJ L 26/7.

3.4. *Enforcement Law in Practice*

However, this three-level process often takes a quite different turn in practice depending on the policy area concerned. Serious problems generally present themselves in the early stages of elaborating common regulatory frameworks. Mutual recognition in enforcement matters therefore rarely occurs. Often harmonisation is incomplete to such an extent that even the ECJ has accepted the fact that enforcement authority remains limited to the nation state of the person involved (home-control principle); the only authority actually capable of supervising and sanctioning. This means that the home-control principle prevails in a number of cases involving the four freedoms and that the freedom at issue is then subject to or limited by the enforcement demands of the home-state.[26] Mutual recognition also implies that a Member State cannot assume the place of other Member States in enforcement matters (enforcement competition) nor can it impose sanction measures as regards other Member States. For example, the UK cannot refuse to issue an export licence for livestock because in Spain a directive on slaughtering animals has been implemented incorrectly.[27] Neither can the UK block financial operations concerning legal pharmaceutical trading with Yugoslavia because the economic operators have not applied for an export licence in the UK, but in Italy, where the UK authorities lack supervision powers.[28] In such cases, other means need to be adopted to require Member States to engage mutual enforcement (such as the Article 169 EC procedure).[29]

Similarly, enforcement co-operation may produce ever more complex and difficult situations. The few EC areas which instituted common regulatory frameworks on enforcement co-operation lines show that this process is very difficult. The enforcement tools ostensibly available are hardly ever used and the follow-up of enforcement results in the Member States (at the jurisdictional level) leaves much to be desired. One of the reasons that procedures often grind to a halt is the different procedural and evidentiary rules involved. In the fisheries sector, for example, a mobile sector, for which a co-operation regime has been developed, it is remarkable how little has been achieved.[30] The same applies to the sector

---

[26] Case C-55/93, *Van Schaik* [1994] ECR I-4837; Case C-384/93, *Alpine Investments* v. *Minister of Finance* [1995] ECR I-1141.

[27] Case C-5/94, *The Queen* v. *Ministry of Agriculture, Fisheries and Food, ex parte: Hedley Lomas (Ireland) Ltd.* [1996] ECR I-2553.

[28] Case C-124/95, *The Queen, ex parte: Centro-Com Srl* v. *HM Treasury and Bank of England* [1997] ECR I-81.

[29] Mutual recognition does not of course preclude conflicts of competence between Member States; co-operation and priority rules, however, may provide solutions in such cases.

[30] Commission Report on the monitoring of the Common Fisheries Policy, COM(96) 100 final and Berg/Vervaele (1994).

of customs, which is traditionally an international affair.[31]

It is not by accident that new co-operation procedures have been introduced for the enforcement of Community law, but rather due to a number of particular conditions: firstly, the legislative activity of the Council and of the Commission in the field of enforcement has considerably increased over the last few years; secondly, the Member States continue to show considerable reluctance to accept Community influence in their legal orders; and thirdly, the effective enforcement of Community law demands close co-operation between Community and Member States' institutions. National enforcement authorities are increasingly confronted with an interdependence of problems in an open market, which may be illustrated by the open frontiers policy, the Schengen police measures and the completion of the Customs Union. As the report by the European Parliamentary Committee of Inquiry on transit customs' enforcement stated:

> "[c]rime is organised at a multinational level whereas the 15 customs authorities of the EU continue to think and act within a framework of national boundaries".[32]

Clearly, the BSE crisis, too, shows the need to handle such enforcement issues in a European setting with common rule-setting and standards and increased co-operation between enforcement authorities.[33]

However, the new enforcement authorities, whether or not active in new policy areas, are often active via informal networks and not only in the European market but also at international level. The money laundering enforcement agencies or the financial information units (FIUs) in Europe,[34] have at short notice built a world-wide network,[35] comparable to that of the securities enforcement agencies[36] with a common regulatory co-operation framework and operational co-operation forms (EGMONT group), similar to the International Organisation of Securities Commissions (IOSCO).[37] The FIUs are new, dynamic and find themselves in the forefront of enforcement due to the high political priority their co-operation receives. Schengen and Europol also have, despite their institutional and operational problems, managed to introduce, within a relatively short time, network structures in traditionally closed enforcement areas. The Community has also encouraged the intensification of co-operation and

---

[31] See Inquiry of the EP, see n. 20 above.   [32] Above, note 19.

[33] Report on the alleged contraventions or maladministration in the implementation of Community law in relation to BSE, without prejudice to the jurisdiction of the Community and the national courts of 7 February 1997, A4-0020/97/A, PE 220.544/fin/A.

[34] See Council Directive 91/308/EEC on prevention of the use of the financial system for the purpose of money laundering, (1991) OJ L 166/77.

[35] Zagaris (1989: 465-552) and (1995).

[36] Mahoney (1970: 305); Salbu (1992: 837); *The International Lawyer*, 1995/5, International Securities Law Symposium.

[37] Bermann (1996: 933-984).

networks by introducing exchange and training programmes at the European level.[38] Such Community activities disclose a growing influence upon legislation and increasing co-operation in operational fields. They are illustrations of shared governance in enforcement issues, concerning both the regulatory enforcement framework and its operational application.

Operational network co-operation is also laid down in the Treaty of Amsterdam, in both the first and third pillars. Administrative and customs co-operation has an independent statutory basis in Articles 66 and 135 whilst Article 280 on fraud provides a statutory basis for horizontal and vertical network co-operation. This is even more the case for the third pillar where police and judicial co-operation now retain fundamental positions (Article 29 ff.). Such co-operation takes the form of "operational co-operation between the competent authorities, including the police, customs and other specialised law enforcement services of the Member States in relation to the prevention, detection and investigation of criminal offences" (Article 30 (1) a).

4. From Shared Governance to Network Co-operation in Action

Enforcement is tightly linked to *ius puniendi*, the repressive competence and powers of the nation state. From a formalist institutional perspective, enforcement discloses a picture of competing competences, a struggle for authority and power, which reflects the institutional struggle between the nation state and the Community. When analysed in factual or functional terms, however, enforcement deploys a very different and new picture of forms of network co-operation with the threefold objective of influencing decision-making processes, defending autonomous organisational interests and developing new forms of inter-agency co-operation.

The steering activities of the ECJ, the Council and most importantly, the Commission in the enforcement field[39] play an important role in this process with far-reaching consequences for both the structure and functions of national enforcement authorities, some of them charged with executing exclusive Community obligations, such as customs and sea fisheries enforcement authorities, *vis-à-vis* their own nation states. Here the Community intervenes in the area of indirect enforcement of Community law, the so-called indirect Community enforcement structure in the Member States.[40] The functional obligation approach imposed by Community law places the Member States in a new institutional setting, which is not dominated by their own national enforcement departments. They are increasingly confronted with an enforcement agenda which does not depend on, nor is

---

[38] See, for example, the Mattheus programme for customs officers, (1991) OJ L 187/41 and the OISIN programme for law enforcement agencies (Joint Action), (1997) OJ L 7/5.

[39] See section 3.   [40] Daintith (1995).

even always in line with, the policy agenda of their national departments. By creating autonomous management structures for administrative co-operation and enforcement, denationalised governance structures are emerging which erode both national and supranational institutions.

Denationalising governance structures implies depoliticising them by transforming regulatory challenges into technical and expertise concepts. Through the use of flexible network structures, parallel to enforcement agencies, with one co-operation centre (which might be the European Commission or independent European agencies), a forum for joint technical expert management is developed. The new techniques for on-line communication play an important role in this model. The Schengen Information System (SIS), the Customs Information System (CIS) and the way Europol functions (with a co-ordination centre in The Hague and satellites in the Member States) are very good illustrations of this evolution. The same model will be used for the enforcement of migration regulation in the European Information System (EIS), based on the pending Convention on External Borders. The effect of this networking between enforcement agencies and from their interlocking is that the enforcement authorities originating in the nation state are integrated in a pattern characterised by transnationalisation. In this process of transnational co-operation, everything starts with decentralised, informal, personal and hierarchically based procedures. The informal character of the way these networks are established and their transnational structure is significant. In view of the sensibilities of the nation states it is generally the pragmatic and only way to proceed. However, also through multi-level interactions civil servants of several national and international administrations become aware of common interests and will thus reinforce trends towards specific forms of power-sharing. Only after such informal consensus building of what to do and how to do it, can they elaborate a framework of entrenched procedural rules, which are in turn the building blocks for agency building. Important in this context is that the position and role of the enforcement authorities will change during the process, though this does not have to mean that they will be separated from their national framework. On the contrary, their respective national departments with their expertise and priority structures will often get carried along in the process of transnationalisation.

This process of interlocking (*Verflechtung, engrenage*), links shared enforcement with interdependent policies and interests, and means that no autonomous European enforcement agencies need to be established. In view of this network-model, enforcement is an area in which the European Commission or the regulatory agencies can play a very substantial role in the achievement of transnational co-operation and co-ordination.[41] Considering

---

[41] Majone (1996a).

the boundary-tied tradition of many enforcement authorities (and of their legal traditions), the European Commission has here considerable latitude to set up original co-operation forms, reflecting an integrated operational approach rather than a hierarchical, institutional Community-state approach. Enforcement co-operation in a European regional context will be less and less dependent on classical state to state approaches, and I see the institutional Community-state approach as a variety of this, but even more as a form of direct operational co-operation between the enforcement authorities themselves. The success of European regulatory efforts will depend less upon the establishment of new supranational European institutions but rather upon consolidating and intensifying integration through multi-level governance structures with strong multi-level interdependence between the various levels of political institutions.[42] It is important that these multi-level governance structures gain and consolidate their institutional integrity in a way that can be fitted into the traditions of democracy (including principles of due process) and democratic administration. In order to obtain and retain the necessary legitimacy and to ensure political accountability, a number of checks and balances will have to be incorporated into these new Community governance structures. This entails a well-detailed task, proceduralised legal requirements and duties of co-operation for the national authorities.

5. Shared Governance and Network-building for the Enforcement of Community Law: Two Case Studies

The state of knowledge on cross-border and transnational administration of Community policy in general is either limited, or, as far as enforcement is concerned, virtually non-existent. For several reasons there seems to be little interest both in legal and social/political sciences in regulatory practices and enforcement agencies. Research still focuses on nation state actors, presupposing that cross-border administrative activities of the administrations are random and have only marginal structural and functional implications. The lack of empirical information on the enforcement of Community policies is partly due to the closed structure of many enforcement authorities, to the technically complex nature of many regulatory programmes, and also to the woeful shortage of transnational and interdisciplinary research structures and tools in Europe.

For this reason, I will present two case studies which illustrate the evolution of shared governance and the strong connections between rule-setting, implementation and enforcement. The first case concerns the pharmaceutical market. It may at first sight seem a typical case of social regulation

---

[42] See Joerges, in this volume.

and administration. However, the licensing of a medicinal product involves a powerful enforcement instrument and its suspension or withdrawal is directly linked to infringements. The second field is a classic, important enforcement field, namely fraud against the EU budget. In this field, we can observe how implementation assessment by the Commission is transformed into real enforcement and how networking leads to the development of a multi-level and multi-agency structure.

5.1. Access to the Pharmaceutical Market[43]

Historically, access to the pharmaceutical market has been strictly regulated by domestic legal regimes, *inter alia* to protect public health.[44] These national regulatory regimes, however, constituted trade barriers to the free movement of pharmaceuticals in the European market. The interest of the pharmaceutical industry to have access to a single integrated European market is evident in view of the costly and lengthy process of product research development. This process, which is to a large extent financed by multi-national companies, is only economically worthwhile if those companies can obtain certainty as regards access to substantial markets for sustained periods of time under standardised conditions. Hence, market integration requires either the replacement of national medicines' registration and control or their refinement with complementary systems compatible with international regulations. Over the years the concept of medicine, the duty to register, the registration criteria and the licence conditions have been harmonised via directives and regulations so as to facilitate access to national markets. The 1965 Directive on medicinal products[45] stipulated that no medicinal product could be placed on the market without prior licence or authorisation and prescribed that the application should be accompanied by specific documentary evidence, guaranteeing safety, quality and therapeutic efficacy. Directives 75/318/EEC and 75/319/EEC[46] harmonised these requirements in more detail and established the Committee on Proprietary Medicinal Products, composed of national representatives. In 1983 these requirements were further substantiated.[47]

In 1993 a centralised authorisation system was introduced at EC level. This step was taken at a rather late stage in the process because a substantial number of Member States very stubbornly resisted this development.

---

[43] Deboyser (1994: 213-217); Vos (1999: Chapter 4).

[44] As for instance the Food and Drugs Acts 1909-49 in the UK, the French Act on the General Statute of Pharmacies of 1941 and the Dutch Supply of Medicines Act of 1958.

[45] Council Directive 65/65/EEC on the approximation of provisions laid down by law, regulation or administrative action relating to proprietary medicinal products, (1965) OJ 22/369.

[46] (1975) OJ L 147/1 and (1975) OJ L 147/13.

[47] Council Directive 83/570/EEC, (1983) OJ L 332/1.

Unsurprisingly, the pharmaceutical industry strictly opposed centralised safety and public health requirements too. Within this system an independent agency, the European Agency for the Evaluation of Medicinal Products (EMEA),[48] was made responsible for European authorisation and licensing in the field of biotechnological medicines (advanced and technical innovations, including the use of genetically modified organisms, GMOs). Harmonisation activity has thus created a new market stratification which is no longer based on the differences between Member States but rather on the differences between products.

As regards the centralised procedure, it is remarkable that within the EMEA the committees and even the national authorities continue to play a very important role. Within the EMEA, which has its seat in London, two committees exist: the Committee on Proprietary Medicinal Products and the Committee for Veterinary Medicinal Products. The Committees have thirty members, two for each Member State. The Committees may establish working and expert groups and establish links with the national marketing authorisation bodies. Applications must be submitted to the EMEA. One of the Committees, depending on the application, examines the application and formulates an opinion. In the case of a negative opinion, the applicant can ask for a re-examination. The opinion of the EMEA is forwarded to the Commission, which adopts a draft decision. After having consulted the Standing Committee on Medicinal Products for Human Use in the framework of the *contre-filet* regulatory committee procedure,[49] the Commission then takes the final decision, which is binding throughout the Community. The positive final decision is entered into the Community Register of Medicinal Products. The EMEA Committees thus function as a bridge between the EMEA and the Member States. In this vein, the national drug regulatory agencies no longer take independent decisions, but are locked into co-operative preparatory work and the implementation of common decisions. This entails that all legal protection is provided by classical Community legislation and not through national laws.

For all other medicines, licence criteria are included in national legislation and the competences lie with the national drug regulatory agencies. However, where a company has already obtained a market licence in one Member State and wants to market this product in one or more other Member States, the Community's decentralised authorisation procedure applies, which is based on mutual recognition. For example, the Dutch Provision of Medicines Act (*Wet op de Geneesmiddelenvoorziening*)

---

[48] Council Regulation (EEC) 2309/93 laying down Community procedures for the authorisation and supervision of medicinal products for human and veterinary use and establishing a European Agency for the Evaluation of Medicinal Products, (1993) OJ L 214/1 and Council Directive 93/39/EEC, (1993) OJ L 214/22.

[49] Comitology Decision, above, note 7.

provides for a procedure in which the Committee for the Evaluation of Medicines (*College ter beoordeling van de Geneesmiddelen*), the Dutch drug regulatory agency, has the task of evaluating and licensing medicines for the Dutch market. If the medicinal product enters the market for the first time, this constitutes a classical licence application to the Dutch drug regulatory agency. Notwithstanding this, Member States and the EMEA must be notified of licences granted. If the medicine is already marketed under licence in another Member State, the Dutch regulatory agency requests the relevant national drug registration authority to send its evaluation report and will usually grant the licence on the basis of mutual recognition. A licence can only be refused on grounds of serious danger to public health or conflicting Community interests. Such a refusal requires consultation with the other Member States and where there is disagreement the matter is brought before the EMEA. Both Community legislation and Dutch legislation provide complaints' or appeals' procedures for both the Dutch regulatory agency and producers as regards decisions of national registration institutions. Having obtained the advice of the Committee for Proprietary Medicinal Products, acting as arbiter, the Commission takes the final decision.

Besides the use of the licence as a steering instrument, which can be used to grant the producer access but also to withdraw it, there are of course the classic enforcement responsibilities and tools. Regarding enforcement the responsibilities are, in line with the state of the art in Community law, rather different. Enforcement is primarily a Member State responsibility, even as regards medicines for which the decision-making competence lies directly with the EMEA. This means that the Member State must provide for an efficient and effective control and sanction system. Thus, for example, Dutch legislation provides for control and investigative powers and penal sanctions. In other words, the European registration regulation requires supervision of national pharmaceutical inspections, even in relation to pharmaceuticals that have been entered in the Community medicine register. In the Netherlands, for example, there is the State Supervisory Agency for Public Health, an independent part of the Ministry for Welfare, Public Health and Sport, which encompasses four inspectorates: the Health Care Inspectorate (*Inspectie voor de Gezondheidszorg*), the Health Protection Inspectorate (*Inspectie Gezondheidsbescherming*), the Veterinary Inspectorate (*Veterinaire Inspectie*) and the Environmental Protection Inspectorate (*Inspectie Milieuhygiëne*). The latter falls under the authority of the Ministry of Housing, Planning and Environment. The Health Care Inspectorate is charged in particular with the supervision and detection tasks relating to food and foodstuffs. The Inspectorate may demand any information and is authorised to initiate investigations as regards producers. It may also provide instructions as well as report offences. In case of infringements, the classical criminal law route is followed (settle-ment, dismissal, prosecution, sanctioning). If regulatory offences are at issue, the maximum penalty is six months imprisonment; this would apply, for example, in cases of non-compliance with the administrative requirements (no licence, non-compliance with licence conditions, etc.). If the life of humans or animals is endangered, general sanctions in the criminal code may be applied which entail far more severe penalties. Besides this national line of enforcement there is also a Community line of enforcement. After all, the EMEA also has a supervisory task and may initiate investigations in the various Member States, either on its own initiative or in co-operation with national inspectorates. At the same time civil servants from other Member States may be involved in such inspec-tions. The EMEA may also conduct investigations with producers in third countries which trade in the internal market. The EMEA has no other independent sanction authority apart from the licence.

This exposition shows that in the European context national markets and regulatory competition between national legislative systems have been ruled out. By extending European legislation to the adoption of genuine European standards and their supervision, not only has a harmonised European market been created but also an integrated approach has been established regarding the consequences for human health. The second aspect is that this harmonised European model is not based on the classic legal-institutional division of authority between the Union and the Member States, but rather on a functional horizontal network that cuts right through the institutional Union-Member States structure. This devel-opment is also obvious in other fields; such as veterinary inspection, the Agency for Trademark legislation[50] and, prospectively, perhaps also the European Environment Agency.[51] Thirdly, this not only involves co-ordina-tion and harmonisation of standards regarding market access (and there-fore, market formation) or health aspects, but also the co-ordination and harmonisation of the supervisory dimension. Only the sanctioning aspects, that is to say the administrative and/or criminal law instruments, remain within the national competence, at least for the time being. Sanctioning via civil law liability has been harmonised since the introduction of the Product Liability Directive.[52] A further striking phenomenon is that committees continue to play an important role in the new horizontal struc-tures. They form bridges between the various horizontal structures and the organisations and actors within the nation state. Thus, not only is national expertise incorporated into the network, but at the same time sufficient support and legitimacy is secured within the Member States.

[50] Council Regulation (EC) 40/94, (1994) OJ L 11/1.
[51] Council Regulation (EEC) 1210/90, (1990) OJ L 120/1.
[52] Council Directive 85/374/EEC, (1985) OJ L 210/29.

5.2 The Protection of the Financial Interests of the EU[53]

5.2.1 The Normative Legal Framework

Although over the years some attempts had been made to combat EU fraud,[54] it was only in the 1990s that a horizontal and integrated approach to this problem was developed. Following the reports by two expert groups,[55] the Council adopted in 1991 a resolution requesting that the Commission conduct a comparative law study on the legal and administrative provisions in the Member States, with a view to co-ordinating anti-fraud legislation. On the basis of this study,[56] proposals were drafted for horizontal framework regulations on inspections and sanctions, covering the enforcement of EC income and expenditure rules in all fields.[57] However, only after the entry into force of the Treaty of Maastricht was the negotiation process continued.[58] The Commission was nevertheless now politically obliged to institutionally divide its proposals between the first EC pillar and the third pillar on issues of justice and home affairs, which has resulted in a horizontal regulation on administrative law sanctioning and a horizontal convention on criminal law sanctioning.[59] As a result, the Member States have again managed to keep criminal law substantially outside the ambit of Community integration and to set the agenda through mutual consultation. This does not have to mean that there is no co-operation whatsoever or that that co-operation has no bearing on the institutional structure of the nation state. Although the entire discussion on Schengen and Europol is centred, particularly by lawyers, around institutional competences and especially on the division of powers between the first and third pillars, the issue of competences, legal protection and legitimacy point beyond such institutional questions towards a truly transnational approach to enforcement.

5.2.2 The Operational Co-operation: From Assessing Implementation to Operational Enforcement

The horizontal and integrated approach not only required integration of the normative framework but also integration of the operational structure

[53] Vervaele (1994b); Dannecker (1995); Harding/Swart (1996).

[54] See for an overview, Vervaele (1994a: 113).

[55] The *ad hoc Droit pénal-droit communautaire* working group of the Working Group *Judicial Co-operation* of the European Political Co-operation (EPC) and the *ad hoc* working group *Cour de Justice et protection pénale*.

[56] Carried out by the Anti-Fraud Co-ordination Unit (UCLAF) and DG XX in strict collaboration with the network of Associations of Jurists: The system of administrative and penal sanctions in the Member States of the European Communities, I-II, Luxembourg, 1994.

[57] See Vervaele (1994c: 185).

[58] See in this context also, for example, Case C-240/90, above, note 18, which concerned the Commission's competence to prescribe such sanctions to the Member States.

[59] Vervaele (1997); Delmas-Marty (1995).

and instruments. Such integration is likeliest as regards financial monitoring. Formally speaking, competences are divided between the Union and its Member States. The latter are primarily responsible for the proper financial management of the Community funds they control. Until recently these were completely separate control systems. Only a short while ago the step was taken to conclude co-operation agreements between the Directorate General for Financial Control (DG XX) and the accountancy agencies in the Member States' ministries of finance. This is a further development of the co-ordination meetings on fraud between the Commission and representatives of the Ministries of Finance within the framework of the Sound Financial Management Group. There are also contacts between the European Court of Auditors and the national Courts of Auditors with a view to co-ordination. The Commission increasingly depends on a horizontal advisory committee which is consulted before the adoption of policies, subsequently in their evaluation, including operational aspects. This new committee was initiated in 1994 and set up under Article 209a EC: the Advisory Committee on the Co-ordination of the Prevention of Fraud (COCOLAF).[60]

Still more interesting are the developments in the field of enforcement. The Commission's competences to execute Euro-controls were, as was mentioned above, elaborated into sectoral regulations. This meant that in the absence of an integrated approach Directorate General Euro-inspectors and/or anti-fraud units were active with diverse competences. In 1988 the Commission established a special Anti-Fraud Co-ordination Unit (UCLAF) within the Secretariat-General. In 1995 the anti-fraud units of the DGs were dissolved and integrated in UCLAF, which means that UCLAF can now boast a staff of over 125 and expertise in a variety of policy fields. It is the start of a horizontal approach within the Commission. Very recently this has also resulted in a horizontal regulation concerning on-the-spot checks and inspections by the Commission for the detection of fraud and irregularities detrimental to the financial interests of the EU.[61]

UCLAF has both preventive and repressive tasks as well as specific operational tasks regarding co-operation. As regards prevention there are both legislative and operational tasks. National information streams form an invaluable source of information for the legislative and operational work of the UCLAF. As regards repression, UCLAF's work also involves part of the enforcement obligations of the Member States. Operational tasks are more complex; here UCLAF may use its Euro-inspection competences but it has no sanction competences. Co-operation on transnational frauds or fraud within a Member State confronts an important problem for which additional reinforcement is very much needed. This means that UCLAF co-ordinates and supports fraud investigations. Often such a fraud

[60] Commission Decision 94/140/EC, (1994) OJ L 61/27.
[61] Council Regulation 2185/96, above, note 17.

investigation is not limited to reclaiming monies or administrative investigation, but also involves judicial and police authorities under the supervision of the Public Prosecutor and/or an investigating judge. UCLAF has no judicial competences; it may not search houses or arrest people. However, UCLAF may co-ordinate actions in co-operation with judicial authorities, in such a way that the national judicial activities have effect and are conducted in a co-ordinated fashion. To that effect it regularly happens that special task forces are established, for instance, on cigarette smuggling. Thus, UCLAF plays a substantial role in pro-actively initiating judicial action and evidence gathering.

Especially interesting in such federal-state enforcement co-operation is that UCLAF has at ita disposal personnel and expertise from the Member States. Officials from national administrations, inspectorates and the judiciary are seconded to UCLAF for several years. They are active as UCLAF officials during that period, but are originally officials of the national departments, of the national inspectorates and of the national Public Prosecutor's Offices. Some investigating judges have even been seconded to UCLAF. This means that UCLAF has at its disposal an extensive network of personnel and expertise, not only horizontally through all the Commission's policy fields but also because of postings within the Member States themselves. This latter expertise is essential for the further expansion of its operational work within the Member States and for co-operation in specific fields. Many of the seconded officers from the national administrations have experience with the Commission and/or Council working groups. In that respect UCLAF may be considered a multi-cultural and multi-functional agency which, as regards competences and expertise, reacts pro-actively and retroactively by means of (within the European federal-state context) a mostly informal network on the enforcement efforts of the Member States.[62] In the current state of affairs this informal horizontal network has proved far more productive than the formalised Europol model with liaison officers, which stranded in endless legal-political debates on competences and legal protection. This explains why there was an increasing demand, also by the European Parliament,[63] to provide for an new statute for UCLAF, enabling it to become an independent enforcement agency with full responsibility and real investigative powers.[64]

---

[62] See Cour Européen des Comptes, Rapport spécial no. 8/98 rélatif aux services de la Commission chargés de la lutte contre la fraude, notamment l'UCLAF.

[63] Bösch, *Draft Report on the independence, role and status of UCLAF, Committee on Budgetary Control*, 13 January 1998, PE 225.069, and Theato, *Projet de Rapport sur les poursuites judiciaires pour la protection des finances de l'Union*, Commission du contrôle budgétaire, 8 January 1998, PE 225.338.

[64] For comments, see Vervaele (1998) see note 3 above.

6. Concluding Remarks

Over the last 10 years some substantial changes have taken place in relation to the enforcement of Community law whereby the various actors have positioned themselves around their various interests. This holds true both for Community organisations and the Member States, although there are no homogenous blocks involved. The tensions within the European organisations are significant and even within the European Commission there are huge differences of opinion between a number of DGs and the Secretariat General on the issue of enforcement. In the Member States themselves, this tension is also apparent between the departments that have to deal with European policies day in day out and the more autonomous departments which can allow themselves the conduct of ideological debates on sovereignty.

This institutional stalemate on competences has contributed to the development of consultation structures and operational methods in practice in which national and Community actors, in mutual consultation, develop policies, implement them and enforce them. The consultation structures within the Commission and Council (comitology, working groups, etc.) play a very important role in this as they are able to depoliticise and denationalise issues. Even though the European dimension of European policies' enforcement is still rudimentary, the first steps towards enforcement networks in Europe have been taken; these can in turn form the basis for agency-building. An advantage of this development is that new regulatory and enforcement frameworks develop, not by opting for supranational institutions, but, as Member States are not willing to loosen their grip on the implementation process, from a co-operation perspective, in which the Member States' authorities are involved to a significant extent.

Compared to the United States[65] the road to be taken seems still arduous. What needs to be done is to strengthen federal-state co-operation regarding enforcement, not by introducing new and complicated treaties but rather via financial incentives which may reinforce network structures and therefore horizontal governance. Only then will we be able to realise an enforcement system above and beyond the nation state, whereby the nation state itself would be transformed from an enforcement authority into an enforcement instrument. After all, within such a model the organs of the nation state have to function within a transnational co-operative approach which distances itself from the nation state model. It seems possible to achieve alternative legitimacy via procedural guarantees and safeguards instead of running after an illusive substantive-value orientated

---

[65] See Berman (1996).

legitimacy. However, that requires that we manage to integrate our principles of due process and justice into the new governance-structures, with judicial review in a transnational setting. The key issue remains: at what level do we have to formalise these procedures? At the same time, there is the risk that juridification would lead to a loss of the informal strength of the networks. Legislation in this context presents possibilities but also constraints. We have also to look at emerging new structures of co-operative enforcement and at the processes and functions of co-operation in the field. It is within that framework that we have to embed procedural safeguards for the citizen and to construct a renewed legitimacy in European integration and European governance.

9

Towards a Legal Concept of the Network in European Standard-Setting

Karl-Heinz Ladeur*

1. Standards and the Transformation of the Common Knowledge Base

1.1 The Difficulties of "Harmonisation"

Until 1985, the predominant strategy of standard-setting in product safety and environmental law was one of comprehensive European harmonisation. In product safety law, the famous *Cassis de Dijon* Case[1] had already paved the way towards a new legislative strategy: European directives were from now on to restrict themselves to formulating "essential safety requirements" which were subsequently elaborated by standardisation organisations, mainly CEN and CENELEC.[2] In environmental law,[3] there has not been such a spectacular transformation of rule making, but instead there has been a shift in emphasis from harmonisation towards procedural measures such as the Directive on environmental impact studies,[4] the environmental information Directive[5], the eco-audit Regulation[6] and the Regulation on the European Environment Agency.[7] The recent discussion on the introduction of integrated pollution control is further evidence that the institutions are focusing on procedural integration and not substantive harmonisation, and this tactic might be a recognition of the fact that

---

* Professor of Law, University of Hamburg and European University Institute, Florence.
[1] Case 120/78, *Rewe-Zentral AG* v. *Bundesmonopolverwalting für Branntwein* [1979] ECR 649.
[2] See Joerges *et al* (1988: 305 ff.); Di Fabio (1996).
[3] See Steinberg (1995: 549, 562); Eifert (1994); generally Rengeling/Gellermann (1996); Schneider (1995).
[4] Council Directive 85/337/EEC, (1985) OJ L 175/40.
[5] Council Directive 90/313/EEC, (1990) OJ L 158/56.
[6] Council Regulation (EEC) 1836/93, (1993) OJ L 168/1.
[7] (1990) OJ L 120/1.

earlier EC environmental law is suffering from increasing difficulties
surrounding its implementation. The continuous control of harmonised
law does not seem to be guaranteed where the will and the administrative
and technical capacity for the implementation of environmental law are far
from self-evident in the Member States – problems which are compounded
by the heterogeneity of general administrative law into which the specific
European norms must be integrated.[8] There are widespread fears that
future attempts to harmonise environmental law will result in the overburdening of the economically weaker Member States, whilst the environmentally more advanced Member States might engage in a race to the bottom.
Furthermore, any proposal must take into consideration the tendency to
block national environmental law by a broad interpretation of the
economic liberties and the limits to commercial discrimination which
could be seen in any kind of environmental regulation. Therefore, the
situation which exists at a European level demonstrates a conflict which is
not essentially different from those which can be observed at the national
level: the technological, economic, administrative and cultural evolution is
increasingly heterogeneous and no longer follows uniform linear trajecto-
ries which represent a common knowledge basis, a shared body of experience linked to an evolving but not fundamentally different search process
which does not question the common definition of danger limits posed by
the technical process.

1.2 "Harmonisation" and the Heterogeneity of the Technological Evolution

Although there has traditionally been a differentiation between stronger
and weaker industries within the Member States, this heterogeneity was
not so important as to prevent the formulation of a shared set of average
expectations, resting on the basis of a linkage of shared assumptions of
probabilities, cost-benefit-comparisons made on the basis of a knowledge
base accessible to the public, and a consensus on the necessity of a
technical evolution following a process of piecemeal engineering and trial
and error. This relatively homogeneous horizon of decision-making has
become a problem at the national as well as the international level because
technical evolution has accelerated and new options are no longer formulated on the basis of common experience but are designed in theoretical
scientific constructions and models. The hierarchy of general knowledge
(experience), and its application or variation in experimental settings is
undermined by challenging innovations; technology no longer follows a
decentralised trial and error process allowing for control within a rather
restricted time frame and with reference to clear criteria defining success
and failure. Instead, the technological process and the safety standards

---

[8] See Breuer (1993); Steinberg (1995: 549, 562); Kahl (1996a).

designed to avoid unintended harmful consequences can no longer be clearly separated. Technologies are becoming more complex: no longer do they comply with the model of mechanical and analytical decomposability into different elements and separate levels of hierarchy (more or less abstract and general rules and their application in concrete cases), and the consensus on the evaluation of technological progress has been severed. This phenomenon is of critical importance when developments in the Member States are taken into account, but it is pertinent to remember that it is not integration as such which has created the problem – integration has only accentuated the heterogeneity of a development which is also occurring within the Member States. The aggravation of the problem created at the European level, however, could stimulate a more profound reflection upon a new productive relationship between private actors, administrators, experts and the public, and lead to a conception which might assist the analysis of national processes of public decision-making on issues of technical safety and environmental protection.[9] Greater heterogeneity at the European level could create an incentive and the possibility to design a more adaptive model of decision-making.

This contribution analyses the co-operation between public and private decision-makers at state level and the changing role of public responsibility when they operate under conditions of complexity. It proceeds to focus on the specific conditions of co-operative standard-setting on the European level and highlights the innovative aspects of European standard setting. The paper considers whether the different national, transnational and supranational components of co-operation should not be integrated into a theoretically more sophisticated and refined version of the network concept which could be instrumental to the ongoing development of a transnational construction of European administrative law which would not rest on traditional understandings associated with either national or supranational levels.

2. Administrative Regulation and Co-operative Decision-making

2.1 Decision-making, Standards and Rules

The phenomenon of co-operation between administration and private firms has been discussed for quite some time in the administrative and constitutional law of the Member States. In Germany, this has given rise to numerous publications on "informal administrative action" (*informales Verwaltungshandeln*) replacing or supplementing authoritative decisions.[10] A whole range of different levels and modes of distributing responsibilities

---

[9] See generally Joerges/Ladeur/Vos (eds.) (1997).
[10] See Schulze-Fielitz (1994); Schneider (1996); Röhl (1996).

between public and private actors has come to the fore:[11] it may concern the collection of facts on which the public decision is based (license), but it may also comprise decision-making and control. The private establishment of expertise and evaluation of risk are two new versions of a kind of "procedural privatisation" (*Verfahrensprivatisierung*), which reduces public normative control of complex technological decisions.[12] At this point, different types of more or less abstract levels of action have to be taken into account and this is particularly so in the case of establishing standards.

Standardisation itself can take on various forms especially with respect to the generation of the knowledge basis: reference can be made to existing experience, to more explicitly agreed upon interpretative practices and even to formalised private or public standards including rules on procedure. Procedural rules come in different forms and in various degrees of legal enforceability: they can be attributed to the explicit force of law,[13] they can have special weight as expertise, or they can be given a presumption of conformity.[14] Norms can be referred to explicitly by way of legal norms (laws) and they can be given legal value indirectly in the form of definitions of legal concepts such as "risk" or "danger". Reference to standards can be static (specific norms) or dynamic (a changing set of standards), standards can be differentiated according to various levels of more or less advanced knowledge (scientific rules). Furthermore, the role of public decisions on norms can vary from control on a case by case basis after the fact, or the mere publication of established private norms to various forms of *a priori* control.[15] The typology[16] could even be differentiated still further, but it would only accentuate the impression that cooperation between private and public decision-makers in standard setting has abolished the hitherto clear-cut separation between binding general rules for which the state can be held responsible, general experience which is beyond the reach of both individual and public decision-makers, and specific facts which were to be gleaned from private addressees of decisions.[17]

The idea that an administration is bound by laws is one which is closely linked to bureaucratic principles of impersonal and detached decision-making which should allow for a decision relating the specific elements of the case to a general rule, thereby transcending personal narrow interests. In the same vein, the broad concept of "danger" which permits intervention in private interests, gains sharper contours within liberal administrative law. It is used for a more specific differentiation between decisions

[11] See Schuppert (1994); idem (1995: 761 ff.).
[12] See Hoffmann-Riem/Schneider (1996).
[13] See *Bundesverwaltungsgericht*, BVerwG 72, 300, 316 ff.; Wahl (1991: 409 ff.).
[14] See Di Fabio (1990).
[15] See Schneider (1991).
[16] See Di Fabio (1994b); Marburger (1979: 395ff.); idem (1982).
[17] See Joerges/Ladeur/Vos (eds.) (1997).

intervening in private action in order to protect an established set of legally attributable public or private goods (from danger), on the one hand, and the prospective improvement of this set of goods.[18] The latter version of administrative action is subordinated to the former inasmuch as it is only used in order to supplement the presupposed tendency of social evolution to return to a stable equilibrium (e.g. by buffering private life risks in a public insurance system). Furthermore, the law of technical safety is characterised by its orientation on a set of experiences which are prone to continual progress but can be used as a stable frame of reference in both private and public decision-making.[19]

The structure of the formation of expectations channelled by this evolution of a shared experience appears to be much more important for the role of public administration than the formal question of whether the administration is bound by the general law: neither in the more active strategies of decision-making nor in the classical domain of interventionist police-law can the law alone give express guidance to decision-makers. The concept of "danger" is necessarily tied to a set of basic assumptions on causal attributions, probabilities of events, decomposability of social complexity into identifiable relationships between causes and effects, and regularities which cannot form an explicit part of the law itself. For this reason Mayer[20] could assume that for German administrative law the "hunger for norms" is not so developed in administration as it is in court procedure. The stability and normativity of structured expectations, of a social knowledge basis allowing for reliable reality constructions and attribution of responsibility according to a concept of social causality is of much more importance for administration. And it is this paradigmatic orientation which structures social complexity: separating universal rules, specific facts and situative adaptation to new possibilities which allows for hierarchical organisation and the implicit differentiation between rules and decisions.

2.2 *Consensual Decision-making and the Transformation of Law*

The push towards a more consensual approach in decision-making can only be described and analysed adequately if the change within the social knowledge basis is considered. Until now, the trend to replace or supplement authoritative decision by bargaining processes has been characterised by approaches which remain as "informal" and conceptually unstructured as are the observed practices of mutual arrangements: "informal" administrative action is regarded as guaranteeing willingness of the addressees to implement established programmes or as being more adaptable to the

---

[18] See the famous *"Kreuzberg"* judgment of the Prussian *Oberverwaltungsgericht*, PrOVG 9, 353, 376 ff.

[19] See Ladeur (1994a: 199 ff.).

[20] See Mayer (1924: 88).

challenges of complicated cases.[21] This new approach is said to fit into a logic of planning, focusing more on setting purposes and aims instead of clearly structured action-oriented norms. Implementing the purposes and aims is said to be left to bargaining processes between private and public decision-makers. Of course, this is not completely wrong, because there are many phenomena which fit into this approach, but it is doubtful whether the complexity of the transformation of administrative decision-making under conditions of uncertainty can be adequately described by this approach. Rather, it has to be recognised that all the phenomena of informal action and bargaining processes mirror a much more profound change which needs new conceptual analysis. The critical point is not the adaptation of general norms to situations, or the definition of purposes by co-ordinated public and private action. What is necessary is rather a shift from a hierarchical substantive orientation, to be found in given rules and aims, to a horizontal heterarchical and procedural approach, operating with the localised and linked potential generated from private and public action and the linkages inherent to them. This means that there are no longer universal rules and substantive aims to be applied or adapted to specific situations but that productive "areas of change" have to be defined in a co-operative process of co-ordination of private and public interests within a common strategy.[22] This is not equivalent to the assumption that public interest consists in nothing else than the reinforcement of private decisions. Rather, the strict separation between private (specific) and public (general) interests is itself undermined by the fact that the orientation by a common knowledge basis, to be found by experiences of steering expectations in private and public decision-making, is replaced, or at least transformed, by constraints to design, construct and experiment with new options generated under conditions of complexity which calls into question the hitherto established lines of separation.

2.3 Technical Safety Law and the Changing Role of Organisations

This changing role of organisations can be seen clearly in the area of technical safety law: the concept of danger and its prevention through police law never consisted in the imposition of a purely external limit on private action protected by civil liberties, but it presupposed a shared common knowledge basis of practical experience. Private and public decision-makers found orientation in their mutual strategies of evaluating and testing the acceptability of new options within a given pool of variety considered to conform to an equilibrium model. The technological paths seemed to evolve on the basis of a trial and error process which allowed for correction within a limited time scale; this model attributed different roles

[21] Dose (1994: 91 ff.); Schulze-Fielitz (1996).
[22] See Schuppert (1994) and (1995).

to private and public decision-makers but at the same time it presupposed a common frame of reference which allowed for mutual observation, trust and co-ordination. Private actors knew in principle where the limits of danger had to be respected and the administrators could decide with reference to a shared body of experience which on the one hand had been generated from private action but which, on the other, contained the potential for self-control because its regularities were beyond the reach of the individuals contributing to its evolution.

It is exactly this common frame of reference which, in recent times, has been shattered by the fact that new technical evolutions seem to conform less and less to the continuity of common experience and established paths of evolution but instead follow complex designs and theoretical modelling. Technology itself calls into question the separation between rules and application; it has to construct, observe and experiment with limits which are no longer evident from rules of experience to be transgressed in a trial and error approach.

In my view, this is the main reason for the development of new forms of co-operation between administration and private actors – a development which also allows a more adequate conceptual reflection of the ongoing transformation. The new comprehensive technological evolution[23] is also undermining the stable frame of reference administrators could rely upon in controlling private action because the guiding light of experience is fading for both public and private actors. Private and public decision-makers are confronted by uncertainty and a multiplicity of options. It is important to accept that the phenomenon is primarily concerning private actors. Because of this fundamental transformation, a merely descriptive phenomenology of the whole range of different distributions and levels of responsibility between state and enterprises is not sufficient. After the rise and establishment of corporatist forms of integration and the participation of representative groups in administration, which was characteristic of the welfare state (trade unions, political parties, and trade associations), we are now confronted with a completely new paradigm of co-ordination.[24] The model of the welfare state was based on the assumption of a balancing of representative interests which had to be collected by intermediary links between the private sphere and the state-oriented domain of public interest. The new forms of co-ordination do not follow the same pattern: the role of representative organisations is diminishing and instead companies, groups of companies and especially citizens' groups are coming to the fore as the main actors trying to co-operate with administration.[25]

---

[23] See Foray/Grübler (1996: 3 ff.).
[24] See Grande (1996).
[25] See Teubner (1993); idem (1996).

3. From Experience to Experimentation with
New Technological Options

The transformation outlined above can be demonstrated in more detail with reference to the example of technical norms[26] inasmuch as they are not only designed to guarantee uniformity of basic characteristics but also to specify safety requirements. The new element in standardisation does not so much consist in a growing dominance of private actors, such as companies, because this was always the case: technical experience as such is a product of private actors, not of public norms. Change rather concerns the multiplicity of options, the different time horizons (short term *versus* long term perspectives) and the weakening integrative force of experience which calls into question the separation of experiential rules and their application. The new technologies are much more likely to generate this charge, as their design creates new paths of evolution and new domains of option which can no longer be observed and evaluated on the basis of a shared knowledge basis, but which create, in an experimental way, their own reference.[27]

This means that the technical rules themselves are no longer out of reach of decision-makers as was the case in the past. The design of technology creates its own frame of reference, but this does not necessarily mean that technical norms formulated by private organisations are equivalent to legal norms in the strict sense and that a public "final responsibility" (*Letztverantwortung*) of public authorities in the form of a "controlled reception" of standards should be insisted on, and that for legal reasons a kind of formal rule of recognition is crucial.[28] This assumption is not very plausible because the complexity of the standard-setting process and the uncertainty of its cognitive basis renders impossible meaningful substantive responsibility of the state. According to my view, the constraints of co-operation as such have not changed in this field of action, the difference resides only in the fact that rules and application in technology are no longer separate, that the evolution is more rapid and that the multiplicity of options allows for more alternatives of compromise between conflicting values and interests (such as cost *versus* safety).[29]

In the past, the administration and the courts have restricted their control to a kind of standard of consistency and plausibility in the sense of guaranteeing a reflected and enlightened practice, with the result that they have not expanded to an autonomous public standard of evaluation of the risks and benefits of technological evolution.[30] This is exactly the point from which, in my view, the design of a new co-operation of private and

[26] See Brennecke (1996).   [27] See Favereau (1989: 21 ff.); idem (1993).
[28] See Di Fabio (1996: 109 and 136 ff.); Nicklisch (1982: 67 ff.); idem (1983).
[29] See Fiorino (1996: 457 ff.).   [30] See Di Fabio (1996); Marburger (1979).

public in this domain could depart: in the same way as administration has drawn its evaluations and assessments on the basis of experience generated from private action in a substantive way, the more complex process of design and experimentation with new technological options could now be structured in a more procedural way by constraints established in order to keep the process itself open to alternatives and thereby guarantee sensitivity for unintended side effects and exploration risks which can no longer be controlled by experience alone.[31]

Proceduralisation in this sense is not only and not even primarily concerned with the establishment of a schematic procedure in a legal sense but should focus on the process of knowledge generation as such, i.e. its productivity, its openness to different search criteria, for self-observation and self-control, for a linkage between design and experimenting with technologies in practice (monitoring) and the integration of systematic risk assessment into the technical process. It is only on the basis of a given prestructure that a meaningful public role in the process of technology can be imagined because the spontaneous character of experience, as a shared public knowledge basis, cannot be presupposed as a starting point.

4. Integrating Knowledge Generation into Decision-making

In recent times, the public regulatory process has often been faced with a twin criticism: its lack of flexibility and the overburdening of private and administrative decision-makers.[32] The multiplicity of alternatives and the strategic character of technical decisions to be made under conditions of complexity have led to an overestimation of the possibility of an autonomous state control based on substantive criteria, with the result that there is a risk of a deadlock of regulatory strategies. An alternative cannot be simply to opt for the flexibility, thereby lowering the standards of public control, although this is a tendency which is quite widespread throughout the Member States.[33] The preferred strategy should rather be to search for a functional equivalent to experience as a common frame of reference for public and private action. This alternative can only be seen in a procedural perspective which would not so much stress the substantive requirements of giving reasons but which would shift the emphasis to the transformation of the process of knowledge generation itself and would therefore try to guarantee the productivity and flexibility of this process, by allowing for the experimental use of new technology on the condition that a systematic post-market control is established so that companies do not just wait for bad experiences to occur.

---

[31] See Denninger (1990).
[32] See only Breyer (1993); Finkel/Golding (1994); Viscusi (1996).
[33] See Trute (1996); Kloepfer/Elsner (1996); see generally Di Fabio (1996).

The solution cannot be found in a kind of pluralisation that would allow for the integration of competing interests because this would amount to a copy of the established model of corporatist administration (and which we might therefore label a micro-corporatist approach). This micro-corporatism does not fit into the framework outlined above because it does not pay sufficient attention to the fundamental changes taking place within the process of knowledge generation itself. Instead, the solution should establish a systematic linkage of the design character of current technology with the plurality of different aspects of empirical, methodological, normative and theoretical concerns. The relationship between private and public decision-makers with reference to experience could be remodelled by a productive combination of the self-regulation of industry and public regulation which complements their differing social functions. But this cannot be achieved by focusing only on substantive requirements or a merely formal responsibility of the state. This strategy would also allow for a more differentiated adaptation of regulations to specific industries taking into account the different level of technological capacities of small, medium and large industry: smaller firms could on the one hand be given incentives to establish circles with a view to searching for flexible solutions for productive safety and environment-related technical problems. On the other hand, smaller firms could be exempted from a basic standard which has already been achieved in larger firms. The development of strategic arrangements encouraging research may be more desirable than the implementation of just one uniform industry-wide standard.[34]

Clearly, the problem of standard setting under conditions of uncertainty has to be reconstructed beyond pragmatic approaches of flexibilisation. This is possible if we attempt to build a bridge between the knowledge problem of the past and its present transformation into the complex technological developments of today. A new strategy can only be designed within a process of a search for a functional equivalent to established modes of co-ordination by a systematic development of the procedural and methodological aspects of the knowledge generation process. The organisational dimension of this strategy could be designed with reference to the network concept.[35] The use of this ill-defined concept, which is already quite familiar to political scientists,[36] seems to focus on the necessity of stable inter-organisational co-operation and an overlap of formal and informal institutional co-ordination. Within the administrative and legal sciences, the concept could rather be productive inasmuch as it could allow for a more temporalised and heterarchical approach, stressing the need to impose new structures on relationships which have developed as informal ones in the shadow of institutionalised responsibility. Furthermore the network concept could serve as a frame of reference for the linkage of

---

[34] See Fiorino (1996: 483); Braithwaite/Ayres (1992).
[35] See Pitschas (1995).   [36] See only Dowding (1995).

different decision-makers (administrative and private actors, experts, citizens' groups) and different types of contributions (procedural criteria, methodological rules, private design of technology, self-regulation of risk-assessment and post-market control, regulation of supplementary public control and group rights, etc.) which are to be tied together within a better-structured process of decision-making under conditions of complexity.

5. In Search of a New Procedural Concept of Public-Private Co-operation

5.1 The Concept of "Network" and its Use in a Flexible Regulatory Approach

The trend towards a more co-operative approach to public action has given rise to a pragmatic descriptive and phenomenological attitude in the administrative and legal sciences. Besides this arid approach, there has also been a normative reflection on how to remodel administrative and public tasks in general. According to the normative account, there is a new conception of a better-defined core of public functions at stake, but a closer look at the arguments advanced by the protagonists of this position might raise some doubt as to whether this is a productive approach[37] because it still seems to start from the assumption of a presupposed hierarchy of public over private decisions. A more sensitive approach must acknowledge that it was the welfare state, and its tendency to end in deadlock, which left out the search for structure which had been inherent to the liberal legal system: majority rule and the concept of positive law are in fact based on the assumption that, within basic institutional rules, it is opinion which lays the ground for public order.

This assumption is also valid for technical safety law because safety standards are linked to experience which combines knowledge with practice but they should not be viewed as a derivative of a hierarchy of values. This assumption can be used as a starting point for the description of the continuing change in the relationship between private and public responsibility: it does not seem to be helpful to set up a more abstract range of values and public interest and to ask for more flexibility in the implementation process. It would be more productive to look back to the liberal idea of process and its generative potential: this idea has to be detached from the hierarchy of the general ideas in the specific situation and from the assumption of the centrality of the public as a central forum of reflection, separating the limited particularities of a case from the rational form of the general law. Similarly, the relationship between shared rules of experience and the specific aspects of an experiment should be

---

[37] See, for a critique, Naschold (1993: 41).

exposed to the test of trial and error. A new version of procedure, of constructing public interests from a process of experimentation, could be based on the assumption that the search process itself should be regarded as operating on the basis of a heterarchical linkage of private and public action and on the hope of finding a productive pattern of self-stabilising co-ordination, generated from emergent effects of self-organisation, instead of a top down rule structuring social complexity. This approach does not mean a plea to adapt to private action, but to follow the line which was drawn by the liberal legal system and to adapt it to changing conditions. "Public interests" should be understood as emanating from a linking of private and public actions, the observation of which allows for the identification of productive co-operative patterns, of tentative or provisional controls on the consistency and circumstantial viability of actions.

5.2 The EC and Openness to Institutional Reforms

On the basis of this assumption, the network concept could gain greater shape as a legal and administrative construction. The State no longer has its place at the centre of society from which the rules for the conservation of the equilibrium of society can be conceived and formulated. Neither inside the public nor the private spheres can order any longer be constructed as hierarchical. The State has to adapt to a new experimental logic of modelling new domains of option beyond experience, and only on the basis of this more general idea is the observation and description of a whole range of different types of public responsibility meaningful.[38] Co-operation is neither collusion nor a farewell to decision-making in the stricter sense but the logic of action changes because the public interest can only be conceived of as a product of a heterarchical relational rationality, of a search for viable patterns actions dependent on modelling, operating with situative constraints and (self-)observation.[39] (Of course, this does not completely exclude substantive criteria which are rather derived from experience as in the past: the value of safety as such need not be generated from a search process but it does not give us much orientation in decision-making.) Furthermore, this approach does not preclude setting priorities, but it means that they cannot be separated from the co-operative search process itself. Consequently, priorities have to be "derived" from the operation with self-generated constraints set by mainly private actors. This "positive" approach can be helpful because it prevents us from the overestimation of values and it places much more pressure on a public policy (particularly its effects) than on a policy which lays claim to high values which of course can be primarily used as an excuse for not attaining them once the project has become so ambitious and its enemies, numerous and powerful.

The same kind of objections militate against the insistence on the

---

[38] See, generally, Crozier (1991).   [39] See Favereau (1989).

superior validity of "public interests" in the established sense of the hierarchy of the public over the private domain:[40] this normative approach can easily end up in a mere illusion of control and at the same time neglect the possibilities inherent in a more modest understanding, playing down the centrality of state power but opening up new possibilities of a procedural co-operative model of decision-making and standard-setting.

Although the dilemma is equally applicable to the EC, it achieves an extra dimension because of the evolving and incomplete nature of the institutional structure of integration. Whilst this growth could be open to new experimental models of decision-making, there is a real risk that continuing to operate on the established state-oriented track will be a less suitable means of dealing with conflicts because of the diverse national and cultural backgrounds. Pursuing this tactic in the area of supranational standard-setting is undesirable because "scientific" and technological "neutral" requirements could superimpose order on a very heterogeneous domain of options[41] with the result that conflicts would be driven into the murky world of implementation.

6. The "New Approach" and the Case for Differentiation

6.1 Uniform Standards and their Heterogeneous Contexts

The area of technical safety law has particular problems which stem from the national and cultural differences in the linkages between risks, norms, products and administrative measures.[42] At a European level, there is no shared knowledge or information, no common framework capable of processing the information that does exist and finally there is no sophisticated administrative control to ensure that the standards conform to the essential safety requirements. In the absence of a shared framework it is difficult to identify these essential safety requirements since there is a close link between normative prescriptions and their cognitive basis. Consequently national administrators will find it almost impossible to contradict the presumption of conformity of European standards with substantive safety requirements formulated in European directives.[43]

6.2 The Necessity to Introduce more Variety into Standard-Setting

The pressure on private enterprises to adapt to standards can be much higher at the European level than with reference to national standards because of the greater degree of uncertainty attached to the administrators

---

[40] See Reichard (1994); Bauer/Reichard (1993); Hood (1991: 3 ff.); König (1995).
[41] See Waterton/Wynne (1996); see Rasmussen (1997: 15-31).
[42] Recent analyses of the New Approach include Falke (1997) and Krieger (1992).
[43] See Breuer (1993); Marburger/Enders (1994).

who elaborate the conformity of alternative safety devices with the basic safety requirements. Although some directives allow for a certification of alternatives[44] beyond European norms, this does not change the underlying problem and it also tends to block technological innovation and diversity because the standards do not have legally binding force. The problem is aggravated by the European process of standard-setting which ignores different groups and types of enterprises present in an industrial sector: smaller and medium-size firms tend not to be represented in the European process.[45] Because of these structural shortcomings in the European standard-setting process, an explicit institutional device guaranteeing administrative assistance for innovative products should be integrated into the procedure. One could even go a step further and create incentives for the organisation of circles of smaller firms trying to develop alternative technologies. The possibility should also be taken into account of favouring quality management procedures rather than specific technology oriented norms; innovative elements of this approach can be found in the Directive on Construction Products.[46] In any event, because the technological process no longer follows established paths, the potentially harmful side-effects of standardisation should be taken more seriously into account, particularly at a European level, and be compensated by strategies explicitly introducing new alternatives into the technical process.

A more open process of standard-setting at a European level could be achieved from a regulatory approach which would shift from substantive safety requirements to more structured procedural and methodological criteria which would pay more attention to the collection of data, assumptions underlying standards, cost-benefit-analysis, priorities underlying decision-making and evaluation of inherent uncertainties, including a prestructure for post-market observation.

7. Transnational Networks as an Alternative to both Supranational and National Decision-making

7.1 Shifting the Stress to Procedural and Methodological Criteria

Given that experience no longer produces practical standards for the assessment and evaluation of risks in relation to competing interests, criteria must be developed within the process of standard-setting itself.

This problem is linked to several uncertainties of different types; empirical, theoretical, methodological, and normative. But this lack of a presupposed separation of different hierarchical levels of decision-making within

---

[44] See Kilian (1996: 360 ff.); Di Fabio (1996: 24 ff.); Kiehl (1990).

[45] See Di Fabio (1996: 43 ff. and 114 ff.); Kilian (1996: 359).

[46] See Di Fabio (1994b).

the European system could be used in a productive way by integrating and structuring the different problems in order to build a bridge to the problem of post-market control and the design of a monitoring structure. This approach would allow for a productive relationship between partial knowledge and the design of a model for (self-)observation of experimental procedures with the intention of finding viable approaches.

Emphasising the need to link different procedural, methodological, cognitive, cultural and normative components of decision-making could also contribute to a specification of the network concept whose productivity consists in the fact that it describes a non-hierarchical relationship among heterogeneous actors generating patterns of interaction which are not to be reduced to mutual exchange processes because they have a productive property calling into question hitherto established limits and the separation of established levels of decision-making. This could mean that stress has to be laid on methodological and procedural aspects of decision-making once new possibilities have to be designed, generated and tested in a more structured way and the orientation potential of experience and rules has faded. An example of the practical consequences of this approach can be found in the change of American and British regulation to cost-benefit-analysis as a method to impose more structure on regulation and which stresses the necessity of observing and evaluating the process of standard-setting and not keeping rules separate from decisions.[47] This procedural approach could also allow for a more promising mode of integration of public interest groups which in fact cannot participate in a meaningful way in all the detailed decisions on standards but structure, method and priorities cannot be taken as a stable and definite frame of reference.

This idea could be linked to the general question of the function of standards: under conditions of growing complexity standards should rather – beyond clearly demarcated danger limits – be designed in a more open and optional way such as to allow for national and technical alternatives. The risks for the internal market inherent in this conception could be reintroduced into the approach itself in a proceduralised version by establishing duties to observe competing norms in view of the potential creation of unintended negative effects for protection from health and comparable risks. The question of the acceptability of supplementary national requirements imposed on products which are in conformity with European norms should also be treated in a less restrictive way; of course, access to markets as such cannot be called into question where the conditions of exemption procedure are not satisfied, but apart from this it is far from evident that taxes and financial discrimination on, for example, environmentally less acceptable products, should be completely excluded.

---

[47] See US House of Representatives March 1995, No. 122.

7.2 Variety, Competition and Comparison in
European Standard-setting

Where legal requirements impose changes in the production and distribution process (packaging) after the barriers seem to have been overcome without unacceptable cost, Article 130r (2) EC presupposes an integrative approach to environmental policy notwithstanding the absence of institutional and organisational conditions. Consequently, Member States should be given greater flexibility to experiment in environmental regulation. It is conceivable that more onerous environmental regimes resulting in additional costs for the introduction of products from other Member States could only be accepted on condition that a transnational co-ordination among several Member States, with a certain percentage of the total EC population, takes place in order to avoid too much heterogeneity and to keep the cost of adaptation to different regulatory regimes low. But why should it not be acceptable to impose, for example, packaging requirements on firms which affect only one third of the EC? Resolving unavoidable conflicts could be the task of an arbitration institution which could decide disputes by majority. Such an institution would appear to be much more legitimate than an awkward compromise on a European standard. Furthermore, this institution could be responsible for evaluating the heterogeneous standards within the EC. Even without an arbitration institution, standard-setting should no longer be so oriented towards uniformity – which in any case is rather fictitious given the degree of economic divergence – except where there are clear risks of blocking market integration. Instead, a more open procedural conception of integration using competition, mutual observation, institutionalised comparison of different rules and constraints to observe the transnational effects of national rules could be considered. Focusing on procedures could help to link European policy more effectively to an all-embracing modernisation strategy including the state level instead of there being a constant search for embarrassing compromises – a strategy which is not really adapted to the above mentioned necessities of adaptation to conditions of uncertainty.

The network aspect of this approach would consist not only in replacing integrated decision-making by co-operation but also in a more fundamental change to a relational logic of search and experimentation, of generating new options and designing new option domains through an a-centric heterarchical trans- and supranational process of self-organisation. The EC would then be understood as a decision-making unit encouraging productive processes of self-transformation in the transnational emergent network of interrelationships between Member States, which are themselves to be viewed as co-operative networks of networks and not as sovereign units.

8. "Co-operative Law" instead of Unification

Abandoning the desire for uniformity is equally applicable to similar ideas for the regulatory conception of the EC itself, particularly in the area of environmental law. The existing paradigm is too much centred on unity, and again it should be clear that the alternative to unity is not just diversity but a more proceduralised process of overlapping search and monitoring processes which the Member States could stimulate by setting different priorities according to different expectations. For example, it is not evident that all the Member States should have the same emission standards for potentially harmful industrial installations. This assumption could be expanded to emission standards as well because of differential cost-benefit relationships. Of course, this does not mean that environmental and technical safety regulations and risk assessment should not be regulated at all at the European level; on the contrary, approaches, methods and priorities should be permitted to be different and at the same time should be mutually linked by obligations to compare, to explain and to evaluate.

One could also think about a compensation model which could set certain standards, but leave Member States the possibility of changing priorities and approaches without abandoning the requirements of the common standard. An independent institution could control the range of possibilities used by a Member State with the result that environmental policy could be encouraged but without running the risk of a huge implementation gap developing behind the veil of compromise. Concentrating on the procedural aspects must be taken seriously, given the differences within the legal and administrative systems of Member States which impose real constraints on achieving strict integration. Clearly, establishing an environmental inspectorate will not be particularly successful unless environmental policy is part of an integrated approach that is accepted by Member States and adapted to their legal and administrative system.

Although the establishment of an environmental inspectorate would not be free from problems, it would at least reveal the risks, thereby making them more observable and manageable. The network conception of integration would not tend to reduce the supranational character of the EC altogether but it would instead attempt to focus on a transnational mutual permeability of administrative organisation and procedure in order to set up a European network-like administration.[48] The supranational component should find a place in this a-centric heterarchical process; simultaneously European law would be able to develop a new vision of administration which would be adapted to respond to the evolution of co-operative administration.

---

[48] See Kahl (1996b); Ladeur (1996b).

Consequently it would be possible to reformulate the link between European law and general principles of national administrative law. Again, the aim should not consist of harmonisation in a traditional state-oriented way because the *effet utile* of secondary Community law must be guaranteed. The arguments to be considered in this respect do not draw on national interest and the preservation of cultural values but rather on the general problem that the complexity of phenomena facing the law can no longer be tackled by classical understandings of law. We need a new approach to the design of a "co-operative law" which transcends pragmatic adaptation to economic constraints. The approach should, in this respect, be directed to the question of whether and to what extent different national versions of implementation of European law risk leading to deadlock in the integration process or whether more heterogeneity could lead to more productive trial and error processes and mutual stimulations of change. An example of the first alternative would be the case of a subsidy granted by national authorities. In this case a protection of formerly legitimate expectations based upon national law cannot be accepted because of the close interrelationship of mutually imposed self-restrictions. On the other hand it is far from evident that the implementation of European environmental law and its effects especially on the procedure of decision-making (e.g. environmental impact assessment) should be the same in each Member State as long as they are based upon doctrinal and systematic deliberations. This assumption presupposes that the integration process should be differentiated with respect to strict and loosely mutual interrelationships. The potential fluctuation of implementation of European environmental law will not necessarily inflict harm on other Member States once a specific margin of manoeuvrability is accepted. The focus should in this case rather be shifted to mutual observation and comparison, creating constraints to expose clandestine presumptions and to integrate a general co-operative, interpretative topos into the legal systems imposing consideration of possible harms inflicted on other Member States. The organisation of mutual self-observation and encouraging transnational exchange, information, comparison and critique could be overseen by the European Environment Agency.[49] Such an orientation could permit a more creative and productive role for this new agency which hitherto has been discussed with reference to a very schematic alternative between information and inspection.[50] In my view, competition of institutions and rules can be a very productive way of integration as long as it is linked to a conception of law-making and learning under conditions of complexity and is not just a simplistic transfer of the concept of "market" to a different issue.

[49] Ibid.   [50] Majone (1997); Shapiro (1997b).

9. Co-operative Learning in Transnational Networks

The modern relationship between private and public, general rules and specific applications, the common knowledge base and private innovation, administration and enterprises, has brought fundamental changes to the legal process which must be reflected within the broader legal system. Rules can no longer be understood as isolated from the specific decision-making process and a component of learning and modelling new option domains without a reliable knowledge basis must be integrated into the legal process. Co-operation must be given a more productive meaning that extends beyond a merely pragmatic constraint on managing implementation problems. The area of European standard-setting has not been shielded from change, with the result that there is a clear need to reformulate administrative responsibility in decision-making to operate under conditions of complexity. Given that this process may not be comprehended at the national level, there is a compelling argument to tackle this problem at the EC level thereby taking advantage of its imperfect and open structure, which could be used in a reforming manner for the design of a new legal approach embracing Supranational and national levels. Within such an approch, public interests can only be formulated in a procedural, heterarchical way.

Procedure is not to be reduced to rules of decision-making which are not outcome-oriented (substantive rule, public interest) but means that proceduralisation is bound to structure different aspects of uncertainty within a co-operative learning-process, generating new option domains and new knowledge for the management of uncertainty. This is the critical issue: "solution" problem solving can no longer be expected from an application of general rules, even where combined with an empirical case analysis, nor from broader participation in decision-making procedures with the hope of finding better outcomes. However, they must rely on procedures which must be designed in an experimental attitude. The clear structure of classical decision-making has to be redesigned and adapted to a network-like procedure for the generation of new options from the experimental operation, with constraints and open possibilities, with the aim of constructing fresh patterns of self-stabilising interrelationships between heterogeneous actors. The political science concept of network can be useful provided it is adapted to the legal system and its constraints. The concept should focus on the institutional components of decision-making and the linkage of heterogeneous actors, resources, stages and levels of the decisional process within a strategy of modelling a co-operative reproductive pattern of interrelationships. For the European Community this would mean that the emphasis should be shifted from separation of national and supranational levels in a state-like approach to a transnational co-operative interrelationship which extends beyond Member States to include private actors with the result that the transnational network forms the core component of European integration and not merely unitary actors representing either supranational or national decision-makers.

SECTION 4

Comitology as Seen by Political Science

10

The European Regulation of Biotechnology by Polycratic Governance

*Christine Landfried**

1. Introduction

This contribution demonstrates that classifying the EU system as a "technocratic regime"[1] is a gross over-simplification of a complex reality. The EU decision-making procedures in the area of biotechnology involve interdependent levels of governance and new heterarchical forms of co-operation between private and public organisations. Significantly, the economic criteria of rationality do not dominate political regulation in the EU structure; ethical, ecological and democratic values are all present in the complex system of national and supranational, political and technical, legislative and executive elements which comprise the EU decision-making procedures.

It is the complexity of European integration, with its periods of stability and of instability and with its interdependencies of different interests and levels of political regulation, that has led to a system of governance which I describe as a "polycracy". Polycratic governance exists when the European decision-making process, at different levels, takes place in what Scharpf has called the "shadow of hierarchy": regulation by self-co-ordination of bargaining collective actors within a hierarchical structure.[2]

Consequently, the theory of "complex systems" is the most convincing concept to explain the integration process in Europe with its mixture of stability and instability. However, what is still missing in the system of European governance is a co-ordination of the existing plurality of ideas and criteria of rationality so as to achieve a greater degree of coherence

* Professor of Political Science, University of Hamburg.
[1] Bach (1993: 264).
[2] Scharpf (1993b: 67).

which, in turn, could inform public debate. A more coherent system would not mean returning to the old hierarchical and centralised system of political regulation if a way could be found of structuring the different levels, networks, interests and ideas which would allow the EU to progress from a polycracy towards a decentralised discourse democracy capable of combining legitimacy with efficiency and effectiveness.

In an attempt to conceptualise European governance, this article draws upon well-established dichotomies which have been used to illuminate the characteristic features of the integration process: national/supranational authority,[3] executive/legislative functions, political/technical decision-making and negative/positive integration. However, in considering these distinctions, greater attention will be paid to the different combinations of elements and the complexity of problems (Section 2), of the behaviour of the European Commission's employees (Section 3) and of the decision-making processes (Section 4). It will be argued that the characteristic feature of governance within the EU in the area of biotechnology is the mixture of national and supranational elements within each single institution, and not merely the relationship between the institutions. Equally, numerous combinations of executive and legislative functions may be identified in decision-making processes.[4] Similarly, the orientation-patterns of élites are not simply national in the Council of Ministers and supranational in the European Commission; again, there are varying combinations. Finally, it is inaccurate to describe members of the Commission as having a technocratic understanding of politics.[5]

The main thesis of this contribution is that we must take note of these various "mixtures" if we wish to understand fully the outcomes of European policy-making processes: social and ethical criteria are beginning to play an important role in European decision-making processes, and thus European governance structures may be argued to be more than a technocratic régime and to do more than merely promote economic rationality and negative integration.[6] Further, this article also examines how these new criteria of ethical and social rationality are developing and under what conditions they might be strengthened. In this vein, the chapter draws upon Lepsius' analysis which warns that the EU will only succeed in managing the contemporary problems of a single market if a variety of guiding precepts (criteria of rationality) can be developed which adequately structure attitudes toward governance. Since it is impossible to construct an internal market which leaves the social costs to the Member States alone,[7] there must be a normative debate on the appropriate combination of

---

[3] Ladeur (1995b: 244), arguing that too much attention has been paid to such a dichotomy.

[4] Bücker *et al* (1996: 55) speak of 'executive legislation within a multi-level system'.

[5] Kohler-Koch (1996: 204).   [6] Scharpf (1996b: 109).   [7] Lepsius (1995: 401).

different leading ideas in the various contexts of European governance and not merely a discussion of how greater efficiency can be achieved from the point of view of a better realisation of the ideas underlying the four freedoms of the single market.[8] An empirical analysis of the extent to which new criteria of rationality are established, and how their relative success might be explained, is an initial step which must be subsequently related to the normative debate on how governance patterns in the EU might best be reformed, because the issues of efficiency and effectiveness of European problem-solving and democratic self-determination are, for European citizens, inexorably entwined.[9] This chapter, however, takes a more modest step and focuses on one specific field of topical importance: biotechnology. Political processes in this area demonstrate that it is incorrect to speak of a purely technocratic regime. Even though exclusively technical questions are becoming increasingly rare, many political questions are nonetheless categorised and labelled as being "technical". Only if we identify the mechanisms and the interests that explain why political issues are often reduced to technical questions, can we develop ideas about how these mechanisms might be altered so that they will address what are essentially political problems in a political and democratic manner within the polycratic system of governance in the EU.

2. Complexity of Problems: Political and Technical Issues

2.1. Definitions

Following Max Weber, a technique may be defined in the following manner: a technique is the complex of means for attaining a designated aim. The technique of an action denotes the most rational way to achieve a purpose in contrast to this purpose itself. Thus, techniques exist for any action one might imagine: the technique of praying, of asceticism, of thinking and researching, of education, of political and bureaucratic ruling, of eroticism, of painting and of playing music, just to cite some of Weber's examples. According to Weber, a technical question must be resolved whenever there are doubts about the most rational way to attain a desired result.[10] Answering a technical question in Weber's sense entails

---

[8] Ibid., 403.

[9] Scharpf (1995: 567): '*wo die Effektivität gegen Null tendiert, da findet auch die Demokratie ihr Ende*'.

[10] Weber (1989: 32): '*Technik eines Handelns bedeutet uns den Inbegriff der verwendeten Mittel desselben im Gegensatz zu jenem Sinn oder Zweck, an dem es letztlich (in concreto) orientiert ist, rationale Technik eine Verwendung von Mitteln, welche bewußt und planvoll orientiert ist an Erfahrungen und Nachdenken, im Höchstfall an Rationalität: an wissenschaftlichem Denken (...) Immer bedeutet das Vorliegen einer technischen Frage: daß über die rationalsten Mittel Zweifel bestehen*'.

deciding upon the most rational means to attain a given purpose in the most appropriate and economic manner, whilst at the same time ensuring the perfection, safety and durability of success.[11]

Applying Weber's definition of technical questions, *mutatis mutandis*, it becomes clear that many questions in the field of biotechnology, which may on the surface appear to be technical, are not technical at all. A question is technical only where the technique or means chosen are neutral with respect to the purpose of the action. A choice of means in the field of biotechnology – for example, the information that is required for the authorisation of certain biotechnological experiments – is nonetheless not neutral with respect to a given objective, where this purpose is not merely progress in research, but also the protection of human health and the environment. Since the consequences of the use of certain means in biotechnology are largely unforeseeable,[12] the goal of any legal regulation will be affected where, despite all uncertainties, its operation requires detailed information on the potential effects of a specific action; the lack of comprehensive information inevitably determining that there be a political and not a technical question. Equally, regulations on biotechnology frequently have several objectives determining that the choice of means will indeed seldom be neutral with regard to the purpose of the regulation. This dilemma is clearly reflected in the German Biotechnology Act of 16 December 1993: Section 16 (1) point 3, states that a release into the environment of genetically modified organisms might be authorised only if, according to current scientific knowledge (*Stand der Wissenschaft*), no detrimental effects to human life or health, to animals and plant life, or to the environment are foreseeable, such effects being unacceptable when compared with the desired aim of promoting research into and exploiting the benefits of biotechnology.

One might, of course, simply abandon the distinction between the polit-ical and technical and presume that all questions are political in character. This solution nonetheless seems unsatisfactory since technical questions do continue to exist and, accordingly, the term does play a role in politics, though often not being precisely defined. Rather than dispense with the distinction, one should note that not many technical questions are left within policies requiring risk assessment and standard setting; and conse-quently, political scientists should address the interesting issues of when,

[11] Ibid., 32: '*Solange die Technik in unserem Wortsinn reine Technik bleibt, fragt sie lediglich nach den für diesen Erfolg, der ihr als schlechthin und indiskutabel zu erstreben gegeben ist, geeignetsten und dabei, bei gleicher Vollkommenheit, Sicherheit, Dauerhaftigkeit des Erfolges vergleichsweise kräfteökonomischsten Mitteln. Vergleichsweise, nämlich soweit überhaupt ein unmittelbar vergleichbarer Aufwand bei Einschlagung verschiedener Wege vorliegt'.*

[12] See Ladeur, who states that '(...) the technological process and the safety standards designed to avoid unintended harmful consequences can no longer be clearly separated'. Ladeur, in this volume, section 1.2.

how and why politicians pretend that they are solving purely technical questions.[13] Equally, however, the distinction between political and technical does not provide a suitable foundation upon which to base the decision as to which might be the correct level or norm for a particular policy-decision. If a political problem needs to be solved, a decision must still be taken to determine which political problems are so important that statutes and legislative procedures are required and which problems can be safely left to regulations or even to administrative guidelines. If technical questions alone were to be decided by regulations and administrative guidelines, legislative decision-making processes could be overloaded with problem-solving. Standard-setting by means of statutes may also prove too inflexible because of the many amendments which the dynamics of techno-logical progress may necessitate.[14] It appears that politicians claim to be dealing with technical rather than political questions since, in such a case, they no longer need to provide detailed reasons why a particular problem may be solved by the executive or administration. The avoidance of complex legislative procedures thus becomes easier. This indicates, however, that there must now be a greater degree of deliberation upon the requirements which determine whether norm-setting requires legislation or may take place at the administrative level, or, indeed, may be conducted by private bodies.[15] To take a purely national example, the constitutional requirements laid down in Article 80 of the German Basic Law no longer seem stringent or sensitive enough to control the delegation of problem-solving functions to the administration.

2.2. *The Case of Genetically Modified Micro-organisms (GMMOs) and Novel Food*

At European level, the tendency of politicians to claim that they are deciding upon technical questions, which are, in reality, political, is readily demonstrated by Directive 90/219/EEC on the contained use of genetically modified micro-organisms (GMMOs),[16] together with the subsequent

---

[13] I would like to thank Martin Shapiro for giving his comments on this point. His arguments convinced me to stick to the distinction between political and technical and then ask the two questions that are relevant for political science: first, the question concerning the pretension of politicians to decide on technical matters, and secondly, the question concerning the way in which technicians solve political problems. In this article, I will only deal with the first question.

[14] Ladeur (1997b: 78).

[15] Denninger (1990: 15): '*Jedenfalls auf allen Ebenen der Normsetzung, bis hinab zum Verordnungs- und Satzungsrecht und bis zur Einbeziehung technischer Regelwerke in das staatliche Normensystem, sind Entscheidungen zu treffen, die auch politischen Charakter tragen, die nicht allein aus der Kenntnis der einzusetzenden Mittel, sondern auch in Verantwortung für die Auswahl der anzustrebenden Ziele zu fällen sind*'.

[16] (1990) OJ L 117/1.

amendments made to it. The Directive established two risk groups of GMMOs (Group I and II), with a simplified procedure being applied for the notification of Group I micro-organisms. Although a decision upon the group to which a GMMO belongs is related to the purpose of protection and is, therefore, a political question, the Directive nonetheless qualifies the classification decision as being of purely technical relevance. According to Article 20 of the Directive, the classification criteria (Annex II) might be amended by a regulatory committee in order to adapt the Directive to "technical progress". Subsequently, the Directive was amended in this manner, and now contains a new classification list and more general criteria which govern the classification of Group I micro-organisms.[17] Meanwhile, plans have emerged to enlarge the scope of Article 20 in such a manner that all and not merely some of the annexes might be amended by the Commission in co-operation with a regulatory committee, so that every annex might be adapted to technical progress through this simplified procedure. Importantly, should this new draft of the Directive be approved, the scope of the application of the regulation of the use of GMMOs (Annex I) will be liable to amendment through the comitology procedure.[18] It should be noted, however, that fierce debate has always surrounded the scope of application of rules for the regulation of biotechnology, with the most recent example being the debate upon the Regulation on Novel Foods and Novel Food Ingredients. The controversial question of the Regulation's scope and the exact range of novel foods and food ingredients which must be labelled, was indeed only finally settled upon after the intervention of the joint Council and Parliament Conciliation Committee.[19] Clearly, which particular organisms and which specific experiments fall under a norm, are not questions which are at all neutral with regard to the purpose of the norm, and secondly, they are political questions of such importance that they should not be tackled by a regulatory committee, but should instead be decided upon by a full legislative procedure. Therefore, we must think about a way to limit the scope of policy-making by committees. Clear criteria for the work of these committees must be developed, and that these criteria must be determined by the legislative is but one of the principles which – besides rules – should be applied to comitology.[20] What Martin

[17] Council Directive 94/51/EC adapting to technical progress Council Directive 90/219/EEC on the Contained Use of Genetically Modified Micro-organisms, (1994) OJ L 297/29.

[18] COM(95) 640 final, 3 and 8.

[19] See the second reading of the European Parliament. Debates of the European Parliament, 12 March 1996, OJ (EC) Annex no 4-478, 8ff and the amended Commission proposal COM(96) 229 final. For the compromise of the Conciliation Committee, see the Press Release of 28 November 1996 of the Fraktion der Sozialdemokratischen Partei Europas.

[20] Toeller/Hofmann (forthcoming) demonstrate that 'principles' have been neglected in decisions on comitology.

Shapiro has demonstrated with the American experiences with the judicial control of science-based decision-making is equally true for the debate on European comitology as well: "Legislatures (...) should specify how they want regulatory agencies to deal with uncertainties, hiatuses and probabilities".[21]

Besides specifying criteria for the decision-making of committees especially with regard to risk-assessment, it would also make sense for members of the European Parliament to participate in the work of the committees. The participation of the MEPs could strengthen the democratic legitimacy of comitology and, at the same time, could make it more difficult for policy-makers to pretend that they are solving technical questions. The important point is to "structure incentives for policy makers that lead them to highlight the elements of discretion in their decisions and not hide them behind false claims of scientific exactitude".[22] The inclusion of MEPs into the decision-making of committees could be such an incentive.

The process of defining political questions as being overwhelmingly technical in character, and thus reducing the transparency of decision-making, might also be observed in Directive 90/220/EEC on the deliberate release into the environment of genetically modified organisms (GMOs).[23] The Directive contains a complex market authorisation procedure for GMOs. Prior to entering the Community market, the producer or importer of a GMO must seek authorisation from a national agency which, subsequently, hands over the documentation on the authorisation process to the Commission. The Commission circulates details of the documentation amongst all Member States. If one Member State objects to market entry, and where this objection is well grounded, a final decision is taken according to the comitology procedure.[24] In other words, a political decision on whether a specific product may enter the European market, which is of great relevance for health protection, has been handed over to the "executive legislation" of the Commission in co-operation with a regulatory Committee. This surrender to comitology is also true for certain of the annexes which may also be adapted to technical progress. Annexes II and III contain a detailed list of the information which must be supplied upon application for the notification of and authorisation for the release of GMOs into the environment and a list of additional information which is required should an application be made to place a GMO on the market. The question as to how much information should be provided for the notification, relates to and seeks to fulfil one of the Directive's objectives: the protection of human health and the environment.[25] However, according to Article 20, the question of adequate information is interpreted as being

---

[21] Shapiro (1997a: 342).   [22] Ibid., 342.   [23] (1990) OJ L 117/15.
[24] Article 13 in conjunction with Article 21 of Directive 90/220/EEC, above, note 23.
[25] Article 1(1) of Directive 90/220/EEC, above, note 23.

technical in nature, and the Directive has consequently been adapted to "technical progress" through the creation of a new category of genetically modified plants, whose release into the environment both for experimental and commercial reasons requires less information for notification than other organisms do.[26]

In addition, however, a growing number of problems in the field of biotechnology are characterised by a close relationship between means and ends. The manner in which risk assessment is structured has consequences for the material objective of a specific policy. The evaluations of the effect of techniques on the purpose may change upon the development of new knowledge, experience or "theoretical scientific construction and models",[27] and thus a temporal factor arises. For example, it has been found that using biological means to reduce pollutants might create potential risks due to the earlier release of certain GMOs into the environment.[28] Thus, this new knowledge determines that the information required under Directive 90/220/EEC in order to assess whether GMOs might be released into the environment, should, in future, also include additional information about the interaction between the biological destruction of pollutants and the release of GMOs.

Yet, there remain no clear criteria governing the process of observation or, indeed, agreement as to the duration of the assessment; consequently, this prevents a coherent determination of the consequences of the release of GMOs into the environment. The field trials of a limited release are not representative because they do not reflect the circumstances surrounding mass commercial production. This is why it has been proposed to institutionalise, parallel to commercialisation, an obligation to observe the interaction between the released GMOs and the environment.[29] A first step in this direction has been undertaken by Commissioner Ritt Bjerregaard with her project to establish a register in order to provide a database with data on the modifications introduced in GMO products released into the environment. With such a register, the European Commission wishes to initiate post-release observation and control of GMOs.[30]

The structure of problems in biotechnology and the difficulties of differentiating first, between political and technical questions, and secondly, between political questions that require legislative procedures and political questions that can be left to executive procedures, make it possible to deploy the power of definitions so as to reduce transparency and restrict democratic procedures. This is clearly the case with regard to the new draft amendment to Directive 90/219/EEC which proposes that, in future, every annex to the Directive, and even its scope of application, are to be classified

[26] Directive 94/51/EC, above, note 17.   [27] Ladeur, in this volume.
[28] Hohmeyer *et al* (1994b: 97).   [29] Gill (1997: 312).
[30] SEC(97) 589 final, 6, Communication of Commissioner Bjerregaard.

as technical in character.[31] Given this possibility, conflicts between the European Parliament and the Commission about the basis of a decision in the Treaties are really conflicts about competence.[32] The European Court of Justice[33] has already considered a complaint from Parliament, which contested that certain measures adopted by the Commission on the basis of the opinion of a committee of national representatives were technical in nature and, consequently, argued that the Commission had misused its powers, the measures deserving the consultation of Parliament.[34] It is likely that this conflict will grow in intensity as Parliament attempts to prevent the Commission from circumventing the normal decision-making procedure by voting against the use of annexes. In the case of the Regulation on Novel Foods and Novel Food Ingredients, Parliament successfully removed two proposed annexes.[35]

The conflict between Parliament and Commission demonstrates that the difficulty of distinguishing between political and technical questions also provides an opportunity to those who might wish to reduce political questions to technical ones. Within the EU, the process of distinction has become part of a political struggle. The growing awareness of the technical and the political questions, together with the implications of this distinction for the adequacy and legitimacy of procedures, has led to the consideration of new criteria of rationality. An international comparison of regulation in the field of biotechnology concludes that European requirements for the authorisation and release of GMOs into the environment are very strict and allow health and environmental aspects to be taken into account. Importantly, this comparison of regulation in the United States, Japan and Europe has also demonstrated that the strict regulation of biotechnology does not influence industry's decision upon the location of its "biotechnology branches", and that the issue of location has to date been greatly over-exaggerated whilst the issue of popular acceptance for biotechnology has been largely underestimated.[36] The acceptance of biotechnology by citizens is especially low when it comes to novel foods.[37]

The practical impact of new non-economic criteria in the context of European politics is clearly demonstrated by close examination of the decision-making process which led to the adoption of a Regulation on

[31] COM(95) 640 final.

[32] Ehlermann (1990: 140 and 144).

[33] Case C-156/93, *European Parliament* v. *Commission* [1995] ECR I-2019.

[34] Ibid.

[35] See EP amendment no. 14 to Article 1 on the Commission Proposal for a Directive on Novel Food (COM(92) 295 final) in the Report of the EP Committee on the Environment, Public Health and Consumer Protection, Session Document A3-0244/93, PE 202.785 fin.

[36] Hohmeyer *et al* (1994a: 189).

[37] Schmitt/Zweck (1996: 6) 'concerning Novel Foods, 28% of the population think them to be useful, but 45.2% hold the opinion that risks are so high that this technology should be rejected'.

Novel Foods and Novel Food Ingredients.[38] The European Parliament was
to recognise that the distinction between technical and political is of vital
importance, concluding that details such as annexes and the enumeration
of which novel foods ought to be subject to labelling requirements are not
technical problems. Though dealt with more fully below, it should be
noted here that comparison between the Commission's original proposal[39]
and the Common Position adopted by the Parliament and the Council[40]
clearly reveals that criteria beyond both technocratic arguments and
economic efficiency played a role and were, in part at least, successful.

The issue of biotechnology also focuses our attention upon the need to
rethink technical aspects in other areas. In my opinion, it is not convincing,
at least not without further empirical evidence, simply to conclude that
European social policy, both with regard to its content and in relation to
the perception which European actors have of it, deals primarily with
"technical matters" and "exclusively serves purposes of market-making or
market accommodation".[41] If Leibfried and Pierson's broad definition of
social policy as including policies that "modify market outcomes to facilitate transactions, to correct market failures, and to carry out regional,
interclass, or inter-generational redistribution"[42] are accepted, then the
suggestion that successful social regulation at European level[43] in fact
means that the social dimension has been "defeated",[44] cannot be simply
accepted. What are the modern "core features of welfare state régimes"?[45]
Might it not be possible that issues which have to date been a matter of
secondary and technical importance, now belong to the "core features"?

3. Complexity of Élite-Behaviour: The Orientation Patterns of Members of the European Commission

"Politicians are around the table of the Commission – technocrats are
everywhere else". This answer from a Member of the Commission to my
question of whether decision-making within the Commission is shaped by
a technocratic understanding of politics, may be exaggerated. But it is
equally overstated to assume that a technocratic élite, especially in the
Commission, is the driving force of a European integration process that
can be characterised as a "technocratic régime".[46] During my survey of ten
Commissioners,[47] two Commissioners answered that the particular policy-

[38] European Parliament and Council Regulation (EC) 258/97 concerning novel foods and
novel food ingredients, (1997) OJ L 43/1.
[39] COM(92) 295 final.   [40] Common Position (EC) no. 25/95, (1995) OJ C 320/1.
[41] Streeck (1995b: 39).   [42] Leibfried/Pierson (1995: 43).
[43] Majone (1993a: 153-170).   [44] Streeck (1995a: 396).
[45] M. Rhodes (1995: 80).   [46] Bach (1993c: 264).
[47] Personal interviews with Members of the Commission in September 1996.

field will determine whether there is a technocratic understanding of politics, one Commissioner held the view that there is a technocratic understanding, whilst seven Commissioners maintained that decision-making in the Commission is political, and even "very political".

Let us first look to the occupational backgrounds and political experience of Commissioners. What do they tell us about orientation-patterns within the Commission? If the careers of all Commissioners, from the establishment of the Commission under the Merger Treaty of 1967 up until 1996, are considered, the following characteristics emerge: more than two-thirds of the 89 Commissioners held a mandate in the national legislature whilst 29% held senior positions in political parties, with the percentage having held a senior party position having grown slightly since 1993. One fifth of Commissioners had been MEPs and here the trend is upward (Table 1). More than half of Commissioners (57%) had ministerial experience before they were appointed to the Commission (Table 2). Most Commissioners have an occupational background in politics (80%),

Table 1 *Political Office held by Commissioners Prior to their Appointment (1967–96)*

Office	Total	as % of Commissioners
National legislatures	59	66
High Party office	26	29
Local government	20	22
European Parliament	19	21
Regional assemblies	7	8
None	19	21
no data	1	1
Total	151*	168*

Source: up to 1993 Page/Wouters (1994). Own calculation of statistics for the period 1993–6.
* Total exceeds 100% because many Commissioners have held more than one political office.

Table 2 *Ministerial Ranking of Commissioners Prior to their Appointment (1967–96)*

Office	Total	as % of Commissioners
Minister	51	57
Junior minister	7	8
Non-ministerial function	30	34
No data	1	1
Total	89	100

Source: up to 1993 Page/Wouters (1994). Own calculation of statistics for the period 1993–6.

Table 3 *Occupational Background of Commissioners (1967–96)*

Office	Total	as % of Commissioners
Politics	70	80
Civil Service	29	33
Diplomat	21	24
NGO	21	24
Law	20	23
Education	20	23
Journalism	10	11
Private Industry	5	6
State Industry	3	3
Other	3	3
Total	202	230

Same source as for Table 2, although in Table 3 the percentage relates to 88 Commissioners, as the data for one Commissioner is missing.

followed by civil service (33%), diplomacy and interest groups (both 24%), law and education (both 23%). 11 % had worked as journalists and 6 % in private industry (Table 3).

From the data, it appears safe to conclude that "the post of Commissioner is largely a political one, filled predominantly by professional politicians".[48]

The question immediately arises: what happens once a Commissioner has worked for some time in Brussels? One view holds that once in Brussels and isolated from their home countries, Commissioners cut themselves off from domestic political life, fill their cabinets with career bureaucrats, and finally engage themselves in bureaucratic and technocratic administration; the absence of party politics and direct public legitimacy having the consequence that the Commissioner's only objectives are closer European co-operation and the realisation of fair trading conditions.[49]

It is true, and this was one of the results of my interviews, that according to the self-assessment of the Commissioners, party-politics do not play an important role within the Commission. Yet, this does not mean that Commissioners either have a technocratic understanding of politics or are only concerned with economic rationality in decision-making. What, after all, do we associate with the term "technocratic understanding of politics"? We can start from the distinction in the first section of this paper between a technical and a political question: politicians who tend to be in favour of accomplishing what is technically feasible and who do not consider whether the technical means to implement a policy are neutral

[48] Ibid., 451.   [49] Ibid., 454.

with regard to the purpose, necessarily have a technocratic understanding of politics. Sometimes, the purpose is nothing more than putting a technique into practice and, to remain with our example of biotechnology, means that the development of research in this field and the marketing of manipulated products becomes an aim in itself. The questions as to whether there is a political desire to further such research, or what the consequences would be were this technique successfully applied on a large scale in areas such as agriculture, are not asked.[50] Accordingly, the first priority of politicians with a technocratic attitude is the realisation of a technique and not the problem of transparency or democratic legitimacy. Technocratic politicians care about experts and bureaucracy and not about the acceptance of a policy by society.

In the case of the two biotechnology directives, the Commission's understanding of politics was, in part, shaped by technocratic elements with the consequence that the transparency of decision-making was reduced. However, as will be demonstrated below, it is equally apparent that the Commission's attitude towards biotechnology is not merely guided by the criterion of economic rationality. There is, thus, a mix of technical and political approaches towards problem-solving within the Commission. Helen Wallace is correct in emphasising that the perception that the Commission defines politics in a bureaucratic manner and relies continuously on experts and comitology, is misleading. Frequently, the Commission reacts faster to new political problems than the Member States do.[51] "I have a decidedly political view of subjects", answered one Commissioner, who similarly criticised the degree of reliance upon committee members, who might have a very short-sighted and technocratic approach and very often do not even represent their country but only the narrow perception of one administrative body. The interviews merely reveal the opinions of individual Commissioners. Yet, the strategies of collective actors cannot be explained without taking into account the views of individual actors at micro-level.[52] Of course, the interviews represent nothing more than the self-assessment of Commissioners. However, including the élite-interviews within policy-analysis gives rise to a more realistic view which also serves to emphasise the thesis that members of the Commission have a mix of political and technical approaches to problem-solving.

---

[50] Von Weizsäcker (1992: 134): '*In der Agrar-Gentechnik liegt eine Tendenz zur weiteren Sortenverarmung von Nutzpflanzen oder -tieren (...) Damit ist eine Gefahr angesprochen, die im bisherigen Regelwerk der Gentechnik noch gar nicht zur Sprache gekommen ist. Bislang beschränkt sich die Gesetzgebung auf die Kontrolle der Mißbrauchs- und Unfallgefahren. Die langfristig größten Gefahren sind vom Gesetzgeber noch nicht einmal angesprochen, eben die Gefahren des flächendeckenden Erfolges*'. See also Winter (1992: 389-404).
[51] H. Wallace (1996a: 149).
[52] Mayntz/Scharpf (1995: 44).

There are also national and supranational elements in the orientation-patterns of Commissioners: there is no such thing as the sudden "isolation"[53] of Commissioners from their own country. As Sir Leon Brittan said:

"I am frequently consulted by Jacques Delors about what is going on in Britain. It would be bizarre if I could not answer (...) I think that it is important that whoever holds my job should play a part in British public life since the EC itself is part of British public life".[54]

Commissioners hover between autonomy and a continuing relationship with their own country.[55] Other Commissioners likewise demonstrate such behavioural patterns. In February 1996, Karel van Miert threatened to sue the Belgian Government since it had failed to comply with European competition rules.[56] Equally, however, Commissioners may also speak out in favour of their own government, and accordingly Keith Middlemas observes that "national interest thus intrudes via procedures, as it does with personalities, especially in disputed cases where the Commission, having full competence, is the last court of appeal".[57] The replies of the Commissioners to my question as to whether they could conceive of returning to national politics were varied. Five Commissioners could envisage such a return move, but five could not. Negative replies range from "[I] prefer to influence European politics", "Never say never, but I cannot really imagine", to:

"I think to return to national politics would be difficult. Once you engage in European politics, you sometimes have to vote against your own country and you cannot make a COREPER out of the Commission. Moreover, one gains some distance from national politics".[58]

Thus, Commissioners are, to a certain degree, remote (rather than isolated) from national politics; a situation which makes a certain degree of sense in view of the supranational elements within their work but which might also prove disadvantageous, there being a lack of in-built knowledge about concrete problems within the Member States.[59]

---

[53] Page/Wouters (1994: 454).
[54] Cited from Donelly/Ritchie (1994: 35).
[55] Lequesne (1996: 405): 'Dans la conduite de leur actions publique, la position des commissaires à l'égard des Etats qui les ont désignés n'est pourtant pas celle d'une soumission pure et simple. Elle illustre plutôt la dualité autonomie/dépendance qui charactérise plus généralement toute l'organisation'.
[56] Ibid., 405.
[57] Middlemas (1995: 234).
[58] Interviews conducted with Members of the Commission in September 1996.
[59] H. Wallace (1996a: 204).

4. Complexity of Structures: New Leading Ideas in Decision-making

Political regulation at European level is initially influenced by the existing national problem-solving philosophies and administrative traditions.[60] Subsequent research likewise demonstrated that the success and acceptance of a regulation in a certain policy-sector depended greatly upon the characteristics of established national regulations in this field. On the one hand, the homogeneous structure of the telecommunication sector was thus a good basis for successful European problem-solving; on the other, heterogeneous national regulatory structures in the electricity sector were to hamper the evolution of a European policy. Yet, despite all the problems deriving from the divergent national regulatory approaches to the electricity sector, there was not simply a return to intergovernmental politics at European level and a supranational solution was nonetheless found. Accordingly, Schmidt concludes that European decision-making in the field of electricity clearly demonstrates the growing influence of a truly supranational approach within the EU.[61] An intergovernmentalist approach[62] would assume that despite qualified majority voting, "the mutual respect for each other's sovereignty would prevent the passing of legislation that contravenes vital interests".[63] However, European legislation on electricity was indeed possible, notwithstanding French resistance to liberalisation.

In addition to the national regulatory characteristics in specific fields, the "constellation of interests among the national governments who have to agree upon effective regulation"[64] need also be examined. Thus, for example, the constellation of interests may result in European regulation based upon higher standards than the lowest common regulatory denominator if the Member States have succeeded, in accordance with Articles 100a and 36 EC, in maintaining their own national regulation and restricting the entry of foreign products into their market which do not satisfy national requirements with regard to health or environmental protection.[65]

I will now proceed to outline the decision-making process in the area of novel foods and novel food ingredients. Prior to the Commission's involvement, this field was not overly regulated by the Member States. However, since the use of such foodstuffs touches upon issues of health and environmental protection, States favouring stringent standards, such as Denmark, were in a position to threaten to draft national laws based upon a level of

---

[60] Héritier/Mingers/Knill/Becka (1994).   [61] Schmidt (1996: 45).
[62] Moravcsik (1995: 29-80).   [63] Schmidt (1996: 9).   [64] Scharpf (1997b).
[65] Ibid. Though regulations in the field of biotechnology might generally be classified as product regulations, they also entail aspects of process regulations.

high protection and then to invoke the exemption clause of Article 36 EC, should the Member States be unable to find a European solution. Accordingly, biotechnology might be identified as a policy-field in which the potential was for a more stringent European solution, and not for a regulatory race to the bottom.[66]

In the novel foods policy-field, only two Member States already had domestic legislation: the Danish Law on Environment and Gene Technology, and the British Food Safety Act of 1990 which merely laid down a voluntary authorisation procedure for genetically modified novel foods.[67] France, Greece, Italy, Spain[68] and Germany had not tackled the issue. The likelihood that a European solution to the problem of labelling novel foods would be forthcoming may explain why the amended German law on biotechnology of 1993 did not contain any provisions on novel food labelling. This presumption may have been strengthened by the participation of European experts such as Kristin Schreiber of DG III, whose responsibilities included the regulatory framework for biotechnology and novel food legislation, within the German legislative debates.[69]

A comparison between the Commission's original proposal on the Regulation of Novel Foods and Novel Food Ingredients in 1992 and the Common Position of the European Parliament and the Council adopted in 1995, reveals that ethics, health, and environmental protection criteria were to play a role alongside once dominant economic criteria. This result – the transcending of technocratic decision-making and negative integration – was possible only because of the existence of a structure of governance which combines national and supranational elements within and between institutions, and encompasses a variety of leading ideas.

In the preamble to the 1992 proposal, the potential risks which novel foods pose to the environment are mentioned, whilst risks to public health are neglected. In the Common Position of 1995, however, there is an extra paragraph in the preamble tackling the protection of public health, and a new Article 3 which states that:

> "Foods and food ingredients falling within the scope of this Regulation must not constitute a danger for the consumer, mislead the consumer, or differ from foods or food ingredients which they are intended to replace in such a way that their normal consumption would be nutritionally disadvantageous for the consumer".[70]

---

[66] Ibid.   [67] Hohmeyer *et al* (1994a: 107).

[68] For purposes of comparison, see the synopsis in: European Parliament, Scientific and Technological Options Assessment, STOA, Bioethics in Europe. Final Report (September 1992: 187).

[69] Schreiber being asked in a public hearing of the German Parliament's Health Committee as to whether the European Community already had a position on this subject, Deutscher Bundestag, 12. Wahlperiode, Protokoll der 66. Sitzung des Ausschusses für Gesundheit (30 June 1993: 15).

[70] Article 3 of the Common Position no. 25/95, above, note 40.

Equally, in the proposal, the categories of food falling within the scope of the Regulation were listed in an annex whilst the Common Position was to incorporate them within Article 1 of the Regulation, thus ensuring that Parliament might not be excluded from any subsequent amendment procedure.

The labelling of novel foods played a very minor role in the proposal, only being briefly mentioned in Article 6 which referred to Council Directive 79/112/EEC on labelling. However, the preamble to the 1995 Common Position emphasised the need to provide specific information in the labelling of novel foods.[71] Article 8, therefore, lists specific labelling requirements. Interestingly, however, whilst the Common Position determined that these labelling requirements should apply when a novel food was "significantly different from an equivalent existing food", a Parliamentary amendment demanded that the word "significantly" should be struck out.[72]

The second reading on the Novel Food Regulation in the European Parliament saw the European Socialist Party (PSE) and the European People's Party Group (PPE) welcome the difference between the Commission's first draft and the Common Position. The reporter Dagmar Roth-Behrendt (PSE) acknowledged that "There has been a touch of insight from the Commission and the Council".[73] Karl-Heinz Florenz (PPE) reminded his colleagues that the Commission's proposal had contained only a "hint of labelling".[74] However, Hiltrud Breyer (Greens) denied that advance had been made and held the opinion that the new draft merely concealed the issues. Further, consumers need not be protected by a paternalistic guardian such as Commissioner Martin Bangemann. Instead, citizens only required the adequate information to enable them to make an informed decision in the market-place.[75] Parliament, being fully aware of its power under the co-decision procedure, accordingly proposed 55 amendments of which only a few were adopted. Whilst a more far-reaching proposal that all foods produced with the aid of biotechnology need be marked as such, failed to attain the requisite absolute majority,[76] an amendment stating that all novel foods and food ingredients differing from existing foods need be labelled was successfully

---

[71] Ibid., Article 8.

[72] Amendment No 32 concerning Article 8 (1) of the Common Position, EP Committee on the Environment, Public Health and Consumer Protection, Recommendation for a second reading on the Common Position adopted by the Council on the Novel Food Regulation, Session Document A4-0050/96, PE 215.404 fin.

[73] Debates of the European Parliament, 12 March 1996, OJ (EC) Annex no 4, 4-478, at 8.

[74] Ibid., 16.   [75] Ibid., 12.

[76] For this more far-reaching amendment, see EP Committee on the environment, health and safety and consumer protection, Session Document, A4-0050/96 of 23 February 1996, no. 35. Labelling should be required for: '(...) food and food ingredients produced from but not containing organisms genetically modified by means of genetic engineering processes'.

carried and was subsequently accepted and formalised by the Conciliation Committee of Council and Parliament in November 1996. Parliament was thus successful in this point.[77]

The move towards labelling requirements was given added impetus by the creation of a Group of Advisers on the Ethical Implications of Biotechnology appointed by the European Commission. The group, comprising two lawyers, three philosophers, two geneticists, a biologist and a doctor, was asked by the Commission for an opinion on the labelling of foods produced through modern biotechnological means. The Commission "directed the Group's attention to the ethical dimension of labelling, to the consumer's right to know as well as to the scope of the duty of adequate information (...)"[78] and in May 1995 an opinion was submitted. The Group concluded that consumers require clear information and that labelling would be appropriate should biotechnology "cause a substantial change in composition, nutritional value or the use for which the food is intended", and that in such cases labelling should not merely highlight alterations in food composition but should also detail changes in the production process.[79] However, the compromise agreed upon in the Conciliation Committee was to be more comprehensive since all novel foods differing from existing foods were to be labelled and the criterion of "substantial change" was to be dispensed with.

Ethical implications of biotechnology are becoming increasingly impor- tant. In January 1998, a physicist in Illinois announced plans to open a clinic for cloning humans. The most convincing argument against the cloning of humans is an ethical one developed by the philosopher Jürgen Habermas. According to his argument, we are responsible for our actions and behaviour because we are born free even if we cannot choose our inherited characteristics. For a cloned human, this would be different. The way a cloned human is born is not contingent but the result of a conscious manipulation by another person. Thus, the cloned human is not born as a free person and cannot be responsible for his life.[80]

In the case of novel foods, it might thus be concluded that ethics, health and environmental protection did indeed play a role alongside the criterion of economic rationality. This naturally begs the question of how this

---

[77] *Süddeutsche Zeitung*, 29 November 1996. 1. Note also the formulation in Regulation 258/97, Article 8 (1) a: 'A novel food or food ingredient shall be deemed to be no longer equivalent for the purpose of this Article if scientific assessment, based upon an appropriate analysis of existing data, can demonstrate that the characteristics *are different* in compar- ison with a conventional food or food ingredient, having regard to the accepted limits of natural variations for such characteristics. In this case, the labelling must indicate the characteristics or properties modified, together with the method by which the characteristics or property was obtained' (emphasis added), above, note 38.

[78] Group of Advisers of the Ethical Implications of Biotechnology of the European Commission, Opinion No. 5 of 5 May 1995, 3.

[79] Ibid., 4.   [80] Habermas (1998: 13).

limited consideration of new leading ideas may be explained and institutionally strengthened. Clearly, the growing influence of the European Parliament, particularly in policy areas governed by the co-decision procedure, is of primary importance.[81] However, if the Parliament is to have a chance "in the uneven battles of information politics that legislatures fight with other organs of government"[82], its powers need be augmented through added emphasis upon the good functioning of specialised legislative committees and the recruitment of expert staff. In this vein, Shapiro has proposed that there should be greater recognition for the special role of legislative committees and that

> "the recruitment and career management of those members of staff (...) should be clearly differentiated (...) from the development of the general EU civil service".[83]

Whilst Parliament continues to fight an uneven battle, its influence should nonetheless not be underestimated: one indicator of its growing power being the lobbying by multi-national enterprises which increasingly devote more time to the European Parliament.[84]

Equally, however, there are greater opportunities for the inclusion of new leading ideas, such as ethical and environmental criteria, within the Community debate which do not solely derive from inter-institutional conflicts between Parliament and Commission. Fresh ideas are also the product of inner-institutional conflicts and debates. Members of the Commission are influenced not only by their supranational obligations but also by national interests and viewpoints. To return to the example of novel foods, four Member States voted against the Common Position: Austria, Denmark, Germany and Sweden. Denmark published a separate opinion explaining its dissent: "the draft does not ensure that the consumer gets sufficient information that novel foods have been produced by genetic process engineering".[85] Members of the Commission were, therefore, aware both of objections within the Council and of the Parliament's proposed amendments.

The Commission was also aware of splits within the organisations operating under its auspices. The Group of Advisers on the Ethical Implications of Biotechnology exists alongside committees on biotechnology created under Directives 90/219/EEC and 90/220/EEC. The committees are composed of delegates from national health ministries (Austria, Germany, Italy and United Kingdom), agricultural ministries (Belgium, France), environmental protection agencies (Denmark and Ireland) and environment ministries (Greece). Issues of biotechnology are also discussed

---

[81] Westlake (1994: 94).   [82] Shapiro (1996b: 18).   [83] Ibid., 18.

[84] Green Cowles (1995: 20).

[85] Council of the European Union, Letter of 13 November 1995 to the President of the European Parliament.

in various Directorate Generals: DG III (industry), DG XI (environment and nuclear security) and DG XII (science, research and development).[86] These different contexts contribute on the one hand, to a fragmented policy-making process; but on the other, they also provide channels of opportunity for diverse rationality criteria. Thus, the Commission is not simply "supranational", nor do the actors within it merely represent the supranational interests of the Community.[87] Edgar Grande's relation of actors to arenas in the multi-level system of the EU so that the Commission and the Parliament emerge as supranational arenas with supranational actors,[88] should be substituted by a more flexible model reflecting the diverse mixture of national and supranational arenas and actors.

The structure of governance enables the Commissioners to engage in a learning process and to develop innovative ideas.[89] Compromises may be formulated which integrate new criteria of rationality. This is true, for example, not only of novel foods but also of the Commission proposal on the legal protection of biotechnological inventions. Whilst an original Commission proposal contained no references to the ethical aspects of the patenting of parts of the human body,[90] the failure of the Conciliation Committee to gain majority acceptance for its text in the Parliament,[91] was to lead the Commission to accept one of the most important parliamentary amendments within its new draft:[92] neither the human body nor parts of the human body will be patentable.[93] Interestingly, the new Commission proposal describes its forerunner as being "(...) largely technical in character".[94] Here again, the complexity of the decision-making process opened an opportunity for the inclusion of new criteria of rationality such as those of an ethical nature.

5. Conclusion

My starting point was the observation that not many problems in the area of biotechnology were exclusively technical in nature, and the interesting question for the political scientist of why politicians on occasions claim that they are solving technical problems. The definition of political issues as technical questions leads to a reduction in the transparency of decision-

[86] European Commission, Guide to Services, March 1995.
[87] Grande (1994: 188).   [88] Ibid., 186.   [89] H Wallace (1996a: 149).
[90] COM(88) 496 final.
[91] Debates of the European Parliament, 1 March 1995, OJ Annex No 4-458. Voting results: Yes: 188, No: 240, Abstention: 23.
[92] COM(95) 661 final.
[93] Dispensing with the formulation 'the human body or parts of the human body as such'.
[94] COM(95) 661 final, 5.

making and the democratic accountability of politics. In the field of biotechnology, such a strategy was to cause conflict between the Parliament and the Commission. At the same time, however, awareness is growing of the relevance of the political-technical distinction to democratic procedures. Interviews with Commissioners demonstrated that the argument which holds that the Commission is dominated by a technocratic understanding of politics is an oversimplification. Rather, elite-behaviour and governance structures within the EU demonstrate a mixture of political and technical approaches to problem-solving.

Where the search for the elusive balance of power between the European institutions has failed,[95] a close study of the mixture ratios of national and supranational, executive and legislative, political and technical in the structures of problems, of elite-behaviour and of governance, might succeed in providing a greater insight into the specific character and results of European integration. The results of European integration prove that compromises which are based upon more than negative integration or the lowest regulatory common denominator may be reached.[96]

Instead of merely condemning the entire political process within the EU as being technocratic, we should neither be blind to elements existing beyond technocratic governance, nor to the existing shortcomings in the technocratic approach. One reason why it may be convenient for actors within the EU to deploy the "technical definition" may be the fact that the solution of a technical problem may safely be left to the administration, committees or experts. In such cases, actors no longer need detailed grounds for the avoidance of time-consuming legislative procedures and the participation of the European Parliament. They might with "good conscience" argue that the complexity of the problem determines that it is unsuited to democratic participation. Although such behaviour might be explained, it need nonetheless be criticised since it necessarily entails a reduction in transparency and democracy. It is the complexity of European integration, with its periods of stability and of instability and with its interdependencies of different interests and levels of political regulation that has led to a polycratic system of governance. The political regulation in such a complex system as the EU has to integrate a new view of causality and must find new combinations of stability and innovation.[97] In spite of the complexity of structures, there must be a way to co-ordinate the different interests and levels of governance into a system that allows co-evolution of the nation states and the European Union.[98] The different interests, levels and new leading ideas and criteria of rationality have so far not been co-ordinated into a coherent concept of European governance. Nevertheless, a public discussion of such a concept is all the more relevant

---

[95] H. Wallace (1996a: 143).   [96] Eichener (1996: 249-280).   [97] Willke (1996: 77ff.).

as Europe progresses beyond an internal market. As long as European integration was limited to economic integration this could be done by the co-operation of functional élites, but with the ongoing transformation into a political and social Europe, the need for democratic legitimacy has increased.[99]

[99] Lepsius (1997: 951).

11

Bargaining, Arguing and Functional Differentiation of Decision-making: The Role of Committees in European Environmental Process Regulation

*Thomas Gehring**

1. Introduction

Committees play an important role in the European Community.[1] In quantitative terms, the estimated number of committees existing under the auspices of the Community institutions ranges between several hundred to a thousand. The committees are regularly attended by more than 50,000 people: scientists, civil servants and representatives of interest groups.[2] In qualitative terms, committees provide the foundation for "bureaucratic" integration theories that emphasise the emergence of a European bureaucratic élite[3] or envisage the "fusion" of national and European state bureaucracies.[4] Based on empirical investigations into committee decision-making in the foodstuffs sector, the members of the Bremen research project have not only claimed that governance by committees is located somewhere between intergovernmentalism and supranationalism[5] but they also believe that some core institutional features of the EC should be read as "supranational versions of deliberationist ideals".[6] In combination with

* Lecturer in International Relations, Department of Political Science, Free University Berlin and Faculty of Administrative Science, University of Konstanz.

[1] See Bertram (1967); Grote (1990); Schaefer (1996).
[2] See Falke (1996: 132-138); Buitendijk/van Schendelen (1995: 40-41); Algieri/Rometsch (1994: 137-141).
[3] See Bach (1992).   [4] See Wessels (1992).
[5] See Bücker *et al* (1996: 39, 45); Joerges/Neyer (1997a).
[6] See Joerges/Neyer (1997b).

European law, committees are expected to transform "strategic interaction into deliberative problem-solving".[7] In this way, a form of governance by committees emerges that need not necessarily reflect an awkward political compromise[8] – in fact, it may approach a normative ideal that is not even attained within the political systems of the Member States.

Committees therefore represent a particular form of institutionalised decision-making for European governance which is only just beginning to be understood. However, it remains largely unclear whether, and why, committees matter for European governance. They will generally be meaningful if they influence the outcomes of decision-making processes.[9] Thus, the question arises, how can committees affect decisions in ways that non-committee decision-making processes cannot, and in what kind of mechanism is their influence rooted? In particular, do the participating actors behave differently in committees than outside, and if so, why and under which conditions? This last question cannot be tackled without a distinct *concept of interaction* among the participating actors.

A methodological problem is that the committees under the EC auspices are so diverse in their nature that it is difficult to develop a concept of "committee decision-making" which is meaningful.[10] Whilst some commit-tees consist of Member States' representatives (hereafter, the comitology committees), others constitute forums for interest groups or independent experts. Not only is the membership of these committees different, the opinions which these bodies adopt are of varying degrees of legal weight. Despite the multifarious nature of committees, they all share one feature in common: a committee is always embedded in, and therefore functionally dependent on, the overall decision-making process. Decision-making processes involving committees are sequenced in one way or another, so that the significance of a committee depends on its specific contribution to a larger decision-making process.

This article explores the relevance of committees in European governance on the basis of two premises. First, it assumes that committees are part of overall decision-making processes and cannot readily be understood in isola-tion from them. Second, it accepts that rational actors do not always act strategically according to their established interests but may, under certain circumstances, also engage in discursive deliberation. In Section 2 the article briefly develops the relevance of sequenced decision-making and introduces two diametrically opposed and ideally constructed modes of interaction among rational actors: "bargaining" and "arguing". Subsequently, the paper proceeds to examine the relevance of committee-based decision-making for

[7] Joerges/Neyer (1997b), also (1997a) and Neyer (1997).
[8] See the frequent criticism of comitology decision-making referring to the exclusion of the European Parliament. See Grams (1995: 119-131).
[9] See van Schendelen (1996: 29).
[10] See van der Knaap (1996).

European environmental process regulation. Section 3 explores the considerable influence of an *ad hoc* advisory expert committee on the negotiation of the Drinking Water Directive of 1980.[11] Section 4 compares three comitology committees in the area of environmental process regulation to examine their impact on the bargaining situation among the Member States. Section 5 examines the informal functions that the comitology committees may fulfil if they meet on a regular basis to determine whether the institutional structure provides sufficient room for the exchange of arguments *not* immediately related to their own formal decision-making.

2. The Influence of Committees in European Policy-Making

Any evaluation of the role of committees in European policy-making cannot be limited to their internal decision-making arrangement. It must begin with the overall decision-making process of which committee interaction forms an important part. The negotiation-system among Member States within the Council constitutes the core component of the normal decision-making procedures laid down in Articles 189a, 189b and 189c EC. However, non-state actors, in particular the Commission and the European Parliament, may have an important impact on outcomes of this system. Therefore, the impact of European committees may be directed at two different points of reference. They may influence the intergovernmental core of European decision-making and modify the outcome of Council negotiations among the Member States. They may also affect the institutional balance that exists between the Council (the Member States collectively), Commission and Parliament. A committee that does not have an impact on either of these points of reference will be largely irrelevant for the EC system and therefore falls outside the scope of this article.

The impact of committees on decisions is closely related to the functional differentiation of decision-making processes. It is difficult to believe that interaction in a committee will differ significantly, if it entirely replaces the normal decision-making process within the Council and deals with an identical set of issues. Thus, meaningful committees exist as satellite bodies in addition to some parallel entities that are frequently positioned higher up in the overall institutional structure.[12] A decision-making process may be sequenced so that a committee intervenes either before or after these other entities act. The mandate of a committee may also be restricted to specific aspects of the general decision-making process so that the committee deals with a particular subset of relevant issues. Finally, the attendance of a committee may systematically differ from that

---

[11] Council Directive 80/778/EEC on the quality of water for human consumption, (1980) OJ L 229/11.
[12] On the functional differentiation of decision-making processes, see Bora (1993).

of the normal decision-making process in order to fulfil its limited function. Thus, the more a committee differs in one or more of these three dimensions (sequence, mandate or attendance) from a (hypothetical) unitary decision-making process, the more the operation of a committee will deviate from the latter.

In order to establish how a committee may alter the interaction among the key European institutions, it is necessary to investigate how these actors *may* interact. Assuming that corporate actors do not easily sacrifice advantages without reciprocal benefits, they may be expected usually to pursue their parochial interests within a Community legislative project. Accordingly, negotiations may be conceived of as "bargaining": the arm-twisting type of interaction among rational utility maximisers to accommodate and balance established interests. Bargaining should be distinguished from unilateral action or competitive behaviour that rules out consensus. Actors bargain not only to collectively establish mutually beneficial co-operation but also to achieve an individually favourable distribution of these gains.[13] The eventual outcome will largely rely on the distribution of bargaining power among the actors that depends, in turn, not least on the number of votes assigned to the Member States and the formal competences granted to the supranational actors. Allowing European committees to participate in decision-making procedures may influence the allocation of bargaining power within the European polity. It may also affect the boundaries of the decision-making situation and modify the preferences of actors[14] even though there is no change in the *mode of interaction* among the participating actors.

However, actors do not always bargain. If uncertainty prevails because of a lack of information or an inability to process the data, even rational utility maximisers may be motivated to question their preferences on the basis of convincing arguments or credible information. In complex situations, actors may also "argue": they attempt to convince their counterparts of the appropriateness of their own points of view. This type of interaction does not preclude actors from pursuing their own interests, but their influence on a collective outcome will be based on the provision of convincing arguments and not on power. In order to collectively remove uncertainty and settle initially disputed issues in a Habermasian type of discourse, actors must have recourse to undisputed criteria.[15] European committees

---

[13] Hence, bargaining creates a tension between a collective and an individual interest that may cause the break-down of negotiations despite existing opportunities for mutually beneficial co-operation. See Scharpf (1992); Gehring (1996).

[14] Adding and subtracting issues is a well-known instrument to influence the probability of successful co-operation. See Sebenius (1983).

[15] In a Habermasian type of discourse, actors settle disputes essentially by individually invoking and collectively applying undisputed criteria located at a higher level of abstraction. See Habermas (1973). On the distinction between the interaction modes of "arguing" and "bargaining", see Gehring (1996).

may provide the forum for this type of interaction based on the exchange of arguments. This function does not rely on formal decision powers. To be meaningful, it merely requires that conclusions are successfully introduced into the formal decision-making process.

The two ideally constructed interaction modes of "bargaining" and "arguing" fulfil very different functions within a comprehensive decision-making process.[16] The former provides a mechanism for the accommodation of established interests in comparatively clear-cut situations, while the latter supports the collective removal of uncertainty and affects the definition of interests. Unfortunately, they require very different behaviour. Arguing presupposes the willingness of the participating actors to question their own views and, if necessary, modify their preferences. In contrast, successful bargaining relies on fixed preferences. Where the modes of interaction are deployed simultaneously, interference will occur.

European committees matter primarily because they influence the organisation of decision-making processes. Furthermore, they may also affect the mode of interaction among the participating actors, if the sequenced approach characterising committee-supported decision-making contributes to separating interaction in the arguing-mode from interaction in the bargaining-mode and promotes deliberative consensus-building, rather than the power-based pursuit of parochial interests.[17] Yet, the mere existence of a committee does not ensure that arguing dominates over bargaining.

3. The Influence of an Advisory Expert Committee; the Case of the Expert Group on Drinking Water

Committees may operate as advisory bodies within a broader decision-making process. In this function, a committee does not need any formal decision-making competences. However, its advice will only be meaningful if it is integrated into the formal decision-making process. The specific way of embedding an advisory committee in an overall process is exemplified in the role of the *ad hoc* Advisory Group of National Drinking Water Experts in the preparation of the Drinking Water Directive.[18]

---

[16] See Gehring (1995: 205-210).

[17] A frequently observed (Neyer 1997: 29-30; Bach 1992) but rarely corroborated third candidate for committee influence is the "socialisation" of committee members over time. For a normative account which approaches "arguing", such as that adopted by the Bremen research group (Joerges/Neyer 1997a and 1997b), systematic European socialisation might cause a serious problem because committee members would no longer fully represent their home countries and committee opinions would lose legitimacy for their home constituencies. However, the effect may be largely overestimated because committee members still spend the bulk of their working time in their home offices and will be socialised predominantly within this framework.

[18] Council Directive 80/778/EEC, above, note 11. On the Directive, see Haigh (1992: Chapter 4.4.).

In preparing the proposal for a Drinking Water Directive, the Commission determined the design of the Directive and elaborated the content of its main body, that would primarily outline the scope of the Directive, as well as central obligations and ancillary duties of the Member States. However, it refrained from selecting the detailed content of a number of annexes intended to define the specific standards for drinking water, in terms of parameters and their limit values, as well as the measurement techniques and analytical methods for the testing of these parameters. Since this task required expert information which it did not possess, the Commission set up the *ad hoc* Advisory Group of National Drinking Water Experts.

The experts attended in a private capacity but they were nominated by the Member States and originated predominantly from specialised state agencies like the German Federal Health Agency (*Bundesgesundheitsamt*). The *ad hoc* Group was given the limited task of advising the Commission on the parameters and figures to be inserted into the annexes. During 1974, the Group met several times and discussed the details of the annexes on the basis of a report written by a French *rapporteur*. The experts reached general agreement on the requirements for healthy drinking water, while some issues remained unsettled.[19] The Commission mainly adopted the experts' conclusions for its proposal of the Directive.[20] It can be seen that, in this case, the expert opinion was assimilated into the formal decision-making process.

The Group had been delegated a limited task embedded within a larger legislative project. It was set up to advise the Commission on the appropriate quality standards for drinking water from a public health point of view, and it was not required to consider a broader range of issues that might also have been relevant for the creation of rules on European drinking water standards. Because of the restricted scope, the experts could rely on established professional criteria concerning such issues as toxicity testing, the credibility of epidemiological studies and consumption usages. In fact, they referred to standards that had been negotiated elsewhere and relied on, in particular, a recommendation of the World Health Organisation (WHO).[21] *Procedurally*, the experts were invited to deliberate and, as far as possible, reach agreement, but they were not mandated to decide anything.

In this type of arrangement, consensus settles issues and increases the relevance of the advisory body at large.[22] When disagreement emerges, the

---

[19] For example, the relevance of regulating the total hardness of drinking water remained disputed, see Veh/Edom (1981: 474-475).

[20] COM(75) 394 final.   [21] Ibid.

[22] See Buitendijk/van Schendelen (1995: 50). Falke/Winter (1996: 567-575) compare the consequences of a successful and a failed attempt to achieve consensus in similar working groups.

Group will be unable to provide clear-cut advice and force the Commission to fill the gap on its own. The Commission had no reason to deviate from the opinion of the national drinking water experts, as far as their consensus reached, but it retained the power to determine the parameters in the event that the experts could not reach agreement. Under these operating conditions, it was not a viable strategy for a stake-holding Member State to send a representative merely to block consensus. This approach could not preclude the emergence of near consensus that might strongly influence the Commission's choice despite some remaining disagreement. In order to promote their interests, Member States would have to influence the deliberation process positively. Therefore, they were better off sending experts capable of *convincing* their colleagues of their opinion. In short, the arrangement was designed to encourage the Member States to send "real" water experts rather than negotiators thereby "forcing" them to argue and to pursue their interests by providing reasonable and convincing arguments on the basis of professionally shared criteria.

If the scientifically sound basis for the parameters and the limit values had been the only relevant criteria for the acceptability of the proposal by the Member States, then there would have been hardly anything left to negotiate within the Council. However, the Expert Group had not discussed a wide range of issues which were important to the overall acceptability of the directive; for example, its influence on the supply of drinking water in the Member States, its impact on domestic legal systems, or the expected improvement costs of upgrading the quality of national drinking water to the proposed minimum standards. On these issues, Member States' interests and national assessments as to the economic, financial and administrative implications of the EC standards varied considerably. Since the costs of achieving the standards were not uniform across the Member States, negotiations in the Council were fractious despite the almost unanimous scientific opinion. For example, the Directive related to more than 60 parameters whereas German law only checked 16 parameters; consequently, Germany felt that the costs following from the regular measurement and analysis of the parameters were too high.[23] Britain campaigned hard for a less stringent limit value on the content of lead in water because much of Britain's water supply is still delivered through lead-pipes.[24] The Netherlands politicised those parameters in the Directive which related directly to the saline content of water because this formed a part of its long-term struggle to desalinate the waters of the River Rhine.[25] It can be seen that the Expert Group did not pre-empt the negotiations in the Council.

[23] For the German position see Stellungnahme des Bundesrates, Drucksache 494/75.
[24] See Haigh (1992: Chapter 4.4).
[25] See Kromarek (1986: 31-32); Veh/Edom (1981: 474).

Because the Directive was based on Articles 100 and 235 EC, before the Directive could be adopted by the Council, unanimity of the Member States had to be achieved. The intense negotiations in the Council took five years of "bargaining": the balancing of established interests. Primarily, the Council considered the main body of the Directive. General concerns of the Member States as to the perceived "rigidity" of the Directive resulted in the incorporation of a number of measures designed to relax the strict legal regime.[26] The Member States agreed to extend the transition period for implementation from two to five years. Furthermore, no less than three new exemption clauses were introduced: under certain conditions, there was a further extension of the transition period; there was also a provision on the temporary infringement of limit values for drinking water abstracted from exceptionally bad surface waters; and, as a safeguard clause, the temporary lifting of the limit values in emergency situations. Besides altering the temporal implementation of the Directive, in some cases, the Council also modified the legal status of parameters; for example, it classified the chloride and conductivity parameters as non-mandatory "guide-values" rather than as binding maximum concentrations. On the issue of lead-pipes, it added a "commentary", in particularly unclear language, on the lead value with the result that the Directive allowed the lead value to be exceeded where there is lead-piping, notwithstanding the fact that the Directive retains the original, scientifically based figure.

In short, the Council significantly amended the Commission proposal and introduced a number of lacunae in order to produce a text that was acceptable to every Member State. It is remarkable, however, that the Council resorted to manipulating the impact of the entire Directive on the domestic water supply systems and largely *refrained from adjusting the figures and parameters elaborated by the advisory Expert Group*. In fact, it was more difficult to bargain over the part of the Directive that had been subject to far-reaching expert consensus than over those parts which had not been previously subject to expert advice. This strategy of the Member States suffered a set back before the European Court of Justice several years later. The Court considered a case concerning the definition of the "emergency situation" in the safeguard clause contained in the Directive.[27] The Court adopted a narrow interpretation of the provision with the result that the most important loophole was effectively closed. Whereas the Council had introduced this provision to relax the strict provisions of the Directive and to facilitate compromise, the Court's interpretation meant that the Member States were more firmly bound to the strict limit values of the Directive. Accordingly, within the institutional framework, the conclusions of the advisory expert committee did not only affect the negotiation process and the design of the Directive. Over time, they also had a serious

---

[26] See preamble to the Directive, above, note 11.
[27] See Case 228/87, *Pretura unificata di Torino* [1988] ECR 5099.

impact on the substantive content of the obligations contained in the Directive as the Court closed lacunae on the Directive's scope.

The long and fierce struggle over the Directive within the Council suggests that the Member States defended important stakes and did *not* refrain from bargaining. The impact of the committee on the outcome cannot simply be explained as an apparently low importance project, nor by a general "problem-solving" attitude of the negotiators; rather, it may be attributed to the particular position of the expert committee within the overall decision-making process. The conscious separation of committee deliberations from Council negotiations had the effect of protecting the professional discourse of water experts as far as possible from bargaining. In the area of drinking water, arguing dominated and facilitated the emergence of a professional consensus. States had to send "real" experts – rather than negotiators pursuing general state interests – to influence the deliberation process. A prerequisite for the dominantly discursive interaction of experts was, however, the embeddedness of their deliberations in a broader decision-making process. States *could afford* to send water experts precisely because they knew that they retained the opportunity to struggle for their aggregate interests in the subsequent negotiations in the Council. If the whole Directive had been negotiated in an expert committee, the Member States would have been encouraged to send "tougher" negotiators. Similarly, if the Directive had been prepared in the Council, national delegations desiring to mitigate implementation costs would have been motivated to question the scientific basis of strict limit values. In both cases, arguments actually intended to convince another party would have been mixed indistinguishably with moves in the bargaining process. The risk of misunderstanding would have increased and the negotiators would have been less inclined to question the preferences of their states as a prerequisite for a meaningful discourse. In these surroundings, the chances of achieving professional consensus would have been seriously reduced.

The degree of professional consensus actually produced by the advisory committee proved difficult to challenge in later stages of the decision-making process. Although negotiators bargained vociferously, they could not simply push aside a consensual and scientifically based conclusion agreed upon by their own experts. However, the professional consensus did not dominate the overall interests of the Member States because it did not cover the entire range of relevant "administrative" aspects. Thus, the experts' conclusions persisted while national representatives bargained over the impact of these conclusions on their domestic water supply systems.

More generally, advisory expert committees may facilitate, and rationalise in the Habermasian sense, decision-making, if their task is deliberately limited to the exploration of one set of relevant aspects according to agreed upon (professional) criteria. The contribution of committees to European governance relies on an institutional barrier that separates their deliberations from the arena of actual decision-making and protects them from being contaminated by the inclusion of extraneous components which belong elsewhere in the overall decision-making process.

4. Decision-making in Comitology Committees

A very different sort of committee is designed to adapt directives to "scientific and technical progress". Committees of this type are envisaged under virtually all of the environmental directives. In 1975, the Environment Council had agreed on a model article[28] according to which these committees would generally operate under what later came to be known as the "regulatory committee (*filet*) procedure" or "the IIIa committee procedure".[29]

Establishing a committee of this type generally modifies the applicable decision-making procedure. This modification may be assumed to be acceptable to the Member States only where benefits of for example, avoidance of stalemate or unforeseen problems, outweigh the costs, such as the loss of bargaining power and an increased risk of undesirable decisions. Generally, this balance will be particularly favourable if at least one of the following three conditions is fulfilled:

a) a common goal renders even an individually costly committee decision generally acceptable, or,

b) the new procedure does not introduce major changes compared to the original decision-making procedure, or

c) the procedure is limited to the adoption of decisions of minor importance.

With respect to the common goal (a), the establishment of a committee touches the distinction between product and process regulation. The Member States will have less difficulty in assigning case-by-case decisions to a European committee, where speedy European decision-making promises to increase benefits from other issue-areas that may be traded off against the risk of undesirable committee decisions. The area of product regulation generally allows this trade-off because it contributes to removing national obstacles to transboundary trade.[30] In contrast, the

---

[28] See Council Resolution on the adaptation to technical progress of directives or other Community rules on the protection and improvement of the environment, (1975) OJ C 168/5.

[29] In accordance with the "Comitology Decision" of the Council, (1987) OJ L 197/33; see Meng (1988); Ehlermann (1988). For a description of the procedures, see Vos in this volume.

[30] On the difference between product regulation and process regulation, see Weinstock (1984); Rehbinder/Stewart (1985); Scharpf (1996b); Gehring (1997). On foodstuffs and the committee-like agency arrangement for pharmaceuticals, see Hankin (1997); Gardener (1996); Joerges/Neyer (1997a).

costs of European process regulation are usually not matched by overall gains in other sectors; consequently, Member States tend, in general, to be more reluctant to assign significant powers to comitology committees in this area. Accordingly, establishing comitology committees in environmental process regulation may be assumed to rest predominantly on the remaining options (b and c). Committees could be expected to be created in areas in which the related modification of decision-making procedures is modest. Furthermore, for less important issues, such as those of a technical nature, it could be expected that decision-making would be left to comitology decision-making. However, it is likely that issues which are more important are dealt with by the unbridled political process. In this Section, the powers and decision-making activities of comitology committees in three areas of environmental process regulation will be examined according to these criteria.

4.1 The Drinking Water Committee

The Commission proposal for the Drinking Water Directive included the establishment of a regulatory committee (IIIa) that would be generally responsible for the adaptation of the annexes to scientific and technical progress.[31] These technical and predominantly science-based parts of the Directive had been elaborated largely by the *ad hoc* Group of National Drinking Water Experts.[32] Any amendment to the annexes would be based on scientific expertise and the specific knowledge of public health experts. However, the Commission proposal was heavily contested within the Council.[33] Eventually, the final version of the Directive adopted by the Council reduced the power of the Drinking Water Committee to the adaptation of only one of the annexes that dealt with measurement techniques and analytical methods. Every other detail encapsulated in the annexes, such as the parameters, the limit values and their legal status (mandatory or advisory values) had to be revised according to the normal decision-making procedure. In effect, the scope of the Drinking Water Committee was not really significant, and in practice the Committee never met.

The Directive suffered from a serious implementation problem.[34] Part of the difficulty was the fact that numerous parameters of minor importance had to be measured regularly and analysed according to specific procedures. Consequently, it became clear that implementation would benefit from separating substantive and formal cases of non-compliance. Therefore, an *ad hoc* group of high-level governmental experts of the Member States agreed that the annexes of the Drinking Water Directive and some other quality standard directives required adaptation and that

[31] Above, note 20.   [32] Above, Section 3.   [33] See Kromarek (1986: 33-36).
[34] See Krämer (1992).

committee-based decision-making was the appropriate way forward. However, it was felt that the committee decisions ought not change the ambition of the directives and should not have economic implications for the Member States.[35] The decisions ought to be limited to "minor" issues. Against this background, the Commission proposed in 1988 to establish a uniform committee procedure which would cover four directives, including the Drinking Water Directive.[36] It was proposed that the committee would participate in the modification of all the annexes of these directives with the result that it would be responsible for changing, adding and removing parameters, limit values and measurement methods. The Commission intended that the committee set up under the directives concerned would operate according to the regulatory committee procedure (IIIa), which is most widely used in environmental legislation.[37] Despite the earlier agreement, a number of Member States blocked the proposal, fearing that the committee might adopt costly decisions.[38] Thus, the attempt to establish a committee competent to modify the relevant annexes failed once again in the Council and the project was eventually abandoned in 1990.[39]

In order to understand this failure to establish a meaningful comitology committee in an area in which an advisory expert committee had been quite successful, it is necessary to consider the role of the committee proposed by the Commission within the larger decision-making process. The function of the proposed committee differed greatly from that of the advisory expert committee. Although any amendment of an annex of the Directive by a committee decision did not preclude other professional advice of drinking water experts being sought, the expert deliberations had to be organised either in the form of a new *ad hoc* committee operating under the auspices of the Commission (beyond the remit of the Drinking Water Committee's control), or in the form of a working group of the committee, thus differentiating its own institutional structure. In both cases, the comitology committee would have been the recipient and not the producer of this advice. Accordingly, the joint committee for the quality standard directives was not designed to benefit the Council negotiations, it was intended to replace them. A Member State intending to pursue its

[35] See the Introductory Note in COM(88) 752 final, 7.

[36] Commission proposal for a Council Directive amending directives 80/778/EEC on drinking water, 76/160/EEC on bathing water, 75/440/EEC on surface water and 79/869/EEC on methods of measurement and frequencies of analysis of surface water, COM(89) 478 final.

[37] Initially, the Commission had proposed to grant the Member States a right of initiative but amended its proposal after an intervention of the European Parliament, see its amended proposal (1989) OJ C 300/13.

[38] See Europe Environment, 27 March 1990.

[39] In 1995, the Commission adopted a different approach and submitted a fresh proposal for a revision of the Drinking Water Directive, (1995) OJ C 131/5, see also its amended proposal, (1997) OJ C 213/8.

overall "national interest", however determined, would have to do so within this committee, because there might not be a second stage of decision-making.

Even though the proposed comitology committee could not operate on the terms of the advisory expert committee, it was also designed to perform a particular function within the larger decision-making process. The committee would have constituted the follow-up stage preceded by political decision-making on the directive according to the normal procedure. It would operate within the margin and according to the criteria contained in the Directive. The political pre-decisions envisaged the switch from unanimity to qualified majority voting which would have had considerable implications for the distribution of bargaining power. The committee would seriously soften the voting requirements for follow-up decisions. Before the introduction of qualified majority voting for environmental matters inserted by the Treaty of Maastricht, the Member States preserved their individual veto power according to the unanimity requirement in Articles 100, 235 and 130s EC, while even the most restrictive comitology committee procedure would deprive them of this power resource.[40]

The proposal to establish a committee with the power to amend all annexes might have been feasible if its activities could have been restricted to issues of minor importance. Unfortunately, the pre-decisions did not clearly distinguish between minor and major decisions. This endeavour was doomed to fail not least because the main body of the Drinking Water Directive does not contain all the important provisions, and the relevance of the annexes is not limited to mere technicalities. Thus, the committee's activity would have been directed only loosely by preceding decisions and the committee would have enjoyed a wide margin of discretion. Formally at least, the committee was rather powerful and, over time, it might well have introduced important changes to the European policy on drinking water. The agreement of the Member States not to change the "ambition" of the Directive by committee decisions and not to adopt costly decisions reflects another attempt to demarcate the line separating minor from major decisions. However, this guideline was not formally binding and could not, therefore, ensure that it was actually followed in the long run.

In short, by agreement on the proposal, the Member States would have had to accept a major procedural change and they would not have been sheltered from undesirable decisions of the utmost national importance.

---

[40] One might even argue that the primary intention of establishing comitology committees in environmental process regulation was to avoid the "joint decision trap" (Scharpf 1985) that occurred as a consequence of the transfer of a competence to the European level *and* the still low problem-solving capacity at that level. The fact that any change of a unanimously agreed directive required once again a unanimous decision threatened to create the "problem of obsolescence" (Rehbinder/Stewart 1985: 279) in as dynamic an area as environmental policy-making.

Therefore, it is not particularly surprising that some of the Member States blocked the envisaged expansion of committee decision-making.

4.2 The Nitrate Committee

The Nitrate Committee is an example of a "powerful" committee in environmental process regulation that was established successfully and has been operating for several years. Late in 1991, the Council adopted unanimously the Nitrate Directive[41] based on Article 130s EEC. The Directive was the first piece of environmental legislation regulating the adverse effects of modern farming practices on the environment. The main body of the Directive obliges the Member States to monitor their water resources for pollution by nitrates, identify areas draining into waters that are vulnerable to nitrate pollution and eutrophication, and elaborate and apply action plans. A number of annexes contain specific criteria for identifying vulnerable areas, the content of action plans, and a code of good agricultural practices. Annex III contains the most far-reaching specific obligation: annual limits on the amount of manure that can be spread. The permitted amounts of manure are gradually lowered: in the first four year period, the amount is 210 kg/ha N; thereafter, the rate is dropped to 170 kg/ha N. In terms of its legal architecture, the Nitrate Directive closely resembles the Drinking Water Directive because core obligations are codified in its annexes.

Somewhat surprisingly, the regulatory Committee established under the Nitrate Directive has far-reaching decision-making competences. It is empowered to adapt, without any further express constraints or guidelines, all annexes to scientific and technical progress. Hypothetically, it could seriously tighten, or weaken, the limit values for manure. It is also not prevented from introducing new policies such as a detailed limitation of the application of industrial fertilisers. The Nitrate Committee, therefore, is very powerful in terms of its formal powers. The extent of powers might suggest that the Member States had been willing to relax their direct control over the future of regulatory processes in the area of nitrates, but this approach appears to be in direct contrast to the approach pursued by the States in the areas of drinking water and the packaging of waste.

This apparent contradiction can be explained by viewing the decision to create the Nitrate Committee against the backdrop of the general decision-making process of an EC policy in the area of nitrate pollution. The negotiations of the Nitrate Directive coincided with the Conference on Political Union[42] that was in the process of drafting the Treaty of

[41] Council Directive 91/676/EEC concerning the protection of waters against pollution caused by nitrates from agricultural sources, (1991) OJ L 375/1. On the Directive, see Conrad (1992: 188-192).
[42] On this conference, see Corbett (1992).

Maastricht. During the course of the Conference negotiations, it became clear that for environmental issues based on Article 130s, the co-operation procedure would be used and that the unanimity requirement for Council decisions would be softened to qualified majority voting. Notwithstanding the fact that the Nitrate Directive itself was still adopted under the old unanimity requirement, it was already clear to the Member States that any subsequent amendments of the Directive would fall under the new procedure contained in Article 130s EC with the result that Member States would no longer be able to use their former power of veto. As the new Treaty had revised the overall decision-making process, the Member States in the Council faced a choice: either the Council could send the amendments through the co-operation procedure, thereby reinforcing the role of the European Parliament; or it could establish a comitology committee with the effect of empowering the Commission. Faced with this decision, the Member States chose to retain control over the development of the Community nitrate policy in collaboration with an empowered Commission by establishing a comitology committee and virtually excluded the Parliament from the decision-making process. However, the Council limited the power of the Commission as far as possible by agreeing to the *contre-filet* variant of the regulatory committee procedure (the "IIIb committee procedure")[43] which gives the greatest possible bargaining power to the Member States. The agreement on the Nitrate Committee and the scope of its powers can be explained therefore as a consequence of the Member States' desire to preserve rather than to change, the established decision-making procedure as far as possible.

Although the Nitrate Committee meets regularly, it has not yet adopted any formal decision.[44] The introduction of new policies or the tightening of existing ones is currently not viable because the Member States already face serious difficulties to implement the existing policy. Meanwhile, the Commission has commenced Treaty infringement proceedings against almost every Member State. Against this background, the Netherlands asked in 1996, on the basis of an exemption clause, for an approval to calculate the limit values for manure in a way that would have the effect of allowing values much higher than those normally permitted. This attempt to dilute the limit values might have jeopardised the European nitrate policy if it had been followed by other Member States. Therefore, the Commission submitted the formal proposal for a decision rejecting the Dutch application to the Committee. Voting was postponed because the Committee members were reluctant to outvote a Member State. However, the Netherlands withdrew its application because it had become clear that

[43] The Commission, however, had proposed a IIIa committee procedure, see (1989) OJ C 54/4.

[44] Information on the actual activities of the Nitrate and Packaging Waste Committees is based on interviews conducted in Bonn and Brussels.

it would not be able to gather a qualified majority in favour of its plan. Hence, it was the lack of support from the other Member States that prevented a serious backtrack from an established policy. The Dutch action emphasises that a Member State may have important interests in a particular committee "decision" and that it may well be determined to use its power resources to influence the outcome even though, in this case, the Dutch move was unsuccessful.

The Nitrate Committee demonstrates the general problem related to decision-making in powerful committees. The power of a committee is rooted in its ability to take important decisions independently and is, therefore, immediately related to a large degree of discretion. Under these conditions, the formal activities of a committee are not strictly governed by criteria established at a higher political level (i.e. the Council). Yet, the less clearly committee decision-making is guided by pre-decisions, the more closely will it resemble normal Council negotiations. Hence, comitology committees that are powerful in the present understanding reflect a low degree of functional differentiation of overall decision-making processes. Somewhat paradoxically, the more powerful a committee is in terms of its formal "decision-making powers", the less far-reaching consequences will the transfer of a decision from the Council to the committee entail.

4.3 The Packaging Waste Committee

The Packaging Waste Committee provides the example of a formally "weak", albeit operating, comitology committee. The Committee was created under the European Parliament and Council Directive 94/62/EC on packaging and packaging waste.[45] This Directive establishes mandatory targets for the recovery and recycling of packaging waste and contains quality requirements for packaging; for example, limit values on the content of certain heavy metals, as well as the general obligation to accept packaging that meets these requirements onto domestic markets.[46] Since the Packaging Waste Directive was adopted under the co-decision procedure, in accordance with the qualified majority rule in Article 100a EC, committee decision-making changed the applicable procedure in a way different to that of the proposed Drinking Water Committee because this Committee was to be adopted under the unanimity rule.

The differences between these two committees were not limited to voting requirements because the Packaging Waste Committee formed part of an

---

[45] (1994) OJ L 365/10. On the directive, see Porter/Butt Philip (1993); Porter (1995); Golub (1996).

[46] This directive combines a process-related and a product-related component. It started as a purely process-related project and moved, during the preparatory process, tacitly toward product regulation. See Gehring (1997).

ambitious attempt to develop a long-term European policy on packaging waste. As the policy requires future revisions according to the normal co-decision procedure, the primary task of the Committee is not the general adaptation of the Directive to scientific and technical progress; it is responsible only for the adaptation to scientific and technical progress of two aspects of comparatively minor importance: a marking system and the building of a data bank. Consequently, the political pre-decisions in the area of packaging waste placed most of the important issues beyond the remit of the Committee and strictly limited its potential autonomy in this area of decision-making.

Instead, the Committee was set up primarily to *relieve* the Council. It may adopt specific measures in a number of areas to solve difficulties arising from the implementation of the Directive. The Committee has been active in these areas and so far it has participated in the adoption of two formal decisions on the marking system and the structure of the envisaged data bank. These decisions had been prepared by extensive discussions and were adopted by written communication. The written communication procedure significantly differs from the normal committee procedure: the Commission communicates the draft decisions to the Committee members but then takes any failure to reply as a positive note. Accordingly, negative rather than positive votes are to be voiced.[47]

Currently, the Committee is in the process of drafting decisions on the exemption of certain glass and plastics packaging from the restrictions in the Directive relating to the content of heavy metals. To prepare these decisions, the Commission has initiated three rounds of open discussion on the subject and collected the points of view of the Member States. Subsequently, it has summarised the debate and submitted its conclusions that were in turn hotly debated in the committee. In a future session of the Committee the Commission is expected to submit informally draft decisions that will gather sufficient support for adoption. Only then will this draft be introduced into the formal committee procedure, pass the relevant Commission units, be translated into the official languages, and thereafter be decided upon by the Committee.[48]

The function of relieving the Council underlines the impact of introducing a separate stage of secondary decision-making into the overall decision-making process. All of the Committee's decisions concerned could have been dealt with by the relevant Council working group, as had

[47] However, no Member State voted in the negative.

[48] Thus, Falke's observation that proposals for decisions submitted by the Commission are rarely rejected (Falke 1996: 138-143) primarily reflects the fact that these decisions are well prepared in light of the constellation of Member States' interests. It does *not* imply that the Member States refrain from employing their bargaining power to promote their interests. See van Schendelen (1996: 32-33).

been initially proposed by the Commission. Instead, the decisions are taken by a very similar group of Member State representatives but within the distinct institutional framework of the Committee. Due to this modification, decisions are no longer part of a comprehensive package involving numerous other issues. For example, when the particularities of the marking system are discussed, the desirability of a European policy on packaging waste and the general approach of the Directive are no longer subject of contention. In this subject-area, the political pre-decisions define a narrow scope for autonomous committee decision-making. Accordingly, introducing a second (committee) stage of decision-making following the preceding "political" (Council and Parliament) stage significantly modifies the surroundings of decision-making in which the stake-holding actors operate.

The surroundings influence those decisions taken within the distinct second stage of a larger process. The more precisely the political pre-decisions structure and direct committee decision-making, the less "powerful" a committee is in terms of its ability to adopt decisions independently. In this sense, the Packaging Waste Committee is a "weak" committee. Nevertheless, "weakness" alone does not promote arguing over bargaining. A Member State that is seriously affected by a decision will mobilise its bargaining power in any type of comitology committee to influence the outcome in its own favour. Admittedly, interaction in weak committees may be less prone to fierce bargaining simply because the decisions are too unimportant due to the small margins of committee autonomy.

However, the more closely guided a comitology committee is by clear-cut and general criteria adopted elsewhere, the more important will be *the transfer* of a decision to a committee. If the Member States agree at the political stage on reasonable general criteria, for example because they are not aware to which cases these criteria will be applied over time and how their parochial interests will be eventually affected, and if committee decision-making is closely governed by these criteria when dealing with specific cases, the division of decision-making between two functionally interdependent stages may well encourage actors to refrain from bargaining *at both stages*. In this case, a committee will be weak in terms of a limited margin of discretion but it will be important because it discharges an indispensable task for an altogether important decision-making process. Therefore, weak committees are not necessarily irrelevant; they may well reflect a more successful functional differentiation of decision-making between the Council (and Parliament) stage and the committee stage.

5. Informal Functions of Comitology Committees

If comitology committees convene regularly, they may fulfil additional functions not formally envisaged in the directives. The Nitrate Committee and the Packaging Waste Committee have evolved into regularly-meeting consultation fora, whereas the policy on drinking water has lacked a comparable forum because of the inactivity of the Drinking Water Committee. The systematic and repeated convening of meetings can be advantageous for Community policy-making. For the Commission, committee meetings constitute a source of information on the difficulties occurring in the implementation process and on the opinion of the Member States on the subject. For the Member States committees provide an opportunity to explain their approaches and voice their concern about the behaviour of other Member States. Within the framework of the Packaging Waste Committee, for example, France questioned the German "*Duales System*" (the "green dot" system) because of its discriminatory effects on foreign producers. The United Kingdom made clear that it interpreted the Directive in such way as to render the Danish ban on beverage cans illegal.[49] Disputes on the appropriate implementation of a directive are thus introduced into the multilateral setting of the Committee and withdrawn from the bilateral relationship between a single Member State and the Commission.

One important source of conflict is the correct interpretation of disputed or unclear clauses. The Nitrate Committee interpreted a number of concepts and clauses that are not clearly defined in the Nitrate Directive. For example, it agreed that the mandatory limit values for the application of manure per hectare had to be achieved only by the end of the four year action programme and were not binding for the whole period. Likewise, it agreed on the transformation of the nitrate target into animal units and settled the question as to whether the figures stipulated in the annex of the Directive applied to the average of a farm or to every part of its lands. Currently, it is discussing the nature and extent of monitoring obligations and the criteria establishing agricultural effects on surface waters. Likewise, the Packaging Waste Committee is endeavouring to elaborate a clear-cut definition of "packaging" that is crucial for the proper assessment of recovery and recycling quota.

Over time, a standard procedure has evolved for the interpretation of disputed clauses in environmental directives. A dispute is first discussed in the committee (stage one). Next, the responsible Commission division summarises the exchange of arguments and states its own interpretation of

---

[49] The British position was established as early as 1987 in the famous *Danish Bottles* case, Case 302/86, *Commission* v. *Denmark* [1988] ECR 4607.

the disputed clause in a working paper to be examined by the legal service of the Commission to check its compliance with European law (stage two). Subsequently, the paper is discussed within the committee (stage three), and, where necessary, this process may be repeated.

This standard procedure contributes remarkably to producing discursively reasonable results. In the first round, the Member States discuss a disputed interpretation with each other. A stake-holding Member State may generate consensus on its preferred view, but to affect the outcome, it must (also) convince the Commission. Hence, it may well pursue its own interests but it is encouraged to provide reasonable arguments rather than rely on its power resources with the effect that the Member State must argue rather than bargain. In addition, the Member States are hindered from agreeing on a "convenient" solution among themselves because the Commission dominates in the second stage. Nevertheless, it would be imprudent of the Commission to adopt any "convenient" interpretation because it will subsequently have to convince the Member States of its choice. Therefore, it is well advised to consider the arguments put forward in the preceding discussion and base its judgement on criteria that are accepted by the Member States. These criteria are basically provided by the directive as well as the *acquis communautaire*, in short by European law that is equally mandatory for all actors involved and enables all actors to challenge any interpretation before the European Court of Justice.

If the Commission reaches and submits to the committee an interpretation that is not convincing according to these criteria, interested Member States may challenge it in the third stage in a – now predominantly legal – discourse on the basis of the same criteria. However, if an interpretation is reasonable and convincing, there will be no point in a stake-holding Member State rejecting it because it contradicts national interests. The interpretation merely indicates an appropriate application of the directive compatible with European law and does not itself oblige the actors to anything. In particular, it does not prevent a Member State from implementing the relevant directive according to its own interpretation, but this decision raises the risk that "deviant" behaviour may result in Treaty infringement proceedings. Likewise, the Commission is not prevented from commencing such proceedings notwithstanding a Member State's compliance with a commonly agreed interpretation, but it risks being unsuccessful before the Court. Hence, a common interpretation is not meaningless; it may affect behaviour because the powerful actors are well advised to *consider* it when deciding upon their unilateral moves.

The standard procedure for the committee-supported interpretation of directives promises to produce altogether "rational" results in the Habermasian sense. It does so by forcing both the Member States and the Commission into an exchange of arguments that makes the pursuit of interests only promising as far as it is based on the provision of reasonable arguments.[50] The influence of comitology committees in this informal function relies on their ability to generate consensus and collectively remove uncertainty. Like advisory committees, they are influential precisely because they do not take the final decisions.

For the process of European governance, the informal activities of a comitology committee may be at least as important as the formal ones.[51] Unfortunately, the formal and informal functions of a comitology committee will frequently operate according to different modes of interaction.[52] Formal decision-making cannot fully avoid bargaining because the Member States will not, and should not, ignore their national interests. Informal functions require arguing because they rely on the emergence of consensus that actually convinces the participating actors; thus, comitology committees are hybrids that must accommodate two different, and possibly conflicting, modes of interaction.

6. Conclusion

The existence of committees indicates that decision-making processes are functionally differentiated. In addition to changes of formal decision-making procedures, European committees may affect outcomes of decision-making processes in two conceptually distinct ways. They may define a particular subset of issues relevant to a larger decision-making process and simply re-shape the decision situation in which the participating actors interact. Under certain conditions they may also provide the foundation for a systematic transformation of the mode of interaction from bargaining to arguing. These two different types of committee influence should be analytically distinguished from each other, even though they may occur simultaneously in a single case.

In environmental process regulation, European comitology committees may be formally very powerful. This is true for the proposed Drinking

[50] Similar to the interpretation of unclear terms, informal committee interaction may lead to agreement on the deficits of a directive and guide the Commission proposal for a normal amendment to be adopted according to the applicable decision-making procedure. This function was less relevant in the present cases.

[51] Indeed, the Commission repeatedly attempted to formalise the informal function. In its proposals on the Nitrate Directive, (1989) OJ C 54/4 and (1990) OJ C 51/12, and the Directive intended to establish a uniform committee procedure for some water directives, COM(88) 752 final, committees were assigned the task of advising the Commission on its request on all matters relating to the implementation of the directives. This expansion of formal committee activity was rejected by the Member States.

[52] Principally, the informal functions could be discharged by additional advisory committees. However, it is much easier to motivate "governments" to participate in a comitology committee than require a group of governmentally designated experts to attend an *ad hoc* committee set up by the Commission.

Water Committee and for the Nitrate Committee. The former was rejected by the Member States because it would also have changed the applicable decision-making procedure significantly, while the latter was accepted precisely because it promised to preserve the established procedure as far as possible. These committees have, or were designed to have, very broad competences to modify and adjust important parts of the respective policies. Their far-reaching formal power is rooted in the absence of strict guide-lines established by pre-decisions taken at a hierarchically higher level. Therefore, committee decision-making involves wide margins of discretion, and decisions may touch important interests of Member States. Accordingly, powerful committees will not dramatically redefine the bargaining situation and formal decision-making may be expected to reflect largely intergovernmental bargaining in the Council. This type of committee is not particularly well suited to transform interaction related to formal decision-making from bargaining to arguing.

Other comitology committees, like the Packaging Waste Committee, are formally quite weak. Their activities are governed by comparatively clear-cut and carefully demarcated powers and decision-making criteria. The decisions of committees of this type will be more closely guided by the relevant political pre-decisions. Accordingly, they enjoy only a comparatively small margin of discretion. Decision-making within a weak committee will differ more profoundly from the original situation than that in a powerful committee. Since a weak committee has less freedom of choice, it will on average touch less important national interests. Yet, this conclusion does not prove the low relevance of these committees; on the contrary, they may well be simultaneously weak in the present understanding and important for the related overall decision-making processes, if the political (Council) stage is largely limited to establishing generally applicable and clear-cut decision criteria, and if committee activity is limited to applying these criteria to specific cases. Accordingly, a weak committee may reflect a more advanced functional differentiation of decision-making.

Finally, European committees may matter, even though they are formally entirely powerless. This is not only true for advisory committees like the *ad hoc* Committee of National Drinking Water Experts but also for comitology committees in areas in which they do not take formal decisions. This advisory type of committee activity is directed at *convincing* decision-makers of the relevance and reliability of the advice given. Interaction in the bargaining mode or the adoption of decisions by voting would merely reflect the distribution of bargaining power. To produce convincing arguments and reliable information, the participants are therefore compelled to interact in the arguing mode. The institutional separation of the advisory and the decision-making functions of an overall decision-making process provides the necessary protection of discursive interaction from undesirable intervention of bargaining. The empirical investigation in this paper suggests that the activities of comitology committees in environmental process regulation are, to a large extent, related to this advisory and informal function.

Clearly, committees may well contribute to eroding the crude pursuit of national interests and thus promote "deliberative problem-solving" in European governance. Generally, this effect may be attributed to the functional differentiation of decision-making processes and the delineation of areas in which bargaining constitutes the less viable mode of interaction for the Member States to pursue their interests. Somewhat paradoxically, formally weak committees that enjoy little or no freedom of independent choice and which are quite strictly governed by general criteria may modify interaction among the participating actors more profoundly than committees with far-reaching formal powers. In this sense, the extent of a committee's formal powers is inversely related to its contribution to European governance.

12

The Comitology Challenge to Analytical Integration Theory

*Jürgen Neyer**

1. Introduction

This essay demonstrates that mainstream political science approaches to European governance have serious difficulties in both coping analytically with the complexities of comitology and providing a normative orientation towards the envisaged reform of comitology. Two theoretical approaches, each modifying more general schools of political theorising, are outlined in the paper and are illustrated by referring to European foodstuff policy: intergovernmentalism with its recent emphasis on principal-agent analysis and supranationalism with its focus on administrative interaction. Both highlight important aspects of the way in which decision-making is conducted under a comitology procedure. Neither of them, however, is able to provide an interpretation of comitology which is analytically as well as normatively sound. In falling short in this respect, more of them can sufficiently respond to current reflections about a reform of comitology. Rather than evaluating the relative merits of the two perspectives and assessing which proves more useful in understanding comitology, the paper therefore proceeds by interpreting comitology in the perspective of "deliberative supranationalism".[1]

This approach starts with conceptualising comitology as a necessarily pluralistic "political administration", which combines political and technical tasks in one procedure without adopting state-like characteristics. Comitology, it is argued, is indicative of the necessity to promote administrative discourses which emphasise the need to facilitate transnational

* Research Fellow and Lecturer, Centre of European Law and Politics, University of Bremen.

[1] The concept of deliberative supranationalism has been elaborated in depth in Joerges/Neyer (1997a) and.

deliberation. Deliberative supranationalism underlines the inadequacies of traditional state-oriented analytical categories for describing and understanding the European polity and proposes a constitutionalist approach which takes into account that institutions need to be simultaneously effective and compatible with the normative requirements of Member State democratic polities. It is argued that neither the supranational administrationalist idea of an independent executive nor the intergovernmentalist idea of comitology as mere intergovernmental co-operation can suffice as blueprints. Both are insensitive to the fact that delegation is not just a technical device for furthering efficiency, but an integral element of legislation. Whereas a supranational administrationalist perspective underrates the political character of implementation, intergovernmentalist approaches have difficulties in taking account of the constitutional dimension of delegation. The essay concludes by arguing that comitology is a necessary and useful procedural supplement for enabling the Community to cope efficiently with complex interdependence among European societies by means of facilitating interadministrative discourse and transnational social integration. The realisation of its normative potentials, however, depends crucially on the degree to which the necessary preconditions of deliberation can be realised.

2. Comitology and Political Science

Research on committees and comitology has for a long time been a neglected issue in European integration studies. Over recent years, however, there has been a marked increase in interest shown in this subject:[2] social scientists and lawyers alike have undertaken quantitative[3] and historical[4] descriptions of the committee system, have searched for the functions which committees perform, and have considered the working style in which interaction in committees is conducted.[5] Fundamental issues have begun to emerge: how far does comitology distort the institutional balance of the Community[6] and does the comitology system lead to a further erosion of democratic governance in the EU?[7] Against this flourishing background of innovative research, it comes rather as a surprise to discover that theoretical approaches to comitology are still heavily dominated by the traditional views of intergovernmentalism and supranational administrationalism.

---

[2] An overview of the literature is provided by Pedler/Schaefer (1996). See also the special issue of (1997) 3 *European Law Journal*. A collection of empirical case studies can be found in van Schendelen (1998).

[3] Dogan (1997); Falke (1996).   [4] Demmke *et al* (1996).

[5] Roethe (1995); Wessels (1996).   [6] Lenaerts (1993); Bradley (1992); Vos (1999).

[7] Bach (1997).

2.1. Comitology: An Intergovernmentalist Approach

In the study of comitology, the recent intergovernmentalist approach relies on principal-agent analysis.[8] This approach assumes that the delegation of the Council's competences to the Commission needs to be controlled by Member States because of conflicting interests: the Commission tends to promote liberalisation whereas Member States must balance their collective interest in deepening the internal market with their particular interests in economic and social protection. Thus it was plausible that Member States should insist on control mechanisms to ensure that the Commission would also pay attention to their respective social and economic interests. It is no surprise, therefore, that the 1987 Comitology Decision[9] was the Council's first decision after the SEA came into force. However, the Council also realised that overly strict controls on the comitology system could produce rigidity and inflexibility and therefore result in the inefficient implementation of Community legislation. Hence, the Council felt that what was needed was an effective and diverse range of control mechanisms that would enable it to exercise the requisite restraint to prevent the Commission from overemphasising its own interest.

Indeed, this simultaneous concern for the risks of delegation and the costs of control goes a long way in explaining the institutional complexity of comitology. The different procedures provided by the Comitology Decision represent specific combinations of autonomy of the Commission and control by the Member States, which in turn differ in their effects on the efficiency of implementation and on the balance between the collective and individual interests of Member States. The advisory committee procedure emphasises efficiency and collective interests by merely requiring the Commission to consult Member States. In the case of the management committee procedure, more extensive consultation is necessary in order to avoid a negative qualified majority in the Council. Lastly, the regulatory committee procedure may not only result in significant delays but it also gives great weight to the particular interests of Member States, making it difficult for the Commission to ensure the collective interest in market integration.[10] It is primarily for this reason that the Commission has never suggested the regulatory committee procedure to the Council, whereas the Council frequently tries to revert to this procedure when it is expected that decisions taken by the Commission may cause domestic problems. As a consequence, the Standing Committee on Foodstuffs (StCF), which deals with a variety of highly sensitive issues such as food additives and genetic

---

[8] See Pollack (1997).

[9] Council Decision 87/373/EC (1987) OJ L 197/33.

[10] For a more extensive description of the different procedures see van der Knaap (1996) and Vos, in this volume.

engineering of foodstuffs, almost always operates as a regulatory committee.

From an intergovernmentalist perspective, the unequal distribution of power among the Member States is an important variable explaining the outcomes of interaction.[11] In comitology, however, preferences cannot be simply asserted but need to be justified by arguments such as health risks which are supported by scientific evidence – a feature that may seem astonishing to international theorists.[12] Thus, relative power needs to be defined with regard to the ability to present and substantiate convincing arguments. Since governments will often depend on information supplied by domestic firms, their ability to present convincing arguments is likely to depend on the degree to which domestic industries are interested in a certain regulatory outcome – which, in turn, depends on its expected economic costs or benefits.[13] Thus, the particular frame within which problems must be defined and dealt with in comitology will favour those Member States that command the most advanced scientific expertise. Because governmental representatives must justify their preferences, those which lack the resources for presenting their policies by legally recognised arguments (i.e., by reference to scientific evidence and agreed-upon standards) face serious difficulties. Since scientific discourse acts as a filter, participants who cannot present generally acceptable arguments will find their submissions easily delegitimated. Therefore, the high level of consumer protection that is characteristically achieved by decisions of the StCF may well reflect the "silencing" of relatively powerless Member States in an intergovernmentalist variant of rational choice explanations.

2.2. Comitology in the Perspective of Supranational Administrationalism

As opposed to intergovernmentalism, a supranational administrationalist argument places strong emphasis on the influence of interadministrative partnership[14] and the importance of the Commission in shaping transnational information exchange. The Commission, it is argued, can do so because it is able to dominate the flow of information and monopolise agenda-setting functions.[15] From the perspective of supernational administration, it is not the Member States' interests which dominate European politics but rather European institutions which have the capacity to

---

[11] See Moravscik (1993).   [12] See Neyer (1998).

[13] This argument is supported by several interviews conducted with representatives from the Bund für Lebensmittelrecht und Lebensmittelkunde (BLL), 14 February 1996, the Confederation of the Food and Drink Industries of the EU (CIAA), 26 April 1996, and an official from the Bundesministerium für Gesundheit, Bonn, 28 February 1996.

[14] See Wessels (1996); Institut für Europäische Politik (1989).

[15] See Bach (1997).

channel and influence Member States' interaction in a way which is compatible with European interests. Indeed, there are important arguments to be made in favour of the bargaining power of the Commission: in preparing proposals the Commission has a powerful tool at its command, the Scientific Committee on Food (SCF). The SCF is a committee which is responsible solely to the Commission and which the Commission can consult whenever it deems appropriate.[16] Arguably, recent case law demands that the SCF must be heard whenever aspects of public health are concerned;[17] but it is the Commission which insists on its competence to decide if this condition is met.[18] Because scientific evidence is accepted to be the most valid currency for effecting convincing arguments in comitology, this is an important bargaining chip which the Commission deliberately employs to support those arguments which are compatible with its general interest of furthering harmonisation. Aside from preparing proposals, the most important function of the Commission is to chair the negotiations regarding the adoption of its proposals and to set the agenda of the committee and the working groups. In combining different topics in one session, the Commission can not only further package dealing among the Member States and itself, but it can also place high demands on the technical expertise of Member States' delegations which the limited resources of the delegations are not always able to meet. It comes as no surprise therefore that overloaded agendas and the pressure of the Commission to proceed according to tight time schedules form some of the central concerns of most of the delegations. The period of time national delegations have to respond to the Commission's proposals and to formulate their own positions is sometimes only a few weeks[19] which often leaves no time to organise domestic consultations with all interested parties.[20] Furthermore, the Commission does not hesitate to take a vote on

[16] Not surprisingly, the Commission explicitly rejects demands for a more autonomous and confident role for the SCF which includes the right of the SCF to give opinions without being requested to do so (see interview conducted with a Commission official at DG III, Brussels, 22 February 1996). The Commission's practice of instrumentalising the SCF is a fact which is heavily criticised by a number of delegates; see interview conducted with official from the Permanent Representation of Germany in Brussels, 26 April 1996.

[17] See Joerges (1997) pointing among other cases to the *Angelopharm* case; Case C-212/91 *Angelopharm GmbH* v. *Freie und Hansestadt Hamburg* [1993] ECR I-171.

[18] Interview conducted with a Commission official at DG III, Brussels, 22 February 1996.

[19] The rules of procedure of the StCF demand that all documents related to committee sessions (e.g. the notice convening the meeting, the agenda, the draft measures on which the committee's opinion is requested) must reach the offices of the permanent representatives of the Member States not later than 21 days before the date of the meeting (Article 3). In urgent cases, however, the chairman of the committee may shorten the time to ten clear working days or even include an item on the agenda for a meeting in the course of that meeting (in cases of "extreme urgency").

[20] This problem is exacerbated for the German *Länder* which need to consult one another before being able to reach common positions. It also highlights the difficulties

proposals if consensus is beyond reach and voting is the only way to succeed within such time constraints. Consequently, almost all delegates express concerns about the Commission being too assertive in pushing for results or for using its competences too extensively.[21] Some even argue that the whole process of negotiation is not merely heavily influenced but in fact dominated by the Commission.[22]

3. Comitology as Political Administration

Intergovernmentalism and supranational administrationalism both highlight important aspects of the practice of the administration of the internal market. None of them represents either the whole or the single empirical truth but signifies just one element of a complex process of European market-building. Both provide important critiques of the claim that the reality of comitology should approach the normative ideal of deliberative supranationalism. Both of them point their analytical finger exactly to those issues which normative theories rather easily tend to underrate: power play among Member States, institutional interests, and the reality of strategic bargaining. This analytical strength of both approaches, however, is at the same time their central weakness: in defining European politics as either the master or the servant of national politics and thereby denying the possibility of argumentative interaction among elected governments and European institutions, both approaches fail to take into account what the social sciences have been pointing to since the time of Emil Durkheim: social systems of any kind are not only the sum of their parts but have an autonomous impact on the way their constituent units behave. One of the main problems of both intergovernmentalism and supranational administrationalism is that they understate the importance of discourse in facilitating social integration and lack the conceptual space for understanding that supranational preference generation is more than just a process of aggregating individual preferences. Due to this shortfall, intergovernmentalism and supranational administrationalism do not only overlook an important explanatory variable of the way delegates as well as

Germany's federal structure faces in being compatible with the demands for decision-making under intense time pressure (see interviews conducted with officials at the Landesuntersuchungsamt für die amtliche Lebensmittelüberwachung, Bremen, 15 January 1996, the Behörde für Arbeit, Gesundheit und Soziales der Freien Hansestadt Hamburg, 29 April 1996, the Niedersächsisches Ministerium für Landwirtschaft und Forsten, Hannover, 3 May 1996, a representative of the Bundesrat, Wiesbaden, 15 August 1996, and the Ministerium für Umwelt, Raumordnung und Landwirtschaft des Landes Nordrhein-Westfalen, 4 June 1996).

[21] Responses of delegates to a questionnaire, distributed in the 52nd session of the StCF. The compilation is published in Joerges/Neyer (1997a: 280).

[22] Ibid.

the Commission behave, but they also fall victim to the analytical trap of equating rational behaviour with strategic behaviour. Rather than treating the two perspectives as mutually exclusive, an adequate analytical approach should aim at incorporating the two into a broader perspective. One way of doing so is to analyse comitology as a reaction of Member States to the need for a decision-making procedure which is simultaneously efficient and respects the intrinsically political character of market-building; comitology, in this light, never had the options available to transform into either a supranational agency (which only puts emphasis on efficiency) or to regress to a purely intergovernmental procedure (reviving the co-operation problems in the Council) but needed to build on the assumption that implementation in a non-hierarchical polity must build on the promotion of deliberative decision-making. Three elements are of particular importance in observing deliberative discourses empirically:

(a) The proposals which the Commission presents to the StCF are, in general, the result of extensive consultations with individual national administrations and independent experts.[23] Particularly in committees like the StCF which act under qualified majority voting, proposals do not only reflect the Commission's interest but also include what it assumes to be in the interest of more than only a qualified majority of the other parties involved. This factor attains critical importance because the effectiveness of any measure adopted depends on Member States transposing the measure adequately into their national legal systems without leaving too many opportunities for evasion[24] and – more importantly – without invoking safeguard procedures. However, in an institutional environment without any effective means of hierarchical enforcement, satisfactory implementation is only likely to happen where delegates see their own legitimate concerns acknowledged and protected in the decision-making procedure.

(b) The importance of the SCF for supporting certain arguments does not derive from any formal power to decide conflicting issues (it has only an advisory status) but from the legal fiction of its scientific expertise and neutrality. Of course, Member States are well aware that the SCF is sometimes used by the Commission as an instrument for furthering its interests and furthermore that its experts do not always comply with the norm of objectivity.[25] Moreover, the BSE case has highlighted the fact that even scientific institutions can easily be captured by certain interest groups

---

[23] Interviews conducted with Commission officials at DG III, Brussels, 22 February 1996, and representatives of the BLL, Bonn, 14 February 1996, BEUC and the CIAA, 26 April 1996, Brussels.

[24] For recent articles highlighting the problems of compliance in the European Union see Mendrinou (1996); P M Haas (1998).

[25] See interview conducted with an official at the Permanent Representation of Germany in Brussels, 26 April 1996.

and be instrumentalised for political purposes by the Commission.[26] The
Scientific Veterinary Committee was not only chaired by a British scientist;
the available records of attendance also show the preponderance of UK
scientists and officials, meaning that the Committee tended to reflect
current thinking at the British Ministry of Agriculture, Fisheries and Food.
Why do Member State delegates nevertheless adhere to the fiction of objective science? To understand this, one needs to consider the functions of
legal fictions: scientific findings are supposed to be accepted by all parties
concerned; science-based discourses have the power of disciplining
arguments; and they allow a clear distinction between legitimate and
illegitimate arguments in cases of conflicts over competing proposals.[27]
Therefore, the fact that the opinions of the SCF have never been seriously
challenged by the StCF may be grounded less in the objectivity of its
opinions than in the function of scientific discourses as a mechanism that
is helpful in overcoming politically constituted preferences by relying on
the fiction of objective science.

How interaction between the StCF and the SCF works in practice can be
illustrated by a case which was dealt with in a session of the StCF in
1994.[28] The Spanish delegation complained about Germany having banned
Spanish baby-food after the German food administration had identified
residues of a pesticide (lindan). After pointing out that according to their
own research, a baby would need to eat 835 jars of the baby-food a day to
reach the critical threshold, the Spanish delegation argued that the German
measures were arbitrary and were not covered by scientific evidence.
Therefore, the German measures were to be viewed as protectionist and
contrary to Article 30 EC. Not surprisingly, the German delegation
responded by pointing to Article 36 EC, and argued that baby-food is to be
viewed as a highly sensitive product which needs more rigorous criteria
than are usually applied to foodstuffs. When the dispute between Spain
and Germany approached the fundamental problem of which criteria were
applicable to baby-food, which of course could not be resolved in the
committee itself, the Commission proposed to ask the SCF to give an
opinion on whether baby-food needed additional criteria that were more
rigorous than those applicable to food in general.

This example underlines an important strength of the comitology procedure: in having the opportunity to rely on an institution which is assumed
among the delegations to base its decision on purely scientific criteria
without taking into account distributional aspects, the rule-making
process in the Standing Committee could be spared from any strategic
bargaining among Member State delegations and be transferred to an

[26] Report of the Temporary Committee of Inquiry into BSE by the European Parliament
of 7 February 1997. See Chambers, in this volume.

[27] See Joerges (1997).

[28] See the minutes of the 47th session of the StCF on 20 to 21 June 1994, Brussels.

independent body for supplying additional criteria. Disagreement about a serious concrete issue was thereby transformed into an agreement about how to solve the disagreement.

(c) International negotiations concerning common solutions to problems of interdependence generally involve two modes of interaction: strategic bargaining to maximise particular utilities at the expense of others and deliberative problem-solving to maximise collective utilities.[29] Empirically, it is important to realise that the relative intensity of both modes may vary, and to identify the conditions which influence them. Whereas the mainstream literature on international negotiations does not acknowledge the possibility of deliberative problem solving but conceptualises international negotiations as a pursuit of domestic policy goals by different means, recent contributions in the literature on epistemic communities highlight conditions under which delegates experience a rather broad range of discretion. The most prominent conditions mentioned are uncertainty about the distributive effects of certain policies, long-term interaction among delegates as well as their mutual socialisation into a community with common problem definitions and collectively shared approaches to dealing with them.[30] Under such conditions governments may be either unaware of what their preferences are, or delegates perceiving themselves as being part of a transnational problem-solving community may be able to change their government's perception of interests or even simply by-pass them.

The condition of high uncertainty about the distributional effects of certain policies is surely not always met; in many cases governments have clear perceptions of the costs certain policy options might impose on them. However, in negotiations in the StCF – and even more so in the SCF – the particular economic costs of policies will be quite diffuse and must not be explicitly discussed – hence information is primarily provided on non-distributional issues. *Ceteris paribus*, therefore, the knowledge of delegates about adequate problem-solving strategies will increase with the duration of negotiations, whereas their *relative* knowledge about economic effects will decline. This change in the perceptions and preferences of delegates becomes increasingly important for shaping national preferences as their informational advantage over their national administration increases with time.[31] It is also important to note that negotiations sometimes last for years among nearly the same set of delegates. Moreover, delegates have established contacts outside the sessions of the Standing Committee; they frequently meet each other in working groups of the Council or advisory bodies of the Commission.[32] In the course of this collaboration, delegates not only learn to reduce differences between national legal provisions but

---

[29] For a recent analysis of international negotiations which takes both elements into account see Chayes/Chayes (1995).

[30] Haas (1992); Lewis (1996).   [31] See note 21.   [32] See note 21.

also to develop converging problem definitions and philosophies for their solution. They slowly proceed from being representatives of national interests to being representatives of a Europeanised interadministrative discourse that is characterised by mutual learning and by an understanding of each others' difficulties in the implementation of specific solutions.[33] For the same reason, even the intergovernmental Committee of Permanent Representatives (COREPER) is jokingly referred to as the "Committee of Permanent Traitors"[34] in the German administration. It is also telling that delegates in the StCF often neither know nor seem to care according to which procedure they are actually negotiating;[35] in practice, it often does not matter whether the Commission has the right or the obligation to take into account their concerns.

3.1. Comitology and Legitimate Governance

Any fusion of legislative and administrative activities into one procedure, however, is a rather problematic issue from a constitutionalist perspective. It escapes the traditional normative requirements of a clear distinction between the first and the second branch of government and therefore indicates a constitutional anomaly. Not surprisingly, comitology has not passed unnoticed by the European legislature but has led to fierce criticisms by the European Parliament concerning its compatibility with the established institutional balance.[36] Whilst Parliament has been unhappy about the whole procedure since its very emergence[37] and as early as July 1987 characterised the Comitology Decision as an "alarm bell demonstrating the manifest lack of political will on the part of the Member States to give practical effect to the objectives of the SEA",[38] its critique has only relatively recently gained momentum with the adoption of the Treaty of Maastricht. Parliament now argues that the third indent of Article 145 EC only refers to acts which the Council has adopted and therefore could not be applied to acts adopted under the co-decision procedure which implies "full equality of Parliament and Council".[39] The Council, however, contends that the execution of legal acts of the

---

[33] See interview conducted with an official from the Bundesministerium für Gesundheit, Bonn, 28 February 1996.

[34] Interview conducted with an official from the Permanent Representation of Germany in Brussels, 26 April 1996. Unfortunately, the pun ("*ständige Vertreter*" vs. "*ständige Verräter*") is lost in translation.

[35] See note 21.

[36] For a critical account of that argument see Vos (1999) and Bradley (1997).

[37] For an excellent and detailed account of Parliament's struggle with the Council and the Commission to become involved in comitology see Bradley (1997). He characterises the overall attitude of the Parliament towards comitology as one of 'deep distrust, boiling over on occasion into barely disguised hostility' (at 231).

[38] (1987) OJ C 246/42.   [39] (1994) OJ C 20/176.

Community is, according to Article 5 EC, the sole competence of the Member States. Only by their autonomous decision do they delegate parts of their sovereign powers to the Commission and only insofar as it seems necessary to them.[40] The Parliament's efforts to enlarge its jurisdiction by participating in the implementation of European legal acts therefore are not covered by the provisions of the European Treaties but need to be viewed as an intrusion into competences of the Member States and, therefore, a violation of Treaty provisions. The Council furthermore argues that it is the Member States and not any European institution which command the expertise to decide on how best to integrate European legal acts into their respective national legal systems. Finally, according to the Council, comitology deals only with the technical implementation of secondary legislation and therefore does not need to be under general supervision of the Parliament, which should restrict itself to co-operate in elaborating basic legal acts and leave the implementation of these acts to the administrative machinery and the deliberations of technical experts.

After Parliament had refused to accept implementing procedures under which the decisional power could revert to the Council alone (procedures II and III) and the first failure of a co-decision procedure had occurred, both institutions agreed on a *modus vivendi*.[41] This provisional agreement was expressed to be without prejudice to the positions of principle of the institutions concerned, and pending any revision to be discussed at the 1996/97 IGC. It provided that Parliament should be informed about all draft general implementing acts and any negative opinion delivered by supervisory committees. Furthermore, the Council should adopt measures being referred to it only after giving Parliament a reasonable time to deliver an opinion and taking due account of the Parliament's point of view. This *modus vivendi*, however, has not resolved the interinstitutional conflict. Not only did it fail to put the Council and Parliament on an equal footing but it has also failed on its own limited terms because the Commission neither provided an adequate flow of information to the Parliament nor always allowed Parliament sufficient time to adopt a position. Although the IGC was expected to solve the interinstitutional problem (probably by changing the third indent of Article 145 EC), it failed to do so and only demanded that the Commission prepare a proposal for a reform of comitology before the end of 1998.

What are the appropriate guidelines for reform? Is Parliament correct to assess that comitology is to be viewed as part of a process of interadministrative fusion, by-passing its right of co-legislation and to be condemned for distorting the institutional balance? Or is it an expression of the need to establish efficient structures of governance which are technically able to cope with complex interdependence as it exists in the EC? Answering these

---

[40] See Jacqué, in this volume.   [41] (1996) OJ C 102/1.

questions is obviously no easy task. Which are the normative criteria to apply to comitology? If they are the criteria of majoritarian democracy, defenders of the comitology procedure are in a difficult position: comitology is neither under the control of the European nor of the national Parliaments; it is neither transparent in terms of openness for the media nor accessible to the general public but takes place behind closed doors, as confidential deliberations among appointed experts.

Any normative critique of comitology needs to confront these issues. Such a critique, however, must start by identifying basic normative criteria, from which implications for the critique can be deduced. These criteria cannot be developed in the void of general reflections about the procedural and substantive requirements of a democracy but need to take account of the very nature of the European polity. But what is the "nature of the beast"? Few issues in European integration studies have attracted more attention and provided less acceptable conclusions. This paper does not want to join the chorus of those trying to analytically capture the whole thing[42] but approaches the problem in a less ambitious way, by highlighting some basic normative underpinnings of EC decision-making systems. The following reflections start with the premise that the most basic task of the EC centres around its ability to provide decision-making procedures which enable the Member States to cope with economic interdependence by means of co-ordinating national policies in a way which is equally effective and respects basic requirements of legitimate governance. Because the EC can be conceptualised as a regulatory apparatus, not substituting Member State polities but adding decision-making procedures to their political systems,[43] a crucial distinction for any normative approach is that between questioning the democratic nature of the EC and its legitimacy. This distinction between democracy and legitimacy is important: democracy as a theoretical concept can be understood as referring to a set of political institutions backed by norms to which consent has been given (constitutionalised norms) which aim at enabling a demos to rule itself. Obviously, one of the things this definition presupposes is that a demos exists at all and that it intends to rule itself. As has been pointed out by a variety of authors, democracy without a demos is a *contradiction in adiecto*, which means simply unthinkable.[44] This, however, is essential to the problem normative theory faces when confronted with the EC: EC decision-making is not about organising the self-governance of a (non-existent) European demos, but about coping with increasing transnational economic interdependence in an identifiable number of issue-areas. The EC is not some newly invented polity, which aims at substituting Member State democracies, but a regulatory apparatus making national markets compatible with

---

[42] For recent attempts see Caporaso (1996); Risse-Kappen (1996).

[43] See Majone (1994a).

[44] See Weiler (1995a); Kielmannsegg (1996); Grimm (1995).

one another.[45] Furthermore, the constitutive characteristic of all democracies that a given majority is in a legitimate position to impose its will on any given minority (restrained only at the margins by the requirement of respecting constitutional rights), is far from being accepted in the EC. Accordingly, supranational decision-making is not to be seen as a virtual democratic procedure, but rather as a more or less legitimate way of making collectively binding decisions among governmental actors.

Arguing that the EC neither is nor wants to become a unitary democratic polity does not imply, however, that its adequate normative yardstick is simply efficiency.[46] Its intrusion into national legal systems, and therefore its impact on the internal public order of the Member States, is so intense that additional requirements such as mechanisms ensuring transparency, accountability, subsidiarity, parliamentary supervision and substantive rationality need to be established. What is needed for guiding normative reflection about decision-making procedures in the EC therefore is an approach to the legitimacy issue which equally takes into account that democracy is a fundamentally demos-bound concept (which cannot be easily translated to the European Community) but also rejects the claim that a sufficient degree of legitimacy of the European decision-making system can be provided by efficiency alone. In contrast to democracy, legitimacy is a much broader concept: it is analytically not restricted to indicating the degree of self-determination which a demos realises in a polity but can be understood as referring to an attribute of a decision-making procedure which denotes the degree to which it can be justified by reasonable arguments and is therefore accepted by the addressees. Significantly, reasonable arguments will normally be those which apply principles of self-determination. Arguments supporting such values are those which are voiced in explaining the reasons for parliaments, referenda, or the application of the principle of subsidiarity. On the other hand, reasonable arguments can also be in sharp contradiction to notions of self-determination: in arguing for the independence of institutions such as courts or central banks, most people today put emphasis on the requirement that neither the general public nor the legislature should be able to interfere with their deliberations. Their legitimacy does not derive from being part of a process of organising self-determination but, on the contrary, is based on an assumed isolation from interference by parliaments or the general public. Asking for the legitimacy of an institution or decision-making procedure therefore does not imply a simple assessment of how far they conform with principles of self-determination; it also

---

[45] See Weiler (1995a: 249): "supranationalism (...) is not meant to eliminate the national state but to create a regime which seeks to tame the national interest with a new discipline. The challenge is to control at the societal level the uncontrolled reflexes of national interest in the international sphere".

[46] But see Majone (1994a).

means relating the claim for self-determination to the equally necessary condition of respecting functional imperatives concerning the problem-solving capacity of decision-making systems.

A third necessary requirement of a legitimate decision-making procedure is its promotion of what Dworkin calls "integrity":[47] integrity as a concept of legitimate decision-making builds on the assumption that any legislative body needs to treat like cases alike. It therefore requires that past legislative decisions do have a restraining impact on the range of options available to legislation. As Dworkin argues, integrity in legislative activity is a necessary political ideal insofar as it is a precondition for a legal act to be recognised as expressing a certain conception of fairness, justice or decency. This requirement, however, is far from being unproblematic: it may not imply that past decisions should be viewed as sacrosanct, removed from the possibility of even major changes and therefore binding legislation to old-fashioned values and/or scientific errors. It only emphasises the need for a coherent legal framework under which society conducts its daily affairs and in which major changes – if assumed to be necessary – need to be backed not only by a majority of opinions but by convincing arguments. Any assessment of the legitimacy of a decision-making procedure therefore needs to take into account at least three elements: a) respect for the principle of self-determination, b) the problem-solving capacity of the procedure and c) the integrity of law.

3.2. Practical Implications of a Deliberationist Approach to Comitology

Neither a supranational administrative nor an intergovernmental decision-making procedure can satisfy this triple requirement by itself: both of them fall short with respect to either the principle of self-determination or a high degree of problem-solving capacity and neither of them possesses procedural guarantees that decisions taken are in principle in accordance with past decisions. A supranational administrationalist perspective, to begin with, starts from the assumption that one of the basic problems of European decision-making derives from the fact that Member States still insist on their national sovereignty. Because they are reluctant to accept that interdependence requires a re-establishment of hierarchical political relationships at the European level, giving clear precedence to supranational majoritarian over intergovernmental consensus principles, the problem-solving capacity of European decision-making systems remains insufficient. Without major reform, so the argument runs, Member States cannot cope efficiently with problems of market failure[48] and will remain imprisoned in what Scharpf has called the "joint-decision trap":[49] they can

---

[47] Dworkin (1991: 164-167).   [48] Majone (1993a).   [49] Scharpf (1988).

in fact neither act unilaterally nor as a group. In that light, what is needed is a broad extension of majoritarian principles and the establishment of a supranational European executive, probably by means of empowering independent agencies.[50] The problem of this perspective, however, is rather obvious: the overwhelming majority of the Member States regards majoritarian governance at the European level as being simply politically unacceptable (i.e. illegitimate) because it does not take account of the fact that democracy is rooted in their national political systems – and not at the European level. Empowering the Community to take collectively binding decisions by means of majoritarian voting would imply a normatively problematic and major shift of emphasis from national self-determination to increasing problem-solving capacity. Both independent agencies and expanded supranational administrative competences therefore can only be viewed as legitimate as long as they remain under supervision of intergovernmental co-operation.

Equally insufficient for satisfying the double requirement of self-determination and problem-solving capacity, however, is simple co-operation. Co-operation denotes a type of decision-making which views individual preferences as being intrinsically legitimate reflections of Member State-based democratic procedures which therefore may not be outvoted. Under a co-operation procedure each and every Member State has the right to veto decisions which means that agreements need to be unanimous. Whilst any outcome of a co-operation procedure is, at least from a formalistic point of view, unproblematic (because all parties have agreed), it carries the risk of lowest common denominator politics, which can be easily instrumentalised by single parties for strategies of obstruction and provides no procedural mechanisms for ensuring that decisions respect the integrity of law. Legal provisions deriving from intergovernmental bargaining are heavily shaped by substantive compromises, package dealing and the logic of two-level-games.[51] Respect for law's integrity is rather detrimental to it and difficult to accommodate. Whilst the extension of qualified majority voting (QMV) by the SEA and the Treaties of Maastricht and Amsterdam has significantly reduced the risk of lowest-common-denominator politics and the danger of obstruction,[52] with regard to safeguarding integrity, however, QMV has changed nothing.

As opposed to both a supranational administrationalist normative perspective (extension of majoritarian elements) and an intergovernmentalist perspective (strategic bargaining, eventually modified by QMV), a deliberationist type of decision-making has the potential to satisfy the triple criteria introduced. Its capacity to do so, however, depends on at least three necessary conditions which can be summarised as those procedural requirements that any deliberative decision-making system needs to incorporate.

---

[50] See Majone (1994a).   [51] Putnam (1988); Zangl (1995).   [52] See Peters (1992).

Probably the most important procedural requirement of a deliberative legislative discourse among Member State delegations is a definition, as concrete as possible, of

a) the collective aim of the participants of the group (for example, finding the adequate balance between Articles 30 and 36 EC) and
b) the substantive boundaries of the discourse.

As Stephen Holmes rightly argues, "a conversation is invariably shaped by what its participants decide *not* (emphasis added) to say".[53] To avoid destructive conflicts and cognitive overload, controversial themes are often suppressed by means of "strategic self-censorship" or – as Rawls has put it – "the method of avoidance".[54] Examples of this occurring are ubiquitous in European politics: most basically they can be found in the principle of limited competences; more concretely in the Commission's new Green Paper on foodstuffs,[55] which states that the only relevant topics for legislative discourses are those which are in direct relation to issues of public health and safety. Accordingly, in the deliberations of the StCF, an important gag rule is not to mention explicitly the distributive implications of measures adopted but only to assess their contribution to health and safety aspects. In determining between legitimate and illegitimate arguments and providing criteria for assessing the validity of an argument (scientific evidence), the bargaining among delegates becomes in fact *constitutionalised*, and decisions being agreed upon can be legitimised by reference to the underlying principle of promoting health and safety. This fact is precisely what the integrity of law demands.

The second most important procedural requirement of any deliberative discourse is the condition that the act of casting votes plays only a minor role in decision-making and is, in importance, subordinated to argumentative interaction. Promoting this requirement entails that the preferences of delegates are not viewed as intrinsically legitimate reflections of the individuality and democratic nature of any Member State's preferences but only as governmental claims which attain their normative status by being convincing to the other delegates. What at first sight seems to be a basic normative problem in terms of responsiveness to domestic constituencies is ultimately a necessary precondition for reaching multilateral agreements above simple aggregation. If all delegates insisted on their status as representatives of an intrinsically legitimate domestic interest, all solutions apart from identifying common denominators would be overruled and excluded. The main decision-making method of a deliberative discourse therefore is to argue, which means that every claim has to be supported by giving evidence for one's propositions. As opposed to a voting procedure in which a slight unhappiness with a provision counts as much as a strong

[53] Holmes (1988: 19).   [54] Rawls (1985).   [55] COM(97) 176 final.

support for it, different intensities of preferences do not need to be ignored but can become an essential issue in a process of pooling individual judgments.[56] The mode in which discourses are conducted in a deliberative procedure can be understood with the help of Dworkin's conceptualisation of legal reasoning:[57] each of the actors in a given legal dispute interprets a given norm relevant for a decision to be taken (in our terms: a substantive definition of the discourse) according to his subjective understanding of its meaning and by openly describing his or her way of deducing implication from a consented norm. By doing so, a number of different interpretations emerge which may only in rare cases converge towards a commonly shared opinion of what kind of concrete measure or behaviour a given norm requires. Legal reasoning by openly describing subjective ways of deducing implication from a norm, however, helps clarify differences of understanding and is accessible for critical evaluation by third parties.

The existence of a neutral third party is a third necessary procedural requirement. It serves the double function of a) giving opinion in cases which would otherwise be unsolvable by means of discourse among the parties themselves and b) providing incentives to actors for behaving in accordance with the requirements of legal reasoning. Analytically, this third party could be, for example, a court (assessing the legal status of arguments), a scientific body (assessing the scientific soundness of arguments), or even the general public (assessing how far arguments are in accordance with a given political will). From a normative point of view, there can be little doubt that in an ideal world it is always the general public which acts as the third party. In doing so it can control whether political agents comply with substantive and procedural requirements of a given definition of discourse and thereby impose political costs on non-compliant governmental actors. In the real world of scarce informational resources and often highly technical matters on the legislative agenda, it may, however, often be the case that neither an interested general public nor interested media actually exist. In these cases, the general public needs to be supported by functionally equivalent third parties which act in its interest. Which of the three possibilities may be the adequate one in a given decision-making system directly depends on the nature of the definitions of a given discourse. If these definitions include, for example, the provision that arguments are only to be viewed as legitimate if they refer to scientific evidence, the adequate arbiter might be a scientific committee. If the definitions are more broad and only provided by secondary or even primary legislation, then a more adequate arbiter would be the ECJ. In all European discourses, above even Treaty law, (for example, IGCs), the arbiter needs to be equally broad and must be the general public or the national legislatures. In all three instances, however, the function of the

---

[56] See Miller (1993: 75-77).   [57] Dworkin (1991: chap. 2).

arbiter is not to give authoritative decisions which lay the ground for executive enforcement, but to provide a disciplinary function for the actors involved in the discourse to refrain from openly selfish arguments and to legitimise their preferences by referring to the normative criteria laid down in the definitions of a given discourse.

4. Conclusions

What is the relevance of the above reflections for suggesting a new normative perspective for comitology? The argument presented so far holds that neither majoritarian nor co-operative decision-making can by itself provide the legitimacy needed for European decision-making but needs at least to be supplemented by elements of a deliberative discourse. Delegation, from this perspective, is not simply to be understood as a kind of outsourcing of those tasks which are of minor importance, and which refer only to technical implementation. Rather, it needs to be understood as structuring the legislative process itself, introducing elements of procedural rationality and substantive integrity to intergovernmental bargaining. Its primary normative function is not merely to delegate the technical aspects of policy-making to apolitical experts, but to restrict the bargaining process in the Council to formulating basic standards and criteria of how to deal with disputed issues. Therefore, it is the essential elements of the problem-solving process itself which are being delegated. The main normative reason for delegating tasks to the Commission is the double acknowledgement of the need for and the difficulty of facilitating deliberative decision-making. Delegation is an expression of the intention to change the logic of the decision-making process from one dominated by strategic bargaining and preference aggregation to one conducted by means of deliberative interaction. Comitology, from this point of view, refers to a set of decision-making procedures which are neither simply characterised by different intensities of Member State control nor can be understood as merely technical devices for propelling implementation. Rather, comitology refers to a redefinition of the terms under which problem-solving is conducted and resembles a kind of intrinsically political administration rather than an apolitical and technical procedure.

It is important to emphasise that intergovernmental deliberation is neither *per se* legitimate nor separate from democratic governance. In the perspective outlined above, it is viewed as a necessary supranational supplement to state-based majoritarian democracy and international co-operation. Its focus is not on substituting state-based majoritarian democracy but on enabling the Community to harmonise equally legitimate but highly diverging preferences of Member States and to cope systematically with the external effects of state-based democratic decisions. Comitology surely is not to be misunderstood as any real world expression of the normative ideals proposed above but as a procedure which is to be legitimised and criticised against the yardstick of its ability to realise the promise of a deliberative decision-making procedure. The appraisal of comitology and its critique are therefore two sides of one coin: its appraisal is the need for deliberation in propelling the efficiency of decision-making; its critique is the degree to which the promise of deliberation remains unfulfilled.

The political price for comitology so far has largely been paid by the European Parliament. Article 145(3) EC can easily be interpreted as a partial negation of the legislative rights which have been given to Parliament by the introduction of Article 189b EC. In agreeing to the comitology procedure, Parliament factually disempowers itself of some of its legislative rights; and Parliament has always made clear that it strongly disapproves of the whole procedure.[58] At least in the long run, comitology implies either the danger of a hollowing out of the co-decision procedure (because important legislative activities are delegated to the Commission), or falls victim to an upset Parliament which rejects any legislative act that does not specify every technical detail. These dangers should (and probably will) be taken seriously when the Commission prepares its proposal for a reform of comitology. This reform should have as its basic element a compromise between Council and Parliament about the conditions under which both can accept delegation. Such a compromise, however, cannot impinge on Article 145 (3) EC (which is in the sole competence of an intergovernmental conference) nor aim at legally enabling the Parliament to broadly participate in executive legislation (for which it is not an adequate institution). A possible way of dealing with Parliament's political demands, without risking either an immediate veto of the Member States or involving a legislative body in mainly executive implementation, may be for both Council and Parliament to introduce a right of revocation for all implementing acts referring to basic legislation conducted under the co-decision procedure. Such a right would entail that both institutions could, under certain specified conditions, require the Commission not to implement its decisions but to refer them back to the legislative procedure. Agreeing on such a proposal would imply that both Council and Parliament could be rather relaxed about the day-to-day practice of comitology and nevertheless remain in a position to enter the decision-making discourse when single topics become of crucial importance to them.

Finally, any proposed reform which is oriented at realising deliberative ideas needs to incorporate increased transparency: until now comitology committees have generally conducted their affairs behind closed doors and

---

[58] See Bradley (1997).

publish neither minutes nor agendas. This practice is, however, unecessary and not useful. Except for deliberations concerning highly sensitive issues, such as the fixing of prices of agricultural products or the allocation of grants under Union expenditure programmes, comitology committees should generally convene publicly, and grant access to the media and interested non-governmental actors. Increased transparency would both encourage the discipline of delegates to behave according to the definitions of given legislative discourses and also provide the Member State legislatures with a more accurate account of what governmental delegates in committees are actually doing. Intergovernmental deliberation without transparency is much closer to Kafkaesque images of 19th century secret diplomacy than to anything compatible with 21st century democracy.

13

Regulatory Oversight in Europe: The Case of Comitology[*]

Michelle Egan[**] and Dieter Wolf[***]

1. Introduction: Governance, Regulation and Control

Control and discretion in the modern administrative state is a concern in most polities. The necessity and effectiveness of controlling bureaucratic discretion and promoting greater political oversight over the administrative process has been debated from different ideological and theoretical perspectives.[1] Thus while Breyer[2] and Ogul[3] focus on the development of an administrative apparatus based on continuity, professionalism, expertise and effectiveness, whereby implementation is carried out by trusted agents with a high degree of congruence of goals and purpose between political and administrative officials, Lowi[4] sees the power of bureaucratic agencies as problematic, since the agencies seem to be gaining power at the expense of the political branches of government and the courts. At a general level, the different theories reflect certain values about the administrative process, the design of accountability systems, and the relations between institutional actors – specifically agencies and bureaucracies, interest groups and experts. As scholars increasingly debate the relationship between political and administrative preferences and goals, along with the institutional design best suited to make the bureaucracy more accountable, transparent and efficient, the debate has assumed greater prominence within the European Union as the growth of regulatory competencies at this level has necessitated a greater role for the bureaucracy in a number of issue areas.

[*] A revised version of the paper presented to the GAAC Summer Institute on "The Political Economy of European Integration", University of Bremen, August 5th–16th, 1996. Both authors acknowledge the financial support of the German & American Academic Council Foundation, Bonn, and the Social Science Research Council, New York. An earlier version was published in the *Columbia Journal of European Law* September, 1998.

[**] Assistant Professor at American University, Washington DC.
[***] Research Fellow and Lecturer, Centre of European Law and Politics, Bremen.

[1] See for example Aberbach/Rockman (1988); Ogul (1976); Moe (1982).
[2] Breyer (1982) and (1993).   [3] Ogul (1976).   [4] Lowi (1969).

While the nation-state has consolidated its activities around distributive and redistributive policies, the EU – as Giandomenico Majone's studies have shown – has chiefly developed its regulatory and rule-making dimension.[5] The growth of regulatory activity has meant increased administrative discretion as agencies, committees, and experts have become increasingly prominent in assisting, advising and interpreting a wide variety of issues related to the implementation of statutory legislation.[6] Since Community legislation provides for the implementation or adaptation of its provisions, just as national legislation allows governments to adopt statutory instruments,[7] there is increasing concern about the adverse consequences of such delegation. Because of the need to delegate day-to-day policy-making to administrative officials, the concern over the loss of policy coherence or the loss of accountability has generated renewed interest in the instruments of regulatory oversight and control at the European level.[8]

While this necessitates more attention being paid to the prospects, problems and possible outcomes upon patterns of European governance,[9] there is no doubt, given the efforts to simplify legislation, devolve responsibility under subsidiarity and challenge community competence, that further debate about the regulatory role of the European Union will be generated, even on those issues which seemingly have been decided. The purpose of this debate is partly symbolic and partly prescriptive, compounded by the fiscal constraints and ideological pressures which have forced governments to achieve new ways of meeting the demands for policy and services that are placed on them. However, it underscores the importance of the on-going institutional debates in Europe, and whether the institutional location of the regulatory function makes a great deal of difference, and whether administrative policy-making ought to be insulated from political control by elected representatives, as governments chafe under domestic political pressures and discontent over the costs of political and economic compliance with European integration.

Though there general support for the overall economic ideals remains, public opinion surveys have found that integration has become increasingly fragile and subject to sudden outbursts, disagreements or rancour over specific issues.[10] One of the most turbulent issues has been the role of the Commission, and the perception of a faceless bureaucracy directing policy from Brussels has generated pressures for administrative reform. Though the Commission has capitalised on its strategic position in the law-making process, guaranteed by the right of legislative initiative, in doing so it has drawn criticism towards its rule-making and enforcement powers in a wide

---

[5] Majone (1996b); (1991).   [6] See Kreher (1997).
[7] Corbett (1989).   [8] Dehousse *et al* (1992).
[9] See Jachtenfuchs/Kohler-Koch (1996a); Marks/Hooghe/Blank (1996); Harlow (1998).
[10] Franklin/Marsh/McClaren (1994).

array of issues areas including subsidies and state aids, competition policy, agricultural levies and quotas.[11]

Despite various conclusions about the power and authority of the Commission,[12] these assessments are grounded in the current debates in integration theory, and do not seek to draw on similar concerns and debates in public policy, public administration and public management about the relationship between politics and administration. One must concede, however, that the issues being raised are not new. The balance between administration and politics or between technocracy and democracy has received a good deal of attention in the American context, and is suggestive of a broader concern about the intersection of governance, accountability and discretion in the modern administrative state. The growth of the administrative state in the US – in part the expansion of federal authority – resulted from a fundamental shift in the constitutional relationship between states and federal government as well as between government and the economy. A great deal of literature looking at the rise of the administrative state in the US has focused on the balance of power between different institutions, and generated a widespread discussion about the role and effect of regulation. The various theories and perspectives that have dominated the American experience (public interest, interest group and administrative control) find echoes in the contemporary debates in Europe.

We briefly consider each of these theories, before turning to an empirical examination of regulatory control in the European Union. In empirical terms, we focus on the "Comitology" procedures of Council oversight as a mechanism of control over bureaucratic discretion. Comitology is essentially the emergence of committees of national civil servants, experts and private interests assisting and advising the Commission in areas where decision-making power has been delegated to Community institutions.[13] The decision-making procedures under comitology essentially fall into two basic types: those that allow the Commission a degree of executive or administrative autonomy and those that reduce administrative discretion and restrict the Commission's room for manoeuvre.[14] The application of regulatory theories to comitology is useful in raising concerns about legitimacy, co-ordination and control. As a result, the following analysis seeks to further identify a series of debates and perspectives in the US that parallel the same kinds of constitutional values, administrative challenges, and political concerns that are being raised in the European political system.[15] Comitology, we argue, is just one additional expression of

---

[11] Harlow (1998).   [12] Pollack (1997); Smyrl (1998).

[13] Vos (1997b); Falke (1996); Egan/Wolf (1998).

[14] See Egan/Wolf (1998) and other articles in this volume.

[15] Majone (1994a); Shapiro (1988), (1996a) and (1997b); Everson (1995a).

controlling bureaucratic discretion as Member States have looked for means to prevent the supranational bureaucracy from overstepping its boundaries, and ensure that the Commission responds to and reflects national Member States concerns when it engages in administrative policy-making.

2. Theoretical Perspectives on Regulation

Generally speaking, the main theoretical approaches to the study of regulation in the US context focus on its origins, practice and consequences.[16] Research on regulatory politics has in recent years sought to test hypotheses about the applicability of different approaches through empirical research.[17] Most of this has concentrated on the American regulatory experience, focusing on its origins, practice and consequences.[18] A core feature of this research is to understand and evaluate the impact of the rise of economic and social regulation on American law and government. These approaches tend to be either bureaucratic or legislative in focus, centering on the behaviour of regulatory agencies and their relation to regulated groups[19] or upon the electoral process and the influence and incentives of legislative institutions.[20] Many focus on certain key actors or stages in the regulatory process, yet attempt to derive general explanations of regulatory behaviour.[21]

2.1 Serving the Public Interest

The notion of public interest seems an unusually vague construct that was initially defined in the nineteenth century to apply to certain types of enterprises as "affected with a public interest" such as banking, utilities and railroads, and therefore subject to a strong application of police powers to prevent destabilising or destructive competition. American law reflected the economic premise of the notion of public interest, which over time had far less utility since some industries were closely regulated and others were not. From an economic perspective, regulation in the public interest was justified in terms of the exercise of collective power to cure market failures, and to protect the public from the effects of monopoly behaviour, destructive competition, the abuse of private economic power, or the effects of externalities.

In the political domain, the notion of public interest is more broadly associated with the public good or general welfare. The classic public interest theory is both a positive theory about what motivates policy

---

[16] Joskow/Noll (1981).   [17] Gormley (1979); Moe (1982).
[18] Joskow/Noll (1981); Mitnick (1980).   [19] Quirk (1981).
[20] Niskanen (1971).   [21] See especially Stigler (1971).

makers and a normative theory about what should motivate them. The theory assumes that political regulation is designed to maximise the benefits to the largest number of individuals. Public interest scholars argue that once the problem is cast in technical terms, regulators can carefully and meticulously consider a response that will produce the maximum aggregate benefit. Thus, they argue that unlike legislatures, regulatory agencies would sit continuously, investigating and deliberating within a universe of dispassionate expertise. As decisions will be determined not by political consensus and bargaining, but rather a technocratic approach – the theory reflects a benign view of interest group competition.

Expertise was said to be vital because regulation involved the interpretation of a wide range of scientific, technical knowledge and social facts. Freedom from political pressure would increase the ability of administrators to exercise regulatory discretion and enable regulators to follow the public interest rather than make policy based on political expediency. This resulted in the creation of public interest era agencies that reflected the classic dichotomy between public regulation and private activity, and employed traditional command and control adjudication and rule-making powers to achieve their market-corrective goals.[22] However, the public interest approach did not consider the implications of vague, ambiguous statutes.[23] While ambiguity was inevitable, since legislation could not cover all contingencies and effects, criticism focused on the insufficient guidance that vaguely drafted legislation provided to regulatory agencies, making it hard to challenge or constrain that discretion.

Advocates of the public interest approach have a great deal in common with functionalist explanations of integration. In the study of the EU, functionalism gives analytical primacy to social and economic co-operation. It is built on the premise that functional integration would be pragmatic, technocratic and flexible; it would deliberately blur distinctions between national and international, public and private, and political and non-political.[24] As with the public interest approach, functionalism focuses on the provision of welfare. It assumes that consensual knowledge and perceptions drive change. Like the public interest approach, functionalists ignore elements of competition and conflict within and between functional agencies. Thus, we would expect comitology committees to be prominent where "problem-solving" rather than political "bargaining" is the dominant policy style.[25]

However, the sheer scope of administrative decision-making raises questions about its efficacy and even political legitimacy. Theoretical objections to the public interest approach focused on the "headless fourth branch of government", that was considered unresponsive to executive leadership.

[22] Rabin (1994).   [23] Lowi (1969).
[24] Pollack (1995); see also E B Haas (1958).   [25] Scharpf (1988).

While tripartite division of powers – legislative, executive and judicial – had been of great importance in justifying the concentration of powers in regulatory agencies, the theory and practice of separation of powers was being undermined, according to critics, as regulatory agencies were not subject to any "checks and balances". As Mashaw summarises the criticism: delegation will delegitimise representative governance and statutory vagueness will lead to an overall reduction in public welfare.[26] This is echoed by Harlow who considers comitology an unaccountable technocracy operating at the heart of the Community, which is incapable of acting fairly and needs to be controlled.[27] Arguing that standard values of openness, impartiality, reasoned and rational decision-making must prevail, Harlow is reflecting the revival of the public interest tradition, whereby public deliberation has increased in saliency in both public policy and public law.[28]

Paralleling these developments, concepts such as policy learning, efficiency, norms and ideas have received widespread interest in international relations and public policy.[29] This has focused attention on patterns of reasoning – determining which assumptions and arguments would form the conceptual basis for public policies or assessing the persuasiveness of the evidence that supports the best means to a given end. In doing so, it recognises the shift towards efficiency as a primary policy goal, and a growing awareness that policy outcomes are not simply the product of group struggle but of rational policy analysis and social responsibility.[30]

In the European context, this renewed attention towards the public interest has been obscured by the focus on the intergovernmental relations between the Member States, and the derivation of legitimacy from the consent of the states to further European integration. The argument put forward by intergovernmentalists that national administrators have a common interest in defending their turf and resisting interference suggests that the trust based systems of public administration, based on rationality, expertise and scientific reasoning, are not in tune with the European policy-making patterns which is characterised by conflict and distributive bargaining.[31] However, there is a growing debate in the legal sphere that "European administrative law must actively seek to identify a series of European constitutional values which it can deploy in order to 'civilise' explicitly political and pluralist administration".[32] The notion that efforts to secure the most effective and legitimate means to balance and consolidate diverse social interests and values are indicative of a shift away from an intergovernmental understanding of administrative control towards a more public interest perspective.

[26] Mashaw (1994a).   [27] Harlow (1998).
[28] Majone (1989a); R B Reich (1988); Breyer (1982).
[29] Goldstein/Keohane (1993); Risse-Kappen (1996); Jachtenfuchs (1995).
[30] Majone (1996b); (1989a).
[31] Scharpf (1988); Wessels (1998).   [32] Everson (1998).

2.2 Lobbying and Interest Group Approaches

While sceptics constantly questioned public interest perspectives, there was constant efforts to support this view, despite increasing work on analysing the ties between regulated and regulator.[33] By the time that the path-breaking work of Olsen[34] and Stigler appeared, a broad re-evaluation of American institutions had begun.[35] Rejecting the validity and efficacy of broad administrative discretion, the basic idea of these interest-based theories of regulation is that regulatory agencies, working on behalf of the public interest are captured by the very interest they are supposed to be regulating. Questioning the rationale that the real purpose of regulation is aggregate social wealth, interest group theories questioned whether interest groups were not using regulatory agencies to serve their own particularistic ends.

Behind the image of pluralism that had so dominated intellectual thought, there was increasing evidence that the regulatory agencies did not match the public interest ideology. Economic theories of regulation, whose near-worship of the market as the most efficient allocator of resources, conceptualised the regulatory process as a form of the market-place where rational self-interested actors maximise their utilities. In these models, regulation is treated as a commodity which could selectively distribute benefits. Unwilling to accept the assumptions of either the public interest or capture thesis, economists (notably Stigler) shifted the focus by assuming that regulators are rational actors trying to maximise the polit-ical benefits from enacting a particular policy. For Stigler, regulation is the result of demands by industry; and the outcome is therefore designed and operated entirely for the benefit of producers, not some broader public welfare.[36] Thus, firms engage in "rent seeking behaviour" and view regula-tion as a means to gain income they otherwise would not enjoy. Stigler's conclusion that "the problem of regulation is the problem of discovering when and why an industry is able to use the state for its own purposes"[37] found its answer in political science and law.

In responding to Stigler's question, Peltzman argued that the regulatory powers of the state can have an impact on the distribution of wealth as well as allocative efficiency.[38] Competing interest groups seek additional benefits through the regulatory process, and to do so, provide benefits and resources, in the form of votes, to receive certain beneficial returns. While again viewing regulation as a form of market-efficiency, with regulators choosing between competing interests and preferences, the debate among lawyers and political scientists centred on due process, reform and legiti-

---

[33] See especially Landis (1938).   [34] Olsen (1965).
[35] Stigler (1971).   [36] Stigler (1975).
[37] Stigler (1971).   [38] Peltzman (1976).

macy, and highlighted the debate between pluralist and anti-pluralist views that seems to have found contemporary echoes in Europe.[39]

Stung by criticism that the supposedly pluralist system did not allow equal access but instead reflected systematic, articulate, well-funded organisation,[40] the increased involvement of the courts sought to ensure that regulators took account of all interests, and in effect substituted judicial for regulatory policy.[41] As a result, rules of standing were expanded to ease access to regulatory policy-making and the reformation of American administrative law resulted in "the provision of a surrogate political process to ensure the fair representation of a wide range of affected interests in the process of administrative decision-making".[42] The increasing substitution of judicial policy-making for administrative and regulatory policy making and the increase in judicial oversight in the 1960s and 1970s was designed to enhance due process and ensure that semi-sovereign bureaucracies review available evidence, engage in reasoned decision-making, and give careful consideration to alternatives.

However, the anti-pluralist indictment inspired not only a judicial response, but also resulted in a period of legislative activism that involved concentrated costs on industry and dispersed benefits to the public – not a scenario predicated by capture theory nor one that traditionally augured well for the enactment of regulatory legislation.[43] Yet a series of regulatory initiatives – on auto safety, product safety, air and water control, and occupational health and safety – marked a return to the policing model inherent in the public interest perspective. By reordering relations between state and society, and blurring the distinction between public and private spheres of activity, the emergence of social regulatory agencies concerned with the long term social consequences of industries imposed significant costs not on a narrow range of industries but more broadly, and can hardly be said to be designed and operated for the benefits of producers.[44] Though the regulatory system – whether dealing with health, safety or environmental issues – operated primarily in an enforcement or policing mode, the judicial activism focused not like earlier public interest periods on the effects of economic regulation, but on questions of how to effectively control the exercise of administrative discretion in cases of scientific and technological complexity.[45] The core of public interest activity is embedded in the new social regulation, in part pushed on by judicial concern over due process, access and fairness. However, this legislative and judicial tandem cannot disguise the remaining biases in resources,

[39] Though current research on European integration does not use this terminology, much of the work on deliberative democracy and administrative law-making is suggestive of similar concerns. See for example, Everson (1998); Harlow (1998); Joerges/Neyer (1997a).

[40] Lowi (1969); McConnell (1966).   [41] Stewart (1975).

[42] Stewart (1975: 1760).   [43] Reagan (1987).

[44] Wilson (1980).   [45] Breyer (1993).

litigation challenges and other benefits that accrue to better organised interests.

Thus, interest group explanations are able to claim theoretical primacy if they can demonstrate that powerful interests – particularly firms – dominate the policy process. In accounts of European integration, EU scholars have highlighted what interest-based scholars would argue is the "capture" of the policy process.[46] As Caporaso and Keeler note: a substantial amount of work had been accomplished by multinationals in preparing the groundwork for the single market. The result has been that economic interest groups play a crucial role in lobbying supranational and national actors.[47] Although the decisions of European firms on investment, employment and output have important allocational and distributional implications which influence public policy,[48] institutions and procedures tend to be portrayed as reflecting the resource-preferences of private actors; and government actors are viewed as carrying out the terms of the reflecting compromises. However, capture theory – because of its American history and intellectual tradition – in many ways does not consider situations where regulatory policy is characterised by an "issue network" that brings together both public and private actors who are mutually interdependent.[49] The policy or issue network literature conveys the image of a complex pattern of interorganisational linkages that can vary across issues and sectors.[50] Policy network approaches hold that the dynamics of regulation are shaped by the institutionalisation of rules and norms based on stable expectations and mutual understandings among the participants. While business can have privileged access as a policy participant, as suggested by the literature on corporatism and private interest government in the European context,[51] the emergence of private regulatory regimes in many industry sectors, setting standards and codes of conduct, raises questions about market governance and the relationship between regulated and regulator in the European polity.[52]

2.3 Principals and Agents: Administrative Theories

In spite of the complexity in rule-making, and the interest in the relationship between public and private interests, there has been a corresponding interest and attention given to the inter-institutional balance in the regulatory process. Contrasting with the debate about the authority and power of interest groups, there has been renewed attention towards questions of control and implementation problems in organisations.[53] Using tools

---

[46] Dehousse (1994b: 125).
[47] See McLaughlin/Greenwood (1995); Cowles (1995).
[48] Lindblom (1977).   [49] Dehousse (1997).
[50] R A W Rhodes (1988).   [51] Streeck/Schmitter (1985).
[52] Haufler (1998); Egan (1998).   [53] Moran (1986).

derived from game theory, microeconomics and social choice of decision-making rules and structures these approaches focus on the degree to which regulatory agencies are responsive, under certain conditions, to efforts at political control of bureaucratic discretion. Many of these theoretical and empirical studies challenge the implicit assumption by capture theorists that all regulatory contexts are characterised by some basic pattern of group interests.

Instead, the inherent problems in the regulatory system are the extent to which agency preference actually reflect that of voters' concerns. The main arguments dominant in the literature draws on principal-agent theory. Interest focuses on whether the abdication or "delegation" of policy-making by the principal (whether voter to government or legislature to administrative agency or bureaucracy) results in policy outcomes that reflect the original intent of the legislation. Because of concerns that agents will engage in either slack (lack of effort) or slippage (discretionary activity), administrative control and oversight is considered a key factor in ensuring compliance.[54] This way of looking at organisations, allows for differentiation in their motivations and incentives that is not fully addressed by capture or public interest theory. In particular, the emphasis on increased scrutiny and interference by courts, executives and legislators has meant an increased focus on institutional design, generating explanations about the activist, regulatory state radically different from that of public interest perspectives.

Pursuit of the public interest as a guide to understanding the structure and behaviour of public institutions is replaced with administrative control theory that focuses on the consequences of delegating decisions to agencies and the methods of institutional design that principals (such as Congress, shareholders, and Member States) can use to increase the likelihood that the consequences are beneficial to them.[55] The political control approach describes a variety of control strategies that can be divided into two broad types: ex post oversight and ex ante administrative procedures.[56] While oversight mechanisms such as budgeting, monitoring and evaluating agency behaviour can provide solutions to the principal-agent problem,[57] create incentives for agents to comply with the principal's objectives and intentions, they depict a situation in which adversarial politics is dominant.

Administrative procedures such as decision-making rules and constraints, openness and transparency, and due process are also important mechanisms for inducing compliance by controlling the institutional environment in which agencies make decisions and thereby limiting the

---

[54] See especially Mitnick (1975).

[55] Mashaw (1994b).

[56] Pollack (1997).

[57] See Weingast (1981); McCubbins/Schwartz (1984); Ogul/Rockman (1990); Weingast (1982).

agent's range of feasible actions. Moreover, administrative reorganisation, procedural reform, changing the mandate and subsidising representation to ensure that agency decisions do not lead to "regulatory capture" can all increase political leverage over bureaucracies or administrative agencies.

Administrative theories, though discussing specific mechanisms of controlling bureaucratic discretion, recognise that it is not costless. The effort that is expended to assure regulatory compliance with stated goals does not really consider that ideas from implementation experience or policy learning over time may enable regulatory agencies to move beyond stated intentions to improve general efficiency or welfare. By limiting the policy entrepeneurship of the European Commission through the extensive network of comitology committees, with their focus on monitoring and control, these administrative efforts may actually deprive the EU of some of the strengths of bureaucratic initiative and innovation.

Yet over the last two decades as criticism of big government has increased, there has been a striking increase in the resources available to control bureaucracies, as well as an increased willingness to do so. Regulatory reform has not only been about retrenchment but also improving efficiency and effectiveness. The result of efforts to increase transparency, openness and fairness in administrative politics in the United States has fostered more cumbersome rule-making procedures.[58] A number of regulatory agencies have been displaced by a judiciary that has assumed the role of policy analyst. Consequently, the effort to increase bureaucratic responsiveness in American politics aimed at ensuring that regulatory agencies do not succumb to pressures by special interest groups may create new problems that studies of regulatory oversight in Europe need to consider. In the US, this has generated a climate of adversarial legalism and increased litigation that has caused tremendous regulatory gridlock as policy-makers have to give detailed reasons for their actions. In assessing the existing system, the structures imposed on agencies may become even more Byzantine and convoluted, and may actually be less-well suited to the achievement of legislatively ordained goals.

It is not surprising given both the foundations and underpinnings of the different perspectives on regulation, that the appropriateness and drawbacks of such a system of comitology in the European context is receiving increased attention. While there has been some criticism of the system, there is as yet little sign that answers to the problems of governance, regulation and control are emerging. Despite generating much criticism for its opaque and undemocratic system, few have offered alternative models of responsive regulation.

---

[58] Shapiro (1997b).

3. Application of Regulatory Theories on Comitology: An Assessment

The history of comitology has been reviewed elsewhere[59] and can be systematised and summarised in Table 1. Despite the paucity of research on the topic, comitology has come to occupy an increasingly important role in decision-making. Negotiations will begin in September 1998 between Parliament, Council and Commission based on the proposal submitted by the Commission in July 1998 under the Amsterdam Treaty.[60] These negotiations for an inter-institutional agreement are expected to be protracted and difficult as Parliament wishes to abolish regulatory committees over which it has no influence, and extend its authority over the decision-making process which it views as opaque and undemocratic.[61]

More importantly for our purposes, are the regulatory theories outlined above useful in explaining the development and politics of Comitology? And if so, how much are they able to explain? While none of these theories are able to explain all aspects of Comitology, our paper seeks to relate each one of the identified phases of comitology development to a specific theoretical approach. Although these theories have been primarily applied and developed in the American system, our chapter seeks to offer an explanation about the development and functioning of comitology in the European Union that seeks to highlight the parallels and concerns about oversight, accountability and participation that have been so strongly articulated in the American context.

The *first phase* during the late 1950s and early 1960s highlights the relevance of administrative and rational choice-approaches, especially principal-agent theory. In the early years of the EC, member governments faced the delicate task of handing over enormous agenda-setting and executive powers to the Commission to foster effective community-wide problem-solving and to ensure Member States' compliance with Community action. The net effect was a loss of important competencies to the supranational level. Some form of delegation to invest the Commission with certain competencies and regulatory instruments was viewed as necessary to prevent free riding or defection on the part of Member States. However, it also created closer ties and interaction between Member States operating within a Community context.

At the same time, national governments felt the necessity to strictly control this independent supranational power to balance its own loss of authority in certain areas. Concern that delegation to the Commission

---

[59] See for example Demmke *et al* (1996); Falke (1996).

[60] See Agence Europe of 25 June 1998. See the Commission's proposal, (1998) OJ C 279/5.

[61] See the Aglietta Report of the European Parliament, Agence Europe of 27 June 1998.

could result in "capture" by some kind of partial interest (such as pressure group, larger Member States), Member States sought to enhance their "voice" at the European level. The Commission, as a fledgling institution, deemed it necessary to cooperate in order to gain the trust of the member governments since it depended not only upon national governments for the flow of information but also for their co-operation in executing and implementing common regulations.

The result of this symbiotic, interlocking relationship was the introduction of the "Comitology" committee system in important Europeanised policy areas such as agriculture, international trade and the customs union. This is best understood in terms of principal-agent theory, since the introduction of these committees highlighted control and oversight issues. The principal (member governments) entrusts the agent (Commission) with the necessary powers to attain pre-defined political goals (for example the power of direct applicability of European law). But at the same time it secures the control and oversight of these powers via committees which essentially consist of national officials and specialists called upon to cooperate with the Commission. By using national experts, the member governments could be sure that the Commission's powers and discretion was used properly, since the committee experts are the national officials with their own stakes in their respective policy fields.

Not surprisingly, this system of transfer and control guaranteed the smooth establishment of several common policy areas despite divergent national structures, administrative practices and traditions. Even with the Luxembourg Compromise, the underlying dispute was not about the transfer of powers to the Commission but about its control via unanimity, since authority still accrued to these European-level committees.[62]

Interest group approaches do not explain much of the development in the first phase (1950s and 1960s) since pressure groups were not visibly active at the supranational level in the early years of the Community. For the most part, they did not have the capacity, resources or interest to really exert influence upon the political decision-making of the Community. Interest groups continued to focus predominantly on their traditional domestic lobbying avenues and tried to readjust their focus to the new European situation. Public interest approaches also do not help our understanding of the early years and development of the comitology process. For example, areas such as the Common Agricultural Policy were from the beginning deliberately built upon the externalisation of costs rather than general public welfare. In order to allow for an increase in farmer incomes, the EC shifted the burden of financing this policy via higher prices, price and export subsidies and agricultural protectionism onto consumers, tax payers and third countries.

---

[62] See Nicoll (1984).

The *second phase* (1970s and early 1980s) regarding the development of comitology practices is characterised by an increasing workload, more tasks, more complexity and more demands on the Community system. The EC was not able to reach all of its intended goals (such as the Common Market and the common currency), but it did consolidate and achieve some of its major policy goals (in agriculture, trade and commercial policy, and the customs union) as well as acquiring new responsibilities or task expansion in research and development, environmental affairs and telecommunications. This led to an increase in the number and scope of committees. Administrative theories of regulation seem to offer the best explanation for this institutional development in the EC. After the establishment of the committee system and the myriad of disputes about harmonisation policies that plagued European integration in the 1970s, the Commission did not have the political will nor the power to fundamentally change the complex web of oversight and control exercised by the principal (Member States) via different committees.[63] The institutional balance that the committee system was designed to achieve was however becoming increasingly difficult given the complexity, diversity, and fragmentation of Member State control via a myriad of comitology committees.

During the 1970s and 1980s, the committees were faced with increased pressures as national administrations sought greater influence and access at the European level. This resulted in a sometimes fierce competition between national departments for the right to represent the member government in their respective policy area. Not only did competition become more intense, but the increased influence of the Community led to new efforts by national administrations and interests groups, to influence the European regulatory process.

This makes interest group theory increasingly relevant. In the early stages of the Community, interest groups were, as previously noted, operating primarily at the national level. The EC tried to foster the presence of such groups at the supranational level via the establishment of the Economic and Social Council, as well as funding certain underrepresented groups.[64] Despite this, the most "privileged" groups were smaller, better organised sectorial interests, in Europeanised policy areas such as agriculture and trade. Not surprisingly, industry, trade and farmer lobbies became the first and most powerfully organised transnational interests.[65]

The establishment of these lobbies and the partial distancing of the agents – the committees – from their (governmental) principals coincided during the 1970s and early 80s with the second phase of the development of the comitology system. Well-resourced transnational interests groups (and their national "constituencies") sought access to the influential

---

[63] See, for instance, Neville-Rolfe (1984).

[64] See van der Knaap (1996: 87–88); Morgan (1991).

[65] Philip (1982); Traxler/Schmitter (1995).

comitology committees in order to promote their ideas about the substance and implementation of European regulations. In the area of agricultural and foreign trade policy, this resulted in the "regulatory capture" of certain committees by respective interest groups. During the 1970s, COPA, the transnational association of farmers unions, managed to block all regulatory attempts to limit the Community's price guarantee for major farm products to certain quantities although the production in the EC already exceeded consumer demand by approximately 120%.[66] Similarly, European textiles interests pressured the EC into rejecting the Multi-fibre Agreement, essentially barring textiles exports of developing countries – for example India or Turkey – into the Community, although Brussels originally had agreed to certain export quotas.[67]

The committees not only gave into political pressure but sometimes even aligned themselves with "their" interest groups, since they considered themselves part of these respective policy communities. Lobbyists promised easy, voluntary and complete compliance with the new regulations if the regulators accepted their reservations. This resulted quite often in the externalisation of costs (to third countries, tax payers or consumers). Since effective counter-lobbying did not (yet) exist, this strategy allowed for cosy and often sympathetic relations between regulators and regulated constituencies. Needless to say, that in this situation, interest group theories are much more useful in understanding the second phase of the development and operation of the comitology committee system.

However, this picture changes in the third phase. With the credible effort to re-launch the European Single Market in the second half of the 1980s, domestically oriented interest groups readjusted to the new situation in which "regulatory capture" became more difficult because practically all important interest groups had established their transnational bureaus in Brussels and monitored not only the decision-making record of the Community but also the implementation of these provisions.[68]

During this more pluralistic period of the EC, the Single Market programme did not result in a "race to the bottom", that is, a reduction of regulatory standards to the lowest common denominator in the Community, as some predicted.[69] In the area of consumer and environmental protection, health standards, biotechnology and technical norms, the EC managed to re-regulate on remarkably high levels that is not readily explained by rational actor nor interest group theories, both of which predicted a massive scaling-down of protective regulations in the wake of the removal of alleged market distortions. Administrative theories, with their focus on oversight, accountability and control, can explain why the Community kept this complex system of committees and did not move

---

[66] Averyt (1977).   [67] Hrbek/Probst (1990).
[68] Kohler-Koch (1994)
[69] See for example Scharpf (1993a); Streeck (1995a).

toward – for example – independent agencies which would further enhance supranational discretion. Because of the original (and still enormously relevant) intention of the member governments to control the agent (Commission), comitology committees ensured that the Commission did not circumvent national demands and preferences in the application and implementation of European administrative law and policies.

It is in this last phase of the development of the comitology system that the public interest theory is relevant. This has nothing to do with some kind of naive idealistic perspective about regulatory oversight at the European level, but fits Joerges and Neyer's assessment that the institutional rise of comitology allows European administrative arrangements to import "rational" scientific and economic expertise into administrative decision-making, and exercise some form of market-management[70] throughout the late 1980s. The multiplicity of actors and interests now mobilised at the supranational level did not allow any single actor to dominate. Even the representatives of powerful interests had to resort to arguments, reasoning and evidence in order to prevail in these discussions. The scientific nature and discussions within some of these advisory committees became important platforms for preliminary decision-making. The solutions offered by these experts were usually accepted by governmental actors as well as interest groups. Thus, it became essential for a successful lobbying strategy to present scientific credible evidence to advance their own interests and policy preferences.

Given these pressures, what resulted was the emergence of policies based on "first mover advantage"[71] or "ratchet effect"[72] which prevented the Community from the predicted "race to the bottom" and allowed for European re-regulation at comparatively high levels. This is exactly what public interest theory predicts: experts in various policy fields are usually inclined to adhere to "state of the art" solutions for technical questions and it takes enormous pressure to force them to settle with less then scientifically sound results. This was noticeably the case in newly developing policy fields (for instance biotechnology) in which scientific evidence was extraordinarily effective and pervasive. Public interest concerns were paramount, and because few national regulations existed, Member States were willing to accept substantial regulatory guidance because the costs of compliance were more widely distributed than areas where there were more entrenched interests.

---

[70] Joerges/Neyer (1997a), Landfried (1997).
[71] Héritier (1997b).   [72] Vogel (1995); (1997); Voelzkow (1996).

4. Conclusion

This contribution attempts to provide a preliminary assessment of the explanatory power of different theories of regulation towards the comitology process. In looking at comitology, we have found evidence of the various approaches to regulation, reflecting the many dimensions of the European administrative state found in the comitology process: its historical origins and political functions, the behaviour of its committees, its policy impacts and the relations among various institutions and processes that the European polity has created. It does not seek to categorise one phase of the development of this committee system to one particular theory. Rather, it offers a brief overview as to the development of what is essentially a complex, interlocking regulatory system (Table 2). None of these theories are able to explain the whole picture, but the article offers some fresh insights into the trade-offs facing the Community and Member States in terms of expertise versus accountability, responsiveness versus deliberation, and particularistic interests versus general welfare. In delegating authority to the European level, member governments have recognised the risk of being faced with policy outcomes that differ from their preferred policy choices. To cope with this, they have created "comitology procedures" to assist, oversee and monitor the activities of the Commission. Increased regulatory demands led not only to the refocusing of lobbying activities to the European level but also to an enormous growth of the committee system in order to cope with both effective administration and implementation as well as guaranteeing the control of the Commission by the Member States. This special mixture of tasks offers an alternative to other administrative structures (such as independent regulatory agencies), albeit it also faces the same pressures that it should rely on scientific reasoning and deliberative processes to foster the public interest rather than narrow particularistic interests.

Scholars of American regulatory politics and administrative law should find strong parallels with EC comitology procedures. As Majone notes, there are available mechanisms of control in the American context such as committee oversight, appointment powers, procedural requirements, judicial review and public participation that can serve as similar checks and balances in the European system. While the characteristics of the American administrative process deserve further comparison with the European "Comitology" experience, there has been growing criticism that the resulting regulatory state – with its necessity of control, oversight and juridification -to ensure accountability is inappropriate.[73]

---

[73] Harlow (1998).

As both search for methods to control "a runaway bureaucracy" or "fourth branch of government", more attention needs to be paid to the implications of such diminished trust in governance for democratic society. As the American case illustrates, efforts to increase transparency, accountability and public participation in the regulatory process were aimed at tackling what Europeans term "the democratic deficit". However, ever intensive efforts to enhance oversight, transparency, and public participation in regulatory decision-making in the US have also increased the number of lawsuits and judicial challenges, and made agencies increasingly cautious.

While Majone argues that it is possible to improve the legitimacy of Community policy-making through a variety of instruments that restrain or moderate regulatory discretion,[74] these "checking mechanisms" such as comitology committees may achieve accountability at the expense of creativity and flexibility. What is clear in evaluating and comparing the administrative or regulatory state in both the US and EU is that it did not evolve in a gradual, deliberative fashion nor is it the product of rational processes of institutional design. Although mechanisms of oversight developed in an effort to resolve political struggles, and provide some coherence to the evolving demands upon governments, concern about the implications of such activity in terms of democratic development has led to pressures for a more deliberative model whereby transnational interest and value formation, deliberative decision-making and scientific reasoning and expertise can be promoted in the area of comitology. As our empirical assessment indicates, one can see in the comitology system a clash between different sets of values, each in its own way geared towards controlling the regulatory environment, but differing as to the rationale, manner and outcome.

[74] Majone (1994a); see also Dehousse *et al* (1992).

Table 1 *History of Comitology*

Phases	Development of the EC/EU	Development of the committee system
Phase 1: late 1950's and early 1960s	Setting-up the basic structures; Europeanisation of agriculture, foreign trade and the elimination of internal trade barriers; diversity of task in regulating the EEC goes beyond the skills of the diplomats, technical expertise necessary to assist and oversee actions of the Commission	Creation of specialised committees to support as well as control the work of the Commission. Member States wanted to prevent the Commission from overstepping its administrative or policy competence.
Phase 2: 1970s and early 1980s	"Dark ages" of EC, Luxembourg Compromise, unanimity, crisis of Bretton-Woods-System, oil crises, EC member governments sought to solve these problems unilaterally: commentators saw the EC on the verge of decay; yet, the EC integrated six new members, consolidated the Community structure and established CAP, Common Foreign Trade Policy, Customs Union, European Political Co-operation, European Monetary System and first steps in European structural and regional as well as research, technology and environmental policy.	Heavy workloads, increasing complexity and diversity of tasks as well as growing demands for monitoring and control called for institutional reforms; but in the view of the crises and already existing conflicts the EC was not prepared to substantially adjust its institutional make-up. It simply increased the number of committees
Phase 3: 1985 and beyond	SEA and Treaty of Maastricht led to the completion of the internal market, the attempt to create a common currency, the creation of the Common Foreign and Security Policy and the introduction of a common internal and judicial co-operation. This multiplied the competencies and responsibilities of the European institutions, especially the Commission, and fostered the re-orientation of interest groups lobbying to the supranational level.	Again, the Member States were eager to increase their control especially over the Commission and relied on the committee system. With the 1987 Comitology Decision the Council essentially confirmed the existence of three types of committees (advisory management, regulatory). Since then, their number increased.

Table 2 *Explanatory Power of Regulatory Theories on Comitology*

Phases of the Development of the Comitology System	Public Interest Theories	Interest Group Theories	Administrative Theories
Phase 1: late 1950s and 1960s	–	–	Committees are created as agents of the member governments to control the implementation power of the Commission
Phase 2: 1970s and early 1980s	–	Regulatory capture of some important committees by special interest groups (industry, farmer)	(administrative self-interest to persist and increase in number and size)
Phase 3: 1985 and beyond	Increasing complexity and multiple interest group pressures lead to more reliance on scientific expertise and reasoning	–	(administrative self-interest to persist and increase in number and size)

14

Comitology as a Research Subject: A New Legitimacy Mix?

*Wolfgang Wessels**

1. On the Joy and Privilege of a Commentator

Comitology committees are a fascinating subject: they offer the opportunity to comprehend and discuss issues of fundamental importance for the European polity and its basic developments. The evolution, salience and forms of these phenomena are considerable: at the end of the 1990s, up to 400 of these committees deal with an ever extending agenda of public policies and in one form or another they are major fora for taking decisions of a binding character for the Member States and the EU citizens. For those analysing the role of administrations and thus the character of the EU's political system, these bodies offer highly valuable insights.

Given the academic and, increasingly, the political relevance of the subject, it is fun to comment on the stimulating contributions at hand. It is the privilege of such an exercise to draw preliminary lessons, to present additional considerations and to sketch further research options without the need to pursue them at once: intellectual associations for new projects abound without the responsibility of having to carry them out.[1]

2. On the Relevance of the Cases: In Search of a Typology for Committees

(a) On a Comparative Approach

Faced with the results of a limited number of case studies on comitology and related committees, one immediate question is the "representativeness" for a broader picture: what is the validity of the empirical material and its surplus for generalising about comitology, EU committees and beyond?

* Jean Monnet Professor, University of Cologne.
[1] For some of the figures and literature referred to see Wessels (1997).

(b) On the Relevance for Comitology Committees

The cases presented[2] offer revealing insights into committees of a certain type, mainly related to regulatory long term tasks[3] in environmental policy fields, which are often perceived as a constituent part of the institutionalisation of the internal market. More than in the literature so far presented, those results urge us to go beyond one policy field with its specific instruments and rules; it is a major incentive to intensify the search for designing a micropolitical typology of committees which goes beyond the formal procedures and cycles and helps us to establish a set of variations and to discern similar and dissimilar features.

If we want to know more about the strategic interactions of civil servants from different levels and if we want to draw lessons for accountability, efficiency and effectiveness of these bodies, we need to enlarge the number and the type of cases to be scrutinised. Thus, we should know more about the functioning of other comitology procedures, especially those management committees in the agricultural sectors with a high frequency of meetings responsible for dealing incrementally with short term issues of positive integration and with considerable direct distributional effects. Confronting several field studies, it will be possible to identify recurrent or diverging patterns of attitudes and behaviour of participants to elaborate more refined hypotheses and test them in the political space of Brussels.

Some of the guiding hypotheses could be deduced from the cases presented here. The results underline fundamental assumptions of political science – especially that we cannot base such a systematic exercise just on the legal provisions. Again, as in earlier studies, the empirical material reveals that the specific legal status of a committee, so intensively and controversially discussed on the Council level, is quite often only of minor importance for the way participants interact in their normal routines and thus for the functioning and productivity of their body.

In spite of all the dogmatic quarrels about the types of formal procedures, day to day business is run apparently in ways for which legal interpretations do not offer sufficient explanatory power. The cases also demonstrate that thinking along traditional lines of national interest is not helpful for understanding the working of at least these kinds of committees.

Following general approaches related to integration studies and neo-institutionalism, we would have to look at several groups of factors for describing, analysing and assessing the real play of the actors in the committees. As for general considerations, some fundamental characteristics of the respective policy field, the kind of instruments being employed by the Community and cleavages between Member States and (perhaps

---

[2] Landfried, Gehring and Neyer, in this volume.
[3] Egan/Wolf, in this volume.

more importantly) between social groups and policy networks should be taken into account.

A closer look at the specifics of each of these bodies is also useful for further studies: the path of the committees, their real and reputational successes and failures as well as their professional composition, the length of individual memberships and the frequency of the sessions could be analysed in view of the interaction style(s) and "culture(s)"; those will in turn shape the behaviour patterns of the actors and influence their role in the policy field. In this context, the legal provisions need to be integrated into the research design and their impact assessed.

Many suggestions derived from the empirical cases could thus be exploited to develop a systematic scheme for comitology committees and help to transfer insights from case studies of one committee to others – similar or dissimilar in their nature and functioning.

(c) Beyond the Cases: Towards a General Typology of Multi-level Committees

Comitology committees are only one way in which national and Community civil servants interact in the EU's policy cycle. The confusing cosmos of administrative set-ups in the EU gives further incentives to do comparative research: the wealth of empirical material invites us to look even more for general features of a multi-level bureaucracy inside the EU system.

To pursue more specific questions: are there any marked differences in the "culture" and performance of these committees to other administrative bodies, especially to the *"groupes d'experts"* called in by the Commission (around 700 in different forms) as well as to the committees and working groups in the Council structure (300 again with different functions), not to mention a large variety of other consultative bodies? Are formal differences – such as the legal basis, voting procedures, the origin of the chairperson – significant for the functioning and performance of these groups; whatever answer we expect, we need to establish some kind of typology which would cut across the traditional categorisation along the phases of the policy cycle. With legal provisions as only one (though probably not negligible) factor a more extended approach for identifying common and different characteristics should be pursued.

The gains of such an exercise will be quite rewarding: it might enable us to transfer lessons from one set-up to another: for example, under which (existing or not) conditions will the Economic and Financial Committee, which will play a crucial role in the implementation of the EMU, pursue a "deliberative" interaction style as identified in some of the comitology committees; which lessons can we draw from the now intensified research on COREPER for the comitology committees and from the studies on the Political Committee – so prominent in the CFSP Pillar of the EU?

Such a comparative survey and analysis should not be restricted to the EU: other experiences of multi-level systems deserve to be added. The extensive administrative infrastructure of international organisations (like the UN and NATO) as well as those of federal states of different kinds offer lessons which can be used for the EU and the comitology committees. But also in the reverse direction: the experimental character of the EU bodies can be used to reassess the general literature on committees, thus being a valid part of a general theory on administrations.

3. Comitology Committees in the Policy Cycle – Variations of the Research Focus

(a) On an Integrative Approach

Beside the comparative approach, the results presented here and elsewhere could be used for an integrated view to analyse the EU's political system from an administrative perspective. The work presented here refers several times to other phases of the policy cycle.[4] From this focus, the way the involved actors interact in these committees can be best understood if they are located in all their networks including also other bodies within the EU-system. Such an approach should observe the actor's involvement at a given period (a static perspective) and the overall patterns of administrative involvement over time (a dynamic view).

(b) A Static Perspective: Integral Parts of Complex Networks

Comitology committees are clearly placed in the implementation phase of the EU's policy cycle; however, as we know from several studies, preparation and decision making are not "isolated" from the work of the Commission and of the committees in a later stage of the policy process. Analytical devices of identifying certain periods along functions pursued should not lead to limited, and therefore distorted, observations: many of the national civil servants are also involved in the Commission's expert groups to give advice for the Commission's draft proposal and in the Council's working groups to prepare and widely shape the legislative act, which then serves as the basis for the work of the comitology committee. Quite often, the actors involved apparently do not care about the exact formal setting they are in. Comitology committees are thus best analysed as part of a complex and overarching network of administrative interactions. Certain features of the relatively smooth and deliberative functioning might then be explained by the "path" of a legislative act: either the "hard" political issues (especially those dealing with distributive issues) have been

---

[4] Neyer, in this volume.

discussed and decided upon elsewhere, or the "technocrats" were able to shift the diplomatically sensitive points from political agendas to their deliberations behind closed doors. Thus, they search for solutions which fit into their epistemic communities and externalise the costs of their decisions.

Members of the committees are also part of an organisation and issue related networks. The civil servants' attitudes will mainly be oriented to the ideology of their "home" department or DG which in many ways will be related to interest groups and other political forces. Thus, the actors involved are not just "experts" without any accountability except to their own professional ethos, they are also not mainly bureaucrats pursuing egoistic material interests, but they could be understood as representatives of "their" political base to which they are in one way or another accountable. Such an interpretation would explain the high degree of politically undisputed work which is performed within these committees.

Linked to that observation is the high degree of decentralisation or fragmentation of the EU's policy process: comitology committees are part of sectorial networks which are likely to compete with each other to use legislative and budgetary instruments of the EC. The "*camaraderie*" among the members of a committee is thus always a function of the in-group feeling vis-à-vis other bodies which are perceived as "hostile" to one's own philosophy, interests and role in the policy cycle. Administrative and indeed ministerial infighting takes place between those set-ups, explaining some of the "cultures" of committees.

(c) A Dynamic Perspective: Indicators for a Horizontal and Vertical Fusion

As mentioned in the contributions to this volume,[5] comitology committees like other administrative and political bodies have grown in number and form over the history of the EC/EU. With the extension of the "acquis communautaire" the number of binding decisions to be implemented and adapted by the Commission grew (perhaps disproportionately) and spread into more and more areas of traditional state activities. Member governments and their administrations are and were not prepared to transfer the use of major policy instruments to the European level without securing an extensive involvement in the relevant policy cycle.

The overall evolution of these administrative phenomena is thus a significant indicator for the EC/EU's process of institutional growth and differentiation. They illustrate major characteristics of the EU's political system. With some specific variations, multi-level committees document in several forms that the responsibility for preparing, taking and implementing

---

[5] See Egan/Wolf, in this volume.

binding decisions is shared by several actors from different settings. National and Community functionaries and experts pool their resources to jointly design and use policy instruments. As observed in this volume, the behaviour patterns of Commissioners also show a mixture between European autonomy and continuous relationship with their own country.

If we take decision-making by the Council and the national end of the policy cycle into account, we witness also in a horizontal view a "hybrid" position of administrations reducing a clear division of labour and responsibilities among politicians and administrators and also diminishing a clear distinction between "technical" and "political" issues and interaction styles. Following experiences of other multi-level systems, horizontal and vertical separation of powers induces at the end a strange merger or *Verflechtung* of responsibilities. With their scope extended, as documented in the three treaty revisions and amendments of the last 15 years, these features are increasingly covering major parts of traditional and modern state sectors. Even more, if we assume that committees are proactive and in competition with each other, committees themselves are dynamic factors in this process and shape the strong administrative nature of the EU system.

In view of a middle range theory explaining the evolution of the EU, the committees are thus valid indicators for a growing process of vertical and horizontal fusion of political responsibilities in using common or shared instruments. In spite, or just because of their complexity, they are also useful to exemplify, explain and evaluate the "strange" system of Brussels and its weak and strong characteristics.

4. On the Relevance for Theories: Constitutional Significance Revisited

(a) On the analytical and normative approach

If (comitology) committees are significant and illustrative indicators for fundamental trends of the EU System, we should look at the relevance for integration related theories and their major analyses and assessments.

Indeed, one of the fascinating aspects of the research done in recent years and presented here in this volume are the arguments about its "constitutional significance".[6] Based on the empirical work, this part of a growing political system is highly relevant for the kind of "polity" we want to live in. Given the importance of the phenomena, it is necessary to discuss the normative issues related to key criteria like legitimacy and democracy. This task is even more stimulating as those committees are partly perceived as an exemplification of a "deliberative democracy"[7] and

[6] Joerges, in this volume.
[7] See Joerges/Neyer (1997a).

thus challenge the traditional notions which characterise those multi-level set-ups as a "mega-bureaucracy" or a "run-away bureaucracy".[8]

(b) Administration Without State?

As the evolution of administrations is generally closely linked to the "state" and its major developments over the last four centuries, the (comitology) committees and the administrative infrastructure of the EU are to be understood as significant indicators for both the role and functions of administrations as well as for the fundamental characteristics of the modern state.

If the European network reflects another and perhaps especially successful attempt of administrations to follow the basic inbuilt instinct of gaining autonomy from their political "masters", the phenomena we observe would indicate a major move to a new European version of a technocracy, or a *Verwaltungsstaat* (administrative state). "Comrades" in attitudes from "Bureaus" of several levels use their EU bodies to emancipate themselves as a group from political (in other words democratic) control; this also explains the unsuccessful attempts made by the European Parliament to gain access. The closed clubs with their technical language, their intrinsic procedures and informal rules are not an example of deliberative democracy, but an immunisation against outside interference; the propensity to transform so-called "political issues" into administrative problems (a major feature of a *Verwaltungsstaat*) is legitimised both in terms of the functional necessity, procedural efficiency and instrumental effectiveness and – in the specific constellation of EU-committees – also for the sake of "Europe" and for guaranteeing positive relations among Member States. In this view the state, especially its features as a "national" and "constitutional" entity, is eroded and replaced by a mere bureaucratic set up hidden behind the illusion of ongoing national control. Without realising it, national governments do allow their own administrations to "usurp" their traditional legitimacy. The counter-bureaucracy established to control the *aréopage technocratique apatride et irresponsable*[9] of the Commission merges with their colleagues from the European level. The intergovernmental strategy of keeping the Member States as "Masters of the Treaty" backfires by its very procedures.

In the same way as we use labels like "governing without government" or "governing beyond the state" one additional characterisation would be "administration without state", thus indicating a new historical stage for both administrations and for the state. The very elements which are positively assessed as "deliberative" would then conceal a plot of bureaucrats and experts.

[8] See Joerges, in this volume, and Egan/Wolf, in this volume.
[9] De Gaulle (1970).

(c) Committees as "Representative" Government?

Another way of interpreting the empirical material is to stress the role of
civil servants as "representatives" of their organisations and with that of
the networks built around formal procedures by the involved and
concerned actors. The positions taken by the official participants would
mirror the interest of the concerned groups and could mobilise public
attention and political support. Without just being "principal agents" of
political masters, the participants – not least the Commission services –
energise the political space and push the relevant groups – defined as
potential veto actors – towards a multi-level consensus, which, after being
established, is regarded as an "acquis" that needs to be protected, if necessary, by incremental adaptations so well performed in the comitology
committees. The lack of attention given to legal provisions is to be
explained by the continuous effort to govern by consensus and not by a
majoritarian rule, in which procedural rules might be used for pushing or
defending one's own position.

(d) On Different Appraisals: Towards a New Legitimacy Mix?

The empirical results and their different interpretations can be seen to have
positive and negative effects in relation to the issue of legitimacy. The
fusion process which is documented and shaped by (comitology) committees needs to be discussed also in view of its normative dimensions.

In view of traditional constitutional principles of a government of, by and
for the people, major criteria such as open access, broad participation and
accountability are less and less guaranteed by these forms of multi-level
administrative governance. Even more, binding decisions are then taken for
a polity without "demos" as political and social preconditions such as
identity, solidarity and a public discourse do not exist and cannot be created
artificially. In spite of those quite convincing arguments, we should not
refrain from pointing at analytical problems and strategic difficulties of
such a fundamental interpretation. The normative framework as it is quite
often presented is designed in an a-historical way as if the "demos" always
existed in a way to fit the nation state and it sets yardsticks which are rarely
met. Thus, in some contributions of this school of thought we face the risk
of being confronted with "utopias" not applicable to Europe at the end of
the 20th century. The poverty of concrete strategies deriving from some of
these assessments to remedy the apparently untenable situation should be
taken as a case for a critical reappraisal of some of these alarmist voices.

Contrary to this approach, another school of thought would claim that
functional necessities and the assumed existence of a European demos – so
far hindered in its right to decide about its fate by national administrations
– demand a real European administration: The (comitology) committees

are then labelled as relicts of a defence strategy by outdated nation states. These neo-functional and neo-federal views quite often also present illusions about what is optimal and feasible for a European polity.

Whatever the demos might look like (be it European or national) the representative of the Member States, governments and parliaments, have clearly agreed in the treaties and their revisions that the institutions of the EU should take and implement binding decisions for the EU citizens – even on expanding areas of public policies. One reason is apparently, that the effectiveness of instruments applied only on the level of the small and medium sized European nations is limited and would be even more reduced without the EU. A government without impact does not act "for" the people. Output legitimacy might be rated as of lower normative value, but it plays, at the end of the day, a quite significant and even necessary role for any government of the people.

Thus, we might start our debate with the puzzle we are apparently faced with: on one side, fundamental critics point at basic democratic deficits and at fundamental shortcomings of the system in terms of legitimacy. At the same time, we witness a considerable dynamic stability: in spite of all negative comments on (comitology) committees, the EU's political system, has at least so far, not been confronted with an existential crisis. In fact the reverse is the case: in the last 15 years, governments and parliaments have even trusted the EU with additional tasks – this transfer of policy instruments has met with some though rarely fundamental opposition.

One explanation, also highly relevant for the debate on committees, refers to the notion of some sort of "representative" government: national and Community actors pool their respective sources of legitimacy – including their functional and technocratic reputation – to make the system acceptable to both the involved and concerned groups and to the population at large. Features known from (neo-)corporatist approaches merge with those of technocratic policy making mixed with parliamentary elements and that of the rule of law. The EU as polity would then be based on a new mix of several and different concepts of legitimacy.

A major precondition and "test" for keeping this pattern is a broad and diffuse "permissive consensus" among the population and/or sufficient trust towards their "representatives"; Councils and committees are then openly or impliedly understood as fora where those who have been given a political mandate, in whatever way, take care of the needs of the people. Thus, the output is for the people, and those exercising the respective power are, in varied forms, mandated by the people.

However, as soon as this group of actors is classified as a "political class" or a "mega-bureaucracy" which uses the complex institutional and procedural set-up to pursue only its own materialistic interests, this broad acceptance (also of committees) will be withdrawn with major consequences for both the Brussels and the national ends of the political system.

Given the close interrelation, as documented in the administrative bodies researched here, both levels will be affected by this kind of popular mistrust. In the general debate about the normative fundamentals of the European polity at all levels, committees and the research about them will remain a major factor.

5. Bibliographical Hints

As the collective bibliography of this volume documents, there is by now an impressive body of literature is available by now. In addition to the works cited in the contributions to this volume,[10] I would like to point to the following literature:

S Bulmer, "The Governance of the European Union. A New Institutionalist Approach" (1994) 13 *JEPP*, 351-380; M Greven (ed.), *Demokratie – eine Kultur des Westens? 20th Wissenschaftlicher Kongreß der Deutschen Vereinigung für Politische Wissenschaft* (Opladen 1998); F Hayes-Renshaw / H Wallace, *The Council of Ministers* (London 1997); A Héritier, "Policy-Netzwerkanalyse als Untersuchungsinstrument im europäischen Kontext. Folgerungen aus einer empirischen Studie regulativer Politik" in A Héritier (ed.), Policy-Analyse. Kritik und Neuorientierung (1993) 24 *PVS*, 432-447; M Jachtenfuchs / B Kohler-Koch, "Regieren in der Europäischen Union – Fragestellungen für eine interdisziplinäre Europaforschung" (1996) 37 *PVS*, 537-556; Keohane R O, *After Hegemony. Corporation and Discord in World Political Economy* (Princeton 1984); B Kohler-Koch, "Catching Up With Change. The Transformation of Governance in the European Union" (1996) 3 *JEPP*, 359-380; G Majone, "The Rise of the Regulatory State in Europe" (1994) 17 *West European Politics*, 77-101; J G March / J P Olsen, *Rediscovering Institutions: The Organizational Basis of Politics* (New York 1989); J G March / J P Olsen, *Democractic Governance* (New York 1995); J G March / J P Olsen, *The Institutional Dynamics of International Political Orders* (Oslo 1998); G Marks / F W Scharpf / P C Schmitter / W Streeck, *Governance in the European Union* (London 1996); B G Peters, "The European Bureaucrat: The Applicability of Bureaucracy and Representative Government to Non-American Settings" in A Blas / S Dion (eds.), *The Budget-Maximizing Bureaucrat* (London 1991); J Richardson, *European Union, Power and Policy-Making* (London 1996); D Rometsch / W Wessels, "The Commission and the Council of Ministers" in G Edwards / D Spence (eds.), *The European Commission* (Harlow 1994); F W Scharpf, "Demokratische Politik in der internationalisierten Ökonomie" in M Greven (ed.), *Demokratie – eine Kultur des Westens?* (Opladen 1998); W Schumann, "Die EG als neuer Anwendungsbereich für die Policy-Analyse: Möglichkeiten und Perspektiven der konzeptionellen Weiterentwicklung" in A

---

[10] In particular, Bach (1992); Blumann (1996); Falke (1996); Haas (1992); Institut für Europäische Politik (1989); Jachtenfuchs/Kohler-Koch (1996b); Joerges/Neyer (1997a); Kielmansegg (1996); Kohler-Koch (1998); Scharpf (1997); Streeck/Schmitter (1991); Vos (1997b); Wessels (1990); Wessels (1998).

Héritier, "Policy-Analyse. Kritik und Neuorientierung" (1993) 24 *PVS*, 394-431; A Spinelli, *The Eurocrats, Conflict and Crisis in the European Community* (Baltimore 1966); G Tsebelis, *Nested Games: Rational Choice in Comparative Politics* (Berkeley 1990); R Vaubel, "The Political Economy of Centralization and the European Community" (1992) 59 *Public Choice*, 151-185; W Wessels, "A Corporatist Mega-Bureaucracy or an Open City? Brussels and the Growth and Differentiation of Multi-level Networks" in H Wallace (ed.) *European Union* (1997), W Wessels, "The Modern West European State and the European Union: Democratic Erosion or a New Kind of Polity?" in S S Andersen / K A Eliassen (eds.), *The European Union: How Democratic Is It?* (London 1996), 57-69; M Westlake, *The Council of the European Union* (London 1995).

SECTION 5

Comitology in the European Polity

15

The European Polity, Deadlock and Development

Adrienne Héritier[*]

1. The Policy Paradox

An observer of European polity and policy development is immediately struck by the contrast between obstacle-ridden and deadlock-prone decisional processes, on the one hand, and institutional change and rapid policy progress, on the other. In this contribution I argue that this parallel presence of deadlock and development originates from two defining properties of the European polity – its diversity and the divergence of the goals pursued by its actors. This gives rise to a fragmented polity and the emergence of consensual decision-making practices to reconcile conflicting goals. The paradox lies in the fact that it is precisely this fragmentation and complexity of the decisional structure, created to accommodate diversity and prone to generate stalemate or a "joint decision trap"[1] in the central decision-making arena (Council), that provides the room and the need for escape routes to circumvent potential gridlock and to accelerate policy developments. This occurs in two ways. First, subterfuge, as it is referred to, is employed by entrepreneurial actors as an intentional strategy to overcome decisional stalemate. This is more easily done in a fragmented and relatively concealed institutional setting of interlocking decision-making[2] where multiple actors are engaged in all kinds of bodies and where issues are effectively disaggregated and pushed down, "from ministerial confrontation to official *engrenage* within a 'hierarchy of committees'".[3] Second, under conditions of institutional complexity and fragmentation, the relative lack of transparency in decision-making allows central actors, such as the Commission, to play on the regulatory competition among Member State actors to initiate a dynamic of policy development.[4]

[*] Professor of Political Science, Director of Max-Planck Project Group "Common Goods: Law Politics and Economics" , Bonn.
[1] Scharpf (1997a).   [2] Wessels (1990: 230).   [3] W Wallace (1996: 449).
[4] Sbragia (1996: 237); Héritier/Knill/Mingers (1996); H Wallace (1996b: 4).

This concomitance of deadlock and development must, however, be placed in a broader temporal context which takes account of the Union's responses over time to new global and regional challenges. The interplay between stalling and speeding in the overall development of the European polity, and in routine policy-making is intensified by the unfinished and open-ended nature of the polity. Thus, the battle to determine the general development of the European polity may – against the background of the diversity of goals pursued and the imminent danger of deadlock – be directed against policy stalling, and rapid developments in policy may in turn induce institutional change in the polity.

In what follows, I analyse the simultaneity of stalling and speeding in the context of an unfinished polity, and study the consequences for polity and policy development. I start by examining Europe as an unfinished polity operating on the basis of interest diversity and institutional fragmentation, and then provide an overview of escape routes used in various policy areas to circumvent stalemate situations.[5]

2. A Polity in Motion

In examining the link between deadlock and development, in the context of an on-going process of change, I distinguish the *polity* from the *policy* level as two distinct, but to some extent parallel and linked, lines of development.[6]

Macro aspects of the polity are defined at the institutional level: membership is delimited, decisional rules are changed, and competences are allocated to specific European bodies. Change at the policy level, by contrast, takes place by establishing new policy areas and modifying existing ones. Changes take place at both levels but at differing speeds and frequency.

Changes are infrequent at the macro level. New members are rarely taken on board and fundamental changes in decision-making rules and the allocation of competences to existing bodies and the creation of new ones seldom take place. At the policy level, however, changes are constantly occurring,[7] with continuous policy expansion, change and innovation.[8]

Up to this point, the two lines of development at the polity and policy level have been considered as parallel. Yet they often interlink, and consti-

---

[5] The policy types analysed here are telecommunications and road haulage for market-making policy; environmental policy for the provision of collective goods; structural funds and social policy for redistributive policy; and research and technology for distributive policy. See Héritier (1997b).

[6] Kingdon (1984).   [7] Peters (1996); H and W Wallace (eds.) (1996).

[8] This does not necessarily mean *more* European intervention. The power to shape policies may also imply the ability to choose instruments which allow for more latitude for Member States in line with the principle of subsidiarity.

tute an important source of change and, indeed, a means of circumventing decisional impasse. There are two modes of linkage: "official
windows of opportunity"[9] where the two lines cross formally and openly
and are debated centre stage, and more stealthy modes of routine inter-
linking and cautious attempts to extend decisional power through
handling policy issues in a specific way, and inversely, by spreading policy
activities in a gradual and inconspicuous expansion of decision-making
powers.

3. Institutional-Constitutional Change as a Window of Opportunity

Actors can exploit the official windows of opportunity opened up by
planned institutional reforms to achieve specific, and constitutional change
to achieve otherwise unrealisable policy goals. Thus, when new members
join the Community, policies are redefined in two ways. First, the acceding
member may lay down policy conditions for its entry to the Union, as in
the extension of the structural funds programme to include the polar
regions in the case of Finland. Second, existing members may stipulate
conditions for their support of the accession of a new member, an example
being the demand made by Italy, Ireland and Greece to establish the
Integrated Mediterranean Programmes when Portugal and Spain, with
their large agricultural sectors, joined the Community.

The reform of decision-making rules often allows policy-makers to
accomplish large-scale policy innovation, frequently as a result of
bargaining. Instances of this second official window of opportunity are the
introduction of the third-pillar policies under the TEU, and the inclusion
of research and technology policy and environmental policy as official
European policy areas under the SEA. Moreover, the reform of an existing
decision-making rule in an established policy area may facilitate policy
expansion. Thus, the introduction of the Social Protocol under the
Maastricht Treaty facilitated development in social policy-making by
allowing the Social Agreement countries to go ahead on their own after
applying the qualified majority rule (QMR), whilst Britain opted out of the
policy-making process.[10]

Finally, policy activities may be expanded by creating new institutions.
Thus, the establishment of independent agencies may have this effect.[11]
For example, the Environment Agency, which gathers information,
monitors activities, and publishes the results, is likely to expand the
environmental policy area and to have an impact on the quality of policy-
making.

---

[9] Kingdon (1984).　　[10] M Rhodes (1995).　　[11] Majone (1996a).

While all official windows of opportunity – enlargement, changes in decision-making rules, and the creation of new institutions – link institutional and policy questions in a straightforward way, the daily interpretation of polity and policy concerns push out the frontiers of European policy-making in a more unobtrusive way.

4. The Routine Interpenetration of Policy and Polity

Some actors, notably the Commission and the European Parliament, seek to enhance their own institutional position by linking the two levels in order to push specific policy issues, and *vice versa*, to expand their own competences. Cases in point are the Commission's entrepreneurial activities to establish and widen policy areas, such as the use of Article 90 (3) EC to by-pass the Council in telecommunications.[12] Similarly, the European Parliament has also been eager to extend its competences by promoting specific policy issues which are in the public eye, such as public health, and immigration and asylum policy. In doing so, the European Parliament has also sought to broaden its powers on a routine basis, by establishing informal rules in the co-operation with the Commission when legislation is drafted.

5. Circumventing Deadlock: Policy-making by Subterfuge

Thus, linking the polity and policy level in a Community which still is not clearly defined may help get a stalled decision-making process moving again. A closer examination of specific policy areas[13] reveals an impressive array of modes to circumvent the potential stalling of decision-making processes, so that, in the words of Brigid Laffan, "[t]here is an enormous dynamic when things get blocked".[14]

Returning to the main propositions that the diversity of institutional and policy goals and the institutional rules of consensual decision-making make the likelihood of deadlock high, given not only the conflict over the material costs of policy implementation, but also the conflict over who gains and who loses decision-making power, and who bears the costs of instrumental adjustment, the question arises: How can one accommodate this diversity of interests, regulatory modes and cultures in policy formulation and implementation? Given the need to make compromises between conflicting goals, how can policy innovations be brought about? Which factors, process patterns and actor strategies promote policy innovation? And finally, with the expansion of the scope of European policy-making,

---

[12] Schmidt (1997); Schneider/Dang-Nguyen/Werle (1994); Natalicchi (1996).
[13] Héritier (1997b).   [14] Laffan (1997).

what attempts are being made – despite the impasse in the main-avenue democratisation process at intergovernmental conferences – to expand public support for existing European policies?

The typical strategies used to accommodate interest diversity and to circumvent a stalling of the decision-making process observed in the policy areas examined here are package deals, framework legislation, phased compliance, optionality and "twin-track" policy-making.[15]

In package deals, compensation is offered to the opponents of a policy who consider themselves to be the losers in order to win their support. Framework legislation soothes conflicts of interests by not specifying the material, decisional and instrumental costs, but leaving these to the implementation phase, leaving the choice of instruments to achieve specific framework policy goals at the Member State level. If legislation is more specific, phased compliance schedules may be introduced to gain the support of policy opponents, or single elements of a policy programme are made optional so that some measures may be chosen, others discarded (*à la carte* legislation). Finally, twin-track policy-making allows policy-makers to build up support within the main conflicting interest associations in the policy area before legislation is considered, or, indeed, instead of legislation.

The institutional avenues for innovation are typically the seizing of "windows of opportunity", the "linking-up strategy" and the "treaty-base-game".[16] Windows of opportunity are opened up by "external events" or "shocks", the pressure of international treaties, or new internal factors such as ECJ rulings. They may be used to widen the European agenda and push policy-making ahead. Frequently a linking-up strategy to programmes which enjoy considerable political support, such as the Single Market Programme (SMP), is used to push ahead policy measures which had previously met with resistance. In this context, policy-makers attempt to channel measures previously dealt with under conditions of unanimity into SMP measures subject to QMR. Similar efforts may be observed in social policy where attempts to play the treaty-base game were made by the Commission to decide contractual labour market issues under the Health and Safety Article which comes under the qualified majority rule.

The more informal strategies of innovation used by the Commission are self-commitment, network-building, insulation and playing on the regulatory competition among Member States. In order to trigger a dynamic of self-commitment the Commission often proposes legislation as a vague framework directive to get a foot in the door. The so-called mother-directive subsequently calls for more specific daughter-directives (the "Russian doll" strategy),[17] a strategy used not only in environmental policy, but also in social policy and telecommunications.

---

[15] M Rhodes (1995).   [16] Ibid.   [17] See Ross (1995); Eichener (1997).

Another common strategy used by the Commission is to build supportive networks to form co-operative relations with sub-national and private actors *before* embarking upon new policy activities, a strategy which has been successfully employed against the will of Member State governments in the fields of telecommunications, research and technology and, to some extent, in structural funds/cohesion.

A further strategy widely used in technologically complex policy areas, is to insulate decision-making in circles of (Member State) experts, which cannot be subsequently challenged in the Council because of lack of knowledge. Moreover, the Commission plays on the regulatory competition among Member States which seek to transfer their own regulatory tradition to the European level, supporting the proposal which best fits its overall programme.[18]

The modes in which substitute forms of legitimation are introduced – in view of the blocked main-avenue reform channels of democratisation – are then the politics of transparency, coalition-formation, and horizontal mutual control.

The Commission has initiated a comprehensive programme of transparency, to spread information on specific policy programmes in environmental, regional and social policy and all single market measures informing citizens of their rights (Citizens First), seeking to bridge the gap between European citizens and the Brussels bureaucracy.

By building up supportive relationships through rounds of consultation for Community programmes, the Commission has sought to enlarge the legitimatory basis for proposed policies. Thus, a supportive network was developed in telecommunications, policy collaboration with private actors has been encouraged in research and technology, key interest associations have been systematically included in environmental policy, and in structural funds/cohesion policy, the "partnership principle"[19] was developed to allow for the participation of sub-national and private actors in the decision-making process.[20]

A final, but little acknowledged, source of democratic horizontal political control is the mutual distrust of national experts and delegates from fifteen countries all carefully watching each mutual policy step in every stage of policy-making. This form of mutual control of knowledgeable actors from diverse backgrounds constitutes a means of holding each other accountable for single policy steps and should not be underestimated as a new mode of "checks and balances".

These unofficial patterns of European policy-making vary to some extent across policy areas. Not all strategies and patterns of interest accommodation, policy innovation and substitute democratic legitimation are equally applicable in all policy areas, but are contingent on specific

[18] Héritier (1997b).   [19] Marks (1992).   [20] Hooghe (1996); Keating/Hooghe (1996).

conditions. Thus, the forming of mutual agreements to reconcile conflicting actors before legislation is initiated and policy expanded, presupposes the existence of associations with reliable membership support. This is the case for social policy, but less so for environmental policy. In some policy areas, such as telecommunications, the Commission however has been eager to promote the consumers and producers organisations to counter the interests of the large state PTT monopolies and to advance interest organisation.

In environmental policy, the cleavage structure of inclusive *versus* exclusive interests in the abatement of industrial emissions, makes the transparency strategy to build support and legitimation through "access to information" particularly effective. Coalitions formed with sub-national actors to accelerate policy expansion are more easily established in regional and social policy given the distribution of financial resources. There are, however, limits to such attempts because Member States guard their competences in social and regional policy jealously because their resource-offering, legitimating roles are more pronounced than in environmental policy.

The use of the impetus of the SMP (linking-up strategy) to facilitate the decision-making process and to generate policy innovation is widely spread across policy areas (transport, telecommunications, social policy). In social benefits policy, it is striking to see that – owing to Member States' reluctance to relinquish competences – expansion usually occurs "by the backdoor". Member States, driven by Court rulings, have been forced to make social policy regimes compatible with a single labour market.[21]

Moreover, some escape routes may be mutually exclusive. Thus, the simultaneous use of opt-outs and package deals preclude each other because those who have opted out can no longer be "bought off",[22] a case in point being Britain when it opted out of the Social Protocol.[23]

Because the use of subterfuge to avoid policy deadlocks is so frequent and ubiquitous in European policy-making, it has become "second nature" to the European polity. The basic preconditions of the existence of escape routes, that is, diversity and a fragmented institutional structure, are likely to persist. Diversity is a constituent and – to many – desirable feature of the Community. The institutional structure will only be subject to incremental changes under the present conditions of unanimity. It is unlikely that the conflicting views – rooted in Europe's diversity – as to the future shape of European institutions, will change drastically in the present and future intergovernmental conferences responsible for redefining the Treaties. In view of the probable persistence of both diversity and

[21] Leibfried/Pearson (1995).

[22] Lykke Friis, in a panel discussion at the conference of the Human Capital Mobility Workshop, University College Dublin, May 1997.

[23] Lange (1992: 24ff.).

fragmented institutional structures, it is highly likely that the use of subterfuge will continue to play an important and strategic role at both the policy and polity level.

16

The Constitutionalisation of European Administrative Law: Legal Oversight of a Stateless Internal Market

Michelle Everson[*]

1. Introduction

In one noteworthy analysis, administrative law is characterised as a derivative of the modern concept of the state.[1] In this view, the incorporation of finite polities within statal structures and the imputation to them of some form of "common will", similarly required the evolution of bureaucratic bodies and a complementary legal *corpus* – administration and administrative law – dedicated to ensuring that the common will of the state/polity be effectively done. Meanwhile, the exact contours of each statal administration, together with their attendant administrative laws, were to be determined by the particular form of state from which they sprung. On the one collectivist[2] or Rousseauean[3] hand, a conflation of the state with the moral will of the political community, primarily gave rise to a function-easing and efficiency-oriented administration and administrative law. On the other, self-limiting and liberal states placed a far greater emphasis upon the establishment of a strictly delineated bureaucracy, forcefully policed by the courts in line with individual rights and/or the rule of law.[4]

Given the intimate relationship between the state and administrative law, the notion of an "administrative law for or of the internal market" may

[*] Jean Monnet Fellow, European University Institute, Florence. Managing Editor, European Law Journal.
[1] Harlow/Rawlings (1984).
[2] So, for example, the reliance of the UK's welfarist post-war state upon a vast governmental bureaucracy to both administer the nationalised industries and effect social programmes – and concomitant hostility towards any (inefficient and imputedly undemocratic) rights-based form of administrative judicial review.
[3] French administrative law still largely being characterised by the eschewal of administrative review instruments which might place individual interest above those of the state.
[4] Typically, a characteristic of US administration.

initially appear to be somewhat misplaced. First, the Community's creation of a single and common economic space, governed by European institutions and guided by a law with a life extending far beyond the normative limits set by its constituent members' notions of statehood, would seem inexorably to confirm Europe's commitment to a "market without a state".[5] And secondly – an inevitable consequence of increasing statelessness – the internal market appears crucially to deviate from conventional state-embedded economic arenas, once structured by and thus in need of guidance from the statal polity via its administration and administrative law. The law of the internal market – or at least its primary and constitutive law – is an essentially atomistic construction;[6] dedicated, not to "administering" or imposing a political will upon economic processes, but rather to ensuring the primacy of individual economic enterprise above the misguided interventionist preoccupations of statal polities.[7]

As a consequence, the pinpointing and formalising of a specific administrative law of the internal market, might also be regarded as little more than a rearguard action undertaken by state-oriented lawyers in a foolish endeavour to re-colonise the ever-expanding world of non-statal international economic-legal orders: a fundamentally mistaken exercise, noteworthy only for its paradoxical attempt to apply legal instruments designed for the very specific needs of a statal world, in an effort to meet the novel legal requirements of a normativised international economic arena. Nonetheless, this paper seeks to argue the case for the evolution of a European administrative law of the internal market for two particular and interrelated reasons.

First, for all that it was born of neo-liberally flavoured rights of personal economic autonomy, the internal market is nevertheless emerging as its own very indeterminate, but decidedly pluralist form of "socialised" or socially-embedded "polity". Both the novel forms of politico-economic interaction observable amongst newly released private economic interests and supranational/governmental actors, and the longevity of more traditional "public" – though also, and increasingly so, "private" – concerns that markets be run in accordance with certain social/ethical criteria, have determined that the internal market now possesses a framework of institutional and substantive regulation largely unforeseen by European treaties. That is, an evolving regulatory structure which is moulded by an as yet indistinct plurality of national, European, public and private interests, and within which the substantive social/ethical features of European economic interchange are being daily determined. Secondly, however, as befits any body of public law, administrative law is not simply a product of the positive state, but might also be characterised as a pivotal mediator of the norms of the "constitutional state": a creature of constitutional law, not

---

[5] Joerges (1991b).   [6] Articles 49, 52, 59, 65 and 30 EC.   [7] Everson (1995b).

only efficiency-seeking, but also equally dedicated to upholding, and ensuring that administrative bodies be committed to, the dual constitutional principles of democratic decision-making and secured individual rights.

The institutional structures around which the emerging European internal market polity gravitates are diverse. Semi-autonomous agencies, committees and less formal (even private) regulatory networks are all engaged in the setting of technical, ethical and social standards, and thus the socialisation of the European market. Though doubts remain as to whether such bodies constitute an administration in the classic sense, or are instead a manifestation of a new and subtle form of European governance,[8] one essential fact is nevertheless clear: increasingly, some mechanism is required to ensure that democratic and rights-based or rule of law values are respected during the process of market regulation. With their roots in the constitution, administrative law and administrative lawyers would seem well-versed in matters of the securing of democracy, the rule of law and individual rights. The trick in the internal market setting, however, will be to find an on-going and explicit mode of "constitutionalising" an evolutionary European administrative law, not with an eye to the particular structures of the finite statal polity, but in line with the peculiar normative requirements of the emerging, indeterminate but pluralist and socialised, or socially-embedded, internal market polity.

2. The Emerging Internal Market Polity: Indeterminate and Pluralist "Socialisation"

2.1 The Internal Market Paradox

The emergence of an indeterminate internal market polity – and with it an uncertain but fundamental reworking of the traditional view of the relationship maintained between markets, politics and society – may be traced to a dual paradox within the legally-inspired process of European economic integration. Certainly, at the time the Rome Treaty was drafted, few would have predicted the curious judicial inventiveness of the ECJ: an institution which chose to interpret the EC Treaty's prohibition of discrimination upon grounds of nationality, not as a simple ban upon tariff barriers to trade in the manner of GATT, but as a positive legal stimulus to cross-border commerce, dismissive of tariffs and old-style, trade-disrupting (interventionist) governmental regulation alike.[9] Equally surprising, however, was the fact that such initial economic rationalisation and a subsequent subjectivisation of market rights,[10] was not simply to result in

---

[8] Below, 3.2.   [9] See Weiler (1999).

[10] That is, the personalisation of and direct effect attributed to the "four freedoms" – Articles 48, 52, 59, 63 EEC.

an ordo-liberal[11] or even neo-liberal internal market construction. The integrated European market is not solely an economic sphere, independent of politics and society alike, where individual market actors conduct their own personal affairs, unmolested by statal polities and constrained only by the formal limits set by the (ordo-liberal) primary European legal order or by the (neo-liberal) judicial breadth endowed upon individual economic rights. Rather, a constitutive law of the internal market, not limited to the opening up of narrow channels of access between individual state-embedded markets, and which instead prises economies out of their national institutional settings to recast them as one common and legally-secured sphere of atomistic economic freedom, is now increasingly being complemented by a complex and "socialising", institutional and substantive framework of technical, social and ethical European regulation.

The reasons for "European re-regulation" are well known. Clearly, the final political impetus for judicial-led "negative" European market integration came in the wake of the 1980s Europe-wide political retreat from redistributive social-welfare models of governance and the once traditional reliance upon ponderous administrations to implement and manage vast programmes of (socially-engineering) economic intervention.[12] The rationalising coalition which saw Member States commit themselves to the Single European Act, and thus give added weight to EC law's forceful integration philosophy, was not, however, to be taken its logical "depoliticised market" conclusion. Pure negative integration instead faltered in the face of a threefold pressure for renewed market regulation. Predictably, governmental withdrawal from the reins of regulatory control did little to alter the basic fact that many market activities continued to be "valued by a public" which demanded that some form of regulatory oversight would still apply.[13] More significant, however, was the large measure of national reluctance to allow the free flow of goods and services across borders prior to the establishment of common regulatory standards.[14] Meanwhile, the Community itself, possibly as part of its search for popular legitimacy, likewise displayed a personal predilection for regulatory activity in eye-catching areas such as environmental protection.

Immediately apparent as the grounds for European re-regulation are, however, its exact ramifications remain somewhat indistinct. Born of personal economic rights and economic rationalisation, the internal market is nonetheless equally subject to certain re-regulatory demands

---

[11] That is, Mestmäcker's vision of an autonomous market secured and regulated not by politics but by formal European law, see Mestmäcker (1994).

[12] Majone (1993a); in this analysis also heralding the rise of the "regulatory state" above its welfarist counterpart. In other words – is this largely true for internal market management – modern regulation is rational, avoiding the conflation of welfarist interventionist economics and simple, market supportive, regulation.

[13] Selznick (1985).   [14] Falke (1996).

expressed through a novel multi-level, national/supranational and public/private, governance structure. Alternatively, in stark contrast to the traditional state-embedded market, clearly governed by a single statal polity with politically predetermined and exact regulatory/interventionist aims, the European market necessarily exhibits a twofold tension. On the one hand, there is doubt about the goal of European economic regulation: is it – in line with negative integration impulses – a mere non-political and technical mechanism, supportive of personal economic autonomy and regulatorily corrective of market failures, or – with an eye to the character of substantive re-regulation – does it also embody "market-external" and possibly even partially-redistributive ethical/social concerns? On the other hand, there is equal uncertainty about who might legitimately claim to be the author of European market regulation: first, individual statal polities in the character of Member State representatives; secondly, a Community integration interest personified by the Commission; thirdly, de-statalised political groupings and Europe-wide interest groups; or fourthly – and with a crucial eye to their supposedly autonomous (of politics and society) status – market actors themselves?

2.2 Committees, Agencies and Networks

This dual tension indelibly marks both the institutions of European regulation, and their substantive policy-making. Though unforeseen by the Treaties and thus clearly creatures of institutional compromise between the Commission and Council,[15] semi-autonomous agencies, committees and less formal semi-private and private networks nonetheless exhibit a far greater degree of heterogeneity in both their activities and composition than can be simply attributed to the contingencies of political horsetrading.

Most famously, continuing uncertainty about the goals of internal market regulation, as well as the character of European regulators, is manifest in the striking functional and compositional divergence between European agencies and committees. Agencies would thus seem to be a simple product of a continuing commitment to economic rationalisation and the protection of private market forces from unwarranted social and political attention. Charged with market entry/exit regulation or more general informal, and policy-informing, information-gathering duties, agencies meet a purely technical demand for market-corrective and sector-specific regulation. As a consequence, their seemingly technocratic and semi-autonomous status gives implicit voice to private market interests, and much credence to the lingering notion that internal market regulation has more to do with the "neutral" sustenance of individual economic enterprise than with the imposition of (collective) political/social direction. Their placement under

---

[15] Kreher (1997).

the Commission's institutional umbrella and the presence of national representatives within their management structures notwithstanding, agencies are thus largely shielded from explicitly political processes by their founding statutes (Council Directives and Regulations), permanent staff, organisational independence, varying degrees of budgetary autonomy and direct networking with national administrators.[16]

Committees, in stark contrast, were born of a strong national desire to retain control over the setting and consequences of European regulatory norms/standards, and thus better embody the functional and structural tensions which characterise internal market regulation. First, they hover between "technical" and "political" considerations in their efforts initially to identify and then – in limited redistributive mode – to apportion the costs of the ethical/social criteria which inform European economic regulation.[17] Secondly, their often very fluid composition not only reflects upon the regulatory endeavour to balance rationalising technical criteria against broader political concerns, but also forcefully highlights schisms between the political interests of those engaged in the process of internal market regulation. Though formally established to pursue the highly administrative goal of overseeing implementing powers delegated to the Commission,[18] committees are thus deeply implicated in political processes and often resemble "mini-councils",[19] being the forum where the battle to balance a European market-integrationist logic against a Member State interest in the substance and costs of consumer protection and cohesive national economic development is daily fought.[20] Institutionally associated with, in this case a politically more upbeat and "agenda-setting" Commission,[21] committees are at the same time subject to a greater degree of Member State influence. The all powerful regulatory committees embrace national governmental representatives, the scientific members of the more "neutral" technical committees are directly nominated by the Member States, and only the weaker advisory committees represent a wider public opinion in the character of "Commission-approved" interest groups.

Less visible but no less significant than the agency-committee divide, however, are similar differences in the intensity and manner with which European administration interacts with a wider public, and more particularly, takes note of "private" expertise and interests within its activities. Divergence extends far beyond a purely efficiency-seeking movement which

---

[16] Ibid, at 235.

[17] That is, determine whether industry, government or consumers should bear the burden of costly regulation, below 3.2.

[18] "Comitology Decision", Council Decision 87/373/EEC, (1987) OJ L 197/33.

[19] Indeed, committees are at times so deeply implicated in political processes that their status as "administrative" bodies has been questioned, see Harlow (1996).

[20] Vos (1999).   [21] Vos (1997b).

sees certain regulatory functions retained in governmental/administrative hands, and others – due to their extremely technical nature – delegated to industry-based bodies such as the private standardisation organisations, CEN and CENELEC.[22] Rather, difference appears also to stem from a limited but fundamental re-working of the once rigidly vertical relationship maintained between regulators and the public, with certain of the heavily networking oriented informational agencies habitually consulting with a far wider range of national administrative and world-wide scientific technical opinion than do the more hierarchically-construed committees and executive agencies. Possibly an innovative response to the very modern challenge posed by regulatory policy-making under conditions of scientific and economic uncertainty,[23] such "heterarchical" regulatory co-operation, however, likewise seems to extend somewhat beyond the risk-responsive collection of data and opinion from "neutral" sources. Instead, certain agencies appear happy to risk a charge of "agency capture", similarly interacting with a large number of private market actors in the shape of industry "clients".[24]

In brief summary, however, agencies, committees and less formal public/private networks are all clearly *ad hoc* creatures of necessity, responding in diverging manners to an unexpected and highly differentiated demand for European market regulation. As such, differences in their composition and mode of operation might initially be attributed to a pragmatic impulse within the EU: a mix and match attitude, reminiscent of the experimental early years of national administration-building, and responsive to national, integrationist, public, private and – where appropriate – market interests in turn. With the internal market in its infancy and the governance system of the EU in evolutionary flux, the development of a wide and colourful range of regulatory bodies is a judicious interim measure: the best available means to satisfy the concerns of all participants within the internal market so as to ensure the continuing dynamic of economic integration. However, to move beyond such immediate pragmatism, institutional and functional diversity might also be characterised as the end-result rather than transient reflection of a fundamental and as yet unsettled re-alignment between markets, politics and society.

2.3 The Socially-Embedded Market Polity

With its judicially secured and economically rationalising base in subjective rights of personal economic liberty, the internal market has finally severed the Gordian and governing knot between statal polities and institutionally embedded national economies. Heralding far more than the mere passing of command economics or interventionist administration, European market

---

[22] Ibid.   [23] Ladeur (1997a).   [24] Kreher (1997).

integration has instead given birth to an extensive and (vitally) socially/politically-detached sphere of private and self-determining economic interaction. Seen in this light, the variety of European regulatory institutions, their contrasting activities and their varying make-ups, may accordingly be argued to represent a vigorous though contested effort to forge new links between society, the political system and the market-place. The re-establishment of relations, or the "socialisation" of the market, however, is greatly complicated both by the complex, evolving and multi-level system of European governance, and by the claim of a newly-liberated internal market sphere to a continuing measure of autonomy. Where the national market was characterised by the simple political pre-determination of social/ethical demands and their subsequent administrative imposition upon market activities, the single market is instead subject to an on-going and openly political, administrative/regulatory process, which is itself the forum in which competing public/private, political/social and national/supranational values and interests are presented, identified and accommodated. The private demand for economic liberty is implicit both in technocratic agency management and in the economically rationalising and "proportionality-imposing"[25] effects of scientific/economic expertise within committees. Equally, a "public" and somewhat old-style national interest in the creation of an ethical and socially-responsive market (sometimes with redistributive consequences) is personified by committees of explicitly polit-ical national representatives; and is similarly counterbalanced against the supranational Commission's institutional influence and promotion of its own – often *per se* economically-rationalising – integrationist demands. Further, post-national private values and interests also find their value and interest-laden voice; not only through semi-official interest groups, but also via less formal networks comprising both general public (and scientific) opinion and market actors themselves.

In conclusion, the internal market and its administration may thus be viewed in one of two ways. First, as a detached private market sphere with an attendant institutional and substantive framework of regulation which is directed towards the market's socialisation, or its re-moulding so as to reflect social, ethical and political pre-occupations. Or secondly – and given the implicit and explicit presence of market actors within administration, more convincingly – as an increasingly socially-embedded "market polity", where market, society and the political system are all engaged in a joint effort to shape private market forces in line both with technical regulatory criteria and with broader social/ethical values and political demands. Whichever characterisation is preferred, however, both administrative actors

---

[25] Joerges/Neyer (1997a). And this point is vital for the continuation of the argument. Alternatively, the importation of scientific/technical expertise into decision-making forces those involved to justify their proposed intervention in scientific/technical terms and thus insulates decision-making from unwarranted governmental interventionism.

or participants within the market polity are possessed of divergent interests and values, and are indistinct but decidedly pluralist; also being to a certain degree (especially as regards private actors within networks) "self-nominating".[26] Equally, the substantive regulatory outcomes of "socialisation", or the established mores of the socially-embedded market polity, are contested and indeterminate: their establishment is a complex matter of on-going interaction between competing values and interests.

3. The Law of Administration: From State to Constitution to Stateless Constitution?

3.1 Transmission: A Dual Genesis in State and Constitution

Conceptually, though simply speaking, the linkage between state and administrative law has found its traditional expression through the legal notion of "transmission" or "transmission-belt administration".[27] In other words, the sovereignty of the statal polity was to be confirmed and strengthened by the creation of an administration to whom the polity's common and indivisible will – expressed through legislative mandate – would be transmitted: a purely delegatee authority charged with imposing a pre-existing statal will upon all segments of national society. Equally, such statal sovereignty was to be protected by a guardian administrative law, dedicated to ensuring that administration neither develop a will of its own, nor deviate from the narrowly-faithful and efficient execution of its legislatively-determined tasks.

Most closely associated with the French state's on-going demand for the forceful execution of the *pouvoir général* – though reaching its undeniable zenith in the post-war European state's collectivist interest in the efficient administration of socially-redistributive economic management – the concept of transmission thus rests primarily upon the postulation of a pre-existing and substantive public good. Inexorably entwined with the notion that groups of citizens can form communities of tangible common interest, and ruthlessly dedicated to the efficient pursuit of that interest, transmission is, above all, a reflection and derivative of the statal incorporation of polities or, more precisely, the statal personification of the putative common will of the community of citizens. However, beyond this incorporative statal impulse, efficiency-seeking and sovereignty-promoting transmission, may nonetheless also be argued to stand in a close relationship with the "constitutional state".

---

[26] That is, actors themselves choose when to become a part of the socially-embedded internal market polity. They are not invited in, but begin to present their interests of their own accord.

[27] Stewart (1975).

Thus, even in its purest form – where administration pursues public interest with little or no regard for individual concerns – administrative legal oversight extends somewhat beyond the simple protection of formal statal sovereignty. The judicial policing of legislative mandates, thus not only secures the state's monopoly of power, but likewise ensures that too independently-minded an administration will not inadvertently, or indeed wilfully subvert the representative and constitutionally-secured democratic process. In other words, administration is as much the handmaiden – rather than the helmsman – of democratically-legitimated policy outcomes, as it is the conduit of the statal will; while the message that "public interest" – as most immediately embodied in a narrow legislative mandate – has a normative/constitutional as well as a substantive/statal connotation, is only given added force by more liberal modifications to the transmission-belt model of administration. Thus, where self-limiting liberalism or the rule of law reign supreme,[28] the administration's faithfulness to the public interest is not merely to be measured in the light of its strict adherence to legislative direction. Rather, judicial administrative review takes place in the twilight zone between individual rights, procedural guarantees and legislative intent. Courts accordingly seek to establish a balance between the administration's proper pursuit of its democratically pre-determined mandate and its necessary on-going respect for those constitutionally-secured individual rights and procedural guarantees which a democratic liberal polity might never alienate.

In its liberal character at least, transmission-belt administration is thus also a highly refined constitutional derivation. The normative construction and task of law is furthermore a dual one, based upon the liberal constitutional compromise between the pursuit of a democratically pre-determined public interest and the safeguarding of more individual – though reflective of a normative general interest – concerns. Not only is administration a neutral delegatee of rigidly defined legislative direction, and not only must administrative law ensure the administration's regard for political mandates. Rather, administration and administrative law need also pay due attention to further core – and on occasions, competing – constitutional values.

3.2 Interest Representation: State and Constitution in Conflict

Moving on to tangible nation states and their law, however, the dual genesis of administration and administrative law in the constitution and the state may similarly be argued to lie at the heart of a growing administrative legal struggle, taking as its focus the functional and normative inappropriateness to a complex modern world, of "simplistic" forms of statal organisation. Conflict has its roots in empirical observations upon

---

[28] The former, a strong feature within US administrative; the latter a characteristic of current UK administrative law.

the operation of the administration, and its tangible expression in the emergence within administrative law, both of various strands of legal pluralism and a growing judicial predilection for the mores of proceduralism. Thus, it mirrors the ever-increasing gap between functionalist, though static, statal thinking and constitutional law's specific pre-occupation with the normative legitimation of the "real-world" institutional structures of social/political organisation. Hence, though administrative law has remained true to its constitutional roots, and has sought to secure both democratic and rights-based values within administration, this effort has similarly led it to place the notion of transmission into doubt; with judicial rethinking tackling exactly those elements within the model which derive most closely from statal thinking. As a consequence, the law has to a certain degree departed from the paradigm of a statal common will expressed through a unitary and representative democratic process.

Historically speaking, this "real-world" pressure upon the transmission-belt model of administration has stemmed from two sources. The first – prevalent in the 1970s – the observation, or at least the belief, that administrative bodies are not simply the servants of a legislative process but also have other masters, still forms the core of a "neo-pluralist" strand within political science: an intensely sceptical body of thought which castes a pessimistic eye over opaque administrative decision-making and argues that the administrative process is *de facto* at the beck and call of various interpolative interests (political, social or economic) the strongest of whom determine the substance of administrative outcomes.[29] Meanwhile, the second is an equally prosaic consideration which maintains that since the regulatory/administrative world is both complex and intransparent, administration is often able to deviate from the mere implementation of narrowly-drawn mandates and instead itself engages in some form of substantive policy-making.[30] Vitally, however, both sources have led to the same transmission-disturbing conclusion: administration does not always involve the neutral execution of the polity's common will, but may itself be a substantive political process, guided by particularist rather than general "public interest" concerns.

Confronted with such transmission-disrupting phenomena, administrative law – above all in the US – was initially to respond with a re-assertion of a somewhat Madesonian vision of normative constitutional, rather than substantive statal public interest. It accordingly chose to place a far greater judicial emphasis on the pursuit of the perennial individualist-pluralist bulwark against the perversion and perverting influence of mass democratic forces, individual rights.[31] A greater court-room pre-occupation with individual *locus standi* thus not only re-invigorated the 18th Century message that true democracy was ever respectful of and indeed based upon

---

[29] For a comprehensive overview, see Croley (1998).
[30] Shapiro (1996a).   [31] Strauss (1984).

extensive and power-diluting personal autonomy, but also furnished the Judges with a cloaked means to depart from their neutral procedural role in order more closely to investigate, and even set aside, the substance of administrative decision-making.[32]

A first hint that the law was prepared to dispense with strict transmission-belt administration in the service of wider normative values, this judicial movement has nonetheless gathered far greater import as it has moved beyond the support of individual rights and has begun equally to develop – through an interest-representation model[33] – an alternative mode of democratic legitimation for, or a substantive public interest within, administration. Thus, though the re-assertion of individual autonomy undoubtedly heralded conflict between constitutional and statal values, the major challenge to transmission and statal thinking has in fact emerged as "public-choice" theories of administration,[34] together with more detailed studies of the modern regulatory challenge under conditions of scientific and economic uncertainty,[35] have not merely exposed the practical shortcomings in pure delegatee authorities, but have likewise suggested that pluralist representation and substantive policy-making are inevitable facets of a modern and responsive administration. That is, they are characteristics to which administrative law can and must respond.

Put simply and briefly, the judicial attempt to evolve an alternative form of democratic control over administration revolves around two mechanisms: the first, the endeavour to give a wider public greater access to the administrative decision-making process through the aggressive application of transparency-securing instruments such as the US Administrative Procedures Act; the second, the use of what were once protective rights of individual liberty to create positive standing for groups of parties with a supposed "interest" in the administrative process.[36] Mirroring that strand in political science which maintains that pluralism will serve a wider form of public interest where the various groups involved in the administrative process engage in a self-limiting exercise – committing their scare resources to the pursuit of self-interest, only where it appears that other groups will not put up costly resistance – transparency-oriented courts thus seek to create as accessible and as pluralist an administrative constituency as possible. Only where administration is transparent, is seen to be such and can easily be challenged on procedural grounds,[37] may multiple and effective interest groupings form to provide the counterbalancing interest

---

[32] Shapiro (1996a).   [33] Croley (1998); Stewart (1975).   [34] Ibid.
[35] Köck (1996).   [36] Stewart (1975).
[37] The idea being that the common structuring of administrative bodies with common procedures, and the provision of a wide right to challenge any abuse of such procedures allows interest groupings to form and be effective: on the one hand, making the activities of administrative bodies highly visible; and on the other leaving much procedural room for the challenging of their decision-making.

pursuit, which seemingly serves as a rough approximation of a general public good.[38] Equally, with an eye to the peculiarities of modern regulatory and administrative problems, the Courts have also extended legal standing beyond individual to wider political interests, largely in an effort to take note of "risk", or scientific and economic uncertainty within the regulatory process. They have thus first, conceded that administration often must engage in substantive policy-making to overcome unforeseen regulatory difficulties; and have secondly, allowed various specialist pressure groupings to challenge the decisions of what is sometimes, and inevitably so, political administration.[39]

Famously characterised as "the provision of a surrogate political process to ensure the fair representation of a wide range of affected interests in the process of administrative decision-making",[40] such latter-day "legal-democratic" activities therefore represent a vital change in the function of administrative law. No longer is it a mere neutral instrument, policing the boundaries of a non-political and autonomy-respecting administration. Rather, given the practical strains upon the notion of transmission, administrative law has also begun to seek alternative means to satisfy its own constitutional vocation for and commitment to ensuring the democratic component within administration. With this, however, the degree of administrative law's identification with the state has necessarily lessened. The state's functional ability to implement, and thus normative claim to embody the general public interest has proven to be somewhat illusory: the mere transmission and implementation of a unitary democratic outcome being subject to the disrupting vagaries of post-legislative regulatory challenges, interest formation and pursuit. As a consequence, an increasingly "constitutionalised" administrative law has withdrawn a degree of its support for traditional (parliamentary) democratic processes and has begun to seek an approximation of the general public interest, or common good, in proceduralism and pluralist representation.

3.3 Normative Demands upon the Internal Market Polity

Admittedly, the slow alienation of administrative law from the state, and its increasing pre-occupation with the securing of eternal constitutional above outdated statal values, has not been without problems of its own. Above all, and correctly so, doubts remain as to whether the attempt to secure an alternative democratic process through procedural mechanisms and a limited measure of pluralist representation within the administrative process, are adequate instruments to ensure administrative respect for the notion of "general public welfare".[41] Alternatively, it may be and is argued

---

[38] Croley (1998).   [39] Köck (1996).   [40] Stewart (1975).
[41] Mostly, a complaint of the left, again for broad details, Croley (1998).

that whilst the transmission-belt model's claim to be implementing the legislatively-established common good, or public interest, is clearly flawed, the developing legal model of interest representation equally does little more than afford more powerful and well-organised interests an added-value voice within administration.[42] Similarly, the danger remains that a procedurally-oriented administrative law will merely substitute the views of the courtroom for those of the legislature. The silent and ever ill-informed majority remains underrepresented; knowingly deprived by a constitution-ally-arrogant and state-usurping administrative law, even of that limited representative voice which unitary political processes have striven – however figuratively – to give it. As a consequence, the divorce between state and administrative law is a necessarily contested one. And yet, with an eye to the legal control of the evolving and substantive framework of internal market regulation, the development of an increasingly constitutionalised and consequently de-statalised administrative law, would seem equally to offer an opportunity positively to structure and "legally-civilise" an emerging and socially-embedded internal market polity.

The internal market diverges in all respects from state-embedded and legislatively-directed economic arenas. Equally, its evolving framework of substantive and institutional regulation in large part encompasses on-going political negotiation rather than neutral implementation processes. Consequently, the evolution of "real-world" modes of social, political and economic organisation within Europe would now seem definitively to have outpaced existing and guiding models of normative governance. The regulation, or the "administering" of the market possesses a depth all of its own: no longer deriving from a clear and single desire to direct market forces, but being framed instead – albeit indistinctly – by an ever-evolving series of national, supranational, public and private interests. In the effort to establish new links between politics, society and the market place, European regulatory institutions have become the focus for an evolving European market polity, bearing little or no relationship with conventional statal polities. Clearly, in such a setting, traditional transmission-belt means of securing the democratic accountability of a burgeoning European "market administration" are somewhat obsolete. With no hint of legislative predetermination and the substantive goals of regulation in on-going doubt, administrative law simply has no single existing democratic mandate to protect. On the other hand, however, the hallmark of a polity remains its respect for some form of democratic process, or overall common good; and here the evolving market polity would appear to be no exception, being subject to an ever-increasing demand that it conduct itself

---

[42] Importantly, an empirical finding of public choice theorists, who admit that trans-parency cannot always be maintained – certain administrative decisions being taken in secretive conditions and still being prey to organised interests, see again for broad details, Croley (1998).

in accordance with a general European public interest.[43] In other words, though divorced from the traditional state and its unitary political will, the internal market and its administration might nonetheless not be seen in isolation from more universal normative concerns about the legitimacy of its regulatory framework. Diffuse and experimental as it may be, the novel internal market polity need nevertheless be directed to some form of acceptable and accepted public interest or common good, with the sole potential guardian of such values within this internationalised economic order being, as ever, European law.

3.4 A Constitutionalised European Administrative Law?

Perhaps the best general indicator of the recent pressure upon an evolving body of European administrative law to exercise normative control over EC/U decision-making processes, are moves amongst administrative lawyers finally to sever the unholy alliance maintained between European law and an efficiency-oriented French mode of administrative thinking, which is still heavily influenced by (Rousseauean) statal presumptions.[44] Such a move is presumably a conceptual response to Maastricht's explicit polity-building aspirations and, more prosaically, is also suggested by the TEU's belated and indirect recognition of a right to "fair administration".[45] As such, the increased emphasis upon wider and constitutionally-derived administrative legal values necessarily reflects the retarded but growing concern that a novel and as yet indistinct supranational organisation, might not simply be viewed as the natural and thus – inefficient tendencies apart – infallible purveyor of an ill-defined European public's somewhat indistinct general interest. Instead, intricate studies upon whether the EC/U's administrative activities would be best governed by the detailed prescriptions of the *Rechtsstaat* or the vaguer principles of the common rule of law,[46] are (albeit implicitly) tackling fundamental questions such as the legitimate breadth of EC/U administrative mandates. That is, who and under what conditions may challenge them.

To be sure, the re-assessment of the general administrative law of the EC/U is very much in its infancy. As such, attempts to extend *locus standi* or clarify which procedural guarantees and individual rights EC/U administration must observe, are limited and theoretically indistinct.[47] The issue

---

[43] And here, the case of BSE is indicative – public concern having led to deep distrust in a committee system which is thought to have privileged the political interests of the UK government above the health of European consumers.

[44] Schwarze (1993).

[45] Via Article F TEU's incorporation within the Union of the European Convention on Human Rights.

[46] Harlow (1996); Schwarze (1993).

[47] Ibid, neither author making clear their underlying preferences.

of whether European administrative lawyers are merely evolving – in rearguard fashion – a Madisonian, rights-based bulwark against the democratic imperfections of supranational decision-making or are instead developing an alternative democratic process to reflect the general interest of the evolving European polity, has yet to be addressed let alone settled. And yet, at the more particular level of internal market regulation, at least three strands of legal thought might be identified which indicate European law's overall vocation for the legal forging of democratisation.

Thus, though not necessarily drawing their inspiration from administrative legal roots,[48] European lawyers have turned their attention to issues such as: first, a Jellinekian mode of securing democracy in the internal market via the extrapolation of unassailable, individual social and ethical "rights" from secondary European law;[49] secondly, the securing of an approximation of a European public interest through greater and legally-guaranteed transparency in the administration of the internal market;[50] and thirdly, greater pluralist representation through the institutional incorporation of "interest-groups" within European regulatory decision-making.[51] Partially a specifically European response to a European problem,[52] partially an echo of administrative themes developed in the national setting,[53] and partially hybridic;[54] all three approaches nonetheless seek to control the institutions of internal market management and thus share a single pursuit – the identification of normative alternatives to the notion of a statal common will expressed through representative democratic processes. Each approach therefore chooses to highlight divergent legal mechanisms for the forging of democratisation, but all are fine-tuned to increase the representation of a European public within the internal market.

1. The first proposes the substitution of substantive rights for substantive politics, and the creation of an individual European with a legally-determined political persona, forged specifically to ensure the crystallisation within the European market of certain social and ethical values.[55]

---

[48] Possibly, a result of the disciplinary rootlessness of European law; and arguably having consequences for the conceptual clarity of various of European law's academic analyses.

[49] N Reich (1997).

[50] Dehousse, in this volume.

[51] Vos (1999).

[52] A Jellinekian constitutional and substantive right-based approach was historically developed in response to the democratic deficit within Germany's turn-of-the Century *Reichsverfassung* – the comparison with the Rome Treaty proves to be irresistible.

[53] An EPA clearly being the younger brother of the US APA.

[54] The notion that interest groups should be institutionally incorporated within administrative bodies, being a subtle variation on a national theme of their judicial representation via a widening of individual rights of standing to include political grouping.

[55] N Reich (1997).

2. The second is based upon a simple acceptance of the fact that internal market administration cannot but be prey to the attentions of a plurality of interests, and tailors its subsequent efforts to ensure an approximation of a general European public interest – or as wide and as pluralist administrative constituency as possible – through a European Administrative Procedures Act.[56]

3. The third entails a clear concession to pluralist representation; though interestingly via its institutional as opposed to judicial formalisation.[57]

In other words, though divorced from the traditional (constitutional) statal setting, European law would nonetheless appear to be attempting to subject the internal market polity to various of the democratic values traditionally secured there. As such, these efforts may likewise be identified as a latter-day endeavour to normativise market regulation – or create a democracy-securing body of administrative law for the internal market polity – in line with the developing mores of a "stateless constitution".[58]

Such legal moves towards the democratisation of the internal market polity cannot but be greeted. Nonetheless, as amply demonstrated in the national setting, the alienation of a constitutionalised administrative law from the state is in any case a troublesome process and, in relation to the internal market polity, may likewise be argued to face very similar difficulties. Thus, though undoubtedly heralding a maturing of European law beyond functionalism and towards sustainable normativity, the threefold legal approach to market democratisation inevitably also suffers from shortcomings very similar to those identified at national level. First, the fear that a judicial crystallisation of various ethical and social values via the creation of subjective rights is, in its effects at least, as great a formalist legal *coup d'état* upon democratic processes, as was the historical courtroom's over-emphasis upon procedural correctness and the primacy of individual autonomy. And secondly, the concern that an acceptance of pluralist representation – however transparent and supposedly well-directed to an approximation of public interest – is a mere blank cheque for more powerful pluralist groupings to pursue their particularist aims. Crucially, however, such concerns are likewise only augmented by specific internal market conditions.

With its constitutive roots in rights of economic autonomy, and yet also playing host to a heterogeneous framework of institutional and substantive regulation, the revolutionary market polity is thus possessed of a high degree of complexity, or an intricacy which is only increased by the wide variety of national, supranational, public and private interest involved. Equally, however, the primary law of the European market was not

---

[56] Dehousse, in this volume.   [57] Vos (1999).
[58] Though only Jellinekean thought is explicit in this regard.

conceived with traditional or, for that matter, any other form of constitutional theory in mind, and thus seems to offer very few definitive normative
waymarkers for the constitutional structuring and control of this complex
polity. Indeed, those few normative pointers that do exist would appear to
be highly contradictory with, for example, the neo-liberally flavoured four
freedoms standing in an uneasy relationship with Article 36 EC's blessing
upon (potentially interventionist) national regulation. As a consequence, it
would only seem meet for any form of European administrative law in
search of stateless constitutional roots, to more closely consider the exact
and possibly contradictory ramifications of the norms upon which it bases
its democratisation efforts. First, in relation to Jellinekian juridification, the
danger that an inviolate crystallisation of social and ethical values within
substantive personal rights will not only undermine the constitutive
economic freedom of the internal market, but may also (perversely) stand in
the way of broader market socialisation efforts.[59] Secondly, with regard to
the strict proceduralism inherent to an EPA, its unwelcome potential to act
as a break upon innovative – i.e., responsive and heterarchical – institution-
building.[60] Thirdly, the lack of regard which institutionalised interest representation would inevitably pay to self-nominating and still-emerging private
interests. And fourthly – and possibly most vitally – the overwhelming legal
disregard for the most pressing problem facing the socially-embedded
internal market polity: the question of the relative weight to be given to
national, community, public and private interest in turn.[61]

In short, or so it may be argued, the internal market is indeed in need of
an administrative law based upon a stateless constitution. However, a far
greater effort is now needed to identify the guiding constitutional norms
which would both satisfy democratisation demands, and be well-suited to
the peculiar structures of the evolving and socially-embedded market polity.

4. Three "Constitutional" Models of the Internal Market Polity?

Clearly, any attempt by administrative lawyers to identify the stateless and
guiding norms upon which they might found their normative control of the
evolving and socially-embedded internal market polity must itself be based
on a wider constitutional view of the process of European market integration. A generalised and generalisable normative/legal framework must be

[59] Would a substantive right to environmental quality act as a break on economic development? Equally, would a right to consumption not stand in the way of the development of
environment policy?

[60] The emphasis on common procedures dampening institutional innovation.

[61] Though here Vos is a very welcome exception, highlighting a "constitutional" balance
between the Member States' continuing responsibility for the welfare of their publics and
the Commission's interest in continuing integration. See Vos (1999).

established which is first, clearly identifying of the outer limits of the socially-embedded polity; and which is secondly, both constituting and apportioning of political power – as well as controlling of the of the means of its exercise – within that polity. Here, however, an unavoidable and interpretative difficulty arises. As noted, significant as the creation of a postnational and legally-secured economic order has proven to be, it was not initially undertaken with any thought of polity-building in mind. Instead, the fundamental and post-statal re-alignment between markets, society and political systems has about it an undoubted air of unexpected incrementalism. As a consequence, there would appear to be a certain mismatch between the few legal norms – a body of European law – created simply to establish a limited international economic order, and the complex subtleties of the emerging and multi-layered market polity. Most clearly manifest in the obvious contradictions between European treaty norms supportive of personal economic freedom and those suggestive of continued national intervention,[62] such incongruity equally acts as an effective foil to formalist legal attempts to derive a generalised and generalisable constitutional framework from primary European law. Although legal provisions of a constitutional nature do exist within the treaties, much interpretative work must nonetheless be undertaken to extract from them a coherent scheme of norms suited to normative market governance through a constitutionalised administrative law. To this end, the following analysis accordingly castes its net widely; seeking to distil suitable constitutional markers for the emerging and socially-embedded internal market polity, not from traditional constitutional law or theory, but from three interdisciplinary models of market regulation.

With its roots in traditional political theory and radical modern economics, the non-majoritarian model of internal market regulation is a subtle blend of disciplines which are harnessed in the service of an "economically-rationalising" view of an internal market polity isolated from all political concerns. The deliberative model of market governance, by contrast, builds both upon European law and international relations theory – with a smattering of sociology thrown in – in its efforts to depict the internal market polity as a "socialised" domain where national governments to a large degree retain the regulatory upper hand. Finally, the heterarchical model of market regulation draws heavily upon post-modern legal theory. As such it is a descriptive rather than normative approach which consequently highlights the often-overlooked "private" rather than "public" facets of political direction within the internal market. No one model is examined in full. Instead, the analysis concentrates upon each body of thought's view upon the legitimate character of the emerging market polity.

---

[62] Several interesting contradictions thus arise. Will traditional national democratic processes have precedence over individual European rights or vice versa. Secondly, is political power in the internal market polity constituted by rights or by politics?

More particularly, it investigates the interrelated questions of which substantive goal the emerging polity should be directed to, and who amongst the variety of interests which focus upon the institutional structures of market regulation, should play a part in securing this goal and how.

4.1 The Non-Majoritarian Model of Market Regulation

Though latterly much embattled, its preferred mode of European market regulation – the fully independent regulatory agency – having met with a certain degree of disfavour in the European arena,[63] non-majoritarian thought nonetheless proves an invaluable point of departure; being an explicit attempt to theorise and normativise the attempt to establish new relations between market, society and the political system without the prop of majoritarian democratic processes.[64]

Though born of modern economics, and more particularly, the notion that the criteria of macro-economic efficiency can guide and shape "non-political" market governance – both guaranteeing aggregate welfare and ensuring that regulation never stray into those redistributive social policy concerns which are ever requiring of majoritarian deliberation[65] – non-majoritarian thought nonetheless also has strong roots in the political constitution. It thus forcefully claims that its isolation of market regulation from political forces serves the goal of democracy, safeguarding the democratically set goals of the polity from the predatory inclinations of a transitory political elite.[66] Accordingly, the oft-made comparison between non-majoritarianism and neo-liberalism is misleading: non-majoritarian thinking placing less emphasis on the unrestrained pursuit of individual economic rights, and more upon the political creation of an autonomised sphere of market activity which is guarded, on the one hand, from disruptive redistributive goals and regulated, on the other, by rational/expert considerations with an eye to increasing overall economic welfare rather than pursuing individual and possibly selfish economic goals.

Translating to the sphere of socially-embedded internal market polity this notion determines equally that non-majoritarian thought parts company with ordo-liberal conceptions of the European market order.[67] On the one hand, it shares with them a desire to conceive of the emerging European market polity outside of the political orders of the Member States. Yet, on the other, it argues that the regulation of the "autonomised" European market sphere is not a simple matter for legal codification, with European rights simply and neutrally securing the boundaries of the market. Instead, it should entail substantive regulatory policy-making with expert epistemic and technocratic communities actively shaping the market in the pursuit of aggregate rather than individual economic welfare.

---

[63] Kreher (1997).   [64] At its most theoretically detailed, Majone (1996a).
[65] Majone (1993a).   [66] Majone (1994b).   [67] Mestmäcker (1994).

Characterising the whole of European Communities as a non-political "fourth branch of government",[68] non-majoritarianism therefore retains faith in the political orders of the Member States, but also serves the economically rationalising elements within the Rome treaties. Thus, the autonomised European market could only come into being following the democratic decision of the national political collectivities that this was an acceptable goal. Equally, it can only remain in being insofar as it is restricted to the macro-economically efficient pursuit of aggregate welfare, and further, does not stray into social or political issues which remain the exclusive concern of national democratic processes. Similarly, however, the scheme of expert and technocratic governance should aid in ensuring that economic activities in Europe no longer be perverted to transient welfarist or simply expedient political goals, and are instead tailored to allow for overall and sustained wealth creation.

Moving on to consider the form of legitimate European market polity which this model envisages – and thus its underlying vision of a constitutional order for that polity – it is at once apparent that the market polity which it postulates is a very limited one whilst the measure of the constitutionality of European administrative law, seen in this light at least, would accordingly lie in its ability to shield this polity from disruptive political concerns and selfish individual economic claims. In other words, neither the Member States nor individual Europeans – through too aggressive a pursuit of their personal economic or even social rights – should be allowed to play a part in the process of market socialisation. Equally, European administrative law need, on the one hand, withdraw from its all too eager attempts to introduce extra private participants into the debate through the juridification of political-social interests. While, on the other, it must also concentrate on the establishment of the legal mechanisms which would not only protect autonomous regulatory European institutions from national political interference, but would also ensure their expertocratic-technocratic "deliberative quality".[69]

In conclusion, however, non-majoritarian thought offers any attempt to develop a European administrative law for the internal market, a subtle and fruitful variation upon a Madisonian theme. To be sure, economically-rationalising market rights and more particularly, the aggregate welfare which their unhampered pursuit will bring, is the final goal of internal market regulation. However, and vitally so, individual economic rights themselves are not the governing locus for legal oversight of the market. Rather, "politics" is to be kept at bay from the socially-embedded market polity via the securing of expert deliberation. Repellent of the disrupting vagaries of a sometimes doubtful political process and the self interest often inherent to economic autonomy alike, the implicit pursuit of a

[68] Majone (1993a).   [69] Majone (1994b).

(substantive) general European public interest in aggregate welfare is instead to be based on the (proceduralist) privileging of the position of those "who can best judge" whether market regulation is truly suited to serving this maximising aim.

4.2 Deliberative Supranationalism: The European Experiment

Interestingly, the deliberatively supranational model of European governance[70] – an explicit rather than implicit attempt to identify constitutional markers for the socially-embedded international market polity – has emerged out of long-standing interaction and disagreement with non-majoritarian thought. Vitally, however, what was once a mere prosaic disagreement on the practical applicability of the macro-economic criterion of aggregate welfare has now taken on normative dimensions with the deliberative school of thought crucially questioning whether "expert-knowledge" is an appropriate yardstick against which the overall democratic and constitutional quality of European deliberation might be measured.

In elucidation: with its lawyerly respect for primary European law, or provisions such as Article 30 EC, the deliberative school of thought has never denied the economically-rationalising effect of European economic rights. On the contrary, it shares with non-majoritarian thinking a vision of the internal market polity as a sphere of private market relations which is overcoming of the economically stagnatory – and quite often unjustified – legal arrangements atrophised in the "welfarist" economic orders of the Member States. However, with a similarly respectful eye to Article 36 EC, and an equally pragmatic suspicion that economic regulation can never effectively be isolated from social or ethical policy concerns, it likewise argues that there is a justified normative dualism within the emerging internal market polity: with Member States, rather than individual Europeans, continuing to possess a "constitutional" right to advance their views where and when this polity addresses issues which lie in the social and ethical sphere.[71] Though not necessarily concerned with social redistribution in the traditional sense, modern markets do inevitably create new and unforeseen risks, thus giving rise to a "limited" redistributive concern in the matter of the allocation of the costs of risk-regulation:[72] are governments,

---

[70] For its now fully (or almost fully) matured contours, see Joerges/Neyer (1997a).

[71] Ibid, and this consideration is vital, not merely being drawn from the prosaic observation that as national governments bear the cost of European regulation they should have the major say in its formulation; but from the far deeper normative contention that the constitutional nation state is still the most effective and legitimate means to balance and consolidate diverse social interests. As such this body of thought comes close to critiques of administrative law's representation model which argue that the limited plural representation provided can never rival the purity of the democratic constitutional state's claim to be acting in the interests of the entire polity, above, 2.3.

[72] Joerges (1992).

consumers or the market to carry the burden of such costs? Accordingly, in the European setting, this immediately translates into the claim that national governments, as the conduit of traditional national democratic processes, must have a major say in an on-going and political process of market regulation – identifying the limits to and allocating the cost of acceptable risk. Yet it also, and crucially so, alters the climate of "European deliberation:" determining that rationalising expert knowledge must always be balanced against legitimate social and ethical policy concerns.

Taking a closer look at the constitutional implications of this model, it thus transpires that the emerging and socially-embedded internal market polity should similarly reflect such dualism with Member States representing the social and ethical concerns of their polities, and the Community institutions seeking to represent and further the "rationalising" goals of European economic integration. Equally, however, the measure of the "quality" of deliberation is not simply to be found in proven expertise, but rather in the institutional processes and political climate which allows such expertise to be balanced against social and ethical concerns. With this, the deliberative model of supranationalism represents a step forward in a search for what might be characterised as a "proceduralised" constitutional order. Beyond its continued respect for the representative function of national governments, it no longer simply postulates public interest in the primacy of collective state-based political decision-making or, indeed, the pursuit of aggregate welfare through expert deliberation. Instead, the measure of deliberative supranational justice is to be found in the supranational process by which political considerations are balanced against expert (rationalising) advice.[73]

In conclusion, however, the deliberative model of supranationalism likewise contains a sting in the tail for any attempt to evolve a constitutionalised administrative law for the internal market. The internal market, it argues, is *per se* a constitutional order.[74] The foundations for normativity within the socially-embedded internal market polity were inevitably laid as the Rome treaties – through their entrenchment of universal economic rights and consequent air of economic rationalisation – solved the dilemma of static state-based organisation, necessarily – though in an unforeseen manner – forcing national polities to modify their own perceived communities of tangible/substantive common interest, in order take the interests of non-nationals into account during the joint effort to establish an economically-rationalising European market. On this score, European law has therefore largely already played out its constitutional role: diluting the homogenising effects of state-based organisation and creating the fora – more specifically, European committees with their division of labour between national political representatives and the rationalising expertise

---

[73] Joerges/Neyer (1997a).   [74] Ibid.

represented by epistemic communities – in which the deliberative play off between rationalising and political interests might take place. Accordingly, beyond its role in continuing to provide the judicial and institutional fora in which diverse views might be aired, there is little left for it to do. The civility and quality of deliberation – or the correct/convincing balancing of interests – cannot be assured by formal legal provisions, but is instead a simple "sociological" result of the plurality and diversity of a European integration process which has forced experts and governments to ground/re-evaluate their interests and ideas through confrontation with many other views.[75]

In this analysis, the institutions around which the socially-embedded internal market polity revolve are thus mechanisms of "governance" rather than "administration". The distinction is crucial, not only confirming the political primacy of national governments and political processes, but likewise denying that the law is required to play any part in overseeing a conventionally political rather than administrative process of market regulation. The socially-embedded market polity is made up of representatives of the national polities and expert representatives of the Community's economically rationalising interest. These two groups alone can furnish – though sensitive debate rather than formalised legal procedure – the delicate and necessary balance between social/ethical considerations and economic rationalisation within the internal market polity.

4.3 Post-Modern Market Regulation: the Liberation of the "Private"?

With its roots in critical legal theory, a specifically "post-modern" assessment of European market regulation would initially appear to have no part to play in the effort to identify a constitutional framework for the emerging and socially-embedded internal market polity: the in-built theoretical pressure to assess norms in the light of facts having, in this body of thought, ultimately resulted in the death of all normativity. Nonetheless, certain post-modern formulations do bring with them a degree of normative power: at least to the extent that they argue that the famous though idealised public/private constitutional divide need now be re-evaluated not merely in pursuit of descriptive real-world accuracy, but also and (vitally so) in an endeavour to secure the integrative efficacy of the law.[76]

In explanation, and immediately translating "post-modern" thought to the internal market setting, this view becomes crucial. First, since it underlines the "real-world" fact that the creation of a socially-embedded European market has sprung the confines of the "public" statal collectivity with certain private interests outgrowing national political processes and instead pursuing their goals – mostly economic but also socio-political[77] –

---

[75] Ibid.   [76] Ladeur (1994b).

[77] And environmental interest is telling here, see Ladeur (1997b).

in the private sphere.[78] Through regulatory networks, they thus attempt directly to influence market forces and decentralised administrative nodes of market regulation. And secondly, since it demonstrates that law – more particularly regulatory law – has established an immediate rather than politically-mediated relationship with such "privatised" interests, mostly through a direct exchange of information on issues such as emerging risks and the best manner in which to regulate them.[79] Such direct exchange subsequently serves the efficacy of law through the evolution of immediate and workable regulatory solutions.

Accordingly, though irrevocably committed to a simple description of the factual process of market integration and the emergence of an increasingly "private" internal market polity, post-modern thinking – and in particular, its observation that law need retain some hold on reality in order to ensure its efficacy and thus power to integrate society – contains lessons for the evolution of a constitutionalised European administrative law. First, though having no vision of a "legitimate" polity of its own, it reminds both non-majoritarian and supranational thought that with so much political-social development now taking place at the level of the private, the national collectivities in which they place so much of their faith are only one element within the emergent market polity. And secondly, since it highlights law's increasingly direct, rather than legislatively mediated, interaction with political and social forces.

5. The Administration of Deliberation?

The large degree of variation in the manner in which each model theorises and normativises the on-going process of the establishment of new links between the market, society and political systems, is itself confirmation of this paper's central claim that the process of European market socialisation is an intensely contested happening. Equally, however, such contradictions highlight various of the models' empirical shortcomings. First, non-majoritarianism's somewhat blinkered view of modern markets, and more particularly, its inability to deal coherently with the redistributive consequences of the risks which would now seem to be inherent to all processes of economic production.[80] And secondly, the somewhat doubtful status of both non-majoritarian theory's and deliberative thought's residual reliance upon traditional national democratic processes within a progressive polity, set in motion by market rights which have liberated private interests from the Member States' public regulatory cocoons.[81]

---

[78] Ladeur (1997a).   [79] Ladeur (1997b).   [80] BSE again being a telling example.
[81] And note, this does not only occur in relation to economic rights but it also visible in the Commission's support for private interests, above, 2.2.

In addition, however, the models may be argued to suffer from various normative lacunae. Thus, most pressingly, while the deliberative school of thought's pre-occupation with governance above administration – and thus politics above law – brings with it a useful bulwark against potentially anti-democratic legal formalism, the sociologically-inspired emphasis placed on the "naturally" civilising effects of debate between experts and politicians, nonetheless courts the risk of confusing *sein* with *sollen*. The fact that deliberation is just and civic now is no guarantee that it will always be so, and some measure of formal legal intervention may nonetheless be required to ensure that the deliberative process does not fall prey to powerful and organised interests.[82] Similarly, post-modernism's excessive concern with description above prescription, might also be argued to give rise to one vital unanswered question: given that the private has been liberated, what mechanisms might be developed to ensure that although the influence of the public sphere has been diluted, the notion of general public interest remains firmly in place? In other words, how can emancipated but potentially selfish private interests be induced to act with some degree of respect for all participants within the socially-embedded internal market polity?

Such contradictions, empirical shortcomings and normative lacunae notwithstanding, the trio of models nonetheless provides certain common and invaluable pointers upon which a constitutionalised European administrative law might build. Tackling their negative prescriptions first, a unanimous refusal to give any political precedence whatsoever to individual rights – social/ethical as well as economic – within the internal market polity, not only demonstrates their authors' unwillingness irrevocably to pre-empt the political result of the process of socialisation through too rigid a judicial formalisation of transient economic and social values; but further, also underlines the message that the effective balancing of the competing values which revolve around substantive and institutional market regulation is a matter for "political" debate rather than law. Similarly, however, their apparent disregard – even in post-modernist mode – for the institutionalisation of private interests within the regulatory process, both underscores the continuing importance of national polities within the socially-embedded market polity, and indicates just how difficult it is effectively to capture – in formal representative terms – the character of emerging private political and social forces.

In positive mode, competing non-majoritarian and deliberative theories also concur in their treatment of the "political" debates – rather than formal rights – which now act as the vehicle for continuing market socialisation. Alternatively, such socialising discourses are not to be seen in a normative vacuum; a mere matter of stand-off between competing values and interests. Rather, in a proceduralist twist, the "civility" and thus

---

[82] And again, BSE is the obvious example.

general public interest-generating character of debate is to be judged in the light of "neutral" and discourse-structuring normative yardsticks. From simple political discourse to civic deliberation: either proven expertise alone, or frank and open exchange between technocrats and political representatives will furnish the internal market with regulation which is responsive to the concerns of all who may be affected by its operations.

Abstracting to the matter of the design of a constitutionalised and state-less administrative law for the internal market, this thus determines that European lawyers should place less emphasis upon the – rights-based or institutionalised – effort to democratise the socially-embedded internal market polity through a Sisyphus-like attempt to give all its diffuse elements voice through various forms of legal standing. Rather, they should seek to structure explicitly political market administration: ensuring that the essentially self-nominating interests and values which have asserted – and which will continue to assert – themselves within the substantive and institutional framework of market regulation, conduct themselves with due regard for all affected by the process of European economic integration.

To be sure, "pluralism" will continue to play its part in an emerging European law dedicated to the administration of deliberation. However, such emergent European legal pluralism must be shielded first, from the discourse-dampening effects of formalised individual-pluralist bulwarks against the supposed tyranny of political processes; and secondly, from simplistic institutional attempts to afford certain but not all interests a privileged voice. The character of the socially-embedded market polity remains contested. Member States – as representatives of their national polities – retain a firm hold on the political process of market socialisation. However, the new and still-emerging private interests liberated by the process of European integration are continuing to find novel means to air their views within the market's administration. To give formal and irrevocable legal precedence to any one of these interests would be no more than an exclusionary privileging of various values above others. Where the true measure of pluralism is the attempt to give all interests/values – including those which have yet to be formed – political voice, the law must dispense with the promotion of any substantive and discourse-disrupting interests/values of its own. The novel socially-embedded internal market polity will very simply define itself. Law, on the contrary, must seek to secure a general public interest through the structuring of deliberation within this emerging, and as yet indistinct, polity.

Primary European law does offer us neutral normative yardsticks for the administration of deliberation. First, the implicit goal of market rationalisation found in the Four Freedoms and Article 30 EC. Secondly, the various provisions indicating that Europe's market must also be a social being.[83] An

---

[83] Most notably, Article 36 EC; but also the various social/ethical provisions of the SEA, TEU and Amsterdam Treaty.

emerging European administrative law would accordingly be advised to ensure that such yardsticks, and more particularly, the universal rational-ising and social/ethical values which they entail, are considered and respected in all discursive fora within the institutional framework of European market regulation. While the few national representatives and expects gathered within committees and agencies may be but a poor reflec-tion of all the actors involved within the socially-embedded internal market – and while the private individual and groups which now focus upon regulatory networks may very well promote individual rather than common concerns – the law can nonetheless ensure a measure of respect for an overall European public interest, or shared treaty aims; subjecting the discursive activities of such groups and institutions to a specific deliber-ative test. Has discussion touched, reflected upon and balanced Europe's dual governing values. Has scientific and technical expertise been consid-ered? Have social and ethical issues been raised? Has a meaningful equilib-rium been established between the two?

6 Conclusion

In a post-statal world of legally-secured international economic orders, administrative law – a derivative of the state – may yet carve itself out a meaningful niche. However, in the face of the novel international attempt to create new links between market, society and political systems, administra-tive law must first, dispense with its traditional adherence to transmission and the primacy of representative democratic processes; and secondly, needs to engage in a radical re-assessment of its endeavours to secure an alterna-tive democratic process through – either rights-based or institutionalised – interest representation. The socially-embedded market polity remains indis-tinct: a complex, emerging, contested and uncertain sphere of social, polit-ical and economic organisation. Accordingly, the normative structuring of this polity cannot but be a complex and on-going matter, while the consti-tutional markers for a stateless administrative law would consequently seem to point in a pluralist but heavily proceduralised direction.

In conclusion, however, it might likewise be argued that a body of law which is now so dependent upon politically-constitutive rather than statal norms, might itself also better be termed constitutional, or public, rather than administrative law. With its traditional efficiency-securing function seemingly largely defunct, and its major role now being one of trustee for political discourse, a putative European administrative would at heart appear to a full-blown matter of the structuring of the "governance" of the socially-embedded internal market polity. The persuasive power of such arguments notwithstanding, the analysis nonetheless finally concludes in support of a European "administrative" rather than "constitutional" or "public" law. First, since European administrative law's on-going support for the market-rationalising values underlying the process of European economic integration necessarily entails traditional considerations of efficient implementation. But secondly, and more prosaically, since the instruments which would aid in "the administration of deliberation" are not the grand provisions of constitutional design, such as individual rights, but are instead workaday legal mechanisms. First, Article 190 EC's "duty to state reasons requirement" – the essential prop upon which judicial review of the quality of deliberation might be founded. And secondly, the evolution of administrative rights of *locus standi* for watchdog/whistle-blowing bodies such as European parliamentary committees; bodies who retain a degree of impartiality within the regulatory decision-making process and who thus are best placed to trigger the judicial review of deliberation.

I would like to dedicate this contribution and my share in this book to Rudolf Wiethölter who would have deserved a whole Festschrift for his 70th birthday on 14th July 1999. The indebtedness of the present essay to Rudolf Wiethölter's work can be easily deciphered. In all of his writings on "Wirtschaftsrecht" Wiethölter has pointed to the tensions between "Law" on the one hand, "governmental" and "administrative" economic policies on the other, and searched for a tertium which would help to realize a "gute Ordnung". As early as 1972 he coined the term "politische Verwaltung" (political administration) to characterise the tasks and dilemmas of juridified problem solving in the field of antitrust (see Rudolf Wiethölter, Artikel "Wirtschaftsrecht", in A Görlitz (ed.), Handlexikon zur Rechtswissenschaft (München 1972) 531–539). And in all of his writings on "Kollisionsrecht", Wiethölter paved the way towards transformation of traditional conceptualisations in private and public international law. In submitting the concept of "good transnational governance" this essay seeks to build upon both dimensions of Wiethölter's ideas.

17

"Good Governance" Through Comitology?*

*Christian Joerges***

1. Introduction

"None other than comitology, that notorious system of inter-bureaucratic
negotiation-diplomacy that even parliamentarians wish to abolish in the
interest of democracy, is supposed to bring an element of democratically-legitimated politics into the Community?"

This reaction by Beate Kohler-Koch[1] to a publication by this author and
Jürgen Neyer[2] perfectly encapsulates the incredulity with which our
findings and their subsequent interpretation were greeted. Quite apart
from the surprise which our publication caused, our fundamental criticisms of the comitology system still hold true: it is probably the least transparent of all of the European institutions; as an institutional innovation it
operates on legally-shaky ground; it is far from clear whether it will, in the
future, continue to be capable of coping with the technically complex and
normatively very sensitive problems of the internal market – especially
since the BSE crisis has shown that the comitology form is in no way a
guarantee of the maintenance and implementation of a responsible risk
policy.[3] Nevertheless, this contribution builds on the theoretical justification for a positive assessment of comitology, as a forum for "deliberative
politics",[4] by making use of the empirical findings of a parallel research
project conducted in Bremen.[5]

---

* Translation by Iain L. Fraser, Florence.
** Professor of Law, European University Institute, Florence.
[1] Kohler-Koch (1998: 277 ff.).
[2] Joerges/Neyer (1997a); (1997b); see earlier Roethe (1994) and Joerges (1995: 45 ff.).
[3] See Chambers, in this volume.
[4] See Joerges/Neyer (1997a); (1997b).
[5] *Die Beurteilung der Sicherheit technischer Konsumgüter und der Gesundheitsrisiken
von Lebensmitteln in der Praxis des Europäischen Ausschußwesens ('Komitologie'),*
conducted in 1995-1998 at the Centre of European Law and Politics (ZERP) with Andreas
Bücker, Josef Falke, Jürgen Neyer and Sabine Schlacke. The project was financed by the
Volkswagen-Stiftung. See Joerges (ed.) (1998).

2. Deliberative Supranationalism and Risk Regulation

The theorem of deliberative supranationalism is privileged in order to offer a conceptional alternative to the well-known dichotomies between functionalism or supranationalism, on the one hand, and intergovernmentalism, on the other, which have dominated integration research in political and legal science until recent times.

2.1 The EU as a Multi-level System

The conceptualisations of the Community which have been developed by legal science have, of necessity, always contained a normative element, and for this reason alone, legal science cannot simply adopt and adapt the distinctly analytical categories of political science and transform them into legal concepts. Nevertheless, the normative concepts of legal science also claim to "meet" the reality reconstructed by political scientists, in such a way that legal concepts – whether affirmative or critical – can become operative in practice.[6] If only for this reason, legal science must take new approaches seriously even where it must work with the political science understanding of the EC as a multi-level system.[7] These shifts in perspective affect the universe of European law's discourse in several fundamental respects. This is true with regard to many analyses which reject the assumption that the integration process might substitute for the withering away of the nation state with some form of "European state formation". In the multi-level analysis this rejection of emerging European statehood determines that its proponents must work without any clear hierarchical co-ordinates. Political scientists tend to point to incentives as a substitute for co-ordination and negotiation, while lawyers emphasise the manner in which all agents are bound to co-operate by legal principles and duties. Equally important, the integration process is in these analyses not reconstructed in the light of some preconceived leitmotiv, but is seen as a contingent process in which governmental and economic agents both define their interests and seek to assert them, and in which institutional alternatives must be discovered and solutions to conflicts be found.

The debate on the strength and weaknesses of the multi-level approach is beyond the scope of this contribution. Rather it suffices to identify the three dimensions of the multi-level analysis which appear adequately to mirror three situations observable in the process of the Europeanisation of law:

---

[6] See Joerges (1996a: 109 ff.); (1996b: 88 ff.).

[7] From the now immense literature, see in particular Scharpf (1994), Marks/Hooghe/Blank (1996), Jachtenfuchs/Kohler-Koch (1996b), Benz (1998) and Neyer, in this volume, all with further references.

1) National regulatory problems are not normally completely pre-empted by European law. Thus, in the area of product regulation, European law concentrates on the question of the marketability of products, while the harmonisation of these requirements with neighbouring regulatory areas remains, in principle, a "national" task – and this is also particularly true for coping with the absorption of the distributive implications of European re-regulation.

2) Such selective European intervention, which claims "primacy" over national law even though it only results in a partial replacement of national regulations, precludes the establishment of hierarchical regulatory structures for interdependent problems within the European multi-level system. Despite the shift of regulatory activities to the Community, the latter remains dependent, specifically for the practical implementation of its regulatory programmes, on the co-operation of administrations and other actors within the Member States.

3) Taking each of these factors together means that the process of market integration continues to remain dependent upon its accompanying political management and supplementary decision-making, but does not itself dispose of any "hierarchically-constructed" basis for regulatory action. An inevitable consequence of such a lack of hierarchical direction is the formation of "networks" in which European and national actors must balance each of their individual competences and pool their resources.

2.2 The Legal Conceptualisation of Governance within the European Multi-level System

While political science's designation of the EU as a multi-level system should not in itself be understood to be a normative perspective which is binding upon legal science, the concept of "deliberative supranationalism" is, nevertheless, intended to serve as a normative yardstick. Deliberative supranationalism entails three elements:

1) It seeks a link to the legal notion of "supremacy" as designating the relationship between European and national law, but attempts to recast and re-interpret that concept.
2) Such a re-interpretation of supremacy embodies a claim of compatibility with "real" approaches to problems of market management in the Community and, in particular, as a response to difficulties arising from the dependency of European solutions upon the constant co-operation of Member States and their administrations; it seeks to link, in legally coherent fashion, the "hierarchical" elements of the Europeanisation process with its dependency on "decentralised" co-operation and the formation of network structures for problem solving.

3) Finally – and this aspect will be developed in detail below – the theorem of deliberative supranationalism strives to create a perspective upon the modes of European integration which entails the potential to legitimise the law governing that process in accordance with the normative requirements which are ever present and constitutive of law within democratic constitutional states.

(a) Delineations

At first sight, this renewed emphasis upon the conditions for the validity of law in democratic constitutional states would appear to place European law upon the horns of the very dilemma which important legal theories of integration sought to avoid: if and because the European Union is not a supranational "state", nor ought ever to become one, the demand for a basis for legitimising supranational law on the same footing as in national law proves impossible to meet, or even appears to be a secretly anti-European strategy of argument.[8]

This is true, first, in relation to the most obvious – and in the public sphere still the most "popular" – answer to the much deplored legitimation deficits of the EU, namely the demand for its parliamentarisation. However, when this demand – and this is a diagnosis on which sociologists and polit-ical scientists, constitutional lawyers and European lawyers ultimately agree[9] – is followed to its logical conclusion, it amounts to nothing more than an abandonment or, at the very least, a weakening of the integration project: "no European demos, thus no European democracy", as this debate can be briefly, albeit not comprehensively, summarised.[10]

Even in the setting of consolidated constitutional states it has long been beyond dispute that parliamentary legislation is an imperfect and even inadequate response to the need to create and legitimise risk regulation which can be only extremely imperfectly guaranteed by involving parlia-ments.[11] This is not, of course, to say that this policy area should be fully detached from the ambit of parliamentary responsibility nor, indeed, that it ought to be but, instead, that parliamentary supervision only imperfectly guarantees the accountability of regulatory processes or, put more funda-mentally and constructively, that the interweaving of normative and cogni-tive questions, particularly typical of risk issues, also act as an impetus for institutional innovation within national constitutional states.[12]

---

[8] The structuring of the considerations below follows Kohler-Koch (1998: 270 ff.)

[9] See only Lepsius (1991); Grimm (1995).

[10] See Weiler (1995a); (1998).

[11] Among many, see Denninger (1990); Ladeur (1995); Köck (1996) with further references.

[12] A full treatment of this point cannot be given in the context of a study concentrated on questions of Europeanisation, although the consistency of theoretical arguments depends on their also starting from factual problems of risk regulation, reaching into the "national" context. See Schmalz-Bruns (1995: 223 ff. and 233 ff.) and (1998); Brekke/Eriksen (1998).

(b) Practical Implications

A reliance upon a "deliberative" generation of law seems, if one focuses solely on the design of the EU's institutional structure, to set lesser requirements than a strategy of parliamentarisation. However, deliberation obviates the need to construct new non-majoritarian institutions, which are envisaged by Majone as the core of a "fourth branch of government".[13] The theory of deliberative politics avoids this dichotomy since it concentrates only in very general terms on guaranteeing rights, or the conditions for equality and fairness in societies, and seeks to avoid universally binding decisions on questions of ethics and the "good life".[14] This is not to suggest, however, that normative issues, such as those of distributive justice or the acceptability of risks, should be delegated to experts or left to voting and/or bargaining rather than deliberative political processes. If the deliberative approach seems in formal terms to set more permissive standards for the further development of the European institutional system than competing concepts, it is nonetheless far more ambitious than either of these theories in relation to the requirements for the justification of decisions taken. "Deliberative politics" is, after all, intended to describe processes in which participants are bound to call their own preferences into question and confine themselves to settling disputes by universalisable arguments.[15] In the light of the requirements placed on those involved in the political process, central importance is attached to laws that define deliberative requirements and requires compliance with them. To that extent, then, deliberative supranationalism, too, has specific institutional prerequisites. If these are not identical with the familiar systems of representative institutions, guaranteeing them is nevertheless a demanding task. Two positive legal approaches to the effective establishment of deliberative procedures should be stressed:[16] first, the indirect structuring of *national* decision-making processes by the imposition of supranational standards such as checks upon parochial interests and consideration for "foreign" concerns; second, the setting up of transnational "regimes", in which legal and institutional measures seek to replace intergovernmental bargaining and the strategic pursuit of particularist interests through the imposition of deliberative problem-solving procedures.

The Community's supranational influence on decision-making processes within the Member States must in each case take such a form as to restrict the constitutionally open political options on grounds that are themselves compatible with democratic ideas. Transnational systems must draw their legitimacy from the deliberative quality of their decision-making processes. This means, however, that they themselves must avoid being bogged down

---

[13] See, for example, Majone (1994a).
[14] See Eriksen (1998); Eriksen/Weigård (1997: 237).
[15] See Gerstenberg (1997: 34 ff.).
[16] See Joerges/Neyer (1997a).

in ethical controversies even to the degree that, where necessary, the search for uniform standards is abandoned. Last but not least, an institutionalisation of decisional venues in deliberative politics cannot come about without setting rules for their procedures and defining participatory rights or opportunities for influence in such a way as to make the "deliberative" quality of the decisions plausible.

3. Normative Perspectives and Factual Circumstances

"How will I know it is deliberation when I see it?"[17] The term "deliberation" has the epistemic status of a regulatory idea according to which the legitimacy of political decisions and legal formulations must derive from a discursive and public process. This criterion cannot be operationalised by unambiguously answering the question of the deliberative quality of observable decisional processes either negatively or affirmatively. What remains possible are descriptions of the course and outcome of agreements on factual and normative questions, which cannot be pronounced plausible if they are to be interpreted not as the outcome of communicative processes but as strategic actions directed at securing one's own interests, or as negotiations. This sort of indirect proof includes statements about factors specific to the problem, and institutional conditions that favour deliberative processes.

The empirical surveys undertaken within the ambit of the Bremen project were required to take into account the status of theoretical considerations as well as the difficulties of confirming them. As a result, they were largely exploratory in fashion, or contented themselves with the pinpointing of indicators that make it, at the very least, plausible to interpret comitology as a forum for deliberative political processes. According to our theoretical premises the quality of governance in the European multi-level system depends, on the one hand, on the "internalisation" of European obligations within Member States and, on the other, on the shaping of transnational "governance structures".

3.1 Repercussions for Domestic Policies and Policy-making Processes

As to the first aspect, we must base our analysis upon somewhat cursory indicators; the more systematic surveys upon which our interpretation is based took note only of the comitology procedures themselves.

The checks on national decisional processes and the legal procedures which serve to curtail the parochial pursuit of "national interest" are, above all, a matter of European primary law. In particular, interpretative

---

[17] Lascher (1996: 503).

approaches are suggested by the prohibitions on discrimination, the anti-protectionist guarantees of economic freedom and the freedom of trade and of contracting within the Community, as well as by the proportionality principle.[18] In this area, there is, accordingly, great need for further empirical research, which would in particular undertake surveys of judicial and administrative practices.

Europeanisation processes might be expected to impact on the approaches and strategies of economic actors in several respects.[19] European law compels the public presentation of one's own position in each individual case, and any criticism of divergent views must use arguments which are compatible with European law, not just with regard to the contents of national legal systems as such, but also with respect to the positions taken by the various interest groups concerned with each issue. All those involved in defending their interests must take account of the fact that Europeanisation processes have similarly precipitated various shifts in competence and that, as a consequence, a strategy purely oriented to "national interests" would simply be ineffective. While our empirical studies did not extend to a systematic investigation of these re-orientations, our interviews continually revealed the extraordinary extent of the power of European law and the concomitant impact of its argumentational requirements. All the actors involved, whether governmental or non-governmental, accept the rules of European law unconditionally. This acceptance applies especially to the fundamental principle that restrictions on freedom of action within the Community can be considered only if based on regulatory interests which are "legitimate" within the meaning of Community law.

This broad recognition for the dispute settlement functions of European primary law does not merely discipline domestic debate, but has its effect upon the presentation of national positions at European level, and therefore also structures the orientation of interest representation by non-governmental actors. This observation concerns not just the argumentative presentation of positions. It also points to the emergence of a European polity and of a public sphere (though admittedly mostly only for the initiated) in Member States, in which European decisional processes are prepared and commented on. One specific feature of this debate seems to be that it perceives of itself, at least as regards scientific standards, as being "homogeneous" (or as relating to a European or international "epistemic community"), but in all other respects it very much operates with due regard for all Member State perspectives, and thus presupposes divergent views or factions within the domestic public even with regard to the same arguments and disputes.

---

[18] See Joerges (1997: 302 ff.); Schlacke (1998: 51 ff.); similarly Maduro (1998: 150 ff.)
[19] From the extensive literature, see Kohler-Koch (1996).

3.2 Decisional Processes within the European Committees

Our surveys of the committee system itself place two questions in the spotlight:

- Can the analytical assumptions and empirical hypotheses concerning the emergence of transnational regulatory systems in the two subject areas studied, be upheld and made specific?
- Can the treatment of risk issues within committees be termed "deliberative"?

(a) Structures

Comitology does not represent some form of hierarchically construed administration placed under the aegis of the Commission. Rather, it can more accurately be portrayed as a network of European and national actors within which the Commission acts as co-ordinator. With its structure being formally matched with the bureaucracy of the Member States, and with its emphasis upon a unitary understanding of "science", the committee system is largely closed to non-governmental actors. Within the Standing Committee on Foodstuffs, the entire policy community can nonetheless voice its concerns, at least indirectly, whether by influencing the administration in Member States or via means of the accompanying experts within the numerous working groups of the Standing Committee on Foodstuffs. Whether these access conditions are transparent and fair, is another question. However, throughout the whole area of standardisation, the co-operation of administrative bodies with private standardisation organisations has become a matter of course in Germany and at Community level. Irrespective of the interests of national standardisation organisations in maintaining their institutional power and independence, there are clear indications of the emergence of a European (specialised) public.

(b) Deliberation

But how might we assess the quality of the decisions arrived at in those networks? The approach in our surveys (interviews/document analyses/questionnaires) and their subsequent evaluation were structured by our theoretical assumptions: we intended to explore whether the conditions under which product regulations are promulgated within the committee structure promote a communicative, co-operative mode of problem-solving. We were concerned to substantiate this hypothesis in the light of our guiding conceptions of legal and democratic theory. Accordingly, we needed to specify the features of "deliberative" processes. Here we were able to refer to studies of the deliberative quality of political processes in general, and of the institutional arrangements for risk regulation in particular, though we were, of course, similarly obliged to relate these studies to the specific conditions of comitology.

According to a much cited definition,[20] "deliberative" decisional processes can be typified as follows:

> "Participants engage in collective reasoning on the merits of public policy; the substance of the discussion involves attempting to achieve some larger public good, independent from (but not necessarily inconsistent with) what is desirable for the participants themselves. Participants make use of information in order to persuade others; at least, legislators themselves maintain open-mindedness and willingness to be convinced by others' analyses of the merits; and the legislators themselves are committed to making their final decisions on policy proposals in accordance with their judgement of the merits".

Definitions like this are inspired by a particular research context – in this case, the American legislature; "deliberation" has always been understood to be a gradual concept: the "correct" compromise between the intensity of communication on the one hand, and information and its discussion on the other, cannot be defined abstractly or universally. All this induced us to concentrate our evaluation on two main questions:

– Do those involved start from fixed positions which they then try as far as possible to push through in the committee meetings, or are they ready to take critical objections to their views seriously and be persuaded by argument?
– Do the discussants recognise standards of argument able to promote the reaching of a basic consensus, shared by all, on the "common weal"?

Further precision in evaluation was made possible by the focus on risk issues. Here, too, the objective of our evaluation was not, nor could it reasonably be, the measurement of risk regulation in practice against ambitious models of "legitimate" risk management. Instead, an attempt was made to verify whether decisional practice within comitology is both open to the various dimensions of risk issues and permits objective debate on these dimensions; in particular, whether they

– guarantee that all the available knowledge which is appropriate to the cognitive dimensions of risk assessment will be taken into account;
– take account of the plurality of the sources of knowledge and are suited to the problem of "dealing with uncertainty";
– co-ordinate expert knowledge with practical and ethical principles and permit balanced consideration of public concerns.

The most important findings can be summarised as follows:

– Both for the areas of foodstuffs and for standardisation, it can be stated

---

[20] Bessette (1994: 46 ff.); Lascher (1996: 505 ff.).

that all actors (surveyed by us) do not merely try to seek confirmation for previously formed views, but frequently enter committee discussions without clear preferences, or are prepared to change their positions. This does not mean, however, that positions and interests play no part whatsoever in committee negotiations. Nevertheless, in a significant number of cases, the main focus was upon the discussion of a problem where solutions had to be found without those participating being able to fall back upon pre-formulated positions. Moreover, all our surveys confirm that comitology operates as a long-term oriented process of working and learning, that has a potential, over time, to condemn and overcome individual attempts on the part of participants to impede reliance upon valid knowledge.

– The questions which arise and are to be solved within committees, by definition, only concern the "implementation" of secondary legislation. Nevertheless, committee discussions, and work in standardisation bodies, require additional criteria even where they formally relate to the interpretation and application of legal acts. In this regard, one proposition, in fact, provides a commonly accepted guideline: committees and standardisation bodies should pay adequate attention to the dual objective of guaranteeing free movement of goods while protecting legitimate regulatory concerns by establishing an acceptable Community-wide "high" level of protection. Seen in this light, the stated objective sets a standard of the "common weal" that all actors, both Commission and Member States, recognise, and to which they may appeal in their arguments.

– An important function in making this standard specific is performed by the involvement of the Scientific Committee on Food, or the expert knowledge available within the standardisation organisations. The fact that in the area of the assessment of foodstuff risks and in the area of standardisation under study here, the specialist debate is conducted at a high level and the European protective standards can accordingly be termed "high", is confirmed by expert interviews with national authorities and with non-governmental organisations.

– The complex structure of comitology, or alternatively of standardisation, as the case may be, takes account of the complexity of risk issues. The invocation of expert bodies can be interpreted as a reference to such standards which may be approved by all concerned. It exhibits a willingness to tackle and decide upon the scientific and technical dimensions of risk regulation without reference to particularist economic interests.

Is comitology, then, a locus of deliberative proceedings? Measuring the findings of our studies against their guiding normative concepts, a series of shortcomings or, at least, uncertainties nonetheless became apparent: failings which must be balanced against the more positive preceding assessment.

- The degree and form of co-ordination between the "cognitive" and the practical, administrative side of risk regulation remains opaque. Certainly, consideration for public anxieties, practical administrative considerations and constraints, and scientific and technical insights cannot simply be aggregated, but can only be collected sequentially. In the period of time covered by our surveys – that is, at least up to the re-organisation of the scientific committees involved with risk assessments and the setting up of the new Scientific Steering Committee on 10 June 1997[21] following the BSE crisis[22] – there was seemingly no clear guarantee that the knowledge available to the competent committees was actually used and that new findings would be responded to. The latent scepticism has not just been nourished by the BSE crisis, but also derives from the much less conspicuous fact that the Commission (and its Legal Service) took the view that it was within their discretion as to whether to consult the Scientific Committee on Food or not.
- However much it might fit the argument of this study that European risk regulation is, in practice, not based exclusively on "non-majoritarian institutions", it is nonetheless questionable whether comitology gives proper expression to the plurality of practical and ethical views which should be included within risk assessment procedures. Certainly, the comitology system cannot be called a closed or homogeneous epistemic and administrative complex.[23] Its openness to the concerns of those involved is, however, limited and haphazard, if not selective.
- Among the most vital of the constitutive rules of committee work is a stigmatisation of particularist, protectionist interests. While this commitment clearly does not rule out the inclusion of economic considerations among the factors to be considered in decisions on the acceptable levels of risk, it nevertheless seems to have had ambivalent implications. All indicators seem to show that all the explicit and transparent cost/benefit considerations which could be exposed to public scrutiny and debate, are rarely heeded. The setting of standards is, in large measure, determined by the representatives of the economically dominant Member States. Evidently, the representatives of smaller Member States are not always in a position to take part in the debate on the appropriateness of a standard. The relationship between the Member States can here be seen as a difficulty which acts as a barrier to the meaningful participation of representatives of social interests in the elaboration of regulatory policies and technical standards – though it should nevertheless be noted immediately that the representatives of all Member States claim undisputed, albeit not equal, rights of political co-determination, whereas the recognition of such rights for non-governmental organisations remains to be clarified.

[21] (1997) OJ L 169/85.
[22] See Schlacke (1998: 331 ff.); also Rack/Gasser (1998), Chambers, in this volume.
[23] But see Bach (1992); (1993b).

4. The Constitutionalisation of Risk Regulation in the Internal Market

Our empirical findings support the thesis that risk regulation, as practised in the comitology context, is in important respects in line with the idea of deliberative politics. The following sections will be concerned with working out more precisely the legal framework conditions to which this potential for promoting deliberative solutions to problems can be ascribed, or to proposing corresponding interpretations, or encouraging innovations. The first step will again deal with the conceptualisation of the conduct required in risk regulation (section 4.1). This is connected with the separation of "regulatory" from "distributive" policies and the widely shared view that the management of the internal market has to neglect industrial policy considerations and distributive objectives or implications (section 4.2). If it is in line with the general normative guiding conceptions of deliberative supranationalism that internal market policy ought not to be administered hierarchically, then, for that very reason, the powers and obligations of the institutional actors involved must be clarified – and debates in this connection are the most important theme in comitology law (section 4.3). By contrast, it is far more important to cope with the various dimensions of risk regulation – consideration for public concerns, integration of expert scientific and technical knowledge, and practical administrative considerations – in a sensible decision-making sequence, to structure co-operation between governmental and non-governmental actors, and to clarify the participatory possibilities of those concerned and their ways of protecting their own rights (section 4.4).

4.1 Towards Good Governance: The "Political Administration" of the Internal Market

Our consideration of risk regulation in the internal market rests upon the premise that this is an ongoing task of "constitutional" importance. Supposedly, committees are engaged with the mere "implementation" of secondary legislation, a task which is far too vast for the Community legislature and which in principle does not deserve such distinguished attention. Nonetheless, the simplistic dichotomy made between legislation issued from a "high level" and dealing with essential questions, and the delegated implementation of legislative instruction does not do justice to the "output" that internal market policy is called upon to deliver. On the one hand, politically sensitive questions continue to arise in the context of implementing activities and even below the attention threshold of the legislature, thus making the term "political" administration an entirely appropriate characterisation; on the other hand, the "implementation" of

Community law requires very much more than the production of rules. Instead, it comprises the solution of technically complex problems, involving, for instance, the integration of expert knowledge with practical application. Thus, while these dimensions of action determine that the execution of a previously given legal programme can be covered by the term "administration", the "implementation" of Community legislation through the committees nonetheless contains an "intergovernmental" component, since it concerns the governments represented on the committees, as well as an "infranational" element, involving governments communicating with a slowly "Europeanising" society. A description of such tasks as "political" is accordingly appropriate where these are associated with Aristotelian connotations of good practice.

Are such considerations overscrupulous? Is national administrative law not also often faced with creative tasks – especially in the domain of "risk administration law" (*Risikoverwaltungsrecht*)?[24] Not only at Community level, but also within the nation state, regulatory objectives are often pursued through the structuring of decisional processes rather than the laying down of their content. To that extent, one could arguably dispense with new terminology. However, the specific intergovernmental and intersocietal co-ordination which comitology secures alongside its politically and legally creative achievements, has no national model. Thus, though the delegation of co-ordinating functions to committees seems regularly to present as few problems as the delegation of implementation activities to the Commission, such function nonetheless may touch upon areas and issues which are irrevocably bound up with important national interests. In other words, that which remains unparalleled is the "conveyance" of law-making powers in a non-hierarchically structured system which, for sound normative reasons, will never transform itself into a unitary polity, and whose structures ought to remain pluralistic. Upon what legitimising power can this form of regulatory achievement be based if not upon a law that calls for and promotes "deliberative" political processes?

Accordingly, the law of comitology must be structured thoroughly. In particular, it must be rooted "constitutionally": above all, committee tasks must be clearly delineated and their solutions to problems legitimated. Comitology must be open to a fine-tuning of its decisional procedures: participation rights must be clarified and demands for judicial protection be met. Methodologically speaking, our perception of comitology as a genuinely European, intergovernmental political administration, determines that, at best, we conceive of the process of the juridification of comitology as a telos of law formation that is evolving through the continuous process of coping with the problems arising from the implementation of EC legislation, which likewise does not seek to copy national models.

---

[24] See Di Fabio (1994a: 445 ff.).

Accordingly, in searching for a legitimate (legitimising) "constitution" for comitology, the vital issue is the creation of a link with existing European primary and secondary law, as well as its judicial interpretation and academic analysis. This form of reconstructive interpretative procedure cannot, of course, give birth to a comprehensive system; however, various elements of a legal constitution of comitology, capable of extension, can be indicated. Admittedly, it is only recently that the law has had to grapple with such practical questions, notwithstanding the fact that these problems had already been identified as being of an urgent nature. One very basic conceptual question, namely the focusing of the internal market policy on market building and questions of risk regulation within comitology has never explicitly been brought up for debate, while much energy has been wasted on weighty institutional controversies which have had very little impact on the performance of committees.

4.2 "Unburdening" Product Regulation from Distributive Questions

Whether and to what extent product regulation in comitology concentrates on technical and scientific questions – even if they also have a normative content – and whether it deliberately neglects the distributive consequences of regulatory decisions is primarily an empirical question. However, a normative problem is also involved: can the compartmentalisation of risk regulation which is isolated from distributive implications be normatively justified, and should it, therefore, be legally and institutionally underpinned? Before taking a position on this question, it is essential to define these "economic" consequences, from which European law commands us to abstract more precisely. Decisions on the safety level of products cause (1) administrative costs (the standards must be developed and implemented); then (2) costs to manufacturers, retailers and consumers; and may finally (3) have implications on industrial or economic policy for a Member State or individual sectors of its economy.

There is no provision to compensate Member States for the extra administrative costs arising from amended and more ambitious regulations in the area of product regulation.[25] Such compensation would hardly be justifiable where such costs stem from "governance" executed jointly by all Member States.[26] With regard to the relationship between manufacturers, traders

[25] If Article 130s (5), second indent EC allows for other options, it should be borne in mind that these apply only to environment protection, but especially that, to date, only the first alternative (allowing transitional periods) has been made use of.

[26] Even if it is true that the regulations laid down in 'Brussels' are 'cheap' because the costs arise in the Member States, this aspect concerns only the decision-making levels. In any case, it should be expected that Member State co-operation in comitology should bring considerable advantages of scale, so that the weaker Member States in particular should be able to feel in a sense 'free riders' in regulatory progress.

and consumers it is just as true as with any national regulations that stricter standards bring so-called consumer rents (to the extent that they prevent well-off, risk-averse consumers from buying the safety level they desire), and that in other respects they restrict the breadth of the product range.[27] Distributive effects of this kind are undoubtedly different from one Member State to another. To neglect these differences means treating European market citizens equally, that is, creating equal minimum protection for them (though this can be exceeded, under the conditions of Article 100a (4) EC, by nations "going it alone"). The mere fact that consumers are protected by a standard that would not have come into being in their own jurisdictions can hardly be presented as a detrimental distributive consequence – what is impacted upon in this connection is the regulatory autonomy of Member States or, to de-nationalise this expression, the constitutional legitimacy of their decisions and the status of their citizens as bearers of political rights ("national citizens"), not as consumers ("market citizens"). These economic consequences which Member State representatives defend as "national" interests typically involve regionally and/or sectorally specific effects.

Articles 30 and 36 EC, in their interpretation by the ECJ,[28] seek to make the anti-protectionist objectives of Article 30 EC, which are directed at promoting integration, compatible with the regulatory powers of Member States: Member States that wish to prevent imports and declare foreign product regulations sufficiently safe, must present generally acceptable "objective" grounds for this; equally, the restrictions placed on individual national regulations by Article 100a (4) EC and the safeguard-clause procedure of European secondary law are to be seen as means to verify regulatory concerns on the basis of mutually recognised criteria. The rejection of regional and sectoral economic arguments thus has a normative basis that simultaneously structures debate on the appropriateness of regulatory standards. It is accordingly defensible that, in principle, only such cost/benefit considerations which are not nationally discriminatory may be taken into account in European risk assessments and that the advantages and drawbacks of a product regulation for a particular economy be treated as legally irrelevant, while transfer payments compensating for the economic disadvantages to a Member State are not provided for. These basic rules are not unfair nor does compliance with them in the committee procedure seem altogether impossible where due attention is paid to the fact that the implementation of Community law is suited to the normal case of implementing uncontroversial framework regulations, and also that transfer payments outside market management in the comitology context are by no means "forbidden", but that, on the contrary, constitutional importance attaches to the precept of promoting the Community's economic and social cohesion. Nor, however, is the validity of those

[27] See Joerges (1986).
[28] On what follows, see Joerges/Neyer (1997a: 296 ff.).

ground rules called into question if it becomes apparent that the economic consequences of measures to reduce risks in the Community interest are concentrated on one Member State, as this state is thus receiving compensation. Taking the example of BSE, Community compensation to the British industries involved can be interpreted as an assumption of insurance functions whereby the appearance of a plague is recognised as a misfortune. The way Britain has promoted this benevolent interpretation[29] is another matter altogether.

4.3 The Accountability of the Internal Market's "Political Administration"

The dispute, ranging over several decades, between the Parliament, Council and Commission has been exhaustively documented and interpreted in this volume.[30] Two issues ought, however, to be addressed because they can be used to clarify in exemplary fashion which consequences arise from the analytical and normative perspectives advocated here. The first is the proper role of the Parliament in the social regulation of the internal market, usually discussed under the heading of "institutional balance"; the second is the anti-delegation doctrine which seeks to assign the responsibility for regulating the internal market exclusively to the institutional actors created by the Treaty. In both areas, the institutional structure of the Treaties is quite obviously not suited to the ongoing task of politically sensitive risk management – certainly not to the fact that this task cannot be handled "centrally" within hierarchical structures, but calls for long-term co-operation between the Commission and the national administrations (and among the latter); and moreover, that this form of "political administration" must make use of the knowledge and the management capacities of firms and non-governmental organisations.

(a) The Proper Role of the Parliament: Monitoring versus Command

In the view developed here, the "political administration" of the internal market is a project with which the Member States "must" collaborate if they are to realise it – in the twofold factual and normative sense of this word: not just because the Community de facto remains dependent on Member States' administrative resources, but also because the so-called implementation of Community law is to be seen as a continuing legal and political process involving not just "correct administration" but "good governance" in an emerging polity.

---

[29] See the references to European Parliament Report PE 220.544 in Rock/Gasser (1998: 422-423); also instructive is the ECJ's very refined discussion in Case C 180/96, UK v Commission [1998] ECR I-431, on Britain's complaint against Commission Decision 96/239/EC, (1996) OJ L78/47.

[30] See Section 2 and also the contribution by Vos, in this volume.

It follows inevitably from the Community's resort to framework regulations which require intensive further elaboration and which, in any case, particularly in the area of risk regulation, must be open to constant revision, that Member States must remain actively present in the "administration" of the internal market, not merely in an advisory capacity but also as political actors.[31] This is not just some policy postulate, but a legal principle of constitutional importance, taking account of the perception that the handling of tasks of Europe-wide market management cannot be exhaustively defined *ex ante* and their implementation then delegated; it is foreseeable that unforeseen problem situations and new interdependencies will arise and will require a re-definition and re-structuring of competences. In the area of risk regulation, Member States' participatory rights find their positive constitutional support in Articles 30 and 36 EC, as well as in Article 100a (5) EC, since the transition to majority decisions.[32] The 1987 Comitology Decision[33] accordingly has a function of supplementing these provisions. Furthermore, it is entirely consistent to regard the Decision's non-specification of the modalities of committee decision-making and its failure to establish a clear connection between committee tasks and such modalities as an issue of constitutional importance.[34] These participatory entitlements of Member States are thus founded not only upon any residual "administrative competence",[35] but on their legislative joint responsibility. This recognition in primary law of Member States as representatives of legislative regulatory concerns is, moreover, supported by a procedural conception of the subsidiarity principle.[36]

However convincing the Parliament's argument that the strengthening of its rights in legislation must also be mirrored by its augmented role in the implementation of Community law may be in principle, it is questionable whether the Parliament, with its attempts to secure direct involvement in the committee procedure, has chosen a strategy which is sensible in the long run. All the experience to date suggests that new participatory rights will yield little since parliamentary committees do not have sufficient resources to engage in the continuous supervision of the Commission's committees.[37] Here, it is sufficient to point to the Commission's response to the Parliament's demand to produce a complete list of the committees

---

[31] See earlier Joerges *et al* (1988: 385 ff., 460 ff.)

[32] For more detailed justification see Vos (1997b: 223 ff.); (1999: 96 ff.).

[33] (1987) OJ L 197/33.

[34] Only in the literature, alas: see Bradley (1997) and also (1989).

[35] See the rejection of Germany's argument by the ECJ in Case C-359/92, *Germany* v *Council (General Product Safety Directive)* [1994] ECR I-3676.

[36] On this aspect see also Vos (1997b: 224 ff.), with further references, and earlier Joerges (1991a: 433 ff.); it is noteworthy that Parliament, too, opts for the regulatory committee procedure in cases where it promises "appropriate" results (see Bradley 1997: 252, with references).

[37] See also Bradley (1997: 237 ff.).

and their decisions.[38] The EP received a two-volume, 2,000 page documentation listing the decisions required – without being able to communicate their substantive contents from this all too brief list. This demonstration cannot simply be dismissed as obstruction on the part of the Commission but ought, instead, to be taken as an indicator of the vast amount of complex work which the committees are required to undertake. The circumstances that led to the transfer of internal market administration to committees cannot be altered. Accordingly, the Parliament should revise its monitoring strategy. A constructive response would concentrate on requiring the actors in implementation policy to define and abide by procedural standards – that is, guarantee the deliberative quality of their decision-making processes – and/or ensure feedback between delegated and conventional law-making.

In addition to its legislative participatory rights under Article 138c EC, the European Parliament

> "may (...) set up a temporary Committee of Inquiry to investigate (...) alleged contraventions or maladministration in the implementation of Community law (...)."

It has recently made use of this right with regard to the BSE crisis.[39] The substantive quality and impact of this initiative derives from the fact that it has made it possible for the Parliament to respond to structural problems of implementing legislation, to the diffusion of political responsibility and the dual administrative/governmental nature of the political administration of the internal market and to the role of expert knowledge and the complexity of decisional processes. Accordingly, it seems appropriate to build upon this positive experience, and to use it as a basis for an institutional innovation: making its supervisory function permanent along the lines of American congressional committees, which regularly engage in the *ex post* monitoring of independent agencies. In so doing, the Parliament could extend its activities beyond the investigation of specific cases, becoming instead a forum for the assessment of successes and failures, and for institutional and organisational questions of risk regulation within the internal market.[40] The creation of the Non-permanent Committee for Further Consideration of Recommendations on BSE[41] would appear to be a step in this direction.

---

[38] (1995) OJ C 18/145, 148.

[39] See the references in Joerges (1993) and (1997: 322 ff.); as well as Beckedorf (1997); Rack/Gasser (1998) and Chambers, in this volume.

[40] See the suggestions in Joerges (1993) as well as (1997: 322 ff.); for a practical example close to this perspective see the "Joint Conference on Foodstuffs Law and Foodstuffs Politics", Brussels 1997, organised at the initiative of the EP Committee for Environment, Health and Consumer Protection together with the European Commission.

[41] B4-0350/97; see the references in Rack/Gasser (1998: 421, 424).

(b) From Prohibiting of "Delegation" to the Structuring of Problem-solving

Disputes on the Commission's possession of implementing powers and the co-decisional powers of the committees which support it, directly concern only the internal relationship between European institutional actors. However, institutional innovations inspired by the deepening of internal market policy are not themselves confined to this realm alone. The completion of the internal market necessitated both a deepened and lasting form of co-operation between the Commission and Member State administrations, and the utilisation of the knowledge and management potential of non-governmental organisations and private firms. Moreover, while the implementation and/or defence of Member States' co-decisional powers was ensured, and is being ensured by means of transparent legal debate, an explicit recognition of regulatory strategies establishing co-operation with non-governmental actors, has proven to be a far thornier legal issue. The continuing validity of the *Meroni* doctrine is unfortunately beyond dispute. By virtue of this doctrine, the *(de facto)* "transfer" of law-making powers, clearly widely present with Community law practice, was habitually concealed with the aid of a classical legal camouflage technique: the scrupulous observance of formal legal assignments of responsibility with a simultaneous transfer of tasks to "non-treaty entities" no longer directly controllable by those formerly competent.[42] If nonetheless the legality of those *de facto* transfers is only rarely questioned in the case law and the literature, this apparently reflects the general view that all attempts to monopolise the production of law by the legislature would be doomed to failure.[43] Scientific co-operation among Member States[44] is just as indispensable for the proper "implementation" in the area of foodstuffs law as is that of non-governmental standardisation organisations with regard to the developing of technical standards. Describing these factual situations as a "transfer" is a legal fiction. What is at stake is the emergence of co-operative arrangements which respond to the fact that the bodies legally competent for law production cannot factually cope with their tasks and thus meet their responsibility only formally. Clearly, the particular response to this fact will depend on the issues concerned, and their regulatory context. The health protection to be guaranteed by foodstuffs law has traditionally been perceived as a governmental and administrative task, while product standardisation is primarily seen as a matter of practical engineering experience. In the case of the shift of the European legal harmonisation policy to the "New Approach" in the 1980s, this traditional

---

[42] This is particularly true of the programming function of the 'essential safety objectives' provided for in the model directive in the "New Approach", and the Commission's decision-making powers in pharmaceuticals licensing; see Vos (1999: 222 ff., 281 ff.).

[43] In general, see Black (1996).

[44] Directive 93/5/EEC, (1993) OJ L 52/18.

dichotomy led to differing patterns in foodstuffs law and in technical safety.[45] The forms of the transfer differ in both areas, and the legal criteria which they have to observe are not simply identical.

(c) The Examples of Foodstuffs Regulation and Machine Safety

This background may explain why the transfer issue has to date rarely been discussed in foodstuffs law; the guaranteeing of foodstuffs safety which all Member States regard as a genuinely public task, formally retained this status under the New Approach, while the more subtle forms of "delegation" of regulatory tasks, through the inclusion of non-governmental organisations and the relocating of control tasks into the production process,[46] are apparently not felt to be similarly troublesome. Accordingly, with regard to foodstuffs, the only legal issue attracting attention remained that of institutional balance, including the Member States' involvement in the committee system.[47]

In the field of standardisation, by contrast, the role of non-governmental organisations and firms in developing standards and in establishing an appropriate safety level has long been noticed; it has been taken to be indispensable and by the same token, deemed to be a commonplace that this collaboration must be legally structured.

At the European level, or at least since the adoption of the "New Approach", the discrepancy between the real-life functions of the standardisation organisations in "making concrete" the legislatively only vaguely defined "essential safety requirements", and the Commission's formal responsibility for ensuring the appropriateness of European standards, has become so drastic that doubts as to the legality of the technique of reference to standards in European law have repeatedly been raised with considerable emphasis.[48] Nonetheless, such objections do not seem to be constructive where they demand that the legally responsible legislative or administrative bodies perform tasks they simply cannot accomplish. Clearly, demands for legal rectification through a detailed Commission review of the contents of standards elaborated by the standardisation organisations,[49] simply ignore the practical reasons for the inclusion of non-governmental organisations in the administration of the internal market. To acknowledge these factual constraints, however, is not to give complete leeway to the Community in organising this co-operation. The ECJ case law already mentioned, which tackles the legal structuring of

---

[45] On technical standards see Bücker (1997: 208 ff.) and on foodstuffs law Schlacke (1998).

[46] See references in Joerges (1994b: 156 ff.); Vos (1999: 184 ff.).

[47] See in particular Case 25/70, *Einfuhr- und Vorratsstelle v Köster* [1970] ECR 1161; Case 5/77, *Tedeschi v Denkavit* [1977] ECR 1555.

[48] See the retrospective in Bücker (1997: 211 ff.).

[49] See for this quest Breulmann (1993: 206, 265 ff.).

such problems, at first glance concerns an apparently remote thematic area: the indirect control of regulatory policy in Member States in the light of the criteria of Articles 5 and 85 EC.[50] We have argued elsewhere that this jurisprudence is nonetheless instructive.[51] The criteria developed by the ECJ in connection with the so-called anti-trust ban on the transfer of powers seem of general significance. They deal with the patterning of the relations between the publicly accountable bodies, on the one hand, and non-governmental self-regulatory bodies, on the other; in addition, and most importantly, they establish legal criteria governing the internal organisational structure of co-operative bodies:

- Organisations entrusted with the performance of regulatory functions must be obliged by legal provisions to uphold interests of the common weal;
- interests relevant in a given sector must be represented in the decision-making processes of those organisations;
- the decision-making bodies must be staffed with experts who remain independent from the economic organisations that support them;
- government offices should be in a position to be involved in the appointment of these experts, to take part in decision-making and, if necessary, to review the outcome of a decision.

It must be kept in mind that this regulatory pattern is derived from the relationship between European competition law and national economic law (forms of economic regulation). The legal criteria which the ECJ developed without further modification cannot be transferred to the area of standardisation; they are neither sufficiently comprehensive to cover all the dimensions of standard setting nor are the regulatory concerns to be respected simply identical.

If the criteria of the path-breaking *Reiff* Decision[52] on the involvement of government bodies in standardisation and their powers of intervention are taken into account, then it should be noted that the control of Member States' economic regulation in competition law relates mainly to corporatist distortions, while in standardisation replacing the co-operative production of standards by government bodies does not come into question – genuine safety interests are guaranteed outside standardisation law on the basis of the Directive[53] on general product safety.[54] Accordingly,

---

[50] Case C-185/91, ECR [1993] I-5801, and since in particular the judgment in Case C-96/94, *Centro Servizi Spediporto* [1995] ECR I-2883.

[51] See in detail Falke/Joerges (1995: 147 ff.); see more recently Bøegh (1998: 275 ff.); Joerges/Schepel/Vos (1998).

[52] Case C-185/91, *Bundesanstalt für den Güterfernverkehr v Gebrüder Reiff* [1993] ECR I-5801.

[53] Directive 92/59/EEC, (1992) OJ L 228/24.

[54] See earlier Joerges/Falke (1991: 176 ff.).

with regard to standardisation, the issue is not the application of general Community safeguards to administrative powers of decision; rather it is much more one of ensuring, through the design of standardisation procedures and the involvement of government bodies or the Commission, that safety and environmental concerns are brought to bear within the standardisation work itself.

This type of *caveat* applies with regard to other principles as well. Thus, the duty to take scientific and technical expertise into account which the ECJ has developed in the field of cosmetic products,[55] can apply only to the *safety dimensions of standards*.

4.4 *Rules and Principles for Europe's "Political Administration"*

Taken together, all these considerations and findings present only a very initial indicator for the legal design of comitology practice. Nevertheless, it seems possible to concretise these beginnings further in a few important respects.

(a) Deliberative Politics and Scientific Expertise

It is beyond dispute that the process of risk regulation must incorporate scientific and technical knowledge. This may be only a truism, but its implications are not. In spelling them out three sets of issues should be distinguished: *When* must the political administration of the internal market take expert advice into account; *how* is that advice to be structured; *what binding effect* is to be attached to it in the decision-making process?

In its attempt to solve the first problem, the ECJ has made recourse to an evident and simple formula: even if secondary Community law does not state this explicitly, a (regulatory administrative) committee, entrusted with the task of adapting directives to technical progress needs to ensure expert advice. The committee:

> "must, in the nature of things and apart from any provision laid down to that effect, be assisted by experts on scientific and technical issues delegated by the Member States. The Scientific Committee, however, has the task of assisting the Community authorities on scientific and technical issues in order to enable them to determine, from a fully informed position, which adaptation measures are necessary".[56]

In this manner, the use of expert advice seems to be transformed into a legal duty; and non-compliance with this duty becomes a *per se* incorrect

---

[55] Case C-212/91, *Angelopharm v Freie und Hansestadt Hamburg* [1994] ECR I-171, at I-211 (para 33).

[56] Ibid, at I-211 (paras 33-34).

exercise of discretion in decision-making. Wishful thinking?[57] It is certainly true that *Angelopharm* related specifically to an already established scientific committee and hence to a context where recourse to scientific advice was statutorily demanded so that the positive impact of the *dictum* just cited might not be as far-reaching as is here suggested. But how would the ECJ rule, were the Community legislature to take it upon itself to license pharmaceuticals without prior expert verification? The absolute indispensability of expert advice in risk decisions is indeed "in the nature of things". That a generalising interpretation of the *Angelopharm* judgment is admissible and required follows also from the fact that the ECJ, in viewing Member States provisions pursuant to Articles 30-36 EC and individual national measures pursuant to Article 100a (4) EC,[58] imposes an obligation on all actors to justify their positions "objectively", taking scientific and technical findings into account – if necessary with reference to the uncertainty of the state of scientific knowledge.[59] And just as the Community uses recourse to scientific knowledge to subject Member States' regulatory policies to the umbrella criteria of rationality, so it now sees itself exposed to similar requirements.[60] Quite irrespective of what the ECJ may still have thought in 1993, today it could no longer oppose an extensive interpretation of its statements today.

It goes without saying that recourse to the quality of scientific and technical advice must have institutional consequences: advice which is within decision-making can be given only by bodies with established competence and who are independent when forming their opinion. Very early on, the ECJ stated the obvious with regard to a blatantly unlawful Commission practice. (Easy cases, too, can make good law:)

> "However, where the Community institutions have such a power of appraisal, respect for the rights guaranteed by the Community legal order in administrative procedures is of even more fundamental importance. Those guarantees include, in particular, the duty of the competent institution to examine carefully and impartially all the relevant aspects of the individual case, the right of the person concerned to make his views known and to have an adequately reasoned decision. Only in this way can the Court verify whether the factual and legal elements upon which the exercise of the power of appraisal depends were present".[61]

---

[57] See the sceptical remarks by Bradley, in this volume.

[58] Case C-41/93, *France* v *Commission (PCP)* [1994] ECR I-1829.

[59] On all this see, in more detail, Joerges (1997), and from the recent case-law see, in particular, Case C-105/94, *Celestini* v *Faber* [1997] ECR I-2971.

[60] See the WTO decision of 16 January 1998 in the hormone dispute with the US, reproduced in extracts in (1998) *Europäische Zeitschrift für Wirtschaftsrecht*, 157-164, and commented on by Eggers (1998), Godt (1998).

[61] Case C-269/90, *Hauptzollamt München Mitte* v *Technische Universität München* [1991] ECR I-5469, at I-5499 (para 14).

Such requirements for the consultation of expert bodies have not yet been explicitly extended to the area of standardisation. It seems to follow nevertheless that such criteria can and should be applied to technical or other products where their risk potential, and its complexity, so requires. These suggestions need, of course, to be specified further with due regard to the connections between standardisation and the economy and the specific design of standardisation work; these require other measures to guarantee plurality of opinion and discourse as between interest bearers, science and officially appointed experts than is the case in the area of foodstuffs regulation.

(b) Deliberation and Interest Group Participation

In the area of risk regulation (and its legal corollaries in *Riskoverwaltungs-recht*), the opening up of decision-making procedures to representatives of social interests is an obvious response to the perception that there are dimensions to the problem of risk assessment which, in view of their practical normative content, ought not to be delegated to expert bodies, no matter how technically competent they may be, but nonetheless cannot be decided *ex ante* by the legislature. It is certainly consistent with the argument so far pursued, to seek the guarantee for the rationality of European decision-making processes not in the inclusion of ever more "interests" but in the further development of principles and rules concerning their "deliberative" nature, or alternatively, the quality of decision-making processes.

The generally valid pragmatic reasons for this approach, which are partic-ularly strong at European level, are obvious: simply because of their cogni-tive content, the correctness of risk decisions cannot be guaranteed by unmediated recourse to interests or their negotiation – or in legal terms, by extending corresponding participation rights and veto positions; and at European level in particular, the identification of representatives of European "interests" is inconceivable. To restate this more constructively, by virtue of its feedback links to Member States, comitology can, in principle, take all social concerns and interests into account while, at the same time, links with science (seen as a social body) can be shaped so as to allow for the plurality of scientific knowledge to be brought to bear. In justifying these approaches theoretically, we repeat: the characteristic feature of the condi-tions for decision at European level lies in the plurality of approaches by the political decision-makers and the experts involved; the chance of estab-lishing a deliberative solution to problems follows from the "constraint" to overcome the divergent opposing practical application of objectives that are, in principle, shared through argument – the legal institutionalisation of a framework that specifically favours this level of decision-making will, *rebus sic stantibus*, be required to pay greater attention to establishing criteria of disciplined argument than to extending the range of those involved.

The situation appears relatively simple in relation to the tasks of scientific committees. Here, the standards of scientifically well-founded assessment already ensure that the validity of the positions adopted by the scientific committee is exposed to a transnational epistemic community and assessed thereby; pluralism of the institutions co-operating in the scientific co-operation[62] seems an adequate guarantee of the representation of all relevant positions.

In technical standardisation, by contrast, extension of participatory rights to a competent public, in particular European associations, should be insisted upon. This postulate is a response not so much to the circumstance that the practical engineering experience on which standardisation is traditionally relied is held to be more strongly marked by culture than scientific knowledge is; this difference will no doubt tend to diminish as the technical complexity of modern standardisation projects increases.[63] What seems even more important is that the European standardisation organisations defend their national internal structure; in as much as they thus continue to represent "national" positions, no genuine interest articulation can be developed at European level.[64]

The most difficult question to answer is that regarding participation in the standing committees. Here, the point is to formalise the, to date somewhat organically established, procedure for including experts, so as to promote the articulation of interests at European level. This could be attained by the Commission's setting up a clearing house made up of members of the standing committee and the Parliament's (specialised) committee, which would review demands for participation, verifying their justification and thus develop standards for guaranteeing consultation rights.

(c) Transparency

In addition to the demand for new participation rights, the quest for greater transparency is an obvious response to the problems of delegated law-making. Such suggestions conform to our theoretical perspectives only where it seems safe to assume that their implementation would promote the "deliberative quality" of problem-solving within committee procedures.

It should be borne in mind that it is not just intergovernmental bargaining but also decision-finding of the judicial branch that takes place behind closed doors; it is widely held that this kind of "non-transparency" protects the consultative freedom within the bodies concerned. Nonetheless, administrative and regulatory committees cannot simply be classified as being commensurate with either of these institutions. Accordingly, confidentiality of the proceedings within the constitutionally bound "political administration"

---

[62] Directive 93/5/EEC, (1993) OJ L 52/18. [63] See Bücker (1997: 44 ff., 52 ff., 70 ff.).
[64] See Falke/Joerges (1995: 156).

should not be refuted *a priori*. On the other hand, it should also be borne in mind that this political administration has far-reaching discretionary room for manoeuvre in decisions. Those subject to and affected by it must accordingly know, at the very least, what questions are being discussed and the reasons for the decisions. Bases in positive law[65] for this postulate follow from Parliament's rights of co-decision, but also from the Community's own commitments.[66] The Scientific Committee on Food (SCF) meets these requirements by publishing its opinions and thus exposing them to public debate that can no longer be restricted. Additionally, the SCF is now also using the Internet to disseminate its findings – the potential of this form of publication in terms of participatory democracy cannot be overestimated.[67]

To date, such requirements are by no means realised. The agenda of the Standing Committee on Foodstuffs about which interested actors need to be informed, can be found only through privileged contact, while privileged contact again tends to determine what will be discussed. Given the diffuse contours of the European public on the one hand, and the nature and extent of the objects of discussion on the other, this official publication is in itself fairly pointless. Nevertheless, here too, the Internet has a great potential. Through this medium, a vast public can be reached and involved. The Commission, at least, has begun to exploit this possibility extensively and competently.[68]

Similarly, the transparency of European standardisation, could and should be considerably enhanced. The production of standardisation programmes by the European standardisation organisations and the issuing of standardisation mandates by the Commission are just as easy to publicise as the opening of public hearings on the basis of draft standards. At present, it is laborious and costly even for firms, individuals or associations not informed of relevant proposals through involvement in national committees, to attain information on the progress in European standardisation work. The fact that the standardisation organisations fund themselves from selling the produce of their labour is not a sufficient argument against the transparency of such delegated law-making.[69]

(d) The Duty to Give Reasons and Individual Rights

In the case of American Independent Regulatory Commissions, rights of complaint for those involved, based on legal requirements to justify

---

[65] For what follows see Schlacke (1998: 327 ff., 337); Dreher (1996); Pernice (1993: 483 ff.).

[66] See in particular the Council Resolution on public access to Council documents, (1993) OJ L 340/43.

[67] See the suggestions in Weiler *et al* (1996).

[68] See the references in Rack/Gasser (1998: 424 ff.) and http://europa.eu/inten/comm /dg24/health/sc/ index.en.html.

[69] On all this, see, in more detail, Falke/Joerges (1995: 161 ff.).

decisions and procedural requirements regarding decision-making, play a prominent role.[70] Even if the repercussions of this form of judicial review for the regulatory practice of the American agencies have, in part, been very critically assessed,[71] the idea of subjecting the "political administration" in the internal market to a European "Administrative Procedures Act"[72] is worth considering. In the conceptual terms adopted here, this would mean directly juridifying the EU's transnational "governance structures" and equipping non-governmental actors within the European polity with appropriate rights.

In comparison with the established system for protecting rights in European law, focused on the European organs and the Member States and referring private actors to a detour through their national systems, this would be a far-reaching innovation. Currently, however, some tentative steps foreshadowing further developments, can already be observed.

The case-law on Article 190 EC deals with the duty to give reasons requirement contained in this provision differentially. Whereas the Council is treated simply like a national legislature and has hence been granted very broad room for discretion,[73] much stricter requirements are placed on the Commission. In *Technische Universität München*, the ECJ pointed out that in "an administrative procedure entailing complex technical evaluations" the Commission must have a power of appraisal in order to be able to fulfil its tasks, but that, precisely because of this room for manoeuvre, those involved have the right "of the person concerned to make his views known", and over and above that a right "to have an adequately reasoned decision", since that is the only way there could be judicial verification of whether "the factual and legal elements upon which the exercise of the power of appraisal depends were present".[74]

The potential for a honing of judicial control over internal market management on the basis of Article 190 EC is enhanced to the extent that private actors are not required to make the detour through national courts when seeking to enforce procedural correctness within the comitology procedure. The recognition of individual rights of action against Community legal acts, which takes account of the perception that de facto "general" legal acts, can have very concrete and individual effects, cannot remain without consequences for the protection of rights against comitology decisions even though, to date, such decisions have been held to be legally unassailable:[75] where, irrespective of the form of executive

---

[70] For a brief survey with further references, see Schlacke (1998: 341 ff.).

[71] Shapiro (1997b).

[72] See Harlow (1996); Dehousse, in this volume.

[73] See only Case C-331/88, *Fedesa* [1990] ECR I-4023, 4036. See, from more recent case-law, for example, Case C-278/95 P, *Siemens v Commission* [1997] ECR I-2507.

[74] Above, note 61, at I-5499 (paras 13 and 14).

[75] Bradley (1998).

law-making, clear rights of the firms concerned or of the representatives of social interests are to be recognised,[76] there must also be protection for rights at European level.

Many further steps towards juridification of the comitology complex are conceivable and foreseeable. Among the issues which will attract legal attention are the Community's liability under Article 215 EC for faulty decisions legally attributable to the Commission, and the liability of Member States in the event of a faulty conversion of European decisions, following the criterion of the *Francovich* case-law.[77] All these approaches could be developed without legislative support, in particular, without some sort of European Administrative Procedures Act.

[76] On the development of the case-law, see Schwarze (1996: 176 ff.); also N Reich (1997: 10 ff.).

[77] Joined Cases C-6 and 9/90 *Francovich* v *Italy* [1991] ECR I-5357.

18

Epilogue: "Comitology" as Revolution – Infranationalism, Constitutionalism and Democracy

J. H. H. Weiler[*]

This volume brings the study of Comitology to maturity and enables us to take stock. The cumulative effect of the contributions to this project is not, in my view, simply the addition of another layer to our understanding of the Community and Union but the confirmation of a veritable and necessary dual revolution. First, a revolution in the thing itself: when you examine the Community through the spectacles of *Comitology*, you no longer observe the more traditional skyline dominated by the distinct outlines of the Commission, the Council, the Parliament, the Member States and their Governments, but an altogether more flattened, albeit complex and hazy, landscape which requires, in turn, a second revolution in the ways we describe, think and conceptualise European integration. In this essay, drawing on the extant research in the Joerges projects in Bremen and Florence in this volume and the earlier *ELJ* special issue (as well as the excellent *Shaping European Law and Policy* by R H Pedler and G F Schaefer (eds.) 1996,) I will sketch a few markers or directions which a discourse revised by the *Comitology* phenomenon may take.

I will first suggest that *Comitology* requires the introduction, alongside intergovernmentalism and supranationalism, of a third paradigm to conceptualise Community government which may somewhat inelegantly be called infranationalism. I will then discuss how this paradigm affects the discourse of constitutionalism and democracy.

[*] Manley Hudson Professor and Jean Monnet Chair, Harvard University.

Infranationalism

Comitology, *stricto sensu*, is a term-of-art defining a discreet set of committees set up by Council Decision 87/373/EEC, which are meant to operate in
accordance with the Decision's famous, or infamous, three procedures and
which are habitually conceptualised within the classical terms of Statal
statecraft – "function" and "power". Typically, Comitology is described as
part of (or an encroachment on) the Commission's implementing function
and an expression of the Council's delegation power. The legal debate
about Comitology mainly revolves around the limits of this power of
delegation and the extent of legitimate encroachment on the function. From
time to time it will look at procedural conformity. The political debate falls
neatly into the supranational-intergovernmental conceptual framework; its
typical vocabulary is institutional balance and its habitual concern is the
delicate relationship of the Member States and their governments (the intergovernmental) to the Community (the supranational).

An expanded discourse – *Comitology* – covers more than the formal
categories of Decision 87/373 Committees. First, it broadens its catchment
to cover the entire universe of Union committees, which shadow all stages of
decision making in both pre- and post- Commission proposal stages, and in
pre- and post- Council adoption stages. Second, it addresses, as relevant
actors, more than the formal committee membership itself and incorporates
all those who come into contact with it – both public officials and private
actors – as a substantive and even defining part of the phenomenon. Finally,
whilst *Comitology* takes an interest in the formal decisional rules, it also
looks, in good realist fashion, at the actual processes in a holistic way.

Two consequences stem from this rejection of the formal Comitology
straitjacket.

First, the simple *factual enormity* of the committee phenomenon is
rendered transparent. *Comitology* is not a discreet phenomenon which
occurs at the end of the decision making process (or at the end of the
chapter on decision making in your typical book, if it appears at all). It is
more like the discovery of a new sub-atomic particle, a neutrino or a
quark, affecting the entirety of molecular physics which requires an
account of both the phenomenon itself and the way it impacts the rest of
nuclear understanding. *Comitology* argues for a rewriting of the entire
decision making field because of the importance of the committee particle
in all its stages. Consequently, the analytical task assumes the same
duality: we require an account of the phenomenon in its own terms (the
internal dynamics of committees broadly understood) and the manners in
which it affects the overall decision making and regulatory process. Last,
but certainly not least, *Comitology* is seen as central to critical areas of
public policy and public administration affecting fateful decisions of risk

allocation, economic (non)redistribution and social organisation within the Union.

Infranationalism, in juxtaposition with supranationalism, tries to point to the *conceptual enormity* of the broadly defined *Comitology* process. Supranationalism is, of course, not a term of art. Though fallen somewhat out of favour in recent times, it is still the preferred term when trying to capture some of the unique features of the Community and Union, features which differentiate it from other transnational organisations, regimes and polities. One way to synthesise the multiple meanings which have been given to supranationalism is to think of it as a paradigm which opposes both Community and State as its central feature and then seeks to show a relationship in which, in a variety of ways – a variety as broad as the many descriptions which use supranationalism – the manner in which States relate to the Community and to other States within the Community differ from one another (and to some, earlier) inter-governmental or international paradigm. Lawyers who find supranationalism a useful concept (though for them the more à la mode term these days is constitutionalism) will use it to describe the special relationship between the Community's legal order and that of the Member States – a relationship which in important aspects "subordinates" individual Member State law to Community law. Political scientists (and politicians) will use supranationalism to describe, say, decisional features such as majority voting, or the special powers of the Commission in Article 189a EC which "subordinate" individual Governmental and/or Statal powers to the Community decisional process. The descriptions are often contested. Some lawyers will argue that the writ of Community law within a Member State derives from national constitutional law and, as such, is ultimately "inferior" to it; political scientists will argue that the supranational thesis is a chimera, and with impressive lexical magic illustrate that both the Community's legal and decisional procedures are willed by States (and their governments!) and would be worthless if this were otherwise. But also this debate (the real one, not the caricature I have presented here) takes place within the supranational paradigm in which the principal, if contested players, are Governments and States, Community and its principal Institutions and the discourse is defined by vertical (Community-Member States) and horizontal (Commission, Council, Parliament) balances.

As noted above, it is, of course, possible to fit *Comitology* into this supranational-intergovernmental framework. The parliamentary debate has been premised on this framework: vertically, *Comitology* is, for example, criticised as introducing an intergovernmental Trojan horse into what is meant to be a Community process. Horizontally, *Comitology* is held to be another Council or Member State Trojan horse in the citadel of the Commission or a means for the Governments to retain control over the regulatory process.

But there is an alternative reading of the world of *Comitology* in which the "balance" between State government and Community (and the concomitant balance between, say, Commission and Council) appears much less critical and enjoys much less explanatory power for the dynamics of Community policy making or, rather, policy making within the Community. One of the principal reasons for the reduction in the importance of the classical supranational balance is that the Institutions which define this balance lose much of their clarity in the *Comitology* process. Notionally, a committee may be a creature of the Council presided over by the Commission. But a close look at the reality of *Comitology*, which the contributions to this project allow us, displays a beast which is quite different from the formal description:

- Process and network are the ontological reality of *Comitology* which put in shadow formal player.
- A distinct and powerful constructivist identity and culture (or subculture) obliterate the plenipotentiary and delegatory aspects of Committee membership. In form they may be representatives of the Member States. In substance they socialise into an independent identity of the committee and its network.
- A rule of informality marginalises formal rules in the decision making process.
- The dynamics that inform outcomes are not a reflection of national interests but of functional deliberation and sectoral pressure.

Most astonishing is the decisional autonomy of *Comitology*. John Le Carré's Cold War novels were characterised by the most intricate stories of espionage in which the double agent, manipulated by one controller and deceiving the other, played a central role. In the post Cold War novels, the erstwhile agents began working for their own devices playing one controller against the other. One gets the impression, by the cosy connivance between Commission and Council that each thinks *Comitology* is their own Smiley or Karla whereas in fact, in the run of the mill cases, the "Committees" composed of mid-ranking officials have long lost their allegiance to their controllers and work very much within their own universe for what they perceive as their function and task. Even the ultimate power brokers, Member State governments elude themselves in this fashion.

Infranationalism would, on this reading, be a third paradigm which addresses a meso-level reality which operates below the public macro and above the individual micro; is not a reflection of the State-Community paradigm and the contours and dynamics of which are ill-served by the perennial supranational-intergovernmental discourse; is, as de Areilza, Dehousse, Everson, Joerges and Vos presciently stipulated long before it was fashionable, more administrative and managerial than constitutional and diplomatic; is polycentric or even non-centric but certainly not dualist;

has dynamics which are neither national or *Communautaire*, but functional and sectoral; has a *modus operandi* which is less by negotiation and more by deliberation.

Infranationalism does not obliterate the intergovernmental or the supranational but operates alongside them. If you think of the Community as governance, infranationalism helps define an important layer in the European multi-layered system. If you think of the Community as polity, it is infranationalism which often conceptualises better a polity in which national controls were not only removed on the highways and at airports. Infranationalism is to Supranationalism and Intergovernmentalism what postmodernity is to modernity: it challenges the epistemic comfort of boundaries – and in this infranationalism becomes, arguably, the most dramatic expression of integration itself.

Constitutionalism

Constitutional or unconstitutional? Formally, the question makes sense. In substance *Comitology* is neither. It is non-constitutional – outside the classical parameters of constitutionalism. Traditionally, constitutionalism is premised on Polity, Institutions and Boundaries. Constitutionality is the condition of respecting such boundaries. Constitutional Courts are border patrols. In its jurisprudence, the European Court of Justice applies the tailor-made constitutional framework developed in the context of supranationalism to the problems of Comitology. Put differently, by using the supranational framework it defines certain types of problems and becomes blind to others.

In the first place, it is a jurisprudence which presupposes ontological boundaries. Committees must be juridical subjects to which, for example, powers may (or may not) be delegated. The question of delegation, central to the formal constitutional discourse, pre-supposes a subject-subject relationship between, say, Council and committee. Juridically, this makes, perhaps, ample sense.

The jurisprudence also presupposes instrumental boundaries – of function and power. For example, the notorious *Meroni* doctrine is premised on the belief in the ability and the necessity of assigning and maintaining certain functions and powers to the sharply defined subjects. The Council may have discretionary power, a committee may not.

Finally, it is a jurisprudence which presupposes or believes in epistemic boundaries, most notably in the ability to differentiate clearly between scientific knowledge and political or value preference.

The constitutional insistence on clear boundaries of subjecthood, of functions and power and of knowledge is, in fundamental respects, at odds with our political understanding of *Comitology*. We understand *Comitology* as process. We also realise that in this process it is fanciful to imagine that functions and powers can be hermetically assigned. And even those, such as myself, who persist in the positivist premise which believes in the separation of facts from opinion, are sceptical about the ability so sharply to differentiate between the "scientific" and the policy preference.

One could regard those differences simply as the benign manifestation of the different disciplinary sensibilities of law and political science. But even if that is their origin, they have profound political manifestations too for they unwittingly camouflage the true Comitology phenomenology, rendering it even less transparent than it is and, ironically, subverting some of the deeper goals of Constitutionalism and Constitutionality, those of constraining political power and protecting fundamental values.

The constitutional fiction of clear ontological boundaries of *Comitology*, that is manifest in the jurisprudence of the Court, privileges the formal actors of the process: Commission and Member State representatives. It obscures the many sectoral informal actors who are an essential part of the committee network. At best, it avoids and, at worst, it contributes to one of the most troubling aspects of *Comitology*, which is unequal access and privileged sectoral influence. The constitutional insistence on the subject thus subverts the constitutional values of transparency, representation and equality. There is something both formal and unreal in the Court's self-confidence that a clear statement of reasons ex Article 190 EC and the possibility of a subsequent judicial action before the Court could undo the deficiencies of the decision-making process.

The constitutional premise of ontological boundaries camouflages another dimension of *Comitology*. It contributes to the fiction that the committee is truly presided over by the "Commission" and that its members truly "represent" their Member States or at least the governments of their Member States. Ontological clarity so demands. Indeed, it is hard to expect the Court openly or even internally to articulate the constructivist insight easily demonstrated in *Comitology* of the development of a value driven, self-generated self-understanding and identity by discreet committees. If committees were truly agents of either the Commission or the Member State they would at least be subject to internal political controls and indirect legitimation derived from their principals. Constitutional ontological boundaries obscure the constructivist autonomy of *Comitology* and, thus, the constitutional value of accountability.

The damage created by the constitutional insistence on instrumental boundaries is no less troubling. Since the boundary is untenable, one resorts to fiction, not to say deceit. The only question is whether the Court knowingly or unknowingly turns a blind eye to the fictions of both the Council and Commission when they apply their *Meroni* circumventions. But the damage is more profound than a simple legal subterfuge. Here, the process is the paradoxical victim of a more alert jurisprudence which looks beyond form into the decision-making process itself (albeit a truncated portion only), insisting on an articulation of rights, a reliance on objective data *et cetera*. Since the Court believes, or is forced to believe in the constitutional grammar, syntax and vocabulary it applies to *Comitology*, that committees do not, indeed, exercise discretionary political power, the Court is obliged to give them a clear constitutional bill of health. This has all the more legitimating specific gravity because the Court has purported to examine the internal committee procedure itself. This diverts attention from the fact that committees *do* exercise considerable political and policy discretion without adequate political accountability.

Finally the epistemic boundaries. One consequence of the Court's *Sciencefest* has been in privileging those actors who are more easily able to access technical expertise. In the formal game this privileges the Commission and large Member States. In the broader network, the Court has privileged the rich who are able to press their case by submitting expensive scientific evidence. But the matter does not end here.

We should not be surprised by the Court's belief in the epistemic separateness of scientific data from political values and its turning to "experts." The origins of this can be found in its own Article 30 jurisprudence where a similar construct is implicitly used as a way of camouflaging the Court's own policy role in policing the boundaries of Member State derogations to free movement.

It was in the exercise of the proportionality test that epistemic boundaries were born. A central feature of the proportionality test is whether a policy objective could be achieved by a measure less restrictive to trade or free movement. Supposedly this is a technical, value free, determination which the Court can make on the basis of evidence submitted to it, or review when made, as a matter of mixed law and fact, by a Member State court. Is the insulating requirement of Member State A on a washing machine excessive? Can the safety of the user be guaranteed by a more modest insulating requirement applied by Member State B on its washing machines? Call in the experts, weigh the evidence and make a determination. That this is deceptive is already noted when we observe, in delicate cases such as *Sunday Trading,* how the hot potato of proportionality is tossed between the national judiciary and the Court; it appears that Member State courts often much prefer the ECJ take those decisions on proportionality. But the reality is far more complex and in countless cases the European Court imposes its values on the level of tolerable risk allocation in society.

Take, by way of example, the least probable case of all, *Cassis* itself. The Court found that the objective of the German government of ensuring that the consumer should not be misled into buying a liqueur, believing it to have a higher alcoholic content, was legitimate. But it also found that that objective could be achieved by a measure less restrictive than the German outright ban, namely by requiring the product to carry a label displaying its alcoholic content. What is involved in this banal and intuitively correct decision? It is clear that even if *Cassis* and other French liqueurs were to carry that label, some consumers would still be misled: some cannot read, others do not read. The communicative effect of labels is notoriously quite limited. What, in effect, the Court decided in *Cassis* was that the German policy of zero-tolerance to any consumer confusion does not override the societal interest in the free movement of goods. Instead, the Court imposed its risk assessment reflected in the label requirement, which, in effect, decided that this was an area in which allowing a certain percentage of consumers to be misled (because of the limited communicative effect of a label) is acceptable.

Who cares? Well, one does care when one moves to the area of automobile safety, of food and beverage additives and the like in which such risk determination can decide, for example, the number of persons who will die on the road each year, the number of persons whose health will be put at risk by certain nutritional substances and the like. And certainly the Court itself feels uneasy in having to take these types of decisions.

Comitology, in some ways, is meant to remove these decisions from the Court to a political, accountable instance of decision-making. The constitutional approach adopted by the Court, with its epistemic boundaries which the Court creates in its "scientific evidence" jurisprudence, coupled with the instrumental boundaries which lead to the fiction of non-discretionary power, de-politicises one of the most important dimensions of Community policy making. One can have sympathy for the Court. How can it recognise the political nature of the risk assessment process in *Comitology* without acknowledging the political nature of risk assessment process in its own Article 30 jurisprudence?

So here, too, constitutional epistemic boundaries most dramatically undermine the fundamental constitutional value of accountable political decision making .

It is evident that unlike some who may celebrate the constitutionalisation of *Comitology*, I regard it as a normative disaster. If constitutionalism is to be brought to *Comitology* without its subversive effects, the Court would have to recognise the infranational character of the phenomenon, which defies the normal constitutional categories laboriously constructed in the context of a supranational understanding of the Community. An infranational adjudication would reverse the current set of priorities and put values before structure. Equality of access, transparency, political accountability should trump considerations of, say, delegation and attribution.

Democracy

The facile democratic critique of *Comitology* as remote, opaque, and unfair and the facile remedies of an American style Administrative Act which would ensure directness, transparency and procedural fairness have been forever shattered by the path-breaking and paradigm-shifting work of Joerges and Neyer. Developed from careful empirical observations their work was able to point to the quality of both process and outcome. Whilst not negating the intrusion of interest, they convincingly demonstrate a quality of conversation which, in its rationality and in its ability to consider (and often accommodate) minority interests, transcends the typical models of power negotiation. In *Comitology* "deliberative" is shown to be not a pious hope but a political reality. Deliberative also means that "national interests" as such often lose their meaning as, inevitably, do national or institutional representation. One consequence of this is a dismantling of the typical intergovernmental and supranational theorems to explain Community processes. I consider the Joerges and Neyer choice to call their model "deliberative supranationalism" a semantic *faux pas* unless it is a failure fully to grasp the real implications of their ground breaking work.

But it is in relation to the discourse of democracy that their work is most tantalising. Lurking in the background in this unlikeliest of places – *Comitology* – and never quite stated as if for fear of wishing away a dream come true, is St Jürgen's noble vision of a deliberative and communicative process through which, and only through which, true democratic discourse can take place. In *Comitology*, Joerges and Neyer find the Habermasian promised land. There is little point in undermining the empirical basis of the Joerges construct because, even if partial and incomplete and not applicable to every single instance of committee work, it has sufficient substance to change the discussion of democracy in relation to *Comitology*.

One set of implications is dramatic. It forces an altogether more careful assessment of transparency, openness and procedural guarantees – since the wholesale enactment of these would inevitably destroy the social and professional fabric of the committees which are the conditions for the emergence of deliberative decision making. And that would be a considerable loss: for the quality of outcome, as the Joerges approach demonstrates, does not only transcend the pitfalls of norms resulting from negotiating national interests. These "national" interests are, frequently, captured by powerful sectarian domestic interests masquerading as national. One of the greatest insights of the Joerges approach is to show how the *transnational* deliberative process is most effective in exposing and stripping the *national* sectarian interest. The results are evident in outcomes which, paradoxically, could not be achieved in any national context.

Yet, without diminishing the importance of any of this, one should be cautious before advocating a generalised normative model of deliberative supranationalism. For even the shiniest of moons has it dark side and even the *Comitology* experience is awash with deep ambivalences. To point some of these out is, in some ways, to do no more than introduce strands from the classical debate between deliberative and representational models of democracy, reflecting, if you wish, the tensions between Government "by the people and for the people".

Here, then, are some considerations which should be factored into any assessment of the virtues of the deliberative model of *Comitology*.

A starting point would be a measure of caution concerning the inevitably elitist nature of all "philosopher king" models of Governance from Plato onwards. Deliberative models are often favoured by the deliberative class – primarily professors who are, naturally, empowered by any process which privileges that which they have and which legitimates, even aggrandises, their status and their actual or pretended *modus operandi*, and in which the model for ideal governance is a well conducted seminar.

For all the attention to the subtle internal dynamics of Comitology procedures and the processes of group socialisation, there seems to be an absence of attention to, or interest in, the social background of the participants themselves. It is striking that in all the empirical work on Comitology with which I am familiar, including the interviews with participants, these parameters were neither explored nor considered relevant. But could, for example, the process of group bonding explained through, for example, long association and shared professional concerns, not also be conditioned or, at least, facilitated by, say, a common socio-economic and educational background (the gymnasium, lycee, liceo class) creating very similar lifeviews and moral preferences? There seems to be a belief that the contours of the deliberation, the options put up for consideration, the economic and moral choices considered – in, say, risk assessment – the shared understanding of what counts as a persuasive argument and what counts as a weak argument can all be decontextualised from the social, class, educational and economic background of those who deliberate. I do not think it can be so decontextualised and from this perspective; the process becomes far more ambivalent and problematic from a democratic perspective.

There is, too, a question of legitimacy both empirical and deontological.

It is possible that the committee members themselves, like the Court in its proportionality determinations, are frequently unaware of the profound political and moral choices involved in their determinations and of their shared biases. This would be especially likely in a group of persons who share common worldviews and a common vocabulary and where, as a result, moral premises are presumed but not discussed. Though scientific analysis can predict how many people will die as a result of adopting this or that safety standard, it cannot determine whether the risk is worth taking or not worth taking. This is a political choice even if at times it is inextricably linked with the scientific data. The biases of the actors in this mixed scientific/political agenda would be crucial. We cannot eliminate bias from political decision making. We can only seek to render it transparent and, at times, to counter it with competing biases. This does not, in and of itself, condemn the *Comitology* process. Someone might advocate that society is better off if such decisions – because of their sensitivity – are taken behind closed doors, by a group of like minded civil servants and "experts" and that such decisions are then camouflaged as "scientific" and, as such, beyond political choice. But we should not hide the utilitarian or social engineering dimension of this governance choice and it hardly provides a basis for a generalised normative model. And there is, at least, a case to be made that in the interest of democracy such decisions should be taken out of the closet and debated openly in our public fora.

Finally, there is the issue of equality of access. One cannot, in the analytic mode, explain *Comitology* as a deliberative network, which inevitably suggests that some interests are included and some are excluded and, in the normative mode, not acknowledging that this is a major problem for democracy. Equally, one cannot affirm that this is a problem for democracy and thus endorse proposals which would ensure transparency, openness and equal access, and not acknowledge that such proposals, if they are to be efficient, would destroy, or at least seriously compromise, the conditions which enable a deliberative process.

Comitology, on this reading, is a microcosm of the problems of democracy, not a microcosm of the solution. The Habermasian noble ideal of deliberation has validity only if assimilated to the Jewish ideal of the Messiah – one fervently believes that the Messiah *will* (future tense) come; the One that actually comes is always false. *Comitology* is just another run of the mill illustration of this truism.

Editorial Note

The editors, and the author likewise, felt that this essay should remain without footnotes. Readers should be able to trace the implicit references easily with the help of our collective bibliography. We add nevertheless:

Both the Comitology Decision of 1987 and the Commission Proposal of 16 July 1998 are documented in the Annexes.

The volume by R H Pedler and G F Schaefer (eds.), *Shaping European Law and Policy. The Role of Committees and Comitology in the Political*

350 J H H WEILER

Process (Maastricht 1996) is a publication of the European Institute of Public Administration, PO Box 1129, NL-6201 BE Maastricht. Presentations of the two research projects on comitology directed by Christian Joerges at the Centre of European Law and Politics, Bremen, and at the European University Institute include: Joerges (1995); Bücker/Joerges/ Neyer/Schlacke, "Formen europäischer Risikoverwaltung: Komitologie im Bereich von Lebensmitteln und technischen Gütern", in: H Schmitt, E Rieger and T König (eds.), *Europäische Institutionenpolitik* (Frankfurt a.M./New York 1997), 289-313. Preparatory and closely related contributions include Falke (1996); Falke/Winter (1996); Roethe (1994). The contributions to the Special Issue of the (1997) 3/3 *European Law Journal* by Vos, Landfried, Bradley and Neyer/Joerges are all cited in the collective bibliography. So are the articles by Dehousse and Everson, who are both represented in this volume.

We refrain from citing J H H Weiler's own work on infranationalism and/or pertinent research he has inspired, with these three exceptions: J de Areilza, "Sovereignty or Management? The Dual Character of the EC's Supranationalism – Revisited", [Harvard Jean Monnet Working Paper 2/95] (Cambridge MA 1995; http: // www.law .harvard. edu/ Programs/ JeanMonnet/papers/95/9502ind.html); J H H Weiler, "The European Court of Justice: Beyond 'Beyond Doctrine' or the Legitimacy Crisis of European Constitutionalism" in A-M Slaughter / A Stone Sweet / J H H Weiler, *The European Court and National Courts—Doctrine and Jurisprudence* (Oxford 1998), 365-191; Weiler/Ballmann/Haltern/ Hofmann/ Mayer, "Certain Rectangular Problems of European Integration" Report to the European Parliament (Project IV/95/02), (Luxembourg 1996; http://www.iue.it/AEL/EP/index.html).

Bibliography

Aberbach J D / B A Rockman, "Mandates or Mandarins? Control and Discretion in the Modern Administrative State" (1988) 48 *Public Administration Review*, 606–612

Albert D, "Supranationale Problemlösung oder nationale Interessenwahrung? Die umweltpolitische Handlungsfähigkeit der EU" (1998) 21 *Integration*, 32–42

Algieri F / D Rometsch, "Europäische Kommission und organisierte Interessen: Die Rolle des 'Ausschußwesens' und Ansätze für einen strukturierten Dialog" in V Eichener / H Voelzkow (eds.), *Europäische Integration und verbandliche Interessenvermittlung* (Marburg 1994), 131–149

Averyt W F, *Agropolitics in the European Community. Interest Groups and the Common Agricultural Policy* (New York 1977)

Bach M, "Eine leise Revolution durch Verwaltungsverfahren. Bürokratische Integrationsprozesse in der Europäischen Gemeinschaft" (1992) 21 *Zeitschrift für Soziologie*, 16–30

―― "Vom Zweckverband zum technokratischen Regime: Politische Legitimation und institutionelle Verselbständigung in der Europäischen Gemeinschaft" in H A Winkler / H Kaelble (eds.), *Nationalismus – Nationalitäten – Supranationalität* (Stuttgart 1993a), 288–308

―― "Transnationale Integration und institutionelle Differenzierung. Tendenzen der europäischen Staatswerdung" (1993b) 14 *Zeitschrift für Rechtssoziologie*, 223–242

―― "Integrationsprozesse in der Europäischen Gemeinschaft: Vom Zweckverband zum technokratischen Regime?" in H Meulemann / A Elting-Camus (eds.), *Lebensverhältnisse und soziale Konflikte im neuen Europa* (Opladen 1993c), 264–266

―― "Transnationale Institutionenpolitik: Kooperatives Regieren im politisch-administrativen System der Europäischen Union" in T König / E Rieger / H Schmitt (eds.), *Europäische Institutionenpolitik* (Frankfurt/New York 1997)

Baldwin R, *Rules and Government* (Oxford 1995)

―― and C McCrudden, *Regulation and Public Law* (Oxford 1992)

Ballmann A, "Infranationalism and the Community Governing Process", annex to J H H Weiler *et al*, *Certain Rectangular Problems of European Integration*, EP Project IV/95/02 (Luxembourg 1996; http://www.iue.it/AEL/EP/index.html)

Bankowski Z, "Subsidiarity, Sovereignty and the Self" in K W Nörr / T Oppermann (eds.), *Subsidiarität: Idee und Wirklichkeit. Zur Reichweite eines Prinzips in Deutschland und Europa* (Tübingen 1997), 23–39

Barents R, *The agricultural law of the EC* (Deventer 1994)

Bauer G / C Reichard (eds.), *Kommunale Managementkonzepte in Europa* (Stuttgart 1993)

Beckedorf I, "Das Untersuchungsrecht des Europäischen Parlaments" (1997) 32 *EuR*, 237–260

Benz, A, "Ansatzpunkte für ein europafähiges Demokratiekonzept" in B Kohler-Koch (ed.), *Demokratisches Regieren jenseits des Staates* (1998) 29 *PVS*, 345–368

Berg A J / J A E Vervaele, *Study report concerning the implementation of articles 29–34 of Council Regulation (EEC) no. 2847/93 of 12 Oct. 1993 establishing a central system applicable to the Common Fisheries Policy* (DG XIV, October 1994)

Berman G A, "Regulatory cooperation between the European Commission and U.S. administrative agencies" (1996) 9 *The Administrative Law Journal of the American University*, 933–983

Bertram C, "Decision-making in the E.E.C.: The Management Committee Procedure" (1967) 5 *CML Rev*, 246–264

Bessette J M, *The Mild Voice of Reason. Deliberative Democracy and American National Government* (Chicago 1994)

Bieber R / R Dehousse / J Pinder / J H H Weiler (eds.), *1992: One European Market? A Critical Analysis of the Commission's Internal Market Strategy* (Baden-Baden 1988)

Bignami F, *The Administrative State in a Constitutional System of Checks and Balances: Lessons for EC Comitology from American Rulemaking* [Harvard Jean Monnet Working Paper 5/gg] (Cambridge MA 1999; http://www.law.harvard.edu/Programs/JeanMonnet/papers/gg/gg0507.html)

Black J, "Constitutionalising Self-Regulation" (1996) 59 *MLR* 1, 24–55

Blumann C, "Le pouvoir exécutif de la Commission à la lumière de l'Acte unique européen" (1988) 24 *RTD Eur*, 23–59

—— *La fonction législative communautaire* (Paris 1995)

—— "Le Parlement européen et la comitologie: une complication pour la Conférence intergouvernementale de 1996" (1996) 32 *RTD Eur*, 1–24

Böhret C / G Konzendorf, *Ko-Evolution von Gesellschaft und funktionalem Staat* (Opladen 1997)

Bora A, "Gesellschaftliche Integration durch Verfahren. Zur Funktion von Verfahrensgerechtigkeit in der Technikfolgenabschätzung und -bewertung" (1993) 14 *Zeitschrift für Rechtssoziologie*, 55–79

Bradley K St C, The European Court and the Legal Basis of Community Legislation (1989) 14 *ELR*, 379–402

—— "Comitology and the Law: Through a Glass, Darkly" (1992) 29 *CML Rev*, 693–721

—— "The European Parliament and Comitology: On the Road to Nowhere?" (1997) 3 *ELJ*, 230–254

—— "The GMO-Committee on Transgenic Maize: Alien Corn, or the Transgenic Procedural Maze" in M P C M van Schendelen (ed.), *EU Committees as Influential Policy-makers* (Aldershot 1998), 207–222

—— and A Feeney, "Legal Developments in the European Parliament", (1993) 13 *YEL*, 383–425

Braithwaite J / J Ayres, *Responsive Regulation: Transcending the Regulatory Debate* (Oxford 1992)

Brekke O A / E O Eriksen, *Technology Assessment and Democratic Governance* (Typescript, Norwegian Research Centre in Organisation and Managment, Bergen 1998)

Brennecke V, *Normsetzung durch private Verbände – zur Verschränkung von staatlicher Steuerung und gesellschaftlicher Selbstregulierung im Umweltrecht* (Düsseldorf 1996)

Breuer R, *Entwicklungen des europäischen Umweltrechts – Ziele, Wege und Irrwege* (Berlin/New York 1993)

Breulmann G, *Normung und Rechtsangleichung in der Europäischen Wirtschaftsgemeinschaft* (Berlin 1993)

Breyer S, *Regulation and Its Reform* (Cambridge MA 1982)

—— *Breaking the Vicious Circle. Toward Effective Risk Regulation* (Cambridge MA 1993)

—— and R Stewart, *Administrative Law and Regulatory Policy*, 3ʳᵈ ed. (Boston 1992)

Bücker A, *Von der Gefahrenabwehr zu Risikovorsorge und Risikomanagement im Arbeitsschutzrecht* (Berlin 1997)

—— and C Joerges / J Neyer / S Schlacke, "Social Regulation through European Committees: An Interdisciplinary Agenda and Two Fields of Research" in R H Pedler / G F Schaefer (eds.), *Shaping European Law and Policy. The Role of Committees and Comitology in the Political Process* (Maastricht 1996), 39–58

Buitendijk G J / M C P M van Schendelen, "Brussels Advisory Committees: A Channel for Influence?" (1995) 20 *ELR*, 37–56

Búrca G de, "The Principle of Subsidiarity and the Court of Justice as an Institutional Actor" (1998) 36 *JCMS*, 217–235

Burley A-M / W Mattli, "Europe before the Court: A Political Theory of Legal Integration" (1993) 47 *International Organization*, 41–76

Caparaso J A, "The European Union and Forms of State: Westphalian, Regulatory or Post-Modern?" (1996) 34 *JCMS*, 29–52

Chayes A / A H Chayes, "On Compliance" (1993) 47 *International Organization*, 175–205

Conrad J, *Nitratpolitik im internationalen Vergleich* (Berlin 1992)

Corbett R, "RE: Comitology", Background Note Socialist Group of the European Parliament (Luxembourg, 23 October 1989)

—— "The Intergovernmental Conference on Political Union" (1992) 30 *JCMS*, 271–298

Cowles M G, "Setting the Agenda for the New Europe: the ERT and EC 1992" (1995) 13 *JCMS*, 501–526

Cranston R F, "Regulation and Deregulation: General Issues" (1982) 5 *UNSW Law Journal*, 1–28

Croley S P, "Theories of Regulation: Incorporating the Administrative Process" (1998) 98 *Columbia Law Review*, 1–168

Crozier M, *État modeste, État moderne* (Paris 1991)

Curtin D, "Civil Society and the European Union: Opening Spaces for Deliberative Democracy" in *Collected Courses of the Academy of European Law*, vol. 7, book 1 (Florence 1999), 185–280

Daintith T (ed.), *Implementing EC Law in the United Kingdom. Structures for indirect rule* (Chichester 1995)

Dannecker G, *Strafrecht der Europäischen Gemeinschaft* (Freiburg 1995)

Deboyser P, "Recent developments in Community law relating to medicinal products" (1994) 2 *Consumer Law Journal* 6, 213–217

De Gaulle C, "Conférence du Presse, 9 Septembre 1965" in Discours et messages, Tome 4 (Paris 1970) 372–392

Dehousse R, "Community Competences: Are there Limits to Growth?" in R Dehousse (ed.), *Europe after Maastricht. An Ever Closer Union?* (München 1994a), 103–125

—— "Constitutional Reform in the European Community: Are there alternatives to the Majoritarian Avenue ?" (1994b) 18 *West European Politics*, 118–136

—— "Regulation by Networks in the European Community: the Role of European Agencies" (1997) 4 *JEPP*, 246–261

—— *The European Court of Justice: The Politics of Judicial Integration* (Basingstoke 1998a)

—— "European Institutional Architecture after Amsterdam: Parliamentary System or Regulatory Structure?" (1998b) 35 *CML Rev*, 595–627

—— and C Joerges / G Majone / F Snyder / M Everson, *Europe after 1992: new regulatory strategies* (Florence 1992)

Delmas–Marty M, *Vers un droit pénal communautaire? Le titre VI du Traité sur l'Union européenne et la matière pénale* (Paris 1995)

Demmke C / E Eberharter / G F Schaefer / A Türk, "The History of Comitology" in R H Pedler / G F Schaefer (eds.), *Shaping European Law and Policy: The Role of Committees and Comitology in the Political Process* (Maastricht 1996), 61–82

Denninger E, *Verfassungsrechtliche Anforderungen an die Normsetzung im Umwelt- und Technikrecht* (Baden-Baden 1990)

Di Fabio U, "Verwaltungsentscheidung durch externen Sachverstand" (1990) 81 *Verwaltungsarchiv*, 193–227

—— *Risikoentscheidungen im Rechtsstaat. Zum Wandel der Dogmatik im öffentlichen Recht, insbesondere am Beispiel der Arzneimittelüberwachung* (Tübingen 1994a)

—— "Rechtsnatur und Rechtsprobleme der bauaufsichtlichen Einführung technischer Baubestimmungen" (1994b) *Jahrbuch des Umwelt- und Technikrechts*, 51–89

—— *Produktharmonisierung durch Normung und Selbstüberwachung* (Köln 1996)

Docksey C / K Williams, "The European Commission and the execution of Community policy" in G Edwards / D Spence (eds.), *The European Commission*, 2nd ed. (London 1997), 125–153

Dogan R, "Comitology: Little Procedures With Big Implications" (1997) 20 *West European Politics*, 31–60

Donelly M / E Ritchie, "The College of Commissioners and their Cabinets" in G Edwards / D Spence (eds.), *The European Commission* (London 1994), 31–61

Dose N, "Kooperatives Recht. Defizite einer steuerungsorientierten Forschung zum kooperativen Verwaltungshandeln" (1994) *Die Verwaltung*, 91–110

Dowding K, "Model or Metaphor? A Critical Review of the Policy Network Approach" (1995) *Political Studies*, 136–158

Dreher M, "Transparenz und Publizität bei Ratsentscheidungen" (1996) 7 *EuZW*, 487–491

Dworkin R, *Law's Empire* (London 1991)

Earnshaw D / D Judge, "Early Days: the European Parliament, Co-decision and the European Union Legislative Process Post-Maastricht" (1995) 2 *JEPP* , 624–649

Egan M, "Regulatory Strategies, Delegation and European Market Integration" (1998) 5 *JEPP*, 485–506

——— and D Wolf, "Regulation and Comitology: The EC Committee System in Regulatory Perspective" (1998) 4 *Columbia Journal of European Law*, 499–523

Eggers B, "Die Entscheidung des WTO Appellate Body im Hormonfall. Doch ein Recht auf Vorsorge?" (1998) 9 *EuZW*, 147–151

Ehlermann C-D, "The Internal Market following the Single European Act" (1987) 24 *CML Rev*, 361–404

——— "Compétence d'exécution conférées à la Commission – La nouvelle décision-cadre du Conseil (1988) *RMC*, 232–239

——— "Die institutionelle Entwicklung der EG unter der Einheitlichen Europäischen Akte" (1990) 41 *Außenpolitik*, 136–146

Eichener V, *Social Dumping or Innovative Regulation? Processes and Outcomes of European Decision-Making in the Sector of Health and Safety at Work Harmonization* [EUI Working Papers SPS 92/28] (Florence 1993)

——— "Die Rückwirkungen der europäischen Integration auf nationale Politikmuster" in M Jachtenfuchs / B Kohler-Koch (eds.), *Europäische Integration* (Opladen 1996), 249–280

——— *Entscheidungsprozesse in der regulativen Politik der Europäischen Union* (Habilitation Thesis, Bochum 1997)

Eifert M, "Umweltinformation als Regelungsinstrument" (1994) 47 *Die Öffentliche Verwaltung*, 544–552

Eising R / B Kohler-Koch, "Inflation und Zerfaserung: Trends der Interessenvermittlung in der Europäischen Gemeinschaft" in W Streeck (ed.), *Staat und Verbände* (1994) 25 *PVS*, 175–206

Eriksen E O, *Towards a People's Europe? On the Problem of Democratic Deficit in the EU* (Typescript. Norwegian Resreach Centre in Organisation and Management, Bergen 1998)

——— and J Weigård, "Conceptualizing Politics. Strategic or Communicative Action" (1997) 20 *Scandinavian Political Studies*, 219–241

Everling U, "Will Europe Slip on Bananas? The Bananas Judgement of the Court of Justice and National Courts" (1997) 33 *CML Rev*, 401–437

Everson M, "Independent Agencies: Hierarchy Beaters?" (1995a) 1 *ELJ* , 180–204

——— "The Legacy of the Market Citizen" in J Shaw / G More (eds.), *New Legal Dynamics of European Union* (Oxford 1995b), 73–90

——— "Administering Europe" (1998) 36 *JCMS*, 195–216

Falke J, "Comitology and Other Committees: A preliminary Empirical Assessment" in R H Pedler / G F Schaefer (eds.), *Shaping European Law and Policy: The Role of Committees and Comitology in the Political Process* (Maastricht 1996), 117–165

——— "Achievements and Unresolved Problems of European Standardisation: The Ingenuity of Practice and the Queries of Lawyers" in C Joerges / K-H Ladeur / E Vos (eds.), *Integrating Scientific Expertise into Regulatory Decision-Making. National Experiences and European Innovations* (Baden-Baden 1997), 187–224

——— and C Joerges, *Rechtliche Möglichkeiten und Probleme bei der Verfolgung und Sicherung nationaler und EG-weiter Umweltschutzziele im Rahmen der europäischen Normung.* Gutachten erstellt im Auftrag des Büros für Technikfolgen-Abschätzung des Deutschen Bundestages (Bremen 1995)

—— and G Winter, "Management and Regulatory Committees in Executive Rule-making" in G Winter (ed.), *Sources and Categories of European Union Law. A Comparative and Reform Perspective* (Baden-Baden 1996), 541–582

Favereau O, "Valeur de option et flexibilité: De la rationalité substantielle à la rationalité procédurale" in P Cohendet / P Llerena (eds.), *Flexibilité, information et décision* (Paris 1989)

—— *L'incomplétude n'est pas le probleme c'est la solution* (Coll. de Cerisy, 1993)

Finkel A N / M Golding (eds.), *Worst Things First? The Debate over Risk-Based National Evironmental Priorities* (Washington DC 1994)

Fiorino D J, "Toward a New System of Environmental Regulation: The Case of an Industry Sector Approach Environmental Law" (1996) 26 *Environmental Law*, 457–488

Foray D / A Grübler, *Technology and the Environment: An Overview, Technological Forecasting and Social Change* (Luxembourg 1996)

Franklin M / M Marsh / L McLaren, "Uncorking the Bottle: Popular Opposition to European Unification in the Wake of Maastricht" (1994) 32 *JCMS*, 455–472.

Gardener J S, "The European Agency for the Evaluation of Medicines and European Regulation of Pharmaceuticals" (1996) 2 *ELJ*, 48–82

Gehring T, "Regieren im internationalen System. Verhandlungen, Normen und Internationale Regime" (1995) 36 *PVS*, 197–219

—— "Arguing and Bargaining in internationalen Verhandlungen zum Schutz der Umwelt. Überlegungen am Beispiel des Ozonschutzregimes" in V von Prittwitz (ed.), *Verhandeln und Argumentieren in der Umweltpolitik* (Opladen 1996), 207–238

—— "Governing in Nested Institutions: Environmental Policy in the European Union and the Case of Packaging Waste" (1997) 4 *JEPP*, 337–354

Gerken L (ed.), *Competition among Institutions* (Houndmills/New York 1995)

Gerstenberg O, *Bürgerrechte und deliberative Demokratie. Elemente einer pluralistischen Verfassungstheorie* (Frankfurt/M 1997)

Gill B, "Hypothetische Risiken: Ansatzpunkte einer vorausschauenden Umweltpolitik. Das Beispiel der Risikokontrolle in der Genforschung" in R Martinsen (ed.), *Politik und Biotechnologie. Die Zumutung der Zukunft* (Baden-Baden 1997), 303–319

Godt C "Der Bericht des Appellate Body der WTO zum EG-Einfuhrverbot von Hormonfleisch" (1998) 9 *Europäisches Wirtschafts- und Steuerrecht*, 202–209

Goldstein J / R O Keohane, "Ideas and Foreign Policy: An Analytical Framework" in J Goldstein / R O Keohane (eds.), *Ideas and Foreign Policy. Beliefs, Institutions, and Political Change* (Ithaca 1993), 3–30

Golub J, "State Power and Institutional Influence in European Integration: Lessons from the Packaging Waste Directive" (1996) 34 *JCMS*, 313–339

Gormley W T, "A Test of the Revolving Door Hypothesis at the FCC" (1979) 23 *American Journal of Political Science*, 665–683

Grams H A, "Komitologie im Gesetzgebungsprozeß der Europäischen Union und die Einbeziehung des Europäischen Parlaments" (1995) 78 *Kritische Vierteljahresschrift für Gesetzgebung und Rechtswissenschaft*, 112–131

Grande E, *Vom Nationalstaat zur europäischen Politikverflechtung. Expansion und Transformation moderner Staatlichkeit: untersucht am Beispiel der*

Forschungs- und Technologiepolitik (Habilitation Thesis, Konstanz 1994)

—— "The State and International Groups in a Framework of Multi-Level Decision-Making: The Case of the EU" (1996) 3 *JEPP*, 318–388

Gray P, "The Scientific Committee for Food" in M P C M van Schendelen (ed.), *EU Committees as Influential Policy-makers* (Aldershot 1998), 68–88

Green Cowles M, *German Big Business and Brussels: Learning to Play the European Game*, American Institute for Contemporary German Studies [The John Hopkins University, Paper Number 15] (Washington DC 1995)

Grimm D, "Does Europe Need a Constitution?" (1995) 1 *ELJ*, 282–302

Gröblinghoff S, *Die Verpflichtung des deutschen Strafgesetzgebers zum Schutz der Interessen der Europäischen Gemeinschaften* (Heidelberg 1996)

Grote R J, "Steuerungsprobleme in transnationalen Beratungsgremien: Über soziale Kosten unkoordinierter Regulierung in der EG" (1990) 4 *Jahrbuch für Staats- und Verwaltungswissenschaft*, 227–254

Haas E B, *The Uniting of Europe. Political, Social, and Economic Forces 1950–1957* (Stanford 1958)

Haas P M, "Introduction: Epistemic Communities and International Policy Coordination" (1992) 46 *International Organization*, 1–35

—— "Compliance with EU Directives: Insights From International Relations and Comparative Politics" (1998) 5 *JEPP*, 17–37

Habermas J, "Wahrheitstheorien" in H Fahrenbach (ed.), *Wirklichkeit und Reflexion, Festschrift für Walter Schulz* (Pfullingen 1973), 211–265

—— "Sklavenherrschaft der Gene. Moralische Grenzen des Fortschritts", *Süddeutsche Zeitung*, 17 January 1998

Haigh N, *EEC Environmental Policy and Britain* (Harlow 1992)

Hankin R, "The Role of Scientific Advice in the Elaboration and Implementation of the Community's Foodstuffs Legislation" in C Joerges / K-H Ladeur / E Vos (eds.), *Integrating Scientific Expertise into Regulatory Decision-Making. National Traditions and European Innovations* (Baden-Baden 1997), 141–168

Harding C / B Swart, *Enforcing European Community Rules* (Dartmouth 1996)

Harlow C, "Codification of EC Administrative Procedures? Fitting the Foot to the Shoe or the Shoe to the Foot" (1996) 2 *ELJ*, 3–25

—— *European Administrative Law and the Global Challenge* [EUI Working Paper RSC 98/23] (Florence 1998)

—— and R Rawlings, *Law and Administration* (London 1984)

Haufler V, *Private Sector International Regime* (Manuscript, 1998)

Héritier A, "The Accommodation of Diversity in European Policy-Making and its Outcomes: Regulatory Policy as a Patchwork" (1996) 3 *JEPP* 149–167

—— "Die Koordination von Interessenvielfalt im Europäischen Entscheidungsprozeß: Regulative Politik als "Patchwork"" in A Benz / W Seibel (eds.), *Theorieentwicklung in der Politikwissenschaft – eine Zwischenbilanz* (Baden-Baden 1997a), 261–279

—— "Policy-Making by Subterfuge: Interest Accommodation, Innovation and Substitute Democratic Legitimation in Europe – Perspectives from Distinctive Policy Areas" (1997b) 4 *JEPP*, 171–189

—— and S Mingers / C Knill / M Becka, *Staatlichkeit in Europa. Ein regulativer Wettbewerb: Deutschland, Großbritannien, Frankreich in der Europäischen Union* (Opladen 1994)

—— and C Knill / S Mingers, *Ringing the Changes in Europe. Regulatory Competition and the Transformation of the State. Britain, France, Germany* (Berlin/New York 1996)

Hoffmann and Töller, "Zur Reform der Komitologie-Regeln and Grundsätze für die Verwaltungskooperations im Ausschußsystem der Europäischen Gemeinschaften", 9 Staatswissenschaften und Staatspraxis 209–239 (1998)

Hoffmann-Riem W / J P Schneider (eds.), *Verfahrensprivatisierung im Umweltrecht* (Baden-Baden 1996)

Hohmeyer O *et al*, *Internationale Regulierung der Gentechnik. Praktische Erfahrungen in Japan, den USA und Europa* (Heidelberg 1994a)

Hohmeyer O *et al*, *Risikobeurteilung und Sicherheitsmaßnahmen bei Einsatz natürlich vorkommender und gentechnisch veränderter Mikroorganismen zum Abbau umweltbelastender Schadstoffe* (Berlin 1994b)

Holmes S, "Gag Rules or the Politics of Omission" in J Elster / R Slagstad (eds.), *Constitutionalism and Democracy* (Cambridge 1988), 19–58

Hood C, "Public Management for all Seasons" (1991) *Public Administration*, 3–19

Hooghe L (ed.), *Cohesion Policy and European Integration: Building Multi-Level Governance* (Oxford 1996)

House of Lords, Select Committee on the European Communities Committee of the House of Lords, 3rd report, Session 1998–1999 *Delegation of Powers to the Commission: Reforming Comitology* (1999)

Hrbek R / C Probst, "Keine Regel ohne Ausnahme? Protektionistische Tendenzen der Bundesrepublik in der Textilhandelspolitik der EG" (1990) 41 *Ordo*, 117–130

Hufen F, "Kooperation von Behörden und Unternehmen im Lebensmittelrecht. Neue Instrumente des Verwaltungsrechts, insbesondere: Akkreditierung, Zertifizierung, Betriebsbeauftragte und kooperative Qualitätssicherung" (1993) 3 *ZLR*, 233–249

Institut für Europäische Politik, *Comitology – Characteristics, Performances and Options*, Research project under contract by the EC Commission, Preliminary Final Report (Bonn 1989)

Jachtenfuchs M, "Theoretical Perspectives on European Governance" (1995) 1 *ELJ*, 115–133

—— "Entgrenzung und politische Steuerung" in B Kohler-Koch (ed.), *Demokratisches Regieren jenseits des Staates* (1998) 29 *PVS*, 235–248

—— and B Kohler-Koch (eds.), *Europäische Integration* (Opladen 1996a)

—— and B Kohler-Koch, "Regieren im dynamischen Mehrebenensystem" in M Jachtenfuchs / B Kohler-Koch (eds.), *Europäische Integration* (Opladen 1996b), 15–44

Jacobs F / R Corbett / M Shackleton, *The European Parliament* (London 1992)

Joerges C, "Quality Regulation in Consumer Goods Markets: Theoretical Concepts and Practical Examples" in T Daintith / G Teubner (eds.), *Contract and Organisation. Legal Analyses in the Light of Economic and Social Theory* (Berlin 1986), 142–163

—— "The New Approach to Technical Harmonization and the Interests of Consumers: Reflections on the Necessities and Difficulties of a Europeanization of Product Safety Policy" in R Bieber / R Dehousse / J Pinder / J H H Weiler (eds.), *1992: One European Market? A Critical Analysis of the Commission's*

Internal Market Strategy (Baden-Baden 1988), 157–225

—— "Paradoxes of Deregulatory Strategies at Community Level: The Exemple of Product Safety Policy" in G Majone (ed.), *Deregulation or Re-Regulation? Regulatory Reform in Europe and in the United States* (London/New York 1990), 176–197

—— "Die Europäisierung des Rechts und die rechtliche Kontrolle von Risiken" (1991a) 74 *Kritische Vierteljahresschrift für Gesetzgebung und Rechtswissenschaft*, 416–434

—— "Markt ohne Staat? Die Wirtschaftsverfassung der Gemeinschaft und die regulative Politik" in R Wildenmann (ed.), *Staatswerdung Europas? Optionen für eine politische Union* (Baden-Baden 1991b), 225–268 (http://olymp.wu-wien.ac.at/eiop/texte/1997–019a.htm)

—— "Product Safety in the European Community: Market Integration, Social Regulation and Legal Structures" (1992) 38 *Journal of Behavioural and Social Sciences*, 132–148

—— "Soziale Rechte und regulative Politik in der Europäischen Gemeinschaft" in SPD-Bundestagsfraktion (ed.), *Besser leben mit Europa? Chancen einer Europäischen Verfassung. Texte der Anhörung am 27. Mai 1993 in Bonn* (Bonn 1993), 24–28

—— "Legitimationsprobleme des Europäischen Wirtschaftsrechts und der Vertrag von Maastricht" in G Brüggemeier (ed.), *Verfassungen für ein ziviles Europa* (Baden-Baden 1994a), 91–130

—— "Rationalisierungsprozesse im Recht der Produktsicherheit: Öffentliches Recht und Haftungsrecht unter dem Einfluß der Europäischen Integration" (1994b) 27 *Jahrbuch des Umwelt- und Technikrechts*, 141–178

—— *Die Beurteilung der Sicherheit technischer Konsumgüter und der Gesundheitsrisiken von Lebensmitteln in der Praxis des europäischen Ausschußwesens (Komitologie)* [ZERP-Diskussionspapier 1/95] (Bremen 1995)

—— "Taking the Law Seriously: On Political Science and the Role of Law in the Process of European Integration" (1996a) 2 *ELJ*, 105–135

—— "Das Recht im Prozeß der Europäischen Integration. Ein Plädoyer für die Beachtung des Rechts durch die Politikwissenschaft" in M Jachtenfuchs / B Kohler-Koch (eds.), *Europäische Integration* (Opladen 1996b), 73–108

—— "Scientific Expertise in Social Regulation and the European Court of Justice: Legal Frameworks for Denationalized Governance Structures" in C Joerges / K-H Ladeur / E Vos (eds.), *Integrating Scientific Expertise into Regulatory Decision-Making. National Traditions and European Innovations* (Baden-Baden 1997), 295–323

—— (ed.), *Die Beurteilung der Sicherheit technischer Konsumgüter und der Gesundheitsrisiken von Lebensmitteln in der Praxis des Europäischen Ausschußwesens ("Komitologie")*, Final Report to the Volkswagen-Stiftung of September 1998, Centre of European Law and Politics (ZERP) (Bremen 1998)

—— and J Falke / H-W Micklitz / G Brüggemeier, *Die Sicherheit von Konsumgütern und die Entwicklung der Europäischen Gemeinschaften* (Baden-Baden 1988) (English version: *European Product Safety, Internal Market Policy and the New Approach to Technical Harmonisation and Standards*, EUI Working Papers LAW 91/10–14, Florence 1991; http://www.iue.it/LAW/WP-Texts/Joerges91/)

—— and J Falke, "Die Normung von Konsumgütern in der Europäischen

Gemeinschaft und der Richtlinienentwurf für die allgemeine Produktsicherheit" in P-C Müller-Graff (ed.), *Technische Regeln im Binnenmarkt* (Baden-Baden 1991), 159–202

—— and K-H Ladeur / E Vos (eds.), *Integrating Scientific Expertise into Regulatory Decision-Making. National Traditions and European Innovations* (Baden-Baden 1997)

—— and J Neyer, "From Intergovernmental Bargaining to Deliberative Political Processes: The Constitutionalization of Comitology" (1997a) 3 *ELJ*, 273-299

—— and J Neyer, "Transforming Strategic Interaction into Deliberative Problem-solving: European Comitology in the Foodstuffs Sector" (1997b) 4 *JEPP*, 609–625

—— and H Schepel / E Vos, *"Delegation" and the European Polity: The Problems of the Law with the Role of Standardisation Organisations in European Legislation*, Paper presented at the RSC Conference on The Political Economy of Standards Setting (Florence, 4–5 June 1998)

—— and E Vos, "Structures of Transnational Governance and Their Legitimacy" in J A E Vervaele (ed.), *Compliance and Enforcement of EC Law* (The Hague 1999), 71–93

Johnston M T, *The European Council. Gatekeeper of the European Community* (Boulder CO 1994)

Joskow P / R Noll, "Regulation in Theory and Practice" in G Fromm (ed.), *Studies in Public Regulation* (Cambridge MA 1981), 1–65

Kahl W, "Europäisches und Nationales Verwaltungsorganisationsrecht – von der Konfrontation zur Kooperation" (1996a) *Die Verwaltung*, 341–384

—— "Stellung und Funktion von Umweltagenturen – Eine rechtsvergleichende Typologie" (1996b) 36 *Jahrbuch des Umwelt- und Technikrechts*, 119–135

Keating M / L Hooghe, "By-Passing the National State? Regions and the EU Policy Process" in J J Richardson (ed.), *European Union: Power and Policy-Making* (London 1996), 216–229

Keohane R O / S Hoffmann, "Institutional Change in Europe in the 1980s" in R O Keohane / S Hoffmann (eds.), *The New European Community. Decisionmaking and Institutional Change* (Boulder CO 1991), 1–40

Kiehl P, "EG-Bauproduktenrichtlinie und ihre Auswirkungen auf die Normungsarbeit" (1990) 69 *DIN-Mitt.*, 250–256

Kielmansegg P G, "Integration und Demokratie" in M Jachtenfuchs / B Kohler-Koch (eds.), *Europäische Integration* (Opladen 1996), 47–71

Kilian W, *Europäisches Wirtschaftsrecht* (München 1996)

Kingdon J W, *Agendas, Alternatives, and Public Policies* (Boston 1984)

Kloepfer M / T Elsner, "Selbstregulierung im Umwelt- und Technikrecht – Perspektiven einer kooperativen Normsetzung" (1996) 111 *Deutsches Verwaltungsblatt*, 964–975

Knaap P van der, "Government by Committee: Legal Typology, Quantitative Assessment and Institutional Repercussions of Committees in the European Union" in R H Pedler / G F Schaefer (eds.), *Shaping European Law and Policy. The Role of Committees and Comitology in the Political Process* (Maastricht 1996), 83–116

Köck W, "Risikovorsorge als Staatsaufgabe" (1996) 121 *Archiv für öffentliches Recht*, 1–23

König K, "'Neue' Verwaltung oder Verwaltungsmodernisierung" (1995) 48 *Die öffentliche Verwaltung*, 349–358

Kohler B, "Ist die EG noch zeitgemäß? Zur Tragfähigkeit der Integrationspolitik" (1984) B 23–24 *Aus Politik und Zeitgeschichte*, 21–30

Kohler-Koch B, "Vertikale Machtverteilung und organisierte Wirtschaftsinteressen in der Europäischen Gemeinschaft" in U von Alemann / R G Heinze / B Hombach (eds.), *Die Kraft der Region. Nordrhein-Westfalen in Europa* (Düsseldorf 1990), 221–235

—— "Interessen und Integration. Die Rolle organisierter Interessen im westeuropäischen Integrationsprozeß" in M Kreile (ed.), *Die Integration Europas* (1992) 23 *PVS*, 81–119

—— "Changing Patterns of Interest Intermediation in the European Union" (1994) 29 *Government & Opposition*, 166–180

—— "Die Gestaltungsmacht organisierter Interessen", in M Jachtenfuchs / B Kohler-Koch (eds.), *Europäische Integration* (Opladen 1996), 193–222

—— "Die Europäisierung nationaler Demokratien. Verschleiß eines europäischen Kulturerbes?" in M Th Greven (ed.), *Demokratie – eine Kultur des Westens?* (Opladen 1998), 263–288

Kortenberg H, "Comitologie: le retour", (1998) 34 *RTD Eur* 3, 317–327

—— "Comitologie: le retour", 34 *RTDEur* 317 (1998)

Krämer L, "Umweltpolitik" in C-D Ehlermann / R Bieber (eds.), *Handbuch des Europäischen Rechts, Vol. "Umwelt"* (Baden-Baden 1992)

Kreher A, "Agencies in the European Community: a Step Towards Administrative Integration in Europe" (1997) 4 *JEPP*, 225–245

Krieger S, "Das technische Umweltrecht der Gemeinschaft nach der "neuen Konzeption"" (1992) 12 *Umwelt- und Planungsrecht*, 401–406

Kromarek P, *Die Trinkwasserrichtlinie der EG und die Nitratwerte* [IIUG Report 86–9] (Berlin 1986)

Ladeur K-H, "Coping with Uncertainty" in G Teubner / L Farmer / D Murphy (eds.), *Environmental Law and Ecological Responsibility* (Chichester 1994a)

—— "Die postmoderne Verfassung" in U K Preuß (ed.), *Der Begriff der Verfassung* (Frankfurt/M 1994b)

—— *Das Umweltrecht der Wissensgesellschaft. Von der Gefahrenabwehr zum Risikomanagement* (Berlin 1995a)

—— "Supra- und transnationale Tendenzen in der Europäisierung des Verwaltungsrechts – eine Skizze" (1995b) 3 *EuR*, 227–246

—— "Sources and categories of legal acts – Germany", in G Winter (ed.), *Sources and categories of European Union Law: A Comparative and Reform Perspective* (Baden-Baden 1996a), 235–272

—— *The New European Agencies – The European Environment Agency and Prospects for a European Network of Environmental Administrations* [EUI-RSC Working Paper No. 96/50] (Florence 1996b)

—— "Towards a Legal Theory of Supranationality: The Viability of the Network Concept" (1997a) 3 *ELJ*, 33–54

—— "The Integration of Scientific and Technological Expertise into the Process of Standard-Setting According to German Law" in C Joerges / K-H Ladeur / E Vos (eds.), *Integrating Scientific Expertise into Regulatory Decision-Making: National Traditions and European Innovations* (Baden-Baden 1997b), 77–100

Laffan B, *Towards a European Model of Internationalisation?*, Paper presented at the Human Capital and Mobility Project Workshop (University College Dublin, May 1997)

Landfried C, "Beyond Technocratic Governance: The Case of Biotechnology" (1997) 3 *ELJ*, 253–272

Landis J M, *The Administrative Process* (New Haven CT 1938)

Lange P, "The Politics of the Social Dimension" in A M Sbragia (ed.), *Euro-Politics: Institutions and Policy-Making in the "New" European Community* (Washington DC 1992), 225–256

Lascher E L, "Assessing Legislative Deliberation: A Preface to Empirical Analysis" (1996) 21 *Legislative Studies Quarterly*, 501–519

Lauwaars R H, "Auxiliary Organs and Agencies in the EEC" (1979) 16 *CML Rev*, 365–387

—— "The 'Model Directive' on Technical Harmonisation" in R Bieber / R Dehousse / J Pinder / J H H Weiler (eds.), *1992: One European Market? A Critical Analysis of the Commission's Internal Market Strategy* (Baden-Baden 1988), 151–173

Leibfried S / P Pierson, "Semi-sovereign Welfare States: Social Policy in a Multi-tiered Europe" in S Leibfried / P Pierson (eds.), *European Social Policy. Between Fragmentation and Integration* (Washington DC 1995), 43–77

Lenaerts K, "Regulating the Regulatory Process: "Delegation of Powers" in the European Community" (1993) 18 *ELR*, 23–49

Lepsius R M, "Nationalstaat oder Nationalitätenstaat als Modell für die Weiterentwicklung der Europäischen Gemeinschaft" in R Wildenmann (ed.), *Staatswerdung Europas? Optionen für eine Europäische Union* (Baden-Baden 1991), 19–40

—— "Institutionenanalyse und Institutionenpolitik" in B Nedelmann (ed.), "Politische Institutionen im Wandel", (1995) Special Issue 35 *Kölner Zeitschrift für Soziologie und Sozialpsychologie*, 392–403

—— "Bildet sich eine kulturelle Identität in der Europäischen Union?" (1997) 42 *Blätter für deutsche und internationale Politik*, 948–955

Lequesne C, "La Commission Européenne entre Autonomie et Dépendence" (1996) 46 *Revue Française de Science Politique*, 389–408

Lewis J, *Constructing Interests: EU Membership, COREPER and the Constitutive Processes of National Preference Formation* (Köln 1996)

Lindblom C E, *Politics and Markets. The World's Political-economic Systems* (New York 1977)

Lowi T J, *The End of Liberalism* (New York 1969)

Ludlow P, *Preparing Europe for the 21st Century: The Amsterdam Council and Beyond* (Brussels 1997)

Maduro M Poiares, *We, the Court. The European Court of Justice and the European Economic Constitution* (Oxford 1998)

Mahoney P G, "Securities Regulation by enforcement: an international perspective" (1990) 7 *Yale Journal on Regulation*, 305–320

Majone G, *Evidence, Argument, and Persuasion in the Policy Process* (New Haven CT 1989a)

—— "Regulating Europe: Problems and Perspectives" (1989b) 3 *Jahrbuch zur Staats und Verwaltungswissenschaft*, 159–177

—— (ed.), *Deregulation or Re-Regulation? Regulatory Reform in Europe and in the United States* (London/New York 1990)

—— "Cross-National Sources of Regulatory Policymaking in Europe and the United States" (1991) 11 *Journal of Public Policy*, 79–106

—— "The European Community Between Social Policy and Social Regulation" (1993a) 31 *JCMS*, 153–170

—— "Wann ist Policy-Deliberation wichtig?" in A Héritier, (ed.), *Policy-Analyse. Kritik und Neuorientierung'* (1993b) 24 *Politische Vierteljahresschrift*, 97–115

—— "The European Community. An "Independent Fourth Branch of Government"?" in G Brüggemeier (ed.), *Verfassungen für ein ziviles Europa* (Baden-Baden 1994a), 23–44

—— *Independence vs Accountability* [EUI Working Paper SPS No. 94/3] (Florence 1994b)

—— *Regulating Europe* (London/New York 1996a)

—— "Public Policy: Ideas, Interests and Institutions" in R E Goodin / H-D Klingemann (eds.), *A New Handbook of Political Science* (Oxford 1996b), 610–627

—— "The New European Agencies: Regulation by Information" (1997) 4 *JEPP*, 262–275

—— "Europe's 'Democratic Deficit': The Question of Standards" (1998) 4 *ELJ*, 5-28

Mancini G F, "Europe: The Case for Statehood" (1998) 4 *ELJ* , 29–42

Marburger P, *Die Regeln der Technik im Recht* (Köln 1979)

—— "Die gleitende Verweisung aus der Sicht der Wissenschaft" in DIN (ed.), *Verweisung auf technische Normen in Rechtsvorschriften* (Köln 1982), 27–39

—— and R Enders, "Technische Normen im europäischen Gemeinschaftsrecht" (1994) 27 *Jahrbuch des Umwelt- und Technikrecht*s, 333–368

March J G, "Footnotes to Organizational Change" (1981) 26 *Administrative Science Quarterly*, 563–577

Marks G, "Structural Policy in the European Community" in A M Sbragia (ed.), *Euro-Politics: Institutions and Policy-Making in the "New" European Community* (Washington DC 1992), 191–224

—— and L Hooghe / K Blank, "European Integration from the 1980s: State Centric vs. Multi-level Governance" (1996) 34 *JCMS*, 341–378

Mashaw J, "Prodelegation: Why Administrators Should Make Political Decisions" in P Shuck (ed.), *Foundations of Administrative Law* (Oxford 1994a), 155–180

—— "Explaining Administrative Process: Normative, Positive, and Critical Stories of Legal Development" in P Shuck (ed.), *Foundations of Administrative Law* (Oxford 1994b), 66–79

Mayer O, *Deutsches Verwaltungsrecht*, Vol. 1, 3rd ed. (Leipzig 1924)

Mayntz R / F W Scharpf, "Der Ansatz des akteurzentrierten Institutionalismus", in R Mayntz / F W Scharpf, *Gesellschaftliche Selbstregelung und politische Steuerung* (Frankfurt/New York 1995) 39–72

Mazey S / J Richardson (eds.), *Lobbying in the European Community* (Oxford 1993)

McConnell G, *Private Power and American Democracy* (New York 1966)

McCubbins M / T Schwartz, "Congressional Oversight Overlooked: Police Patrols versus Fire Alarms" (1984) 28 *American Journal of Political Science*, 163–179

McLaughlin A M / J Greenwood, "The Management of Interest Representation in the European Union (1995) 33 *JCMS*, 143–156

Mendrinou M, "Non-Compliance and the European Commission's Role in Integration" (1996) 3 *JEPP*, 1–22

Meng W, "Die Neuregelung der EG-Verwaltungsausschüsse. Streit um die 'Komitologie'" (1988) 48 *ZaöRV*, 208–228

Mény Y, *The People, The Elites and the Populist Challenge* [Jean Monnet Chair Papers RSC 98/47] (Florence 1998)

Mestmäcker E-J, "On the Legitimacy of European Law" (1994) 58 *RabelsZ*, 615–635

Micklitz H-W, "Consumer Rights", in A Cassese / A Clapham / J H H Weiler (eds.), *Human Rights in the European Community: The Substantive Law* (Baden-Baden 1991), 53–109

—— and Th Roethe / S Weatherill (eds.), *Federalism and Responsibility. A Study on Product Safety Law and Practice in the European Community* (London/Dordrecht/Boston 1994)

Middlemas K, *Orchestrating Europe: The Informal Politics of the EU 1973–1995* (London 1995)

Miller D, "Deliberative Democracy and Social Choice" in D Held (ed.), *Prospects for Democracy* (Stanford 1994), 74–92

Mitnick B M, "The Theory of Agency. The Policing "Paradox" and Regulatory Behavior" (1975) 24 *Public Choice*, 27–42

—— *The Political Economy of Regulation: Creating, Designing and Removing Regulatory Forms* (New York 1980)

Moe T, "Regulatory Performance and Presidential Administration" (1982) 26 *American Journal of Political Science*, 197–224

Moran M, "Theories of Regulation and Changes in Regulation: the Case of Financial Markets" (1986) 34 *Political Studies*, 185–201

Moravcsik A, "Preferences and Power in the European Community: A Liberal Intergovernmentalist Approach" in S Bulmer / A Scott (eds.), *Economic and Political Integration in Europe* (Oxford 1995), 29–80

Naschold F, *Modernisierung des Staates – Zur Ordnungs- und Innovationspolitik des öffentlichen Sektors* (Berlin 1993)

Natalicchi G, *Telecommunications Policy and Integration Processes in the European Union* (Ph.D. Thesis, New York 1996)

Neergaard U B, *Competition and Competences. The Tensions Between European Competition Law and Anti-Competitive Measures by the Member States* (Copenhagen 1998)

Nehl H P, *Procedures Principles of Good Administration in Community Law* (LLM Thesis, Florence 1997)

Neyer J, "Administrative Supranationalität in der Verwaltung des Binnenmarktes: Zur Legitimität der Komitologie" (1997) 20 *Integration*, 24–37

—— "The Standing Committee for Foodstuffs: Arguing and Bargaining in Comitology" in M P C M van Schendelen (ed.), *EC Committees as Influential Policy Makers* (Aldershot 1998), 148–163

—— "Supranationales Regieren in EG und WTO Soziale Integration jenseits des demokratischen Rechtsstaates und die Bedingungen ihrer Möglichkeit", in J. Neter, D. Wolf, M. Zürn (eds.) *Recht jenseits des Staates*, Zerp-Diskussionpapier 1/99 (Bremen, 1999).

Nicklisch F, "Zur rechtlichen Relevanz wissenschaftlich-technischer Regelwerke bei der Genehmigung technischer Anlagen" in F Nicklisch / D Schottelius / H Wagner (eds.), *Die Rolle des wissenschaftlich-technischen Sachverstandes bei der Genehmigung chemischer und kerntechnischer Anlagen* (Heidelberg 1982), 67–97

—— "Funktion und Bedeutung technischer Standards in der Rechtsprechung" (1983) 38 *Betriebsberater*, 261–269

Niskanen W, *Bureaucracy and Representative Government* (Chicago 1971)

Ogul M S, *Congress Oversees the Bureaucracy. Studies in Legislative Supervision* (Pittsburgh 1976)

—— and B A Rockman, "Overseeing Oversight: New Departures and Old Problems" (1990) 15 *Legislative Studies Quarterly*, 5–20

Ogus A I, *Regulation - Legal Form and Economic Theory* (Oxford 1994)

Page E C / L Wouters, "Bureaucratic Politics and Political Leadership in Brussels" (1994) 72 *Public Administration*, 445–45

Pedler R / G F Schaefer (eds.), *Shaping European Law and Policy: The Role of Committees and Comitology in the Political Process* (Maastricht 1996)

Pedler R H / M P C M van Schendelen (eds.), *Lobbying the European Union. Companies, Trade Associations and Issue Groups* (Aldershot 1994)

Peltzman S, "Toward a More General Theory of Regulation" (1976) 14 *Journal of Law and Economics*, 109–148

Pernice I, "Maastricht, Staat und Demokratie" (1993) 26 *Die Verwaltung*, 449–488

Peters B G, "Bureaucratic Politics and the Institutions of the European Community" in A Sbragia (ed.), *Europolitics. Institutions and Policymaking in the "New" European Community* (Washington DC 1992), 75–122

—— *Development of Theories about Governance: Art Imitating Life?*, Paper presented at the Conference "Ten Years of Change" (University of Manchester, September 1994)

—— "Agenda-Setting in the European Union" in J J Richardson (ed.), *European Union: Power and Policy-Making* (London 1996), 61–76

Philip A B, "Pressure Groups and Policy Formation in the European Communities" (1982) 10 *Policy and Politics*, 459–475

Pierce R J, "The Fiftieth Anniversary of the Administrative Procedure Act: Past and Prologue Rulemaking and the Administrative Procedure Act", (1996) 32 *Tulsa Law Journal*, 185– 201

Pitschas R, "Europäische Integration als Netzwerkkoordination komplexer Staatsaufgaben" (1995) 8 *Jahrbuch zur Staats- und Verwaltungswissenschaft*, 379–416

Pollack M A, *Obedient Servant or Runaway Eurocracy? Delegation, Agency, and Agenda Setting in the European Community* [Harvard Working Paper Series 95–10, Center for International Affairs] (Cambridge MA 1995)

—— "Delegation, Agency and Agenda Setting in the European Community" (1997) 51 *International Organization*, 99–134

Porter M, "Scientific Uncertainty, the Role of Expertise and North–South Variations in the EU Environmental Process: The Case of Packaging and Packaging Waste" (1995) 8 *Zeitschrift für angewandte Umweltforschung*, 516–531

—— and A Butt Philip, "The Role of Interest Groups in EU Environmental Policy Formulation: A Case Study of the Draft Packaging Directive" (1993) 3 *European Environment*, 16–20

Prechal S, "Institutional Balance: a Fragile Principle with Uncertain Contents" in

T Heukels / N Blokker / M Brus (eds.), *The European Union after Amsterdam - A Legal Analysis* (The Hague 1998), 273–294

Putnam R, "Diplomacy and Domestic Politics: The Logic of Two-Level Games" (1988) 42 *International Organization*, 427–460

Quirk P, *Industry Influence in Federal Regulatory Agencies* (Princeton 1981)

Rabin R, "Federal Regulation in Historical Perspective" in P Shuck (ed.), *Foundations of Administrative Law* (Oxford 1994), 30–55

Rack R / C Gasser, "Mehr Transparenz und mehr Verantwortlichkeit im Gemeinschaftsrecht. Die beiden BSE-Ausschüsse des Europäischen Parlaments und die Auswirkungen auf das Gemeinschaftsrecht" (1998) 9 *EuZW*, 421–426

Rasmussen J, "Risk Management Issues: Doing Things Safely with Words, Rules and Laws" in C Joerges / K-H Ladeur / E Vos (eds.), *Integrating Scientific Expertise into Regulatory Decision-Making. National Experiences and European Innovations* (Baden-Baden 1997), 15–37

Rawls J, "Justice as Fairness: Political not Metaphysical" (1985) 14 *Philosophy and Public Affairs*, 223–251

Reagan M D, *Regulation. The Politics of Policy* (Boston/Toronto 1987)

Rehbinder E / R Stewart, "Environmental Protection Policy" in M Cappelletti / M Seccombe / J Weiler (eds.), *Integration through Law. Europe and the American Federal Experience, Vol. 2* (Berlin 1985)

Reich C, "Le Parlament européen et la comitologie" (1990) *RMC*, 313–323

Reich N, "Public Interest Litigation before European Jurisdictions", in H-W Micklitz / N Reich (eds.), *Public Interest Litigation before European Courts* (Baden-Baden 1996), 3–20

—— "A European Constitution for Citizens: Reflections on the Rethinking of Union and Community Law" (1997) 3 *ELJ*, 131–164

Reich R B, *The Power of Public Ideas* (Cambridge MA 1988)

Reichard C, *Umdenken im Rathaus? Neue Steuerungsmodelle in der deutschen Kommunalverwaltung* (Berlin 1994)

Rengeling H W / M Gellermann, "Gestaltung des Europäischen Umweltrechts und seine Implementation im deutschen Rechtsraum" (1996) 36 *Jahrbuch des Umwelt- und Technikrechts*, 1–32

Rhodes M, "A Regulatory Conundrum: Industrial Relations and the Social Dimension" in S Leibfried / P Pierson (eds.), *European Social Policy: Between Fragmentation and Integration* (Washington DC 1995), 78–122

Rhodes R A W, "Interorganisational Networks and the "Problem" of Control in the Policy Process: A Critique of the 'New Institutionalism'" (1988) 11 *West European Politics*, 119–130

Risse-Kappen T, "Exploring the Nature of the Beast: International Relations Theory and Comparative Policy Analysis Meet the European Union" (1996) 34 *JCMS*, 53–80

Roethe T, *EG-Ausschußwesen und Risikoregulierung: Ein Problem von Handlungsstruktur und Rationalität* [EUI Working Paper LAW 94/7] (Florence 1994)

—— "Management von Gefahrstoffrisiken in Regelungsausschüssen der Europäischen Gemeinschaft" in G Winter (ed.), *Risikoanalyse und Risikoabwehr im Chemikalienrecht: interdisziplinäre Untersuchungen* (Düsseldorf 1995), 115–164

Röhl H C, "Staatliche Verantwortung in kooperativen Strukturen" (1996) *Die Verwaltung*, 487–510

Ross G, "Assessing the Delors Era in Social Policy" in S Leibfried / P Pierson (eds.), *European Social Policy: Between Fragmentation and Integration* (Washington DC 1995), 357–388

Salbu S R, "Regulation of insider trading in a global marketplace: a uniform statutory approach" (1992) 66 *Tulane Law Review*, 837–869

Sauter W / E Vos, "Harmonisation under Community Law: The Comitology Issue", in P Craig / C Harlow (eds.), *Law-making in the European Union* (London/The Hague/Boston 1998), 169–186

Sbragia A M (ed.), *Euro-Politics: Institutions and Policy-Making in the "New" European Community* (Washington DC 1992)

—— "Environmental Policy" in H Wallace / W Wallace (eds.), *Policy-Making in the European Union*, 3rd ed. (Oxford 1996), 235–255

Schaefer G F, "Committees in the EC Policy Process: A First Step Towards Developing a Conceptual Framework" in R H Pedler / G F Schaefer (eds.), *Shaping European Law and Policy. The Role of Committees and Comitology in the Political Process* (Maastricht 1996), 3–23

Scharpf F W, "The Joint-Decision Trap: Lessons from German Federalism and European Integration" (1988) 66 *Public Administration*, 239–278

—— "Koordination durch Verhandlungssysteme: Analytische Konzepte und institutionelle Lösungen" in A Benz / F W Scharpf / R Zintl (eds.), *Horizontale Politikverflechtung. Zur Theorie von Verhandlungssystemen* (Frankfurt/M 1992), 51–96

—— *Autonomieschonend und gemeinschaftsverträglich: Zur Logik der europäischen Mehrebenenpolitik* [MPIFG Discussion Paper 93/9] (Köln 1993a)

—— "Positive und negative Koordination in Verhandlungssystemen" in A Héritier (ed.), *Policy-Analyse. Kritik und Neuorientierung* (1993b) 24 *PVS*, 57–83

—— *Mehrebenenpolitik im vollendeten Binnenmarkt* [MPIFG Discussion Paper 94/4] (Köln 1994)

—— "Demokratische Politik in Europa" (1995) 4 *Staatswissenschaft und Staatspraxis*, 565–591

—— "Democratic Policy in Europe" (1996a) 2 *ELJ*, 136–155

—— "Politische Optionen im vollendeten Binnenmarkt" in M Jachtenfuchs / B Kohler-Koch (eds.), *Europäische Integration* (Opladen 1996b), 109–140

—— *Games Real Actors Play. Actor-Centered Institutionalism in Policy Research* (Boulder CO 1997a)

—— "Introduction: the Problem-solving Capacity of Multi-level Governance" (1997b) 4 *JEPP*, 520–538

—— and B Reissert / F Schnabel, *Politikverflechtung: Theorie und Empirie des Kooperatives Föderalismus in der BRD* (Kronberg 1976)

Schendelen M P C M van, "EC Committees: Influence Counts more than Legal Powers" in R H Pedler / G F Schaefer (eds.), *Shaping European Law and Policy. The Role of Committees and Comitology in the Political Process* (Maastricht 1996), 25–37

—— (ed.), *EU Committees as Influential Policy-makers* (Aldershot 1998)

Schindler P, "The problems of decision-making by way of the management committee procedure in the European Economic Community" (1971) 8 *CML Rev*, 184–205

Schlacke S, *Risikoentscheidungen im europäischen Lebensmittelrecht: Eine Untersuchung am Beispiel des europäischen Zusatzstoffrechts unter besonderer Berücksichtigung des europäischen Ausschußwesens ("Komitologie")* (Baden-Baden 1998)

Schmalz-Bruns R, *Reflexive Demokratie. Die demokratische Transformation moderner Politik* (Baden-Baden 1995)

—— "Grenzerfahrungen und Grenzüberschreitungen: Demokratie im integrierten Europa?" in B Kohler-Koch (ed.), *Demokratisches Regieren jenseits des Staates* (1998) 29 *PVS*, 369–380

Schmidt S, *Sterile Debates and Dubious Generalisations: An Empirical Critique of European Integration Theory. Based on the integration processes in Telecommunications and Electricity* [MPIFG Discussion Paper 96/5] (Köln 1996)

—— *Die wettbewerbsrechtliche Handlungsfähigkeit der Europäischen Kommission in staatsnahen Sektoren* (Ph.D. Thesis, Hamburg 1997)

Schmitt J / A Zweck (eds.), *Statusbericht zur Akzeptanz der Bio- und Gentechnologie in der deutschen Öffentlichkeit* (Düsseldorf 1996)

Schmitt von Sydow H, *Die Verwaltungs- und Regelungsausschußverfahren der Europäischen Wirtschaftsgemeinschaften* (Brussels 1973)

Schneider J P, *Nachvollziehende Amtsermittlung bei der Umweltverträglichkeitsprüfung* (Berlin 1991)

—— "Öko-Audit als Scharnier einer ganzheitlichen Regulierungsstrategie" (1995) *Die Verwaltung*, 361–388

—— "Kooperative Verwaltungsverfahren" (1996) *Verwaltungsarchiv*, 38–67

Schneider V / G Dang-Nguyen / R Werle, "Corporate Actor Networks in European Policy-Making: Harmonizing Telecommunications Policy" (1994) 32 *JCMS* 473–498

Schulze-Fielitz H, "Kooperatives Recht im Spannungsfeld von Rechtsstaatsprinzip und Verfahrensökonomie" (1994) 109 *Deutsches Verwaltungsblatt*, 657–667

Schumann W / P Mehl, "Bundesdeutsche Interessen und gemeinsame Außenhandelspolitik der EG" (1989) B 24–25 *Aus Politik und Zeitgeschichte*, 36–46

Schuppert G F, "Die Privatisierungsdiskussion in der deutschen Staatsrechtslehre" (1994) *Staatswissenschaften und Staatspraxis*, 541–564

—— "Rückzug des Staates" (1995) 48 *Die öffentliche Verwaltung*, 761–770

Schwarze J, *European Administrative Law* (London 1992)

—— "Developing Principles of European Administrative Law" (1993) *Public Law*, 229–239

—— "Länderbericht Deutschland" in J Schwarze (ed.), *Das Verwaltungsrecht unter europäischem Einfluß. Zur Konvergenz der mitgliedstaatlichen Verwaltungsrechtsordnungen in der Europäischen Union* (Baden-Baden 1996), 123–228

Sebenius J K, "Negotiation Arithmatics: Adding and Subtracting Issues and Parties" (1983) 37 *International Organization*, 281–316

Self P, *Government by the Market? The Politics of Public Choice* (Boulder CO 1993)

Selznick P, "Focusing Organizational Research on Regulation" in P Noll (ed.), *Regulatory Policy and the Social Sciences* (Berkeley/Los Angeles 1985)

Shapiro M, *Who Guards the Guardians: Judicial Control of Administration* (Athens GA/London 1988)

—— "Codification of Administrative Law: The US and the Union" (1996a) 2 *ELJ* 26–47

—— *Law Making in the EU: The Politics of Information: U.S. Congress and European Parliament*, Paper presented to the Institute of Advanced Legal Studies (London 1996b)

—— "The Frontiers of Science Doctrine: American Experiences with the Judicial Control of Science-Based Decision-Making" in C Joerges / K-H Ladeur / E Vos (eds.), *Integrating Scientific Expertise into Regulatory Decision-Making: National Traditions and European Innovations* (Baden-Baden 1997a), 325–342

—— "The Problem of Independent Agencies in the United States and the European Union" (1997b) 4 *JEPP*, 276–291

Shepsle K A / B R Weingast, "The Institutional Foundations of Committee Power" (1987) 81 *American Political Science Review*, 85–104

Shrader-Frechette K S, *Risk and Rationality: Philosophical Foundations* (Berkeley/Los Angeles 1991)

Smiley D V, *Canadian in Question: Federalism in the Eighties* (Toronto 1980)

Smyrl M E, "When (and How) Do the Commission's Preferences Matter?" (1998) 36 *JCMS*, 79–99

Steinberg R, "Probleme der Europäisierung des Deutschen Umweltrechts" (1995) 120 *Archiv des öffentlichen Rechts*, 549–594

Steunenberg B / C Koboldt / D Schmidtchen, Beyond Comitology: a comparative analysis of implementation procedures with parliamentary involvement (1997) 52 *Aussenwirtschaft*, 87–112

Stewart R, "The Reformation of American Administrative Law" (1975) 88 *Harvard Law Review*, 1667–1813

—— "Madison's Nightmare" (1990) 57 *Chicago Law Review*, 335–356

Stigler G, "The Theory of Economic Regulation" (1971) 2 *Bell Journal of Economics and Management Science*, 3–21

—— *The Citizen and the State: Essays on Regulation* (Chicago 1975)

Strauss P L, "The Place of Agencies in Government: Separation of Powers and the Fourth Branch of Government" (1984) 84 *Columbia Law Review*, 573–669

Streeck W, "From Market Making to State Building? Reflection on the Political Economy of European Social Policy" in S Leibfried / P Pierson (eds.), *European Social Policy. Between Fragmentation and Integration* (Washington DC 1995a), 389–431

—— "Neo-Voluntarism: A New European Social Policy Regime?" (1995b) 2 *ELJ*, 31–59

—— and P C Schmitter, "From National Corporatism to Transnational Pluralism: Organized Interests in the Single European Market" (1991) 19 *Politics and Society* 2, 133–164

Sunstein C R, *After the Rights Revolution. Reconceiving the Regulatory State* (Cambridge MA 1990)

Teubner G, "The State of Private Networks – The Emerging Legal Regimes of Poly-Corporatism in Germany" (1993) *Brigham Young University Law Review*, 553–576

—— "The Global Bukowina: Legal Pluralism in the World Society", in G Teubner (ed.), *Global Law without a State* (Aldershot 1996), 3–28

Thise J, *The BSE crisis: policy failure in multi-level governance* (Bruges 1996–97)

Timmermans C W A, "General Institutional Questions: The Effectiveness and Simplification of Decision-Making" in J A Winter *et al* (eds.), *Reforming the Treaty on European Union – The Legal Debate* (The Hague 1996), 133–146

Tinbergen J, *International Economic Integration*, 2ⁿᵈ ed. (Amsterdam 1965)

Toeller A E / H C H Hofmann, "Democracy and the reform of comitology" in M Adenas / A Türk (eds.), *The delegation of legislative powers* (London, forthcoming)

Traxler F / P C Schmitter, "The Emerging Euro-Polity and Organized Interests" (1995) 1 *European Journal of International Relations*, 191–218

Trute H H, "Die Verwaltung und das Verwaltungsrecht zwischen gesellschaftlicher Selbstregulierung und staatlicher Steuerung" (1996) 111 *Deutsches Verwaltungsblatt*, 950–964

Veh G M / E Edom, "Die neuen Vorschriften der EG zur Trinkwassergüte" (1981) 33 *Wasser und Boden*, 472–476

Vervaele J A E, *Fraud against the Community. The Need for European Fraud Legislation* (Deventer 1992)

—— *La fraude communautaire et le droit pénal européen des affaires* (Paris 1994a)

—— *Handen en tanden van het (gemeenschaps)recht. Beschouwingen over publieke rechtshandhaving* (Deventer 1994b)

—— "Administrative sanctioning powers of and in the Community. Towards a system of European administrative sanctions?" in J A E Vervaele (ed.), *Administrative law application and enforcement of Community law in the Netherlands* (Deventer 1994c), 161–202

—— "Law enforcement in Community law within the first and third pillar: do they stand alone?" (1997) VII *Finnish Journal of International Law*, 353–368

—— "Community regulation and operational application of investigative competences. The gathering and use of evidence with regard to the infringement of EU financial interests" in J A E Vervaele (ed.), *Transnational enforcement of the financial interests of the EU. Evolution in the Treaty of Amsterdam and the Corpus Juris* (Antwerp, forthcoming)

—— (ed.) *Compliance and Enforcement of European Community Law*, Kluwer European Monographs 20 (The Hague, London, Boston, Kluwer Law International, 1999)

Viscusi W K, "Regulating the Regulators" (1996) 63 *University of Chicago Law Review*, 1423–1461

Voelzkow H, *Private Regierungen in der Techniksteuerung. Eine sozialwissenschaftliche Analyse der technischen Normung* (Frankfurt/M 1996)

Vogel D, *Trading up. Consumer and Environmental Regulation in a Global Economy* (Cambridge MA 1995)

Vos E, "Market Building, Social Regulation and Scientific Expertise: An Introduction" in C Joerges / K-H Ladeur / E Vos (eds.), *Integrating Scientific Expertise into Regulatory Decision-Making. National Traditions and European Innovations* (Baden-Baden 1997a), 127–139

—— "The Rise of Committees" (1997b) 3 *ELJ* , 210–229

—— *Institutional Frameworks of Community Health and Safety Regulation: Committees, Agencies and Private Bodies* (Oxford 1999)

Wahl R, "Risikobewertung der Exekutive und richterliche Kontrolldichte" (1991) 10 *Neue Zeitschrift für Verwaltungsrecht*, 409–418

Wallace H, "Die Dynamik des EU-Institutionengefüges" in M Jachtenfuchs / B Kohler-Koch (eds.), *Europäische Integration* (Opladen 1996a), 141–163

—— "Politics and Policy in the EU: The Challenge of Governance" in H Wallace / W Wallace (eds.), *Policy-Making in the European Union,* 3rd ed. (Oxford 1996b), 3–36

—— "The institutions of the EU: experience and experiments" in H Wallace / W Wallace (eds.), *Policy-making in the European Union,* 3rd ed. (Oxford 1996c), 37–68

—— and W Wallace / C Webb (eds.), *Policy-Making in the European Community,* 2nd ed. (Chichester 1983)

—— and W Wallace (eds.), *Policy-Making in the European Union,* 3rd ed. (Oxford 1996)

Wallace W, "Government Without Statehood: The Unstable Equilibrium" in H Wallace / W Wallace (eds.), *Policy-Making in the European Union,* 3rd ed. (Oxford 1996), 439–460

Waterton C / B Wynne, "Building the European Union: Science and the Cultural Dimensions of Environmental Policy" (1996) 3 *JEPP*, 421–440

Weber M, edited by J Winckelmann, *Wirtschaft und Gesellschaft. Grundriß einer verstehenden Soziologie,* 5th ed. (Tübingen 1989)

Weiler J H H, "Does Europe need a Constitution? Reflections on Demos, Telos and the German Maastricht Decision" (1995a) 1 *ELJ*, 219–258

—— *European Democracy and Its Critics – Five Uneasy Pieces* [Harvard Jean Monnet Working Paper 1/95] (Cambridge MA 1995b; http://www.law.harvard.edu/Programs/ JeanMonnet/papers/95/9501ind.html)

—— "The European Union belongs to its citizens: three immodest proposals" (1997) 22 *ELR*, 150–156

—— "Europe: The Case Against the Case for Statehood" (1998) 4 *ELJ*, 43–62

—— "The Constitution of the Common Marketplace: Text and Context in the Evolution of the Free Movement of Goods" in P Craig / G de Búrca (eds.), *The Evolution of EU Law* (Oxford 1999), 349–376

—— and A Ballmann / U Haltern / H Hofmann / F Mayer, *Certain Rectangular Problems of European Integration. Empowering the Individuals: The Four Principal Proposals,* European Parliament, Directorate General for Research (Project IV/95/02) (Luxembourg 1996; http://www.iue.it/AEL/EP/index.html)

Weingast B R, "Regulation, Reregulation and Deregulation: the Political Foundations of Agency Clientele Relationships" (1981) 44 *Law and Contemporary Problems*, 147–177

—— "The Congressional-Bureaucratic System: A Principal-Agent Perspective" (1982) 44 *Public Choice*, 147–192

Weinstock U, "Nur eine europäische Umwelt? Europäische Umweltpolitik im Spannungsfeld von ökologischer Vielfalt and ökonomischer Einheit" in E Grabitz (ed.), *Abgestufte Integration. Eine Alternative zum herkömmlichen Integrationskonzept?* (Kehl/Rhein 1984), 301–344

Weizsäcker E von, *Erdpolitik: Ökologische Realpolitik an der Schwelle zum Jahrhundert der Umwelt,* 3rd ed. (Darmstadt 1992)

Wessels W, "Administrative Interaction" in W Wallace (ed.), *The Dynamics of European Integration* (London 1990), 229–241

—— "Staat und (westeuropäische) Integration. Die Fusionsthese" in M Kreile (ed.), *Die Integration Europas*, (1992) 23 *PVS*, 36–61

—— "Verwaltung im EG-Mehrebenensystem: Auf dem Weg zur Megabürokratie?" in M Jachtenfuchs / B Kohler-Koch (eds.), *Europäische Integration* (Opladen 1996), 165–192

—— "An ever closer fusion? A dynamic macropolitical view on integration processes" (1997) 35 *JCMS*, 267–299

—— "Comitology: Fusion in Action. Politico-administrative Trends in the EU System" (1998) 5 *JEPP*, 209–234

Westendorp C (Chairman), *Report of the Reflection Group for the IGC*, Brussels, 5 December 1995, reprinted in J A Winter *et al* (eds.), *Reforming the Treaty on European Union – The Legal Debate* (The Hague 1996), 481–518

Westlake M, *The Commission and the Parliament. Partners and Rivals in the European Policy Making Process* (London/Dublin/Edinburgh 1994)

—— "Mad cows and Englishmen: the institutional consequences of the BSE crisis" in N Nugent (ed.), *European Union 1996: Annual Review of Activities* (1997) 35 *JCMS*, Annual Review, 11–36

Willke H, *Systemtheorie II: Interventionstheorie*, 2nd ed. (Stuttgart 1996)

Wilson J Q, *The Politics of Regulation* (New York 1980)

Winter G, "Brauchen wir das? Von der Risikominimierung zur Bedarfsprüfung" (1992) 25 *Kritische Justiz*, 389–404

Wissenschaftlicher Beirat beim Bundesministerium für Wirtschaft, *Stellungnahme zum Weißbuch der EG über den Binnenmarkt* (Bonn 1986)

Wood B D, "Principals, Bureaucrats, and Responsiveness in Clean Air Enforcements" (1988) 82 *American Political Science Review*, 213–234

Zagaris B, "Dollar diplomacy: international enforcement of money movement and related matters – A United States perspective" (1989) 22 *The George Washington Journal of International Law & Economics*, 465–552

—— "The emergence of an international anti-money laundering regime: implications for counselling business" in R D Atkins (ed.), *The alleged transnational criminal* (The Hague 1995), 127–217

Zangl B, "Politik auf zwei Ebenen. Hypothesen zur Bildung internationaler Regime" (1994) 1 *Zeitschrift für Internationale Beziehungen*, 279–312

—— "Der Ansatz der Zwei-Ebenen-Spiele. Eine Brücke zwischen dem Neoinstitutionalismus und seinen KritikerInnen?" (1995) 2 *Zeitschrift für Internationale Beziehungen*, 393–416

List of Contributors

Kieran St Clair Bradley
Court of Justice
Chambers of Advocate General Fennelly
Palais 228
L-2925 Luxembourg

Graham R Chambers
European Parliament
Schuman Building
Plateau Kirchberg
L-2929 Luxembourg

Giuseppe Ciavarini Azzi
Secretariat-General
European Commission
200, rue de la Loi
B-1049 Brussels

Renaud Dehousse
Institut d'Études Politiques
Centre Européen de Science Politique
5 Place Saint-Thomas d'Aquin
F-75007 Paris

Michelle Egan
AICGS
John Hopkins University, Suite 420
1400 16th Street NW
Washington DC 20036
USA

Michelle Everson
European University Institute
Law Department
C.P. 2330
I-50100 Firenze-Ferrovia

Thomas Gehring
Freie Universität
FB Politikwissenschaft
Ihnestraße 22
D-14195 Berlin

Adrienne Héritier
Max-Planck-Projektgruppe
Recht der Gemeinschaftsgüter
Poppelsdorfer Allee 45
D-53115 Bonn

Jean-Paul Jacqué
Council of the European Union
Legal Service
Rue de la Loi 170
B-1048 Brussels

Christian Joerges
European University Institute
Law Department
C.P. 2330
I-50100 Firenze-Ferrovia

Karl-Heinz Ladeur
Universität Hamburg
FB Rechtswissenschaft II
Edmund-Siemers-Allee 1 (Pavillon Ost)
D-20146 Hamburg

Christine Landfried
Universität Hamburg
Institut für Politische Wissenschaft
Allende-Platz 1
D-20146 Hamburg

Jürgen Neyer
Centre of European Law and Politics
Universitätsallee GW 1
D-28359 Bremen

John A E Vervaele
Centre for Enforcement of European Law
Boothstraat 6
NL-3512 BW Utrecht

Ellen Vos
University of Maastricht
International and European Law Dept.
P O Box 616
NL-6200 MD Maastricht

J H H Weiler
Harvard Law School
Cambridge MA 02138
USA

Wolfgang Wessels
Universität Köln
Forschungsinstitut für Politische Wissenschaft und Europäische Fragen
Gottfried-Keller-Str. 6
D-50931 Köln

Dieter Wolf
Centre of European Law and Politics
Universitätsallee GW 1
D-28359 Bremen

Annex 1

COUNCIL DECISION 87/373/EEC

laying down the procedures for the exercise of implementing powers conferred on the Commission

(1987) OJ L 197/33

THE COUNCIL OF THE EUROPEAN COMMUNITIES,

Having regard to the Treaty establishing the European Economic Community, and in particular Article 145 thereof,

Having regard to the proposal from the Commission,[1]

Having regard to the opinion of the European Parliament,[2]

Whereas, in the acts which it adopts, the Council confers on the Commission powers for the implementation of the rules which the Council lays down; whereas the Council may impose certain requirements in respect of the exercise of these powers; whereas it may also reserve the right, in specific cases, to exercise directly implementing powers itself;

Whereas, in order to improve the efficiency of the Community's decision-making process, the types of procedure to which it may henceforth have recourse should be limited; whereas certain rules governing any new provision introducing procedures for the exercise of implementing powers conferred by the Council on the Commission should therefore be laid down;

Whereas this Decision must not affect procedures for implementing Commission powers contained in acts which predate its entry into force; whereas it must be possible, when amending or extending such acts, to adapt the procedures to conform with those set out in this Decision or to retain the existing procedures,

HAS DECIDED AS FOLLOWS:

Article 1

Other than in specific cases where it reserves the right to exercise directly implementing powers itself, the Council shall, in the acts which it adopts, confer on the Commission powers for the implementation of the rules

---

[1] (1986) OJ C 70/6.   [2] (1986) OJ C 297/94.

which it lays down. The Council shall specify the essential elements of these powers.

The Council may impose requirements in respect of the exercise of these powers, which must be in conformity with the procedures set out in Articles 2 and 3.

Article 2

Procedure I

The Commission shall be assisted by a committee of an advisory nature composed of the representatives of the Member States and chaired by the representative of the Commission. The representative of the Commission shall submit to the committee a draft of the measures to be taken. The committee shall deliver its opinion on the draft, within a time limit which the chairman may lay down according to the urgency of the matter, if necessary by taking a vote.

The opinion shall be recorded in the minutes; in addition, each Member State shall have the right to ask to have its position recorded in the minutes. The Commission shall take the utmost account of the opinion delivered by the committee. It shall inform the committee of the manner in which its opinion has been taken into account.

Procedure II

The Commission shall be assisted by a committee composed of the representatives of the Member States and chaired by the representative of the Commission. The representative of the Commission shall submit to the committee a draft of the measures to be taken. The committee shall deliver its opinion on the draft within a time limit which the chairman may lay down according to the urgency of the matter. The opinion shall be delivered by the majority laid down in Article 148 (2) of the Treaty in the case of decisions which the Council is required to adopt on a proposal from the Commission. The votes of the representatives of the Member States within the committee shall be weighted in the manner set out in that Article. The chairman shall not vote. The Commission shall adopt measures which shall apply immediately. However, if these measures are not in accordance with the opinion of the committee, they shall be communicated by the Commission to the Council forthwith. In that event:

Variant (a)

The Commission may defer application of the measures which it has decided for a period of not more than one month from the date of such communication;

The Council, acting by a qualified majority, may take a different decision within the time limit referred to in the previous paragraph.

Variant (b)

The Commission shall defer application of the measures which it has decided for a period to be laid down in each act adopted by the Council, but which may in no case exceed three months from the date of communication. The Council, acting by a qualified majority, may take a different decision within the time limit referred to in the previous paragraph.

Procedure III

The Commission shall be assisted by a committee composed of the representatives of the Member States and chaired by the representative of the Commission.

The representative of the Commission shall submit to the committee a draft of the measures to be taken. The committee shall deliver its opinion on the draft within a time limit which the chairman may lay down according to the urgency of the matter. The opinion shall be delivered by the majority laid down in Article 148 (2) of the Treaty in the case of decisions which the Council is required to adopt on a proposal from the Commission. The votes of the representatives of the Member States within the committee shall be weighted in the manner set out in that Article. The chairman shall not vote. The Commission shall adopt the measures envisaged if they are in accordance with the opinion of the committee. If the measures envisaged are not in accordance with the opinion of the committee, or if no opinion is delivered, the Commission shall, without delay, submit to the Council a proposal relating to the measures to be taken. The Council shall act by a qualified majority.

Variant (a)

If, on the expiry of a period to be laid down in each act to be adopted by the Council under this paragraph but which may in no case exceed three months from the date of referral to the Council, the Council has not acted, the proposed measures shall be adopted by the Commission.

Variant (b)

If, on the expiry of a period to be laid down in each act to be adopted by the Council under this paragraph but which may in no case exceed three months from the date of referral to the Council, the Council has not acted, the proposed measures shall be adopted by the Commission, save where the Council has decided against the said measures by a simple majority.

Article 3

The following procedure may be applied where the Council confers on the Commission the power to decide on safeguard measures:

– the Commission shall notify the Council and the Member States of any decision regarding safeguard measures.

It may be stipulated that before adopting this decision the Commission shall consult the Member States in accordance with procedures to be determined in each case,

– any Member State may refer the Commission's decision to the Council within a time limit to be determined in the act in question.

Variant (a)

The Council, acting by a qualified majority, may take a different decision within a time limit to be determined in the act in question.

Variant (b)

The Council, acting by a qualified majority, may confirm, amend or revoke the decision adopted by the Commission. If the Council has not taken a decision within a time limit to be determined in the act in question, the decision of the Commission is deemed to be revoked.

Article 4

This Decision shall not affect the procedures for the exercise of the powers conferred on the Commission in acts which predate its entry into force.

Where such acts are amended or extended the Council may adapt the procedures laid down by these acts to conform with those set out in Articles 2 and 3 or retain the existing procedures.

Article 5

The Council shall review the procedures provided for in this Decision on the basis of a report submitted by the Commission before 31 December 1990.

Done at Brussels, 13 July 1987.

For the Council

The President

P. SIMONSEN

Annex 2

Proposal for a Council Decision laying down the procedures for the exercise of implementing powers conferred on the Commission

COM(98) 380 final, (1998) OJ C 279/5

(Submitted by the Commission on 16 July 1998)

THE COUNCIL OF THE EUROPEAN UNION,

Having regard to the Treaty establishing the European Community, and in particular the third indent of Article 145 thereof,

Having regard to the proposal from the Commission,

Having regard to the opinion of the European Parliament,

Whereas, in accordance with Article 145 of the Treaty, in the instruments which it adopts, the Council confers on the Commission powers for the implementation of the rules which the Council lays down; whereas the Council may impose certain requirements in respect of the exercise of these powers; whereas it may also reserve to itself the right, in specific and duly substantiated cases, to exercise directly implementing powers;

Whereas the Council adopted Decision 87/373/EEC of 13 July 1987 laying down the procedures for the exercise of implementing powers conferred on the Commission;[1] whereas that Decision has limited the number of procedures for the exercise of such powers;

Whereas declaration No 31 annexed to the Final Act of the Intergovernmental Conference which adopted the Amsterdam Treaty calls on the Commission to submit to the Council a proposal amending Decision 87/373/EEC;

Whereas the first purpose of the proposed amendments is to clarify the criteria determining the choice of one or other of the procedures provided for the adoption of implementing measures;

Whereas, in this regard, implementing measures and management measures must be taken by a procedure ensuring decision-making within suitable periods;

[1] (1987) OJ L 197/33.

Whereas measures of general scope designed to implement, adapt or update essential provisions of basic legislative instruments should be adopted by a procedure allowing involvement of the legislative authority, be it the Council or the European Parliament and the Council;

Whereas the advisory procedure should be followed where the management or regulatory procedure is not or is no longer considered appropriate; whereas account should be taken of experience already gained in the implementation of the relevant instruments;

Whereas the second purpose of the proposed amendments is to simplify the set of requirements for the exercise of implementing powers conferred on the Commission; whereas it is accordingly necessary to reduce the number of procedures and to adjust them in line with the respective powers of the institutions involved;

Whereas, in this spirit, the European Parliament should be informed of committee proceedings on a regular basis;

Whereas simplification of the exercise of implementing powers means that this Decision should apply to the implementing rules in force prior to the adoption of this Decision; whereas it follows that all such instruments will need to be adjusted in accordance with this Decision;

Whereas certain provisions of Community legislation, particularly health protection, require a decision to be taken rapidly; whereas, therefore, it is necessary to provide that those cases are to be subject to a decision-making process which allows the fundamental objectives of the legislation to be observed;

Whereas committees set up by the Council otherwise than in accordance with the third indent of Article 145 are not affected by this Decision; whereas the same applies to the specific committee procedures created for the implementation of the common commercial policy and the competition rules laid down by the Treaties;

Whereas Decision 87/373/EEC should be repealed,

HAS DECIDED AS FOLLOWS:

Article 1

Other than in specific, duly substantiated cases where the Council reserves the right to exercise directly certain implementing powers itself, such powers shall be conferred on the Commission in accordance with the relevant provisions in the basic instrument.

Where the basic instrument imposes specific procedural requirements for the adoption of implementing measures, such requirements shall be in conformity with the procedures provided for by Articles 3 to 6, and determined in accordance with the criteria laid down by Article 2.

Article 2

Implementation and management measures, and in particular those relating to common policies such as the common agricultural policy, to the implementation of programmes with significant budgetary implications, or to the grant of substantial financial support, shall be adopted by use of the management procedure.

Measures of general scope designed to apply, update or adapt essential provisions of basic instruments shall be adopted by the use of regulatory procedure.

The advisory procedure shall be applied where the management or regulatory procedure is not or is no longer considered appropriate.

The safeguard procedure may be applied where the power to decide on such measures is conferred on the Commission.

Article 3

Advisory Procedure

The Commission shall be assisted by an advisory committee composed of the representatives of the Member States and chaired by the representative of the Commission.

The representative of the Commission shall submit to the committee a draft of the measures to be taken. The committee shall deliver its opinion on the draft, within a time limit which the chairman may lay down according to the urgency of the matter, if necessary by taking a vote.

The Commission shall take the utmost account of the opinion delivered by the committee. It shall inform the committee of the manner in which its opinion has been taken into account.

Article 4

Management Procedure

The Commission shall be assisted by a management committee composed of the representatives of the Member States and chaired by the representative of the Commission.

The representative of the Commission shall submit to the committee a draft of the measures to be taken. The committee shall deliver its opinion on the draft within a time limit which the chairman may lay down according to the urgency of the matter. The opinion shall be delivered by the majority laid down in Article 148(2) of the Treaty. The chairman shall not vote.

The Commission may adopt measures which shall apply immediately. However, if these measures are not in accordance with the opinion of the committee, they shall be communicated by the Commission to the Council forthwith. In that event, the Commission may defer application of the measures which it has decided on for not more than three months from the date of such communication.

The Council, acting by a qualified majority, may take a different decision within the time limit provided for by the third paragraph.

Article 5

Regulatory Procedure

The Commission shall be assisted by a regulatory committee composed of the representatives of the Member States and chaired by the representative of the Commission.

The representative of the Commission shall submit to the committee a draft of the measures to be taken. The committee shall deliver its opinion on the draft within a time limit which the chairman may lay down according to the urgency of the matter. The opinion shall be delivered by the majority laid down in Article 148(2) of the Treaty. The chairman shall not vote.

The Commission may adopt the measures envisaged if they are in accordance with the opinion of the committee.

If the measures envisaged are not in accordance with the opinion of the committee, or if no opinion is delivered, the Commission shall not adopt the measures envisaged. In that event, it may present a proposal relating to the measures to be taken, in accordance with the Treaty.

Article 6

Safeguard Procedure

The Commission shall notify the Council and the Member States of any decision regarding safeguard measures. It may be stipulated that before adopting its decision, the Commission shall consult the Member States in accordance with procedures to be determined in each case.

Any Member State may refer the Commission's decision to the Council within a time limit to be determined in the instrument in question.

The Council, acting by a qualified majority, may take a different decision within the time limit determined by the instrument in question.

Article 7

Each committee shall adopt its own Rules of Procedure on the proposal of its chairman.

The European Parliament shall be informed of committee proceedings on a regular basis. To that end, it shall receive agendas for committee meetings, draft measures submitted to the committees for the implementation of instruments adopted by the procedure provided for by Article 189b of the EC Treaty, and the results of voting. It shall also be kept informed wherever the Commission transmits to the Council measures or proposals for measures to be taken.

Article 8

The Council, or the European Parliament and the Council, acting on a proposal from the Commission, shall without delay adjust provisions relating to committees assisting the Commission in the exercise of implementing powers provided for by instruments predating this Decision in order to align them on it.

Such adjustment shall be made in compliance with the obligations incumbent on the Community institutions. It shall not have the effect of jeopardising attainment of the objectives of the basic instrument or the effectiveness of Community action.

Article 9

Decision 87/373/EEC is repealed.

Annex 3

Note from the Editors:

Thanks to Director Ciavarini-Azzi of the Commission's Secretariat-General we are able to reprint here the new Comitology Decision, which formally repeals Decision 87/373/EEC from which our project started. It was at a very late stage in the publication process (June 1999) that we received the new text and Giuseppe Ciavarini-Azzi was the only contributor in a position to react to the new text in his proofs. We do not think, however, that the messages of individual contributions or our whole project are in any substantial sense affected. The new decision clarifies in a very flexible fashion the reasons that should guide the choice of a particular procedure. It expressly mentions the European Parliament without defining precisely its institutional role. The search for an adequate 'juridification', or, to resume our more ambitious language, for the 'constitutionalisation' of comitology will remain on the European agenda for the foreseeable future - and the Statements on Article 7 make it clear that all the institutional actors are aware of that challenge.

COUNCIL DECISION
laying down the procedures for the exercise of implementing powers conferred on the Commission

THE COUNCIL OF THE EUROPEAN UNION,

Having regard to the Treaty establishing the European Community, and in particular the third indent of Article 202 thereof,

Having regard to the proposal from the Commission,[1]

Having regard to the Opinion of the European Parliament,[2]

Whereas:

(1)   In the instruments which it adopts, the Council has to confer on the Commission powers for the implementation of the rules which the Council lays down; the Council may impose certain requirements in respect of the exercise of these powers; it may also reserve to itself the right, in specific and substantiated cases, to exercise directly implementing powers;

---

[1] (1998) OJ C 279/5.
[2] Opinion delivered on 6 May 1999.

(2) The Council adopted Decision 87/373/EEC of 13 July 1987 laying down the procedures for the exercise of implementing powers conferred on the Commission,[3] that Decision has provided for a limited number of procedures for the exercise of such powers;

(3) Declaration No 31 annexed to the Final Act of the Intergovernmental Conference which adopted the Amsterdam Treaty calls on the Commission to submit to the Council a proposal amending Decision 87/373/EEC;

(4) For reasons of clarity, rather than amending Decision 87/373/EEC, it has been considered more appropriate to replace that Decision by a new Decision and, therefore, to repeal Decision 87/373/EEC;

(5) The first purpose of this Decision is, with a view to achieving greater consistency and predictability in the choice of type of committee, to provide for criteria relating to the choice of committee procedures, it being understood that such criteria are of a nonbinding nature;

(6) In this regard, the management procedure should be followed as regards management measures such as those relating to the application of the common agricultural and common fisheries policies or to the implementation of programmes with substantial budgetary implications; such management measures should be taken by the Commission by a procedure ensuring decisionmaking within suitable periods; however, where nonurgent measures are referred to the Council, the Commission should exercise its discretion to defer application of the measures;

(7) The regulatory procedure should be followed as regards measures of general scope designed to apply essential provisions of basic instruments, including measures concerning the protection of the health or safety of humans, animals or plants, as well as measures designed to adapt or update certain nonessential provisions of a basic instrument; such implementing measures should be adopted by an effective procedure which complies in full with the Commission's right of initiative in legislative matters;

(8) The advisory procedure should be followed in any case in which it is considered to be the most appropriate; the advisory procedure will continue to be used in those cases where it currently applies;

(9) The second purpose of this Decision is to simplify the requirements for the exercise of implementing powers conferred on the Commission as well as to improve the involvement of the European Parliament in those cases where the basic instrument conferring implementation

[3] (1987) OJ L 197/33.

powers on the Commission was adopted in accordance with the procedure laid down in Article 251 of the Treaty; it has been accordingly considered appropriate to reduce the number of procedures as well as to adjust them in line with the respective powers of the institutions involved and notably to give the European Parliament an opportunity to have its views taken into consideration by, respectively, the Commission or the Council in cases where it considers that, respectively, a draft measure submitted to a committee or a proposal submitted to the Council under the regulatory procedure exceeds the implementing powers provided for in the basic instrument;

(10)   The third purpose of this Decision is to improve information to the European Parliament by providing that the Commission should inform it on a regular basis of committee proceedings, that the Commission should transmit to it documents related to activities of committees and inform it whenever the Commission transmits to the Council measures or proposals for measures to be taken;

(11)   The fourth purpose of this Decision is to improve information to the public concerning committee procedures and therefore to make applicable to committees the principles and conditions on public access to documents applicable to the Commission, to provide for a list of all committees which assist the Commission in the exercise of implementing powers and for an annual report on the working of committees to be published as well as to provide for all references to documents related to committees which have been transmitted to the European Parliament to be made public in a register;

(12)   The specific committee procedures created for the implementation of the common commercial policy and the competition rules laid down by the Treaties that are not currently based upon Decision 87/373/EEC are not in any way affected by this Decision,

HAS DECIDED AS FOLLOWS:

Article 1

Other than in specific and substantiated cases where the basic instrument reserves to the Council the right to exercise directly certain implementing powers itself, such powers shall be conferred on the Commission in accordance with the relevant provisions in the basic instrument. These provisions shall stipulate the essential elements of the powers thus conferred.

Where the basic instrument imposes specific procedural requirements for the adoption of implementing measures, such requirements shall be in conformity with the procedures provided for by Articles 3, 4, 5 and 6.

Article 2

The choice of procedural methods for the adoption of implementing measures shall be guided by the following criteria:

(a) management measures, such as those relating to the application of the common agricultural and common fisheries policies, or to the implementation of programmes with substantial budgetary implications, should be adopted by use of the management procedure;

(b) measures of general scope designed to apply essential provisions of basic instruments, including measures concerning the protection of the health or safety of humans, animals or plants, should be adopted by use of the regulatory procedure;
where a basic instrument stipulates that certain nonessential provisions of the instrument may be adapted or updated by way of implementing procedures, such measures should be adopted by use of the regulatory procedure;

(c) without prejudice to points (a) and (b), the advisory procedure shall be used in any case in which it is considered to be the most appropriate.

Article 3

Advisory Procedure

1. The Commission shall be assisted by an advisory committee composed of the representatives of the Member States and chaired by the representative of the Commission.

2. The representative of the Commission shall submit to the Committee a draft of the measures to be taken. The committee shall deliver its opinion on the draft, within a timelimit which the chairman may lay down according to the urgency of the matter, if necessary by taking a vote.

3. The opinion shall be recorded in the minutes; in addition, each Member State shall have the right to ask to have its position recorded in the minutes.

4. The Commission shall take the utmost account of the opinion delivered by the committee. It shall inform the committee of the manner in which the opinion has been taken into account.

Article 4

Management Procedure

1. The Commission shall be assisted by a management committee composed of the representatives of the Member States and chaired by the representative of the Commission.

2. The representative of the Commission shall submit to the committee a draft of the measures to be taken. The committee shall deliver its opinion on the draft within a timelimit which the chairman may lay down according to the urgency of the matter. The opinion shall be delivered by the majority laid down in Article 205(2) of the Treaty, in the case of decisions which the Council is required to adopt on a proposal from the Commission. The votes of the representatives of the Member States within the committee shall be weighted in the manner set out in that Article. The chairman shall not vote.

3. The Commission shall, without prejudice to Article 8, adopt measures which shall apply immediately. However, if these measures are not in accordance with the opinion of the committee, they shall be communicated by the Commission to the Council forthwith. In that event, the Commission may defer application of the measures which it has decided on for a period to be laid down in each basic instrument but which shall in no case exceed three months from the date of such communication.

4. The Council, acting by qualified majority, may take a different decision within the period provided for by paragraph 3.

Article 5

Regulatory Procedure

1. The Commission shall be assisted by a regulatory committee composed of the representatives of the Member States and chaired by the representative of the Commission.

2. The representative of the Commission shall submit to the committee a draft of the measures to be taken. The committee shall deliver its opinion on the draft within a timelimit which the chairman may lay down according to the urgency of the matter. The opinion shall be delivered by the majority laid down in Article 205(2) of the Treaty in the case of decisions which the Council is required to adopt on a proposal from the Commission. The votes of the representatives of the Member States within the Committee shall be weighted in the manner set out in that Article. The chairman shall not vote.

3. The Commission shall, without prejudice to Article 8, adopt the measures envisaged if they are in accordance with the opinion of the committee.

4. If the measures envisaged are not in accordance with the opinion of the committee, or if no opinion is delivered, the Commission shall, without delay, submit to the Council a proposal relating to the measures to be taken and shall inform the European Parliament.

5. If the European Parliament considers that a proposal submitted by the Commission pursuant to a basic instrument adopted in accordance with the procedure laid down in Article 251 of the Treaty exceeds the implementing powers provided for in that basic instrument, it shall inform the Council of its position.

6. The Council may, where appropriate in view of any such position, act by qualified majority on the proposal, within a period to be laid down in each basic instrument but which shall in no case exceed three months from the date of referral to the Council.

If within that period the Council has indicated by qualified majority that it opposes the proposal, the Commission shall reexamine it. It may submit an amended proposal to the Council, resubmit its proposal or present a legislative proposal on the basis of the Treaty.

If on the expiry of that period the Council has neither adopted the proposed implementing act nor indicated its opposition to the proposal for implementing measures, the proposed implementing act shall be adopted by the Commission.

Article 6

Safeguard Procedure

The following procedure may be applied where the basic instrument confers on the Commission the power to decide on safeguard measures:

(a) the Commission shall notify the Council and the Member States of any decision regarding safeguard measures. It may be stipulated that before adopting its decision, the Commission shall consult the Member States in accordance with procedures to be determined in each case;

(b) any Member State may refer the Commission's decision to the Council within a timelimit to be determined within the basic instrument in question;

(c) the Council, acting by a qualified majority, may take a different decision within a timelimit to be determined in the basic instrument in question. Alternatively, it may be stipulated in the basic instrument that the Council, acting by qualified majority, may confirm, amend or revoke the decision adopted by the Commission and that, if the Council has not taken a decision within the above mentioned timelimit, the decision of the Commission is deemed to be revoked.

Article 7

1. Each committee shall adopt its own rules of procedure on the proposal of its chairman, on the basis of standard rules which shall be published in the Official Journal of the European Communities.

   Insofar as necessary existing committees shall adapt their rules of procedure to the standard rules.

2. The principles and conditions on public access to documents applicable to the Commission shall apply to the committees.

3. The European Parliament shall be informed by the Commission of committee proceedings on a regular basis. To that end, it shall receive agendas for committee meetings, draft measures submitted to the committees for the implementation of instruments adopted by the procedure provided for by Article 251 of the Treaty, and the results of voting and summary records of the meetings and lists of the authorities and organisations to which the persons designated by the Member States to represent them belong. The European Parliament shall also be kept informed whenever the Commission transmits to the Council measures or proposals for measures to be taken.

4. The Commission shall, within six months of the date on which this Decision takes effect, publish in the Official Journal of the European Communities, a list of all committees which assist the Commission in the exercise of implementing powers. This list shall specify, in relation to each committee, the basic instrument(s) under which the committee is established. From 2000 onwards, the Commission shall also publish an annual report on the working of committees.

5. The references of all documents sent to the European Parliament pursuant to paragraph 3 shall be made public in a register to be set up by the Commission in 2001.

Article 8

If the European Parliament indicates, in a Resolution setting out the grounds on which it is based, that draft implementing measures, the adoption of which is contemplated and which have been submitted to a committee pursuant to a basic instrument adopted under Article 251 of the Treaty, would exceed the implementing powers provided for in the basic instrument, the Commission shall review the draft measures. Taking the Resolution into account and within the timelimits of the procedure under way, the Commission may submit new draft measures to the committee, continue with the procedure or submit a proposal to the European Parliament and the Council on the basis of the Treaty.

The Commission shall inform the European Parliament and the committee of the action which it intends to take on the Resolution of the European Parliament and of its reasons for doing so.

Article 9

Decision 87/373/EEC shall be repealed.

Article 10

This Decision shall take effect on the day following that of its publication in the Official Journal of the European Communities.

Done at,

> For the Council
> The President

DECLARATIONS ON COUNCIL DECISION 1999/468/EC
laying down the procedures for the exercise of implementing powers conferred on the Commission

1. *Commission Statement* (ad Article 4)
Under the management procedure, the Commission would recall that its constant practice is to try to secure a satisfactory decision which will also muster the widest possible support within the Committee.

The Commission will take account of the position of the members of the Committee and act in such a way as to avoid going against any predominant position which might emerge against the appropriateness of an implementing measure.

2. *Council and Commission Statement*
The Commission and the Council agree that provisions relating to committees assisting the Commission in the exercise of implementing powers provided for in application of Decision 87/373/EEC should be adjusted without delay in order to align them with Articles 3, 4, 5 and 6 of Decision 1999/ /EC in accordance with the appropriate legislative procedures.

Such adjustment should be made as follows:

– current procedure I would be turned into the new advisory procedure;
– current procedures II a) and II b) would be turned into the new management procedure;
– current procedures III a) and III b) would be turned into the new regulatory procedure.

A modification of the type of committee provided for in a basic instrument should be made, on a case by case basis, in the course of normal revision of legislation, guided *inter alia* by the criteria provided for in Article 2.

Such adjustment or modification should be made in compliance with the obligations incumbent on the Community institutions. It should not have the effect of jeopardising attainment of the objectives of the basic instrument or the effectiveness of Community action.

3. *Commission Statement* (ad Article 5)

In the review of proposals for implementing measures concerning particularly sensitive sectors, the Commission, in order to find a balanced solution, will act in such a way as to avoid going against any predominant position which might emerge within the Council against the appropriateness of an implementing measure.

Index

Index